Bit-Mapped Graphics

typo

hsing

vsing

Also for Megan
Who observed that computer books
rarely manage a satisfying level of
gratuitous sex, suspense, or witchcraft.
Perhaps just this once . . .

Bit-Mapped Graphics

Steve Rimmer

FIRST EDITION
THIRD PRINTING

Library of Congress Cataloging-in-Publication Data

Rimmer, Steve.
    Bit-mapped graphics / by Steve Rimmer.
      p. cm.
    Includes index.
    ISBN 0-8306-3558-0 (pbk.)
    1. Computer graphics. I. Title.
  T385.R55   1990   90-38960
  006.6—dc20   CIP

TAB Books offers software for sale. For information and a catalog, please contact
TAB Software Department, Blue Ridge Summit, PA 17294-0850.

Questions regarding the content of this book should be addressed to:

Reader Inquiry Branch
Windcrest Books
Blue Ridge Summit, PA 17294-0850

Acquisitions Editor: Stephen Moore
Technical Editor: Eileen P. Baylus
Production: Katherine G. Brown
Series Design: Jaclyn J. Boone

Contents

Introduction

Computer graphics is becoming one of the most interesting fields of microcomputer application. There probably are all sorts of good reasons for this, ranging from the growing availability of computers with enough power to handle graphics right on up to the growing availability of potential users who really aren't computer literate enough to handle a lot of text. There's much to be said for the first case and nothing really wrong with the second. Accountants account, designers design, and politicians court the true meaning of entropy—none of them should have to become programmers to use the power of personal computers.

Of course, none of them will ever know the profound zen-like satisfaction of getting a 12-bit string compression table algorithm to work properly at two in the morning, but we all choose our paths and walk 'em.

The reality of graphics on a PC is that they're a fantastic chaos of formats, standards, patches, and revision levels, making the big bang look like a well-rehearsed chamber orchestra by comparison. More daunting than their profusion of different types, however, is the lack of any sort of accessible documentation for much of the graphic environment that PCs live in. Want to know how to unpack a PC Paintbrush file? I think I read a message on a bulletin board in Omaha that talked about that. Maybe not—try Chapter 4.

This book is a compilation of formats, standards and—perhaps most important—source code to deal with graphics on a PC. It will let you make sense of five of the most popular image file formats, including some of the really impenetrable ones, like GIF. It will show you how to drive the popular display cards in all their mysterious graphics modes. It will tell you how to print graphics to most of the common hard copy devices, including nasties like PostScript printers. It will even show you how to dither.

If you're writing applications that use graphics beyond that which you can manage with the graphics library that accompanies your C compiler, this book will hand you the research you need, all tied up and helpless. It will save serious programmers hundreds of hours of fiddling with nasty little functions.

On the other hand, if you just like to write programs, this book will turn you on to a whole exciting world of code. Graphics are fantastically challenging and extremely interesting. Think of a computer game in which the rules keep changing and the conclusion of every quest reveals a new secret passage, with a whole new game beyond it.

If you do a lot of writing at two in the morning you'll find that you start thinking like this after a while. The shadows move a bit, the cat sneaks into the room, and suddenly your test images start appearing in places other than on your monitor.

I hope that you have as much fun with the programs in this book as I had creating them. Long before you finish the book, you probably will have abstracted a few of the more interesting ones and started writing something around them. There are so many applications for computer graphics that haven't been done yet.

Steven William Rimmer

1
CHAPTER

An Introduction to Imaging

Build a system that even a fool can use and only a fool will want to.
—Murphy's Laws of Computers

Despite our assertions to the contrary, human beings are still very primitive creatures at heart. Although we have developed the ability to deal with symbols and abstractions—words, for example—we might not necessarily want to do so all the time. Concrete, sensual information that doesn't require a lot of thought to appreciate usually is a lot more effective than words, columns of numbers, or pages of formulas.

Visual images probably are the most easily understood form of information; humans have pretty acute visual senses. We can't see terribly well, but we've got the process of understanding what we see down pat. Much of the abstraction of words serves as an approximation of visual senses. Often we write about things because there wasn't a camera handy.

Consider Fig. 1-1. One of these forms of communication is obviously easier to fully understand than the other. Consider receiving the image on the left on a postcard.

Computer graphics are a powerful facility for all sorts of reasons, but I suspect that the major appeal of computer images is that they allow one to perceive things through a computer visually rather than analytically. In addition, pictures can look analog—they contrast nicely to our largely digital perception of computers as a whole.

Computer graphics usually refers to programs that draw things. Books that discuss computer graphics usually talk about drawing bar charts, scatter graphs, and so on, because business graphics are both in demand and not terribly difficult to achieve at a programming level. Computer images, which is what this book is about, are a somewhat different field.

This book deals with bitmaps, that is, with images that have been represented in digital form and stored as arrays of pixels for ultimate display

They

have very

weird

hotels here

Fig 1-1   Two ways of expressing a similar idea, one using graphics and one using text

on a monitor or for printing in the graphics mode of a printer. Rather than dealing with lines and circles—visual objects that can form a drawing—bit-mapped images are a digital analog to the way we see things.

Most of the problems in handling bitmaps are related to specific pieces of software. Programs such as MacPaint and PC Paintbrush, for example, store bitmapped images in specific formats. If you want to use these files in your own programs or to convert them for use in other commercial applications that have different file format requirements, you must understand the structures of the files and have some code to work with them.

If you want to view image files, you also must know how to work with the oftentimes poorly documented graphics modes of the various popular PC display cards. Printing pictures involves using the even more poorly documented graphic facilities of printers.

There are a lot of graphics file formats, with more cropping up every day. These formats come both from PC-based programs and from foreign applications, such as MacPaint on the Apple Macintosh, the files from which often migrate into the PC environment over computer bulletin boards. This book will get into the details of the five most popular ones: MacPaint, Digital Research's GEM/IMG, PC Paintbrush PCX, Compu-Serve's GIF and TIFF, or the Tagged Image File Format.

It also will discuss how to deal with display cards and printers. Finally, it will discuss some relevant areas of image processing, most notably dithering.

Your application for the code and techniques in this book will be determined by the sorts of programs you want to write. You'll notice as you work your way through this book that much of the field of bit-mapped graphics is influenced by the amorphous world of public domain software and image files. The GIF file format was created wholly for use in the public domain, and many other file formats, such as MacPaint on the PC, owe their popularity to the countless bulletin boards that distribute these images.

Most of the illustrations in this book have been drawn from the public domain, and will serve as examples of the sorts of pictures you can find with a modem and a bit of patience. I should also note that I've attempted to ascertain that these pictures were copyright free before using them. However, unlike software, image files need carry no copyright information at all unless their originators felt like including it. As such, many of the pictures that one discovers on bulletin boards will seem to have "just gotten there," with no record of their sources.

One day soon, a lot of lawyers are going to get rich because of this.

HOW IMAGE FILES WORK

A bit-mapped image can be anything that can be displayed in the graphics mode of a display card. For the sake of this initial discussion, let's assume that the image file under discussion will store a picture the size of your screen when it's in its graphics mode.

Let us further allow that by means as yet unfathomable, the picture in Fig. 1-2 has appeared on your screen. This picture is, in fact, shown here with the dimensions of an EGA card. If you have a CGA card in your computer you would not be able to see the whole picture—you'll have to imagine you have slightly different hardware for a moment.

Because of the limitations of this book, which is all in black and white, this picture is shown here in monochrome. It might well have been in color on the EGA card. Let's ignore this possibility for a moment. It looks like an

Fig 1-2 A graphic the size of an EGA screen. Note all the white space. This picture was downloaded from Rose Media (416) 226-9260

old woodcut (it actually is an old woodcut) and woodcuts were the Hercules cards of their day, that is, wholly monochrome.

The dimensions of the EGA card's screen are 640 pixels across by 350 pixels down, for a total of 224,000 pixels. The screen data on a display card is stored in memory just like the kind that stores programs and data, that is, as a string of 8-bit bytes. Each bit maps onto one pixel in a monochrome image, hence the term "bit-mapped graphics." With eight pixels to a byte, you could store this bitmap in a disk file of about 28k.

This would be a very easy program to write. Knowing that the EGA card stores its images starting at segment A000H, all you'd have to do would be to copy 28,000 bytes from this location in memory into a file, like this:

```
FILE *fp;
if((fp = fopen("SCREEN.BIN","wb")) != NULL) {
        fwrite (MK_FP(0xa000,0),1,28000,fp);
        fclose(fp);
} else puts("Error creating file");
```

Don't worry if a few aspects of this are as yet unclear.

This program would be very fast, but, upon reflection also very wasteful. Look again at the picture. Most of it's white. Even in the areas that are largely occupied by some degree of unicorn, there are huge white bits. In simply storing the image in a file like this, you'd be stashing away voluminous amounts of redundant data.

The later chapters of this book get into full color images that occupy half a megabyte or more in their "raw" forms. Obviously, being concerned about storing more data than is required is important, or soon will be.

The first scan line of the picture of the unicorn is completely white. It occupies 80 bytes. It could be easily *encoded* into two or perhaps even one byte. Suppose the program that placed the picture back on the screen at a later date was reasonably intelligent, and rather than just copying the disk file back into the screen memory from whence it came, it also interpreted the data to some extent.

Here's a simple encoding scheme for picture data. This is actually pretty close to the way MacPaint files are encoded. Let's assume that the picture data that was once on the screen and is now in a file has previously been encoded, and that the program under discussion will be decoding it, that is, restoring it to the screen. Image file compression is a lot easier to follow if you start with the decoding part of the story.

All the data in the encoded image file will be of three types in this example. These are the following:

- **Key bytes**: These tell the decoding what to do with the next *packet* of data it sees
- **Index bytes**: These tell the decoder how much of the rest of the file should be included in the current packet
- **Data**: This is what will be decoded to make up the restored picture

A packet is a collection of bytes that are all dealt with in the same way. A packet can be as long as a scan line, or it can be quite a lot shorter if the scan line in question lends itself to being encoded more effectively by using a combination of several different types of packets.

This example will have two types of packets. The first is a *run of bytes* packet, which will be three bytes long. The first byte will be 0xff, telling the decoding routine that it is looking at a run of bytes packet. The second byte will be a number between one and 80, to indicate how many bytes on the screen are involved. Obviously a zero length packet would be of no use, and for this example no packet can exceed one scan line in length.

The third byte is the actual data byte. If the decoder routine encountered the following packet:

  0xff 0x09 0x55

it would write 9 bytes of 0x55 to the screen. The value 0x55 is useful as screen data in image files, as it has every odd numbered bit set and thus paints a 50 percent grey area on any part of the screen filled with it.

The second type of packet deals with screen areas that cannot be compressed into run of byte packets. It's called a *string* packet. A string packet, in this model, can be from three to 82 bytes long. The first byte is 0x00, indicating that the packet is a string packet. The second byte contains the number of subsequent bytes in the packet, and therefore to be written to the screen. The rest of the packet contains data that could not be compressed, and is to be written to the screen "as is."

If the decoder encountered this packet:

  0x00 0x09 0x65 0x12 0xa6 0x77 0x01 0x76 0x69 0xf1 0x98

it would copy the nine bytes from 0x65 through 0x98 to the screen.

Having dealt with one packet, the decoder simply reads the next byte from the file and treats it as the key byte for the following packet.

Figure 1-3 is a flow chart that illustrates how this simple encoding scheme works. You'll find one of these flow charts for most of the real image file formats in this book.

Practical Considerations

This hypothetical image file format has a number of flaws. The first is that it ties up a lot of data with things that aren't, strictly speaking, necessary. It could combine the key byte and the index byte into a single byte, for example. Because the index byte will never be asked to hold numbers greater than 80—the length of a single scan line on an EGA card—the format could be structured so that the high order bit of the key byte served as a flag to indicate whether the packet is to be a run of bytes or a string. The remaining seven bits could serve as the index when the flag bit was ANDed off. This would save one byte per packet, which is a meaningful amount of space in a complex picture with many packets.

You will find that practical image file formats usually go to great

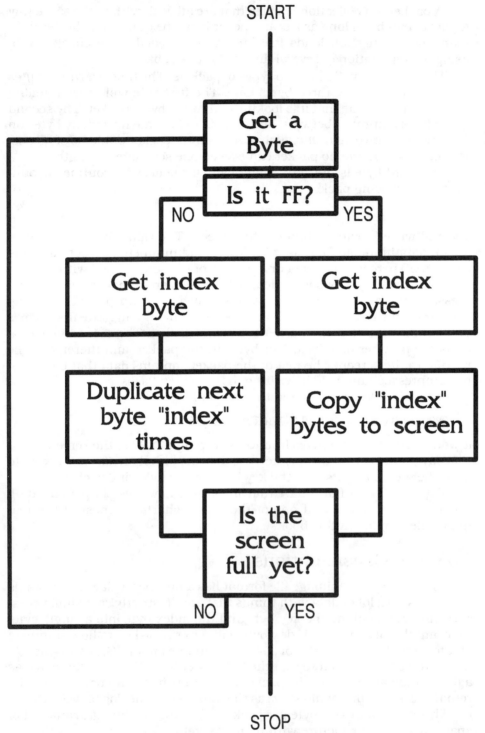

Fig 1-3   A hypothetical image unpacking procedure

lengths to squeeze a little more efficiency out of their encoding schemes with bitwise tricks like this one.

The second and rather more practical problem is that this image file format only works with EGA cards. If you were to attempt to decode it into the screen buffer of a Hercules card, for example, the result would be rather more like bad abstract art than your original image. A Hercules card has screen dimensions that differ from those of an EGA card. A Hercules card also has an internal buffer structure that differs from that of an EGA card, but you can ignore this for a moment.

The dimensions of the image in this hypothetical image file are only what they are because the decoder routine is working with an EGA card. The file is in no way portable—a decoder routine running on another computer with a different size screen would not be able to decode the picture successfully because the image file contains no record of the original picture dimensions.

A third potential problem is that this hypothetical decoder routine has no reliable way of knowing that what it's presented with as being an encoded image file really is. Its input file could, in reality, be a WordStar overlay, the text file for the fifth chapter of this book or a patch file to cheat on Arkanoid. The decoder, unable to distinguish between a real image file and something else, would attempt to decode potentially erroneous data. Decoders frequently find ways to crash their host computers when this sort of thing happens.

The solution to these problems is to equip this image file with a *header*. A header is simply a bit of data that is structured in an agreed upon way and contains the original image dimensions as well as something that the decoder can identify as being its own *signature*. This signature might be a unique string of bytes.

Here's a potential candidate for an image file header:

```
typedef struct {
        char signature[5];
        int width,depth;
} HEADER;

HEADER myHeader = {"PCTR",640,350};
```

If whatever encoded the picture wrote this header to the file first, the image file would carry along with its image data the means to identify itself and a record of its actual dimensions.

Most headers are quite a bit larger than this. There are all sorts of other things that might be included in a header, and image file formats usually find reasons to do so.

C PROGRAMMING CONSIDERATIONS

This is not a programming book for beginners. You will want to understand the C language moderately well to really make use of the examples presented here. You also will require some understanding of assembly language if you want to modify the more advanced programs in the book, although to a large extent you probably will find that the assembly language functions can be used as is.

The programs in this book have been written in Borland's Turbo C using the interactive environment. The assembly language modules have been written for Microsoft's MASM assembler. The C programs really are generic, and will port easily into just about any other C environment with little modification. Just about any C compiler that supports standard object file linking will be able to deal with the assembly language code.

Appendix A discusses those functions and conventions that are specific to Turbo C and their equivalents in Microsoft C.

There is something of an upheaval going on in C programming at the moment, with the introduction of ANSI standard C changing the way one "should" write C programs. The examples in this book don't use the ANSI extensions very much.

One of the powerful aspects of C is the flexibility of the language. Depending upon how you write C programs, the compiler will offer you varying degrees of protection from yourself. For example, you can declare void functions to keep yourself from using the return values of functions that don't actually return anything. This is one of those ANSI things that does not appear in this book.

This is a conventional C function:

```
show_picture(filename)
        char *filename;
{
        /* some code goes here */
}
```

This function might or might not return something. By default, C thinks it returns an int. However, if you don't care what it returns, you can just ignore its returned value entirely.

Under ANSI C, you would write the function this way:

```
void show_picture(filename)
        char *filename;
{
        /* some code goes here */
}
```

This function will cause the compiler to complain if you attempt to use the value that this function returns, as by declaring it void you've told C that its return value is meaningless.

There are those who will argue that a well-organized programmer will never make the sorts of mistakes that the aforementioned example is designed to trap. Assuming that you understand the functions you have written, you won't attempt to use their return values if they don't actually

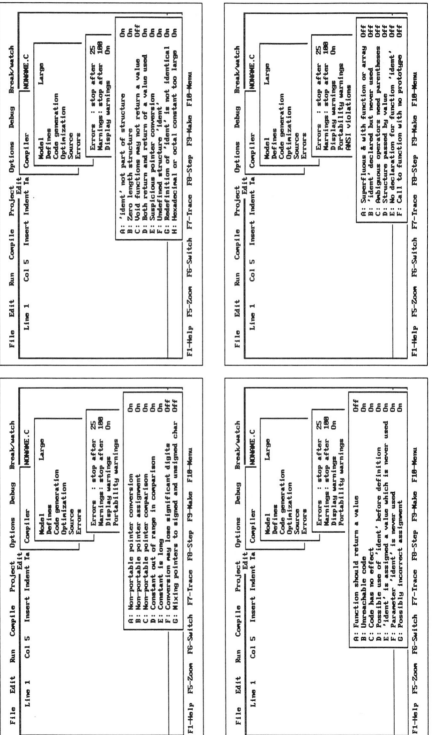

Fig 1-4   How to set up Turbo C version 2.0 for the programs in this book

have any. This is probably less true if you're writing a large application with a number of other programmers, a project in which you can be expected to call functions that other people have written.

To keep the examples in this book down to a manageable level of complexity and hugeness, they are written in pure C, with as few of the ANSI extensions as possible. If you go to use the examples, you can either add the ANSI extensions if you prefer them or you can simply shut off the ANSI features of your compiler. Figure 1-4 illustrates the settings for Turbo C version 2.0, which will disable the ANSI features such that the example programs in this book will compile without any ANSI warnings or errors.

C Programming Style

Everyone who does any substantial amount of C programming will develop his or her own style of programming. C doesn't particularly care whether you put the curly brackets immediately after a while statement, whether you indent nested loops and so on. How you actually write your code largely will be determined by what you find easiest to read. You are strongly urged to modify the code in this book so it conforms with your programming style.

Being able to read a program easily is very important when you begin dealing with a lot of code. Applications that do anything more than trivial bit-mapped graphics functions invariably require a lot of code. One of the limiting factors to the readability of a program is the amount of code you can look at on your screen at a time.

Because of its extreme flexibility, C allows programmers a great deal of slack in how complex expressions are structured. You can compress your code to make several things happen on a line, with the result that a lot more can be read in the 25 or 43 lines visible at one time.

Inexperienced C programmers are frequently baffled by these sorts of expressions. For example, to open a file under C one might do this:

```
FILE *fp;

fp = fopen("PICTURE.MAC","rb");
if(fp = = NULL) puts("Error opening file");
else {
      /* some code goes here */
}
```

The same expression can be compressed a bit to require fewer lines:

```
FILE *fp;

if((fp = fopen("PICTURE.MAC","rb")) != NULL) {
      /* some code goes here */
} else puts("Error opening file");
```

Because the nature of the code in this book presupposes that the programmers using it will have a bit of C under their belts, most of the examples here use the latter sort of C structure. Once again, you might want to modify the code to suit the way you like to write in C. Neither of the previous examples can be said to be preferable over the other in terms of the final code it generates.

Memory Models and Other Low Level Things

Bit-mapped graphics are big. Even small bit-mapped graphics are big. Big bit-mapped graphics are immense. Immense bit-mapped graphics require Cray supercomputers that are probably too expensive for most programmers to own, and will not be discussed here.

Refer again to Fig. 1-1. The image on the left requires 41,722 bytes. The one on the right requires 33 bytes. One of the potential drawbacks of visual communications probably will be apparent.

The memory structure of PCs has been derided at length over the years and probably doesn't need another jeering here. Suffice it to say that objects smaller than 64k in size are handled substantially differently than those that exceed this boundary. An object that fits in 64k is said to reside in a single memory segment. Because most image file formats can contain pictures that are bigger than a single memory segment, one must assume that all of them will and thus allow for large data objects.

Large data objects are awkward.

The C language does not allow for segmented memory directly, and the implementation of Turbo C has some holes in it when it's confronted by the sorts of immense memory buffers required for handling big images. It copes with them differently depending upon which memory model you choose.

Memory models are very important to graphics programming.

In a very simple—and compact—C program, everything will fit in a single 64k memory segment. For example, if you declare some data, like this:

```
char buffer[64];
```

and a pointer to it:

```
char *p = buffer;
```

the actual structure of p will be a 16-bit number. In the early days of microcomputers, when a fully loaded computer only had 64 kilobytes of memory, pointers and integers were often illegally interchanged for this reason.

This starts to fall apart if buffer is either located in another segment of memory that is more than 64k away from the part of the program that will use it or if buffer is expanded so that it's bigger than 64k in size. In either case, a 16-bit pointer would be unable to properly address it.

Having everything fit into a single memory segment is called the *small* memory model. It has not only the aforementioned pointer problem, but also some difficulties should your code get big enough to exceed 64k.

The *large* memory model uses both 32-bit pointers and 32-bit addresses. In theory it can deal with a megabyte of code and a megabyte of data—arguably a little tricky in a machine with just over half a megabyte of memory, but never mind this.

A large memory pointer consists of two 16-bit numbers called the *segment* and the *offset*. The segment value is the number of 16-byte blocks between the very bottom of memory and the location being pointed to. The offset value addresses the 64k immediately above this point. Both can be regarded as unsigned integers and on occasion you will have cause to treat them as such.

Note that using integers to hold the component parts of a large pointer is not the same as simply assigning a pointer to an integer. The former case is acceptable because it's done under circumstances that imply that the programmer knows what he or she is doing.

If you're wondering why the segment value moves in 16-byte intervals, observe that 65,535—the largest number that can be stored in a single 16-bit integer—multiplied by 16 works out to 1,048,560, or one megabyte. This is the size of the total basic memory bus area addressable by an 8086 series microprocessor.

It would be a lot more convenient for the purposes of this book if C could do *linear addressing*, that is, if memory could be addressed by simple long integers. In fact, it can—the huge memory model uses *pointer normalization* to convert between linear addressing and the PC's internal segment and offset notation. However, the normalization process is extremely slow if a program has to do it every time it wants to address something.

In a practical sense, it's faster to use large memory addressing, awkward though it can be, and handle those few instances of huge buffers and addresses by hand when they crop up.

You might not be completely clear about why the large memory model poses so many problems when dealing with big buffers. Here's an example that might help explain it. In this example, *p* points to the base of a very large buffer:

```
p+ =0xffff;
++p;
```

Now, you might think that p would point to the 0x10000L'th byte in the buffer after this, but, in fact, it does not. It points to the start of the buffer again, or possibly even to before the start of the buffer.

Under Turbo C, pointer operations only affect the offset of a large memory model pointer because you can only add and subtract pointers and integers, not pointers and longs. This means that C allows one no obvious way to access more than 64k of contiguous memory using conventional pointer arithmetic.

This is a problem, as bit-mapped graphics programs insist on your being able to do this.

The solution to this problem is in a little function that will crop up throughout this book. This function will add a long integer to a pointer:

```
char *farPtr(p,l)   /* return a far pointer p + l */
    char *p;
    long l;
{
    unsigned int seg,off;

    seg = FP_SEG(p);
    off = FP_OFF(p);
    seg + = (off / 16);
    off & = 0x000f;
    off + = (unsigned int) (l & 0x000fL);
    seg + = (l / 16L);
    p = MK_FP(seg,off);
    return(p);
}
```

The FP SEG and FP OFF functions are provided by Turbo C to extract the segment and offset values from a large memory model pointer. Having reduced a pointer to its component parts, it's a fairly simple process to modify it. To add the long value l to the segment and offset of a pointer, you would figure out how many 16-byte blocks exist in l—divide it by 16—and add this value to the segment. Whatever's left over—l % 16—must be added to the offset.

There's a catch to this. If the initial offset of the pointer was pretty high—within sixteen bytes of the top of the segment—adding the new offset represented by the remainder of l could cause it to wrap back around past zero, which would produce an erroneous pointer when the adjusted segment and offset values are recombined. As such, before the value of l is added to the segment and offset values, the values are fudged so that the offset is reduced as much as possible, increasing the segment proportionately.

This also means that subsequent parts of the program using this function can safely add any value up to 0xfff0 to the pointer returned by farPtr without worrying about its offset value wrapping around past zero.

Fudging the segment and offset values like this is perfectly acceptable, even if it seems a bit peculiar; bear in mind that any number of different combinations of segment and offset values can point to the same place in memory.

With the segment and offset values calculated, the Turbo C MK_FP function can be used to combine the two integers back into a pointer.

The use of this function will be further explained when it turns up in the example programs in this book.

The choice of memory models also affects the way in which assembly language code interfaces to a C program. For this reason, it's essential that you make sure your compiler is set up for the large model before you attempt to use any of the programs in this book.

ASSEMBLY LANGUAGE CONSIDERATIONS

Assembly language can be a bit nasty if you haven't done much of it before. Assembly language that is to be linked to a C program is nastier still. The assembly language functions in this book have been written to be both easy to understand if you find you have to do so and completely unnecessary to understand if you don't. If some of the following section seems a bit incomprehensible, don't worry. It will become clearer through this book. Furthermore, if you just don't get along well with assembly language in general, you can probably skip much of this part altogether, at least for now.

The latest generation of C compilers, such as Turbo C version 2.0, have in-line assembly language facilities. You can include assembly language fragments in your C programs, rather than linking in external assembly language modules. The examples in this book don't handle assembly language modules in this way—despite their convenience, they make the code so written exceedingly nonportable. Portable code is one of the more powerful features of C. Besides which, there are still lots of programmers using earlier versions of Turbo C and other compilers that don't support in-line code, especially in their integrated development environment versions. External assembly language modules are a great deal easier to adapt to different compilers.

The assembly language modules in this book even can be linked to programs written in order languages, such as Pascal or compiled BASIC. There are several reasons for using assembly language rather than C for some functions of a program. The most obvious one is speed. You can fine tune an assembly language function much more effectively than you can a similar function in C. In graphics functions that handle a great deal of information or ones that perform complex operations many times—the LZW decompression functions of a GIF file decoder quickly come to mind in this respect—the amount of time saved by an assembly language function over some equivalent C code can be quite significant.

Assembly language code usually is a lot smaller than C code.

There are things that are difficult or impossible to do in C. The extended memory interface code in Chapter 11, for example, makes use of a process pointer provided by the XMS driver that would be a bit awkward in C. In this case, an assembly language driver saves a lot of head scratching and potential bugs.

Writing assembly language functions for use with C programs is a complex and particularly thorny subject because you have to know a lot about the low level aspects of a PC and about how C works internally, two things that programming exclusively in C insulates you from. Modifying existing assembly language functions is quite a lot easier; if this area is new to you, you might want to start by tinkering with the code in this book before you try writing something from scratch.

In writing an assembly language function, all you're really doing is to synthesize a C function or, more precisely, to sidestep the work that a C compiler does for you and arrive at the same results—hopefully rather more tightly coded.

There are a number of important conventions that assembly language functions must follow. These concern the ways in which assembly language code interfaces with C code.

C is called a *stack-oriented* language, and despite the initial complexity of using the stack, you'll find that assembly language functions work well if you make them stack oriented too.

In passing data to and from functions, C passes values on the stack and returns them in registers. This simple bit of C code involves passing an argument to the function putch:

putch('A');

The equivalent assembly language for this would look a little strange:

```
MOV        AL,'A'
PUSH       AX
CALL       _putch
POP        AX
```

The putch function will retrieve the argument passed to it by peeking back up the stack and copying the contents of the appropriate location of stack memory.

In reality, this example probably would be written like this:

```
MOV        AL,'A'
PUSH       AX
CALL       _putch
ADD        SP,2
```

When a function is called like this, its arguments are pushed up onto the stack. When the function returns, the arguments are "thrown away." In the first example, this was done by simply popping them off the stack. If there had been four arguments on the stack, this would have required four pops. Because each argument must be one word—2 bytes—the stack can simply be adjusted by adding the appropriate number of bytes to the stack pointer, SP. This saves three instructions.

Note that the stack starts at the top of its memory segment and grows down. If SP was 0FFFFH initially, pushing a value onto the stack would leave it at 0FFFDH. To simulate popping something off the stack you must add to the value of SP.

A 32-bit pointer is passed as two words on the stack. The first word is the offset and the second the segment. Long integers also are passed as two words. If you were to write a machine language equivalent to the farPtr

C language function—not a bad idea, actually—it would only have two arguments from C but it would actually have four arguments, or more correctly four words passed to it on the stack, in assembly language.

Because they're just words on the stack, a function can meddle with its arguments if it so desires. Because they're to be thrown away when the call to the function is complete, altering their values will not affect the values of things in the calling code. This also is how an assembly language function copes with local variables.

If the assembly language function that you're writing requires a place to store numbers temporarily, you can allocate some permanent storage in memory for it. This is equivalent to C language static data. This is wasteful of space, however, because the static data will remain even when the function in question isn't doing anything.

A better way is to allocate space on the stack. If your assembly language function begins by decrementing the stack pointer by two bytes—and finishes by adding those 2 bytes so your computer doesn't crash when the function attempts to return—there will be a one word gap in the stack. This word is free for use as a local variable. Because the stack pointer points to beyond this word, it will not be overwritten before the function returns.

This is exactly what C language functions do when you allocate local variables. These stack variables behave in the same way whether they're being used by C or assembly language functions. You can allocate any reasonable amount of storage on the stack.

When an assembly language function wants to return a value it loads the value into the AX register just before returning. In a C program, something like this:

```
a = getch( );
```

really means to execute the getch function and then load whatever happens to be in the AX register into the variable a.

Assembly Language and Compiler Conventions

The sample assembly language module shown in Fig. 1-5 illustrates a complete, linkable assembly language program. This implements a simple PC Paintbrush PCX file decoder. The principle behind this will be explained in detail in Chapter 4. You might want to look at this example program here, though, to see how things are handled in an assembly language module.

When it's linked to a C language program, this function would appear as UnpackBits. Under Turbo C, all external functions have an underbar attached to the beginnings of their names. Hence, an assembly language function must place the underbar in function names that might be called explicitly from a C program if the compiler is to recognize them.

This is a useful feature, because it means, for example, that you could write a function called putch in an assembly language module for use only within that module and not have it interfere with the library function putch that C uses.

You must tell the assembler that UnpackBits will be called from an external module and that it is to be regarded as a Far procedure. This latter designation means that it will be called by a C program compiled with the large memory model. Local assembly language routines that you write for use just within an assembly language module can be near procedures. Procedures that are declared as near can be called with short calls— 16-bit addresses—which allows them to execute faster.

The public designation indicates that UnpackBits is externally callable.

There are three declared segments in this module, in keeping with the segment structure of Turbo C large model programs. The code segment, UNPACK_TEXT here, is where all the action takes place. The Turbo C convention for naming this segment for the large memory model is to call it something with ''_TEXT'' tacked onto the end.

The other two segments, down at the bottom, are for initialized and uninitialized data respectively. Because assembly language modules usually are stripped down for speed, it's more practical to put all your static data in the _DATA segment, whether or not it's initialized, rather than having to swap the DS register value around to address two segments. This approach only gets to be a problem when the contents of the _DATA segment exceed 64k which is unlikely to happen using the example programs in this book.

When this module is linked to a C program, its contents will be split up into three parts, one for each segment, and added onto the code and data segments that have come from the C part of the program being linked.

Handling the Stack

When a C language program calls UnpackBits, the program pushes any arguments it has onto the stack, as you've seen. Next, the PC's processor pushes two words, or four bytes, onto the stack. These are the segments in which the calling code resides and the offset of the place where the call is to return to. When the assembly language part of the code wants to look back up the stack to find its arguments, it has to keep in mind that there are four more bytes up there than would be immediately apparent.

Actually, there will be six bytes, because every assembly language function pushes a minimum of one word onto the stack before it starts doing anything. This will be discussed momentarily.

In a small model program, one in which there was no need to remember the segment of the calling code, there only would be four bytes on the stack. As such, it's a good idea to represent this stack offset as an equate value, such that if you ever did want to modify this assembly language module for use with small model programs you could just change the equate. The equate used in this book is _AOFF.

The way in which an assembly language program gets at the stack is to index off a register that points to the current stack pointer location as of the time the function was called. The obvious choice for this would seem to be the stack pointer, or SP register, but this turns out not to be the case. There are two reasons for this. The first is that the stack pointer is actually constantly in flux, even when the computer appears to be idle. Every time you strike a key, for example, things get pushed onto and popped off the stack as the keyboard handler interrupt is dealt with. Second, the SP register cannot be indexed.

The processor has another register to handle this, the base pointer, or BP register. This is a 16-bit register just like AX or DI, except that it's rarely used for anything other than stack manipulations. It has the peculiar property of always referring implicitly to things in the stack segment. In addition, it can be indexed.

Every procedure in a stack-oriented language uses the BP register to address the stack. As such, an assembly language function like this one must preserve the BP register by saving it on the stack before it mangles it, such that the calling C code will be able to continue to address its stack once UnpackBits returns.

The first important thing an assembly language function does is to copy the stack pointer into the base pointer. Subsequently, all stack operations can be handled by the base pointer.

The first argument on the stack can be loaded into the AX register like this:

```
MOV   AX,[BP + _AOFF + 0]
```

Obviously, you need not have the zero in there—it's done for the sake of consistency. The second argument on the stack could be loaded into the BX register like this:

```
MOV   BX,[BP + _AOFF + 2]
```

As you get into all this stack juggling you'll find that you need not retrieve things from the stack as often as you might think. It's very often more convenient to use them where they stand. For example, the obvious way to multiply the first two arguments on the stack together would be to do this:

```
MOV     AX,[BP + _AOFF + 0]
MOV     BX,[BP + _AOFF + 2]
MUL     BX
```

In fact, it could be done with one less instruction:

```
MOV     AX,[BP + _AOFF + 0]
MUL     WORD PTR [BP + _AOFF + 2]
```

It's important to keep in mind that the stack is just memory, and that the PC's processor is loaded with instructions to let you treat it as such.

The example function in Fig. 1-5 uses several stack variables that it allocates for itself. It does this by subtracting a number of bytes from the stack pointer at the start of the function. You can see how this works. In the course of using this function, the stack might bounce around as various interrupt handlers and TSR programs operate in the background of your computer, but the stack will never get any higher than the point established by this assembly language function. As such, the stack variables so allocated will be safe for the duration of the function.

Fig 1-5   An example of how assembly language modules are written for linking to a C program

```
;
;        A Greatly simplified PCX decoder
;

_AOFF           EQU     6         ;STACK OFFSET TO FIRST ARGUMENY

;THIS MACRO FETCHES THE DATA SEGEMENT
DATASEG         MACRO
                PUSH    AX
                MOV     AX,_DATA
                MOV     DS,AX
                POP     AX
                ENDM

UNPACK_TEXT     SEGMENT BYTE PUBLIC 'CODE'
                ASSUME  CS:UNPACK_TEXT,DS:_DATA

;THIS FUNCTION UNPACKS A BIT MAPPED PCX IMAGE
;               CALLED AS
;               Unpackbits(source,dest);
;               char *source,*dest;
;
                                  ;LOCAL VARIABLES FOR THIS PROCEDURE
IMAGE_DEEP      EQU     2         ;DEPTH OF PICTURE IN LINES
IMAGE_WIDE      EQU     4         ;WIDTH OF PICTURE IN BYTES
IMAGE_PLANES    EQU     6         ;NUMBER OF PLANES IN THE PICTURE
IMAGE_COUNT     EQU     8         ;NUMBER OF BYTES WRITTEN IN THIS LINE
IMAGE_ADJUST    EQU     8         ;AMOUNT OF STACK SPACE TO RESERVE

                PUBLIC  _UnpackBits
_UnpackBits     PROC    FAR

                PUSH    BP
                MOV     BP,SP
                SUB     SP,IMAGE_ADJUST      ;ADJUST THE STACK POINTER
                                             ;FOR LOCAL VARIABLES
                DATASEG

                MOV     SI,[BP + _AOFF + 0]  ;OFFSET OF SOURCE
                MOV     DS,[BP + _AOFF + 2]  ;SEGMENT OF SOURCE
```

Fig 1-5   continued

```
            MOV     DI,[BP + _AOFF + 4]       ;OFFSET OF DESTINATION
            MOV     ES,[BP + _AOFF + 6]       ;SEGMENT OF DESTINATION

            SUB     AX,AX
            MOV     AL,[SI+66]                ;GET THE BYTES PER LINE
            MOV     [BP - IMAGE_WIDE],AX      ;SAVE THEM

            SUB     AX,AX
            MOV     AL,[SI+65]                ;GET THE NUMBER OF PLANES
            MOV     [BP - IMAGE_PLANES],AX    ;SAVE THEM

            MOV     AX,[SI+10]                ;GET THE IMAGE DEPTH
            MOV     [BP - IMAGE_DEEP],AX      ;SAVE IT

            ADD     SI,128                    ;POINT TO FIRST BYTE OF DATA
            SUB     BX,BX                     ;ZERO THE LINE COUNTER

            MOV     AX,[BP - IMAGE_DEEP]
            MUL     WORD PTR [BP - IMAGE_PLANES]
            MOV     CX,AX                     ;GET THE NUMBER OF LINES
                                              ;TO UNPACK

MUP1:       PUSH    CX                        ;SAVE THE LINE COUNT
            MOV     AX,[BP - IMAGE_WIDE]      ;RESET THE WIDTH COUNTER
            MOV     [BP - IMAGE_COUNT],AX

            INC     BX                        ;BUMP THE RUNNING LINE COUNTER

MUP2:       LODSB                             ;GET A BYTE FROM THE SOURCE

            MOV     AH,AL                     ;SEE IF IT'S A PATTERN CALL
            AND     AH,0C0H
            CMP     AH,0C0H
            JNE     MUP3                      ;NOPE... DIRECT WRITE

            AND     AL,3FH                    ;OTHERWISE, GET THE COUNT
            SUB     CX,CX
            MOV     CL,AL                     ;PUT IT IN CX
            SUB     [BP - IMAGE_COUNT],CX     ;SUBTRACT IT FROM THE RUNNING
                                              ;...WIDTH COUNTER

            LODSB                             ;GET THE PATTERN BYTE
            CMP     BX,[BP - IMAGE_PLANES]    ;CHECK THE RUNNING LINE COUNTER
            JL      MUP4                      ;... AGAINST THE PLANE COUNT
                                              ;THROW AWAY ALL THE COLOUR
            CLD
    REPNE   STOSB                             ;WRITE THE PATTERN

            JMP     MUP4

MUP3:       MOV     CX,1                      ;COME HERE TO DO A DIRECT
            SUB     [BP - IMAGE_COUNT],CX     ;...BYTE COPY
```

```
                CMP       BX,[BP - IMAGE_PLANES]  ;THROW AWAY THE COLOUR DATA
                JL        MUP4

                CLD
       REPNE    STOSB                             ;AND SAVE IT

MUP4:           CMP       WORD PTR [BP - IMAGE_COUNT],0
                JG        MUP2                     ;KEEP GOING

                CMP       BX,[BP - IMAGE_PLANES]
                JL        MUP5                     ;DON'T LET LINE COUNTER WRAP
                MOV       BX,0

MUP5:           POP       CX                       ;LOOP 'TIL LINES ARE UNPACKED
                LOOP      MUP1

UPX:            DATASEG
                ADD       SP,IMAGE_ADJUST          ;RESTORE THE STACK POINTER
                POP       BP
                RET
_UnpackBits     ENDP

UNPACK_TEXT     ENDS

DGROUP          GROUP     _DATA,_BSS

_DATA           SEGMENT WORD PUBLIC 'DATA'

_DATA           ENDS

_BSS            SEGMENT WORD PUBLIC 'BSS'

_BSS            ENDS
                END
```

Figure 1-6 illustrates the geography of the stack while UnpackBits is operating.

Again, the BP register is used to address the stack variables. Note how the stack variables are named using equates, so that they're fairly easy to keep track of.

You will notice that the BP register was explicitly saved on the stack in UnpackBits. There are other registers that could be saved on the stack. These tend to vary from compiler to compiler. Under Turbo C, the SI and DI registers are used by the C parts of a program as register variables. As such, they must be preserved by any assembly language program that might mangle them. Alternately, you can just switch off the register variables in Turbo C using the Options menu.

In most cases, turning off the register variables improves the performance of graphics programs, because it relieves all the functions in a program of the necessity of having to preserve them. In this book, all the programs are designed to be compiled with the register variables turned off.

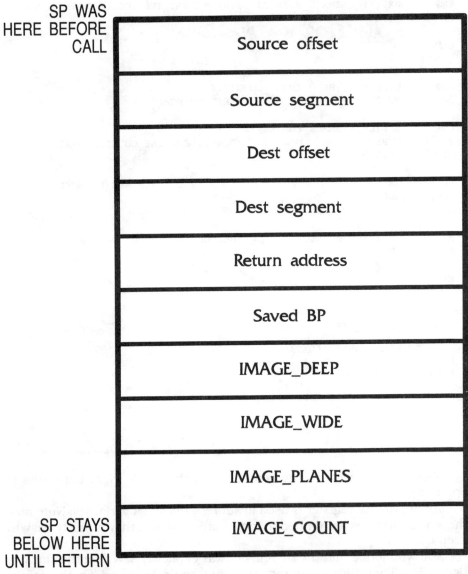

SP WAS
HERE BEFORE
CALL

SP STAYS
BELOW HERE
UNTIL RETURN

Fig 1-6   What the stack looks like while the assembly language PCX decoder is working

Linking Code Modules

When you write a simple C program, such as the following:

```
main ( )
{
    puts("Hello");
}
```

the compiler compiles your source file and creates an object file based on it. This object file is almost pure machine language but, for example, it contains a note to the linker that says "there ought to be a function called puts... find it and put a call to it in the code."

The function puts is called an *external reference*. C is set up so that any function that is called but not defined in the program you're writing is assumed to be external. In this case, the compiler assumes that finding puts is the linker's problem.

You can write a program using UnpackBits by just using it as if it was a function provided by your C compiler. You, too, can assume that finding UnpackBits is the linker's problem, at least for now.

When Turbo C is finished compiling your code—assuming that no errors cropped up—it will subsequently start trying to resolve those functions that were not defined in your program. This is the process known as linking. In a simple program like the one just shown, it would look to the various *libraries* that came with the compiler.

A library is a collection of commonly used functions. When the linker finds a function whose name corresponds to one of the unresolved functions in your program, it copies the function from the library, adds it to your current code segment and replaces all the notes regarding that function with the actual address of the function in your code.

The linker only takes those parts of a library that are needed to resolve the references in your program. It doesn't link in the whole library.

The UnpackBits function is not in a library; it's in another object module. Turbo C does not know this, and, as such, a simple program that attempts to call UnpackBits will run afoul of the linker, because UnpackBits will remain unresolved. In this case, you must direct the linker to include an extra object module in the linking process. This is handled under Turbo C through the use of a project file.

Let's assume that the assembly language module example was typed into a text file called UNPACK.ASM, and subsequently assembled using MASM leaving you with UNPACK.OBJ. You are going to write a program called SHOW-PCX, which will unpack and display PCX files. You would, as such, create a text file called SHOW-PCX.PRJ. It would contain the following lines:

```
show-pcx
unpack.obj
```

You would make this the current project by assigning the project name using the project menu of Turbo C.

If you are using Turbo C version 1.5, note that the linker for this version will not automatically check the GRAPHICS.LIB library when it's attempting to resolve external references. This library contains all the functions for the Turbo C device independent graphics facilities. If you attempt to compile any of the example programs in this book that use the Turbo C graphics facilities using Turbo C version 1.5, you must add this library to their project files.

If the SHOW-PCX program were to require Turbo C's graphics, you would write its project file like this for compilation under version 1.5:

```
show-pcx
unpack.obj
graphics.lib
```

Turbo C version 2.0 onward corrected this. Unless you will be linking in extra object modules such as UNPACK.OBJ, simple C programs that use Turbo's graphics don't require project files at all under version 2.0.

Note also that Turbo C version 1.0 had no graphics support at all. Some of the programs in this book don't use Turbo's graphics, and you can compile them under version 1.0. Those few that do will not be usable with this version of the compiler.

While the linker can resolve external functions without any mention of their external location in your C program, it can't deal with external variables quite so easily. Let's say that UNPACK.ASM had two numbers that represented the image width and depth, and that it wanted to make available to the C program this will be linked to it. First off, you would have to name them in a way that Turbo C agreed with, that is, with underbars before them. They might be defined something like this:

```
_WIDTH   DW   ?
_DEPTH   DW   ?
```

You also would have to tell the assembler that they're for external use, like this:

```
PUBLIC _WIDTH, _DEPTH
```

Let's assume that these variables live in the _DATA segment.

Finally, you would have to tell your C program about the existence of these external variables:

```
extern int WIDTH,DEPTH;
```

Note that the underbars have disappeared. When the linker attempts to resolve any external reference, it adds the underbars. This also is true for external functions.

Debugging Assembly Language Subroutines

One of the powerful features of C is a structure that inhibits the creation of bugs. Inventive programmers usually find a way around it, and for this reason most of the latest generation of C compilers come with sophisticated debuggers that allow you to work at something like the C language level while you step through your program looking for problems.

Assembly language has no reservations about allowing you to install bugs in your programs. It seems to enjoy letting you do so. Because graphics programs invariably use assembly language to deal with the very lowest level of your computer, occasionally bypassing even the BIOS and talking directly to your system hardware, bugs that creep into graphics assembly language routines often are particularly nasty.

The largest part of the problem with debugging an assembly language routine is in finding the actual code to be debugged after the linker has combined it with the C language part of your program. There's a simple trick for handling this in DEBUG.

This section will deal exclusively with DEBUG, which is usually adequate for simple, low debugging. However, DEBUG runs into severe problems if you happen to be debugging on a Hercules card. On any other sort of card, interrupting a program while it's in graphics mode so you can see what it's up to will cause the BIOS to print text to the graphics screen, albeit rather slowly. This facility is not available to Hercules card users, because Hercules cards are not supported by the PC BIOS.

There is no easy way around this should you want to apply the following techniques to a Hercules environment when your program is in graphics mode.

Under DEBUG, executing a specific range of code with an instruction like this one:

```
- G = 100,2FF
```

causes DEBUG to replace the instruction at the second address, 02FFH in this case, with the machine language instruction INT 3. Having done this, DEBUG starts executing the program at location 0100H by simply jumping to it.

When DEBUG is running, the interrupt vector for INT 3 points back into DEBUG, so that when an INT 3 is called, DEBUG stops the execution of whatever threw the INT 3 and returns you to the DEBUG command line prompt. It then replaces the original bytes in memory that were displaced by the INT 3.

You can cause any program to break at a specific point under DEBUG by simply simulating this process. To install a breakpoint in a program containing both assembly language and C, put the instruction INT 3 wherever you want the code to stop. Assemble the assembly language module. Compile and link the program and either exit or shell out of Turbo C. Run DEBUG and load the program under Scrutiny. Let the program run by issuing the G command. The program will run until it encounters your INT 3 instruction. You can trace through the subsequent code by simply starting 2 bytes beyond the location pointed to by IP when the INT 3 instruction was encountered.

From this point on you can debug the assembly language function you've interrupted as you would any assembly language program. There are no real rules to this process . . . debugging is very much an intuitive art.

As a rule, three quarters of all the problems that plague assembly language functions are caused by segment registers. There are a lot of segments in a large model C and assembly language program. These include the stack segment, where arguments are passed and temporary variables are stored, the _DATA segment where static data is stored, the _BSS segment that might get used for uninitialized static storage and, most important, the segment values passed as pointer arguments to your functions. None of these can be assumed to be the same.

In addition, some registers implicitly address particular segments. For example, this line:

```
MOV     [SI],AL
```

will store the contents of AL in the data segment. This line:

```
MOV     [DI],AL
```

will store it in the extra segment. Even if SI and DI are the same, they won't point to the same place unless DS and ES also happen to be equal.

If your assembly language functions fail to behave or, worse, crash your computer, make sure the segment registers are pointing where you expect them to.

COOKBOOK

Don't be too concerned if some of the things in this introduction have seemed a bit intense. They'll crop up throughout this book, but in their future occurrences you'll be able to see them in the context of actual functioning programs. It's a lot easier to see what things do when you're about to watch them at work.

How much or how little of the low level details of this book you have to cope with will be determined largely by how much you have to modify the programs. In many cases you'll be able to simply port the functions in their entirety to your own programs.

In this case, you can use this as a sort of graphics cookbook and get on with the original parts of the application you're writing.

2

CHAPTER

The Secrets of
MacPaint Files

Time is an illusion perpetrated by the manufacturers of space.
—Murphy's Laws of Computers

MacPaint files didn't originate on a pc; they came from the Apple Macintosh. At least until quite recently, with the advent of the graphically more powerful MAC II, MacPaint files were the only bit-mapped image file format to be used with any consistency. In many ways this is extremely powerful, because virtually all Macintosh applications that deal with graphics accept this common file format.

Unlike on the PC, of course.

The interesting thing about MacPaint files is that there are so many of them. Gigabytes worth of interesting pictures exist in the public domain in the MacPaint format. You can download them from bulletin boards and possess an instant clip art collection without having to mortgage your cat.

Figure 2-1 illustrates a typical public domain MacPaint picture, and several others will crop up throughout this book.

In most respects, the MacPaint file format is less flexible than any of the others to be discussed in this book. It's inherently black and white, for one thing. A full page of MacPaint information is only a full page if you print it at about 75 dots per inch. At 300 dots per inch—the maximum resolution of most reasonably priced laser printers—MacPaint pictures appear 2 by 2½ inches.

Unlike all the other common image file formats, MacPaint pictures have a fixed size. No matter what's in one picture, it will be 576 pixels across by 720 pixels deep.

There are a number of interesting elements to the MacPaint format, and, specifically, to the version of it that makes its way across to the PC. For example, when you load a MacPaint picture into MacPaint on a Macintosh, the paint program displays 38 patterns as well as the picture itself. If

Fig 2-1   This is a typical public domain MacPaint picture—sort of. Actually, the great majority of typical public domain images are of nude women. The bottom of this picture bore the following credit: ''From a photo by Tom McHugh, Photo Researchers, in *Natural History* 9/60. (In search of Ancient Pack Rats, Jim I. Mead)''

you edit the patterns associated with a particular picture, they stay edited. MacPaint pictures carry their patterns with them.

This is an unusual feature, and of very little use to the programs you probably will create as a result of reading through this chapter. However, if you can think of an application for them, there are 38 pattern definitions in every MacPaint image file. There's some code coming up that will let you see them.

On a Macintosh, all files are stored in two chunks, called *forks*. These are the data fork, which contains, among other things, picture information, and the resource fork, which contains code. A MacPaint file consists entirely of data fork—the resource fork is said to be empty.

When a MacPaint file is ported to some other system, such as a PC, it's sent a single file. This file consists of the contents of both forks plus a MacBinary header that records how the file is to be split if it returns to a Macintosh, so that the two forks can be regenerated. The MacBinary header also records what sort of file was ported—a MacPaint file rather than, say, a MacWrite file—and the original file name. Macintosh file names can be up to 31 characters long.

The MacBinary header is not, strictly speaking, part of the file format. In fact, it's not even a data structure that officially exists in the voluminous documentation of the Macintosh. Nonetheless, it will be treated as part of the file here because it appears at the start of most of the MacPaint files one is likely to encounter on a PC.

There's a complete description of this structure at the end of this chapter.

The actual picture data in a MacPaint file starts after both the MacBinary header and the pattern data. It's compressed in an unusually simple format, which is why it will be the first image file format to be discussed. The picture data occupies the rest of the file.

THE HEADER

Before a program can begin to look at any image file format, it will have to do some housekeeping. This involves making sure that the file in question is actually what it purports to be, for example, so that the program doesn't attempt to display as image data something that started life as the object code for a video game. In the case of image formats that support variable dimensions, it also must ascertain what the dimensions associated with the file in question actually are. All MacPaint pictures are of the same dimensions, so software that unpacks them needn't worry about this aspect of housekeeping.

The MacBinary header contains two long integers that define the Macintosh file type and the file's creator. The Mac has a rather unusual system of maintaining this data. Each unique file "type" is assigned a 4-byte code; these 4 bytes are treated alternately as 4 bytes or as one long integer, depending upon which is most convenient at the time. Each program that generates files also has a 4-byte signature, or *creator* field. The file type for a MacPaint file is PNTG. The creator, if the file originated with MacPaint, is MPNT. However, there are several Macintosh applications that generate MacPaint format files, so you can't assume that the creator field will be MPNT.

The type field of a MacBinary header exists at bytes 0041H through 0044H. Thus, if the 4 bytes starting at this location are PNTG, you can

assume that you have a MacPaint image file and proceed to decode the
beast.

The original name of a Macintosh file ported to a PC is stored in the
MacBinary header starting with the second byte in. The first byte in the
header is always a zero. The name is stored as a Pascal-style string, that is,
with the first byte in the string being the length of the rest of the string.
The string is not necessarily terminated by a zero.

Finally, the pattern data starts 132 bytes into the file, that is, 4 bytes
past the end of the MacBinary header. Each pattern is 8 bytes long.

To start with, let's look at a simple program to read in the header of a
MacPaint file and do some of the aforementioned housekeeping. It's shown
in Fig. 2-2. This code uses the Turbo C graphics library to keep it simple.
The later chapters of this book will illustrate faster ways to move graphics
data to the screen.

Fig 2-2   A program to look at MacPaint file patterns

```
/* A program to look at MacPaint file patterns */
#include "stdio.h"
#include "alloc.h"
#include "graphics.h"

/* how big each swatch will be */
#define blockSize     32

char header[640];          /* where the header lives */

main(argc,argv)
    int argc;
    char *argv[];
{
    FILE *fp;

    if(argc>1) {
        /* attempt to open the file */
        if((fp=fopen(argv[1],"rb")) != NULL) {
            /* read the first 640 bytes */
            if(fread(header,1,640,fp)==640) {
                /* see if the type is right */
                if(!strncmp(header+0x0041,"PNTG",4)) {
                    /* make the name a C string */
                    header[2+header[1]]=0;
                    /* say what the Mac name was */
                    printf("The Mac file name is %s.\n",
                        header+2);
                    /* wait for a key press */
                    getch();
                    /* and show the patterns */
                    showPatterns();
                } else printf("Not a MacPaint file.\n");
            } else printf("Error reading %s.\n",argv[1]);
            fclose(fp);
```

```
        } else printf("Error opening %s.\n",argv[1]);
    }
}

/* show the patters stored in the header buffer */
showPatterns()
{
    int i,j;

    /* graphics on */
    init();

    /* use the patterns for fill data */
    setfillstyle(USER_FILL,getmaxcolor());
    for(i=0;i<38;++i) {
        /* invert each pattern */
        for(j=0;j<8;++j)
          header[132+(i*8)+j]=~header[132+(i*8)+j];
        /* make it the default fill */
        setfillpattern(header+132+(i*8),getmaxcolor());
        /* fill a swatch with it */
        bar(blockSize+((i/2)*blockSize),
            blockSize+((i%2)*blockSize),
            (blockSize*2)+((i/2)*blockSize),
            (blockSize*2)+((i%2)*blockSize));
    }
    /* wait for a keypress */
    getch();
    /* graphics off */
    deinit();
}

init()          /* turn on graphics mode */
{
    int d,m,e=0;

    detectgraph(&d,&m);
    if(d<0) {
        puts("No graphics card");
        exit(1);
    }
    initgraph(&d,&m,"");
    e=graphresult();
    if(e<0) {
        printf("Graphics error %d: %s",
          e,grapherrormsg(e));
        exit(1);
    }
    setcolor(getmaxcolor());
}

deinit()    /* turn off graphics card */
{
    closegraph();
}
```

This program checks to see whether the header it has read in came from a proper MacPaint file, prints the original file name, and puts your PC in graphics mode to show you what the patterns look like. The patterns can vary from picture to picture. A typical pattern set is shown in Fig. 2-3.

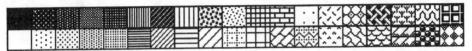

Fig 2-3   A set of patterns from a MacPaint file. These vary from file to file

One useful thing to note about this program is that it inverts all the bytes in the pattern before it displays them. The patterns, as with Mac-Paint pictures themselves, are inverted from what you'd expect picture data to be on a PC. On a Macintosh the screen is white by default; writing a pixel to it will make a black dot appear. On a PC, the opposite is true: the hardware of a PC's display adapter makes the screen black with white pixels. If you display a Mac picture—or Mac picture patterns—directly from their files, they'll look like negatives.

This creates some difficulties in writing fast machine language display routines. You can move blocks of data to the screen very quickly using the 8088 MOVSB instruction. However, in order to move *and* invert it, you must do so one byte at a time, which is much slower. It's often more practical to store MacPaint pictures in memory already inverted, so that they can be updated to the screen more rapidly.

UNPACKING THE PICTURE

All image files use some form of algorithmic compression to reduce the size of the images they contain. It's especially easy to see this work in the MacPaint file format, because its images are so simple and predictable. Figure 2-4 illustrates the process, although you'll probably have to read through the next few paragraphs to properly understand it.

By the way, it's worth noting that one of the several compression techniques used by the much more complicated TIFF file format, which will be discussed later on in this book, deliberately copies MacPaint compression.

A raw image of the size of a MacPaint picture would occupy more than 50k of memory or disk space. In practice, it's rarely necessary that a disk file containing a MacPaint image be anything this big. For example, if the first line of a picture is all white, it can be stored in 2 bytes, rather than the 72 it occupies in its unpacked form. The first byte is called the *index*, and would be 72 in this case. The second byte is the *data* that will be written to the unpacked image 72 times to form the first line.

The image data in a MacPaint file is treated as 720 individual 72-byte scan lines. Each line can contain as many data *fields* as is necessary. A

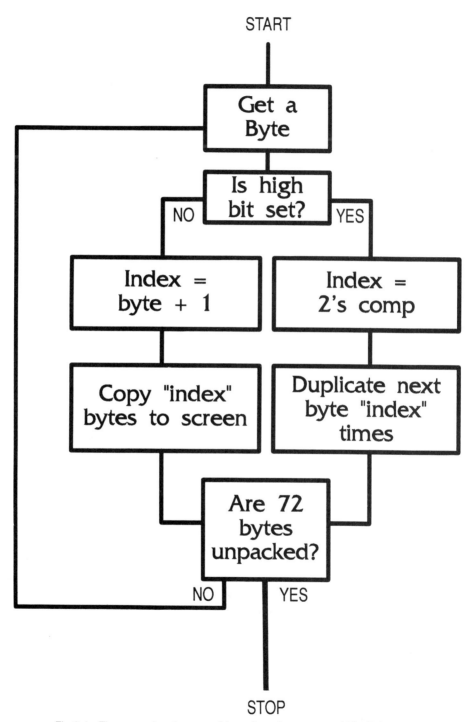

Fig 2-4   The procedure for unpacking a line of compressed MacPaint data

field either can be a run of identical bytes or a string of bytes to be copied "as is" into the unpacked image. Thus, the definition of a particular line might be to write 5 white bytes, 6 grey bytes, to copy the next 20 bytes "as is" from the source file, and to write 41 black bytes, for a total of 72.

The format for defining these fields in a MacPaint file is fairly elegant. Inasmuch as a line can be no longer than 72 bytes, the format can define any field length easily with 7 bits. Seven bits can hold numbers from 0 to 127. Thus, the index byte of any field is defined as being 7 bits for the actual index and the eighth bit, or *high order* bit, as a flag. If the high order bit is set, the field is a run of bytes. In this case, the next byte is repeated index times in the scan line. If the high order bit is clear, the next index bytes are copied "as is" from the source to the destination.

Actually, it's a little more complicated than this. The value of the index is one greater than the number in the first seven bits of the index byte. Presumably this is based on the assumption that there is no such thing as a zero length field. As such, not wishing to waste a perfectly good number, the designer of the format allowed that an index of zero actually indicates a field length of one.

To further complicate things, if the high order bit is set, the index value is actually the two's complement of the byte.

It's interesting to observe that image compression usually results in MacPaint files smaller than the raw images would have been, but not always. There are pathological cases in which the screen data is not compressible, in which case the file compression routine will wind up copying the screen verbatim into the file—plus 720 index bytes. A picture of completely random data would be such a pathological case.

This is not as unlikely as it might seem. Scanned photographs that have been *dithered* to distribute their scanning errors often wind up as very large files. Although the data is not really random, it's so unpredictable as to stymie this approach at compressing it. Both dithering and compression techniques that get around this will be discussed later in this book.

Figure 2-5 illustrates part of a MacPaint picture that started life as a photograph. There is relatively little opportunity for compression here.

The function in Fig. 2-6 is a routine to unpack one line of compressed MacPaint picture information from a file into one line of a raw bitmap. The file pointer is assumed to be pointing to the first byte in the actual image data of the file the first time this is called. It will leave the file pointer at the beginning of the compressed data for the next line.

This routine will return 72 if the field unpacks properly and zero if the end of the file has been reached; this would only happen if the file has been corrupted or truncated. It assumes that *p* points to a buffer at least 72 bytes long.

Fig 2-5   This picture has been scanned and dithered. The image area presents few opportunities for compression. This picture was downloaded from Canada Remote Systems (416) 629-0136

Fig 2-6   A function to unpack one line of a MacPaint file

```
ReadMacLine(p,fp)
        char *p;
        FILE *fp;
{
        int c,i,n=0

        do {
                /* get one byte from the file */
                c=fgetc(fp) & 0xff;

                /* see if the high order bit is set */
                if(c & 0x80) {
                        /* if it is, derive index */
                        i = ((~c) & 0xff)+2;
                        /* get the byte to repeat */
                        c=fgetc(fp);
                        /* and copy it into memory i times */
                        while(i--) p[n++] = c;
                }
                else {
                        /* otherwise get the index */
                        i=(c & 0xff)+1;
                        /* and get i bytes from the file */
                        while(i--) p[n++] = fgetc(fp);
                }
        /* keep at it until one line has been unpacked */
        } while(n < 72);
        if(c==EOF) n=0;
        return(n);
}
```

UNPACKING A WHOLE IMAGE

To unpack a complete MacPaint file into a raw bitmap, you would call this thing 720 times, that is, once for every line in the file. Assuming the file pointer is 640 bytes into the file, that is, that it's past the MacBinary header and the patterns, the function in Fig. 2-7 would unpack the whole file.

Fig 2-7   A function to unpack all the image data in a MacPaint file

```
UnpackMacFile(p,fp)
        char *p;
        FILE *fp;
{
        int i,n;

        for(i=0;i<720;++i) {
                if((n=ReadMacLine(p,fp)) != 72) break;
                p+=72;
        }
        return(n);
}
```

This function assumes that p points to a buffer at least 51840 bytes long—that's 720 lines times 72 bytes. When it's done—assuming that it didn't encounter an error—it will return 72 and the buffer at p will contain a raw bit-mapped image of the original MacPaint picture.

To complete the story, the program in Fig. 2-8 will drive the previous two functions. It will load and unpack a MacPaint image file and display the top of it on the screen. Once again, this program uses the Turbo C graphics library.

This program uses the routines discussed previously in this chapter plus few more. The code to detect the presence of a suitable MacBinary header is more or less unchanged from the pattern display program. In this case, however, the code must allocate a chunk of heap space big enough to hold the unpacked MacPaint picture—plus 4 bytes, for reasons that will become obvious in a second. The actual unpacking process should be familiar by now.

The Turbo C graphics library includes a function called putimage that will copy a bitmap of any size from memory to the screen. It uses the device independent drivers that come with Turbo C's graphics library, so your program needn't worry about which actual graphics card is in use. It also clips any images that are too large for the screen, so you can simply tell it to show the whole picture and allow the code for the function itself to figure out how much of it will fit on your tube.

The bit maps that putimage puts are supposed to be excised from the screen and placed in memory by another function, getimage. In this case,

Fig 2-8   A program to view the top of a MacPaint file

```
/* A program to look at MacPaint pictures */
#include "stdio.h"
#include "alloc.h"
#include "graphics.h"

char header[640];          /* where the header lives */

main(argc,argv)
        int argc;
        char *argv[];
{
        FILE *fp;
        char *p;

        if(argc > 1) {
                /* attempt to open the file */
                if((fp=fopen(argv[1],"rb")) != NULL) {
                        /* read in the header */
                        if(fread(header,1,640,fp)==640) {
                                /* check to make sure it's a picture */
                                if(!strncmp(header+0x0041,"PNTG",4)) {
                                        /* allocate a big buffer */
                                        if((p=malloc(51844)) != NULL) {
                                                /* unpack the file */
                                                if(UnpackMacFile(p+4,fp)==72)
                                                        /* show the picture */
                                                        ShowMacPicture(p);
                                                free(p);
                                        }
                                } else printf("Not a MacPaint file.\n");
                        } else printf("Error reading %s.\n",argv[1]);
                        fclose(fp);
                } else printf("Error opening %s.\n",argv[1]);
        }
}

ShowMacPicture(p) /* display the top of the picture */
        char *p;
{
        /* graphics on */
        init();
        /* set image size */
        memcpy(p,"\077\002\000\132",4);
        /* show the picture */
        putimage(0,0,p,NOT_PUT);
        /* wait for a key press */
        getch();
        /* graphics off */
        deinit();
}
```

Fig 2-8   continued

```
ReadMacLine(p,fp)
        char *p;
        FILE *fp;
{

        int c,i,n=0;

        do {
                c=fgetc(fp) & 0xff;
                if(c & 0x80) {
                        i = ((~c) & 0xff)+2;
                        c=fgetc(fp);
                while(i--) p[n++] = c;
                }
                else {
                        i=(c & 0xff)+1;
                        while(i--) p[n++] = fgetc(fp);
                }
        } while(n < 72);
        if(c==EOF) n=0;
        return(n);
}

UnpackMacFile(p,fp)
        char *p;
        FILE *fp;
{

        int i,n;

        for(i=0;i<720;++i) {
                if((n=ReadMacLine(p,fp)) != 72) break;
                p+=72;
        }
        return(n);
}


init()              /* turn on graphics mode */
{
        int d,m,e=0;

        detectgraph(&d,&m);
        if(d<0) {
                puts("No graphics card");
                exit(1);
        }
        if(d==EGA) {
                d=CGA;
                m=CGAHI;
        }
        initgraph(&d,&m,"");
        e=graphresult();
        if(e<0) {
```

Fig 2-8   continued

```
                printf("Graphics error %d: %s",
                  e,grapherrormsg(e));
                exit(1);
        }
        setcolor(getmaxcolor());
}

deinit()   /* turn off graphics card */
{
        closegraph();
}
```

though, you will want to make putimage think that the unpacked MacPaint file came from getimage. For purely monochrome bit maps, the data that getimage creates is straight black and white bytes that correspond exactly to the data generated by unpacking a MacPaint file. The only qualification is that the first four bytes of the buffer that putimage puts must contain two integers. The first is one less than the original horizontal dimension of the image, and the second is one less than the original vertical dimension of the image. These values would be 575 and 719 respectively, for a MacPaint picture.

Obviously, you can't get all 720 lines on the screen at once. The putimage function ignores the ones that don't fit.

This is why you must allocate a buffer that is four bytes bigger than the uncompressed picture will be. The picture is unpacked into the buffer starting four bytes from its base, and the dimension integers are added afterward. In this program, they're defined as a byte string. The memcpy function serves to slip them into the buffer.

You could write a program to page through an entire MacPaint file using the techniques in this sample program. In practice, moving large amounts of picture information to the screen using putimage isn't all that desirable, because it's quite slow, even on high end machines. The putimage function does a lot of things that aren't required simply for stuffing bitmaps into the screen buffer. Chapter 8 discusses writing much more streamlined graphics drivers in assembly language.

If you look at the init function in Fig. 2-8, you'll note that the screen is forced into CGA monochrome graphics mode if the graphics drivers detect an EGA card. This does not make for the most elegant looking screen display, because the image area will be only 200 lines deep. An EGA card running in EGA graphics mode could manage 350. Unfortunately, it would want to manage them in 16 colors. A 16-color putimage buffer is structured differently than is an unpacked monochrome bitmap.

It's quite possible to convert monochrome data for use with putimage on an EGA card. Chapter 4 discusses how to synthesize a color putimage buffer. Unfortunately, putimage can only deal with image fragments that occupy less than 64 kilobytes of memory. Converting 350 lines of a Mac-Paint file to 16 colors, even if 15 of the 16 colors are unused, would require over 100 kilobytes.

This is another good reason for writing custom machine language drivers.

Figure 2-9 illustrates the differing image areas that are offered by CGA, EGA, and Hercules cards. This is simply the top of the same Mac-Paint file looked at on three different display adapters. The best view actually is to be had by a Hercules card, but Herc cards have the disadvantage of being wholly monochrome. The CGA display is pretty small by comparison; if you have an EGA card, it's desirable to find a way to use it.

Once again, a complete discussion of how to handle your screen graphics elegantly will have to wait for a while, but you can see roughly how it will be done by looking at the next program.

MacPaint Files on an EGA Card

If you want to be able to look at a MacPaint picture on an EGA card without skipping ahead and peeking at the machine language stuff, you will have to cheat. In programming circles this is usually referred to as something like "adaptive algorithmic synthesis" so it sounds better, although it's still cheating. In this case, cheating will result in both a faster program and a bit of prescience about the workings of display cards.

The display buffer memory structures of earlier display adapters behaved a bit weirdly in their graphics modes. An EGA card, by comparison, is elegantly simple. The first line of graphic information is stored in the first 80 bytes, the second in the next 80 bytes, and so on. In fact, there are four-paged display buffers in there—one for each color plane—but if you ignore this, an EGA can be treated as a very simple monochrome graphics display.

Figure 2-10 illustrates the MacPaint display program modified to drive an EGA card directly. It does not use the Turbo C graphics library, but rather, accesses the hardware directly. The init and deinit functions make direct calls to the PC's BIOS to change modes, and the code that displays the top of the MacPaint picture is written with a number of assumptions about the EGA card in mind.

The EGA card keeps its graphics buffer at segment A000H. The Show-MacPicture function uses the MK_FP function to return far pointers into the screen buffer and memcpy to copy lines from the image file to the screen.

This approach is a great deal faster than using putimage was. Its only drawbacks are that it only works on an EGA card, and that it requires considerable knowledge of how an EGA card functions.

Further Unpacking

You can write a much more streamlined MacPaint unpacking routine in assembly language. The functions discussed thus far are elegant and

Fig 2-9
The amount
of a MacPaint file
visible at once using
three popular
graphics cards

CGA card display: 640 by 200 pixels

Hercules card: 720 by 348 pixels

EGA card: 640 by 350 pixels

Fig 2-10 The MacPaint viewing program modified to drive an EGA card directly

```
/* A program to look at MacPaint pictures on an EGA card */
#include "stdio.h"
#include "alloc.h"
#include "dos.h"

char header[640];               /* where the header lives */

main(argc,argv)
        int argc;
        char *argv[];
{
        FILE *fp;
        char *p;

        if(argc > 1) {
                /* attempt to open the file */
                if((fp=fopen(argv[1],"rb")) != NULL) {
                        /* read in the header */
                        if(fread(header,1,640,fp)==640) {
                                /* check to make sure it's a picture */
                                if(!strncmp(header+0x0041,"PNTG",4)) {
                                        /* allocate a big buffer */
                                        if((p=malloc(51840)) != NULL) {
                                                /* unpack the file */
                                                if(UnpackMacFile(p,fp)==72)
                                                        /* show the picture */
                                                        ShowMacPicture(p);
                                                free(p);
                                        }
                                } else printf("Not a MacPaint file.\n");
                        } else printf("Error reading %s.\n",argv[1]);
                        fclose(fp);
                } else printf("Error opening %s.\n",argv[1]);
        }
}

ShowMacPicture(p) /* display the top of the picture */
        char *p;
{
        unsigned int i;

        /* graphics on */
        init();

        /* invert the buffer */
        for(i=0;i<51840;++i) p[i]=~p[i];

        /* copy the graphics to the screen */
        for(i=0;i<350;++i)
                memcpy(MK_FP(0xa000,i*80),p+(i*72),72);

        /* wait for a key press */
```

Fig 2-10 continued

```
          getch();
          /* graphics off */
          deinit();
   }

ReadMacLine(p,fp)
          char *p;
          FILE *fp;
   {
          int c,i,n=0;

          do {
                  c=fgetc(fp) & 0xff;
                  if(c & 0x80) {
                          i = ((~c) & 0xff)+2;
                          c=fgetc(fp);
                          while(i--) p[n++] = c;
                  }
                  else {
                          i=(c & 0xff)+1;
                          while(i--) p[n++] = fgetc(fp);
                  }
          } while(n < 72);
          if(c==EOF) n=0;
          return(n);
   }

UnpackMacFile(p,fp)
          char *p;
          FILE *fp;
   {
          int i,n;

          for(i=0;i<720;++i) {
                  if((n=ReadMacLine(p,fp)) != 72) break;
                  p+=72;
          }
          return(n);
   }

init()            /* turn on graphics mode */
   {
          union REGS r;

          r.x.ax=0x0010;
          int86(0x10,&r,&r);
   }

deinit()  /* turn off graphics card */
   {
          union REGS r;

          r.x.ax=0x0003;
          int86(0x10,&r,&r);
   }
```

easy to follow, but they're not as fast as they might be. Because a MacPaint file will fit into a single segment, and the resulting image also will fit into a single segment, a program can load the source file using a single INT 21H call and unpack it into a buffer very quickly indeed.

Figure 2-11 is an assembly language function to unpack MacPaint files.

Fig 2-11   A very fast MacPaint unpacking function in assembly language

```
;THIS FUNCTION UNPACKS A BIT MAPPED MACPAINT IMAGE
;              CALLED AS
;              Unpackbits(source,dest,length);
;              char *source,*dest;
;              long length;
;
               PUBLIC   _UnpackBits
_UnpackBits    PROC     FAR

               PUSH     BP
               MOV      BP,SP

               MOV      SI,[BP + _AOFF + 0]
               MOV      DS,[BP + _AOFF + 2]      ;SOURCE
               MOV      DI,[BP + _AOFF + 4]
               MOV      ES,[BP + _AOFF + 6]       ;DEST

               CLD
UP1:           LODSB                             ;GET INDEX
               TEST     AL,80H                   ;TEST HIGH BIT
               JZ       UP2
               XOR      CX,CX
               MOV      CL,AL                    ;SET LENGTH
               NEG      CL
               INC      CX                       ;TWO'S COMP
               MOV      BX,CX                    ;SAVE LENGTH
               LODSB                             ;GET BYTE TO WRITE
               NOT      AL                       ;PRE-INVERT IT
        REPNE  STOSB                             ;COPY IT CX TIMES
               JMP      UP3                       ;GO TO NEXT FIELD

UP2:           XOR      CX,CX
               MOV      CL,AL                    ;GET LENGTH
               INC      CX                       ;PLUS ONE
               MOV      BX,CX                    ;SAVE IT
UP2A:          LODSB                             ;COPY BYTE
               NOT      AL                       ;INVERT IT
               STOSB                             ;STORE IT
               LOOP     UP2A

UP3:           SBB      [BP + _AOFF + 8],BX
               JNB      UP4                       ;LONG COMPARE
               DEC      WORD PTR [BP + _AOFF + 10]
```

80 → FF

00 → FF

Fig. 2-11   continued

```
UP4:            CMP     WORD PTR [BP + _AOFF + 10],0000H
                JNL     UP1

                MOV     AX,_DATA
                MOV     DS,AX
                POP     BP
                RET
_UnpackBits     ENDP
```

You would call this code having allocated two buffers. The dest buffer must be 51840 bytes long, that is, the size of the unpacked MacPaint image. If you want to integrate this machine language module with the example using putimage, above, you will want to increase this by four bytes. The source buffer should contain the MacPaint file without its headers or patterns. It's desirable to allocate dest first, because source won't be needed once the picture has been unpacked—at which point the program calling this function can deallocate it and not have a fragmented heap.

The third parameter is a long integer that contains the number of bytes to be unpacked. This value doesn't have to be a long integer, strictly speaking, but it makes the assembly language code a great deal less complicated if it is.

Now, this function is a good example of doing things wrong for the right reasons. It doesn't unpack the picture one line at a time, but rather assumes that it's one big chunk of compressed data. In fact, as it was compressed one line at a time it will uncompress one line at a time, and so this cheat works. It also doesn't count the number of uncompressed bytes, but, rather, simply uncompresses everything in the file.

This code has rather poor error recovery for these reasons, but it is incredibly fast. It can unpack a whole MacPaint file in less than a second, compared to four or five seconds for the top down, properly written C language example discussed previously. Your timing examples might vary depending upon the machine you run this code on.

You also should note that this routine preinverts the image it unpacks, for the reasons discussed previously.

PACKING IT UP AGAIN

Packing an image into a MacPaint file isn't really all that much more involved than unpacking it. The example code to pack a MacPaint file will be handled in C. It's certainly practical to write it in assembly language, but it would be much harder to follow.

To properly analyze a line of picture information, a packing algorithm must start at the first byte and decide whether the subsequent bytes would be more efficiently packed as a run—one byte repeated multiple times—or as a string—some number of bytes copied verbatim into the packed file. Each line can contain combinations of these two field types.

In practice, a packing function will compress a line of data by counting the bytes for as many bytes as match the first byte. If the resulting count is greater than zero, it will write a run field to the file. If it isn't, it will save the first byte in a buffer and increment the start. Prior to writing a run field to the file, it will write a string field if the buffer has any bytes in it.

This sounds a little funky, but it works.

The function in Fig. 2-12 will compress one line of a MacPaint image into a file.

Fig 2-12   A function to pack one line of image data into a MacPaint file

```
WriteMacLine(p,fp)
        char *p;
        FILE *fp;
{
        char b[72];
        unsigned int bdex=0,i=0,j=0,t=0;

        do {
                /* zero the line index */
                i=0;
                /* check for a run */
                while((p[t+i]==p[t+i+1]) && ((t+i) < 71)) ++i;
                /* if there's a run... */
                if(i > 0) {
                        /* check for a previous string */
                        if(bdex) {
                                /* if there's a string... */
                                fputc(((bdex-1) & 0x7f),fp);
                                j+=1;
                                /* write it to the file */
                                fwrite(b,1,bdex,fp);
                                j+=bdex;
                                bdex=0;
                        }
                        /*...and then write the run */
                        fputc((~i+1),fp);
                        fputc(p[t+i],fp);
                        j+=2;
                        t+=(i+1);
                } else b[bdex++]=p[t++];
        } while(t<destBytes);
        /* check for any pending strings */
        if(bdex) {
                fputc(((bdex-1) & 0x7f),fp);
                j+=1;
                fwrite(b,1,bdex,fp);
                j+=bdex;
                bdex=0;
        }
        return(j);
}
```

This assumes that p points to the start of a line of a raw bit-mapped image file—of the right dimensions—and that fp is the handle of a file opened for writing in binary mode. Note that the function must check bdex, the index into the string buffer, even after the entire field has been analyzed to make sure that the line didn't end with an as yet unwritten string.

This function is used much as was the ReadMacLine function. To pack an entire raw image file into a MacPaint file, you would use the function in Fig. 2-13.

Fig 2-13   A function to pack an entire 576-by-720-pixel image into a MacPaint file

```
PackMacFile(p,fp)
        char *p;
        FILE *fp;
{
        int i,n;

        for(i=0;i<720;++i) {
                if((n=WriteMacLine(p,fp)) == 0) break;
                p+=72;
        }
        return(n);
}
```

In practice, you must first create a suitable MacBinary header and a set of patterns in the file before you start compressing data to it. The patterns can be irrelevant to any PC based applications you have for MacPaint image files, but they're necessary space fillers. The horrifying mess in Fig. 2-14 is a complete MacPaint header.

Fig 2-14   The entire MacPaint file header, including suitable patterns

```
char MACheader[640] = {
        0x00,0x00,0x00,0x00,0x00,0x00,0x00,0x00,
        0x00,0x00,0x00,0x00,0x00,0x00,0x00,0x00,
        0x00,0x00,0x00,0x00,0x00,0x00,0x00,0x00,
        0x00,0x00,0x00,0x00,0x00,0x00,0x00,0x00,
        0x00,0x00,0x00,0x00,0x00,0x00,0x00,0x00,
        0x00,0x00,0x00,0x00,0x00,0x00,0x00,0x00,
        0x00,0x00,0x00,0x00,0x00,0x00,0x00,0x00,
        0x00,0x00,0x00,0x00,0x00,0x00,0x00,0x00,
        0x00,0x50,0x4E,0x54,0x47,0x4D,0x50,0x4E,
        0x54,0x01,0x00,0x00,0x00,0x00,0x00,0x00,
        0x00,0x88,0x00,0x00,0x00,0xBA,0x00,0x00,
        0x00,0x00,0x00,0x9D,0x85,0xB7,0x56,0x01,
        0x1C,0xB0,0xCB,0x00,0x00,0x00,0x00,0x00,
        0x00,0x00,0x00,0x00,0x00,0x00,0x00,0x00,
        0x00,0x00,0x00,0x00,0x00,0x00,0x00,0x00,
        0x00,0x00,0x00,0x00,0x00,0x00,0x00,0x00,
        0x00,0x00,0x00,0x03,0xFF,0xFF,0xFF,0xFF,
        0xFF,0xFF,0xFF,0xFF,0xDD,0xFF,0x77,0xFF,
```

Fig 2-14 continued

```
0xDD,0xFF,0x77,0xFF,0xDD,0x77,0xDD,0x77,
0xDD,0x77,0xDD,0x77,0xAA,0x55,0xAA,0x55,
0xAA,0x55,0xAA,0x55,0x55,0xFF,0x55,0xFF,
0x55,0xFF,0x55,0xFF,0xAA,0xAA,0xAA,0xAA,
0xAA,0xAA,0xAA,0xAA,0xEE,0xDD,0xBB,0x77,
0xEE,0xDD,0xBB,0x77,0x88,0x88,0x88,0x88,
0x88,0x88,0x88,0x88,0x4E,0xCF,0xFC,0xE4,
0x27,0x3F,0xF3,0x72,0x80,0x10,0x02,0x20,
0x01,0x08,0x40,0x04,0xFF,0x88,0x88,0x88,
0xFF,0x88,0x88,0x88,0xFF,0x80,0x80,0x80,
0xFF,0x08,0x08,0x08,0x80,0x00,0x00,0x00,
0x00,0x00,0x00,0x00,0x80,0x40,0x20,0x00,
0x02,0x04,0x08,0x00,0x82,0x44,0x39,0x44,
0x82,0x01,0x01,0x01,0xF8,0x74,0x22,0x47,
0x8F,0x17,0x22,0x71,0x55,0xA0,0x40,0x40,
0x55,0x0A,0x04,0x04,0x20,0x50,0x88,0x88,
0x88,0x88,0x05,0x02,0xBF,0x00,0xBF,0xBF,
0xB0,0xB0,0xB0,0xB0,0x00,0x00,0x00,0x00,
0x00,0x00,0x00,0x00,0x80,0x00,0x08,0x00,
0x80,0x00,0x08,0x00,0x88,0x00,0x22,0x00,
0x88,0x00,0x22,0x00,0x88,0x22,0x88,0x22,
0x88,0x22,0x88,0x22,0xAA,0x00,0xAA,0x00,
0xAA,0x00,0xAA,0x00,0xFF,0x00,0xFF,0x00,
0xFF,0x00,0xFF,0x00,0x11,0x22,0x44,0x88,
0x11,0x22,0x44,0x88,0xFF,0x00,0x00,0x00,
0xFF,0x00,0x00,0x00,0x01,0x02,0x04,0x08,
0x10,0x20,0x40,0x80,0xAA,0x00,0x80,0x00,
0x88,0x00,0x80,0x00,0xFF,0x80,0x80,0x80,
0x80,0x80,0x80,0x80,0x08,0x1C,0x22,0xC1,
0x80,0x01,0x02,0x04,0x88,0x14,0x22,0x41,
0x88,0x00,0xAA,0x00,0x40,0xA0,0x00,0x00,
0x04,0x0A,0x00,0x00,0x03,0x84,0x48,0x30,
0x0C,0x02,0x01,0x01,0x80,0x80,0x41,0x3E,
0x08,0x08,0x14,0xE3,0x10,0x20,0x54,0xAA,
0xFF,0x02,0x04,0x08,0x77,0x89,0x8F,0x8F,
0x77,0x98,0xF8,0xF8,0x00,0x08,0x14,0x2A,
0x55,0x2A,0x14,0x08,0x00,0x00,0x00,0x04,
0x00,0x00,0x00,0x04,0x00,0x00,0x00,0x04,
0x00,0x00,0x00,0x04,0x00,0x00,0x00,0x04,
0x00,0x00,0x00,0x04,0x00,0x00,0x00,0x04,
0x00,0x00,0x00,0x04,0x00,0x00,0x00,0x04,
0x00,0x00,0x00,0x04,0x00,0x00,0x00,0x04,
0x00,0x00,0x00,0x04,0x00,0x00,0x00,0x04,
0x00,0x00,0x00,0x04,0x00,0x00,0x00,0x04,
0x00,0x00,0x00,0x04,0x00,0x00,0x00,0x04,
0x00,0x00,0x00,0x04,0x00,0x00,0x00,0x04,
0x00,0x03,0x00,0x0C,0x00,0x3C,0x00,0x00,
0x00,0x01,0x00,0x00,0x00,0x00,0x00,0x13,
0x00,0x16,0x00,0x33,0x01,0x58,0x02,0x33,
0x01,0x0A,0x01,0xC0,0x00,0xAC,0x00,0x0A,
0xFF,0xED,0x00,0x00,0x01,0x52,0x02,0x0F,
```

Fig 2-14 continued

```
            0x00,0x00,0x00,0x04,0x00,0x00,0x00,0x04,
            0x00,0x00,0x00,0x04,0x00,0x00,0x00,0x04,
            0x00,0x00,0x00,0x04,0x00,0x00,0x00,0x04,
            0x00,0x00,0x00,0x04,0x00,0x00,0x00,0x04,
            0x00,0x00,0x00,0x04,0x00,0x00,0x00,0x04,
            0x00,0x00,0x00,0x04,0x00,0x00,0x00,0x04,
            0x00,0x00,0x00,0x04,0x00,0x00,0x00,0x04,
            0x00,0x00,0x00,0x04,0x00,0x00,0x00,0x04,
            0x00,0x00,0x00,0x04,0x00,0x00,0x00,0x04
                    };
```

This wasn't actually typed—it was swiped from a MacPaint file. As such, the name and data fork size fields must be filled in if the header is to be complete, that is, if this file is to be of any use should it be ported back to a Macintosh. The name part of the process is dead easy—you can use the name of the original DOS file prettied up a bit so it looks like something a Macintosh might have created. The size field is a little more difficult, because the packing function won't really know what it is to hold until after the file has been written.

Figure 2-15 illustrates a function that initially writes the header. Its arguments are the file pointer of a file open for binary writing and a pointer to a string that contains the name of the DOS file being created.

Fig 2-15   A function to write the MacPaint header

```
WriteDestHeader(fp,s)
        FILE *fp;
        char *s;
{
        char *p,b[64],r=0;

        /* copy the DOS file name */
        strcpy(b,s);

        /* make it lower case... Macs like lower case */
        strlwr(b);

        /* make the first character upper case */
        b[0]=toupper(b[0]);

        /* make the first character of
        the extension upper case */
        if((p=strchr(b,'.')) != NULL) p[1]=toupper(p[1]);

        /* zero the name field in the header */
        memset(MACheader+1,0,16);

        /* put the name there */
        memcpy(MACheader+2,b,strlen(b));

        /* put the length byte in place */
        MACheader[1]=strlen(b);

        /* write the header to the file */
        return(fwrite(MACheader,1,640,fp));
}
```

This function will return 640 if all is well.

Next, the packing function will have to set the data fork size field in the MacBinary header. The easiest way to determine the value for this is to read the position of the end of the file—which is where the file pointer will be when all the data has been written—and subtract from this value the 128 bytes that comprise the MacBinary header.

The function in Fig. 2-16 should be called after PackMacFile, above, to set this field. It just seeks back to the appropriate part of the MacBinary header 83 bytes in and writes the long integer value—backwards, because it's in Motorola format. Motorola format numbers will be discussed shortly.

Fig 2-16   A function to fill in the data fork size of the MacPaint header when creating a file

```
WriteDestSize(fp)
        FILE *fp;
{
        long l;

        /* locate the end of the file */
        l=ftell(fp)-128L;
        /* seek back to the data fork field */
        fseek(fp,83L,SEEK_SET);
        /* write the size into the file */
        fputc((char)(l>>24),fp);
        fputc((char)(l>>16),fp);
        fputc((char)(l>>8),fp);
        fputc((char)l,fp);
}
```

You might want to be extremely thorough and write in the Macintosh style creation and modification dates of the file, which are part of the Mac-Binary header. These are described in the next part of this chapter. If you do not elect to go to this extreme, the file you've just created will still behave properly if it's ported to a Macintosh some time in the future. Macintoshes, like PC's, don't care if they're presented with files having wildly inaccurate date stamps. Consider that, as you'll see momentarily, time begins for a Macintosh in 1904.

The file can now be closed.

Secrets of the Header

The MacBinary header was created originally to allow Macintosh files to be ported out into a non-Macintosh universe and subsequently returned to a Macintosh intact. It allows the two forks of a Mac file to be combined into a single file, along with such things as the file's original name, creation date, modification data, type, and creator. The resulting file can exist on a PC.

The header also contains enough information to allow a Macintosh to split the two forks apart and reconstruct the file as it originally existed on a Mac.

The MacBinary header is not an official Macintosh data structure. It was created by the author of a telecommunications program. This provides one with a bit of insight into the nature of its design. It was intended to be sent as the "zero'th" sector of a file being transferred to or from a computer bulletin board, such that the receiving program, if it happened to be receiving the file on a Macintosh, could read the information from the header and reconstruct the received file in Macintosh form as it came down the wire.

The basic XMODEM file transfer protocol moves data around in 128-byte blocks. Not surprisingly, then, this turns out to be the size of a MacBinary header. In fact, nowhere near this much space is needed for the information that the header holds. Much of it is filler to pad it out to the length of one XMODEM block.

You already know enough about the MacBinary header to work with MacPaint files. A great deal of what it has to say is irrelevant to someone writing a PC program that reads or writes Macpaint files. Should you want to know more about it, however, you might want to have a look at the data structure in Fig. 2-17, which represents a MacBinary header in C.

Fig 2-17   The MacBinary header

```
#define C_STYLE              /* set false for Pascal style data */
                             /* (the struct is the same: this just */
                             /* alters how it's used.) */

typedef struct {
        char zerobyte;               /* always zero */
        #if C_STYLE
        char length;                 /* 0- 31 */
        char name[63];               /* name and some filler */
        long type;                   /* Mac file type */
        long creator;                /* Mac file creator */
        #else
        char name[64];               /* name and some filler */
        char type[4];                /* Mac file type */
        char creator[4];             /* Mac file creator */
        #endif
        char filler1[10];
        long datafork_size;          /* length of Mac data fork */
        long rsrcfork_size;          /* length of Mac resource fork */
        long creation_date;          /* time of file's creation */
        long modif_date;             /* time of file's modification */
        char filler2[29];
        } MACBINARY;
```

The first byte of the header is always zero. If a Macintosh telecommunications program that reads the MacBinary header sees a zero byte in the first location of the zero'th block of a downloaded file, it assumes that the rest of the block is a MacBinary header.

The next byte is the length of the original Macintosh file name. This has little to do with whatever name the file might have been stored under on your PC. The name can contain up to 31 characters. Any printable characters, except for colons, can be used in a Macintosh file name.

The next field is the name itself. It's a good deal longer than it needs to be. The latter 32 bytes of the name field are filler, and are not actually used.

The type and creator fields can be thought of as being either long integers or arrays of chars four bytes long.

The data fork size field already has been discussed. If you wanted to, you could use this value as a check on the process of unpacking a MacPaint picture.

The resource fork size field should be zero on a MacPaint file.

The creation and modification date fields probably won't pertain to anything you're likely to write on the PC, although you could use them if you really wanted to. They represent the applicable times and dates as Motorola style long integers. The values of the long integers hold the number of seconds between midnight January 1, 1904 and the time of the creation and most recent modification of the file as it existed on the Macintosh from which it was ported.

The little program in Fig. 2-18 illustrates how to read the time and date values from a MacBinary header. Given a path to a MacPaint file, it will read in the first 128 bytes, store them in a struct of the type MACBINARY, and allow you easy access to the data therein.

Fig 2-18   A program to read the MacPaint file creation and modification date stamps

```
#include "stdio.h"
#include "time.h"

#define mac2pc_date     2082830400L

typedef struct {
        char zerobyte;          /* always zero */
        char length;            /* 0- 31 */
        char name[63];          /* name and some filler */
        long type;              /* Mac file type */
        long creator;           /* Mac file creator */
        char filler[10];
        long datafork_size;     /* length of Mac data fork */
        long rsrcfork_size;     /* length of Mac resource fork */
        long creation_date;     /* time of file's creation */
        long modif_date;        /* time of file's modification */
        char filler2[29];
        } MACBINARY;
```

Fig 2-18   continued

```
long motr2intel();

main(argc,argv)
        int argc;
        char *argv[];
{
        FILE *fp;
        MACBINARY m;

        if(argc > 1) {
                /* open the file */
                if((fp=fopen(argv[1],"rb")) != NULL) {
                        /* read in the header */
                        if(fread((char *)&m,1,sizeof(MACBINARY),fp)
                                == sizeof(MACBINARY)) {
                                /* get the dates in Intel longs */
                                m.creation_date=
                                        motr2intel(m.creation_date)-
                                        mac2pc_date;
                                m.modif_date=
                                        motr2intel(m.modif_date)-
                                        mac2pc_date;

                                printf("File creation date: %s",
                                        ctime(&m.creation_date));
                                printf("File modification date: %s",
                                        ctime(&m.modif_date));

                        } else printf("Error reading %s.\n",argv[1]);
                        fclose(fp);
                } else printf("Error opening %s.\n",argv[1]);
        } else puts("I need an argument.");
}

/* convert between Motorola and Intel longs */
long motr2intel(l)
        long l;
{
        return(((l & 0xff000000L) >> 24) +
                ((l & 0x00ff0000L) >> 8) +
                ((l & 0x0000ff00L) << 8) +
                ((l & 0x000000ffL) << 24));
}
```

There are a number of interesting things going on here. The most obvious one is that rather large, peculiar number defined at the top of the program.

This program makes use of the Turbo C ctime function, which converts a PC time value in a long integer into a string that expresses a time and date in English. This is based on the PC's clock, which will return a long integer containing the number of seconds between midnight January 1,

1970 and the present. To convert a Macintosh date stamp into a PC date stamp, all you need do is subtract the number of seconds that elapsed between midnight January 1, 1904 and midnight January 1, 1970. This number is 2,082,830,400.

It probably does not take into account leap seconds.

You also will notice the function motr2intel, which converts Motorola long integers into Intel long integers, that is, it reverses the order of the bytes.

If wish to set the creation or modification dates of a MacPaint file, you can, of course, use this process in reverse. Take the PC date stamp—as returned by the time function under Turbo C—add the constant mac2pc date to it to move the beginning of the universe from 1970 to 1904 and run the resulting number through motr2intel once again. Although its name implies that it only converts numbers from the Motorola format to the Intel format, it actually goes both ways, because one is simply the complement of the other.

It might seem that using the MacBinary structure shown here would be a great deal easier than using that massive header we looked at a few pages back. It would be, expect that the MacBinary header was only part of that huge clump of data. It also contained the default patterns for a Mac-Paint file, which is why it was so big.

By the way, you do find MacPaint files floating around in the public domain without their MacBinary headers from time to time. The PFS:First Publisher package uses this format for its graphics files. You can translate from the MacPaint format discussed in this chapter to this alternate form by simply removing the first 128 bytes of the file and writing the remainder back to the disk.

A MacPaint file without its MacBinary header can be identified by the software that's reading it by checking out the first 4 bytes of the file—they should be 3 zero bytes followed by a byte containing 02.

Mac No More

You've probably had enough of MacPaint files and their dark secrets to last you a lifetime. They'll crop up again briefly in chapter 12 in conjunction with file conversion, but they can be laid to rest for a while now. The next chapter will feature a similar look at GEM/IMG picture files, the format used by Ventura Publisher, and those of the Digital Research applications that use bit-mapped pictures. Much of what you saw happening in MacPaint files will be applicable to IMG files—with a slightly more complex encoding scheme, variable sized pictures and so on.

3

GEM/IMG Files and the Ventura Connection

rep
run
pattern
string

"A man with a watch always knows the time. A man with two watches is never sure."
—Murphy's Laws of Computers

The principle drawbacks to MacPaint files as a universal monochrome graphics format are fairly easy to enumerate. Its fixed image size is a definite problem, because big graphics—especially those from scanners—are both common and interesting to play with. It also insists on carrying around an exceedingly large file header if you include the MacBinary header and its paint patterns.

Finally, there are few PC applications that really want to accept Mac-Paint files. Some will do so if you insist, but they all have other first choices.

The GEM/IMG image file format is one of those other first choices, and is in many respects everything that's good about MacPaint—efficient image compression, an easily decoded format and so on—without the drawbacks. The IMG format allows for images of any size and only has a header of 16 bytes, the smallest of any of the image file formats discussed in this book.

Despite their features, IMG files are not all that popular outside desktop publishing circles. If there is a universal image file format for the PC it's probably the PC Paintbrush PCX format, which will be discussed in detail in the next chapter. The IMG format usually is associated with software from Digital Research, which uses its GEM windowing environment, and with Ventura Publisher, which also runs under a modified version of GEM.

If you plan to write software that works with images for the Ventura Publisher package, dealing with IMG files probably will be essential. Ventura handles its image files in a peculiar way. It purports to read IMG, Mac-Paint, TIFF, and PCX images for inclusion in desktop publishing documents, but in reality it only works with IMG files. When asked to read the other three types of files it converts them into the IMG format each time a file is imported. This means that if you want to include a PCX file in a Ventura document, you must have space for both it and its IMG equivalent on whatever disk the image file resides, a decided drawback.

It's much more desirable to work in the format that Ventura really understands. This saves both disk space and conversion time.

Figure 3-1 illustrates a typical IMG file.

Fig 3-1   An example IMG file. This picture was downloaded from Rose Media (416) 226-9260

DECODING IMG FILES

As with the MacPaint format, it's probably easiest to start with decoding IMG files. Once you understand the format, the code to pack them back up again should be fairly simple to get your head around. Many of the concepts embodied in the MacPaint format will crop up here, too.

The first thing you'll encounter in any IMG file is its header. The IMG file header is particularly easy to handle because there's so little of it, but it involves several things that are peculiar to the IMG encoding process. It's structured like this:

```
WORD      0001H  ⎫  IMG pic type
WORD      0008H  ⎬
WORD      0001H  ⎭
WORD      PATTERN_LENGTH
WORD      PIXEL_WIDTH
WORD      PIXEL_DEPTH
WORD      LINE_WIDTH
WORD      IMAGE_DEPTH
```

This description uses the designation WORD rather than the more common assembly language DW directive because of an initial peculiarity of IMG files. All eight of the 16-bit numbers in the header are stored with their bytes in the inverse order of the usual Intel storage format. This makes accessing them a bit more difficult than it seems; it would be convenient to read the header into a C language struct and access its fields as ints, but there's really very little point.

The first three words are always one, eight, and one. This serves as a signature by which software can identify an IMG file. This is important, because there are several other sorts of files that crop up around Ventura that have the extension IMG. For example, when Ventura read in a PostScript file with a preview image (PostScript previews will be discussed in Chapter 10) it copies the preview into a file with an IMG extension, although it's not structured like the IMG files to be discussed here. Your programs can distinguish between these IMG files and real IMG files by checking out the first three words of the header.

The next field in the header is the pattern length. This usually will be one. You will recall from the discussion of MacPaint files that in a run of bytes field the second byte in the packet was repeated by the number of times defined in the index. In an IMG file, any number of bytes—called a *pattern*—can be repeated in a run of bytes field. The number of bytes in a repeating pattern is set globally for the file by this field in the header.

The pixel size defines the size of each pixel in microns. These two fields usually will be 0055H, or 85 microns. This corresponds to 1/300'th of an inch, one dot at the resolution of most laser printers. In displaying IMG files you might ignore this field and simply map each pixel of the image to one pixel on the screen. Software that uses IMG files, such as Ventura, frequently does look at this field to determine the default scale of the image. It's a lot easier to work with bit-mapped images in Ventura if the pixel size is set small and Ventura is allowed to scale the image up, rather than the other way around.

The line width is defined in pixels, not bytes, which can present software that decodes IMG files with a slight problem. A line being decoded has to go somewhere, and that somewhere will be a buffer defined in bytes. As such, you will need a way to determine how many bytes are required to contain an arbitrary number of pixels.

This is not as easy as it seems. If you divide the number of pixels by eight you'll get the correct number of bytes if the line length happens to be an even multiple of eight and one byte sort if it doesn't. The following function is useful in determining the real number of bytes required:

```
pixels2bytes(n)
    unsigned int n;
{
    if(n & 0x0007) return((n>> 3) + 1);
    else return(n >> 3);
}
```

If you're a bit new to C, pixels2bytes might seem a bit obtuse. Assuming that n is the number of pixels in question, at least one of the three least significant bits will be set if the number is not evenly divisible by eight. The number seven has all three of these bits set, so if you AND n with seven, the result will be true if one or more of these bits is set.

The notation n >> 3 simply divides n by eight, that is, it shifts it right by three places.

This function will appear in several other chapters of this book.

The last field in the header defines the number of horizontal scan lines in the image, or in other words, the depth of the picture.

The encoding scheme of the actual images in IMG files is a bit more involved than MacPaint was. Decoding it isn't all that tricky, but you'll find that there are some tradeoffs to be considered when you go to write an encoding function. The IMG format allows you to achieve some extremely tight image file compression, as run length encoded formats go, but at a considerable penalty in the time it takes to encode a file.

As with MacPaint, IMG files are encoded into packets, each of which consists of a key and then some information that pertains to the key. There are four sorts of packets in an IMG file, of varying sizes.

IMG files always are encoded one scan line at a time. As such, the longest possible chunk of decoded data can also be determined by taking the LINE_WIDTH word, inverting the order of its bytes and running it through pixels2bytes.

The first packet in a scan line can be a *replication packet*. This tells the decoder that having decoded the line that's to follow, it's to replicate it for some number of additional lines. The form of this packet is as follows. Note that all the image data is defined as bytes, not words, so the peculiar structure of an IMG file's 16-bit numbers doesn't affect the actual image:

```
DB      00H,00H,0FFH,REPLICATION_COUNT
```

There is no other case where the first three bytes shown here can be encountered at the start of a packet. The replication count is, of course, the number of times the following scan line is to be repeated.

If no replication packet is encountered at the start of a scan line, the replication count defaults to one, that is, the line is used only once.

There are two types of solid run packets, each of which is only a single byte long. If the decoder encounters a byte other than 00H or 80H as the first byte of a packet, it will know that it has a solid run.

If the high order bit of a solid run byte is set, that is, if the byte is larger than 80H, the run is a run of black bytes, with all the pixels in the byte set. For example, if the byte was 86H, you would mask off the high order bit by ANDing the byte with 7FH and take the remainder—06H—as an index. The next 6 bytes in the current scan line would be set to 0FFH, all pixels on.

If the byte was 06H there would be nothing to AND off. The next 6 bytes in the scan line would be set to zero, all pixels off.

Clearly, this is a very efficient way to encode solid black or white areas.

A *pattern run* packet tells the decoder to duplicate one or more bytes one or more times along the scan line. The number of bytes in the pattern to be duplicated is defined by the pattern length field in the header. It's usually one. The structure of this packet is as follows:

```
00H,RUN_LENGTH,FIRST_BYTE , . . . . . , LAST_BYTE
```

Having patterns larger than one byte rarely is all that advantageous, especially in scanned pictures that have complex dither patterns associated with them.

Finally, a *string* packet simply copies data as is from the image file to the scan line being decoded. This packet is used for data that resisted compression by one of the means previously discussed. It's structure is as follows:

```
80H,RUN_LENGTH,FIRST_BYTE , . . . . . , LAST_BYTE
```

You probably will find this encoding system a lot easier to understand once you've seen the function that deals with it. Figure 3-2 illustrates how it works.

Fig 3-2   A function to decode one line of an IMG file

```
ReadImgLine(p,fp)              /* read and decode a GEM/IMG line into p */
        char *p;
        FILE *fp;
{
        char *pr;
        int j,k,n=0,c,i;
```

Fig 3-2   continued

```
        memset(p,0,bytes);

        /* set the default replication count */
        repcount=1;

        /* loop 'tl the line's all decoded */
        do {
                c=fgetc(fp) & 0xff;

            if(c==0) {                                    O O
                    /* it's a pattern or a rep */
                    c=fgetc(fp) & 0xff;
                    if(c==0) {                       O O O O
                    /*it's a rep count change*/
                    fgetc(fp);
                    /* throw away the ff */        O O O O F F □
                    repcount=fgetc(fp) & 0xff;
                }
                else {
                        i=c & 0xff;
                        pr=p+n;

                        j=patternsize;                    get pattern
                        while(j--) p[n++]=~fgetc(fp);

                        k=i-1;
                        while(k--) {                   copy it X times
                                memcpy(p+n,pr,patternsize);
                                n+=patternsize;
                        }
                }
        }

        else if(c==0x80) {
                /* it's a string of bytes */
                i=fgetc(fp) & 0xff;
                pr=p+n;
                j=i;
                while(j--) p[n++]=~fgetc(fp);
        }

        else if(c & 0x80) {
                /* it's a solid white run - note that
                   it's artificially inverted here */
                i = c & 0x7f;
                pr=p+n;
                j=i;
                while(j--) p[n++]=~0xff;
        }
        else {
                /* it's a solid black run */
                i = c & 0x7f;
```

```
            pr=p+n;
            j=i;
            while(j--) p[n++]=~0x00;
        }
} while(n < bytes);

/* this should be equal to bytes - it might not be if
   the line was corrupted */
return(n);
}
```

The Decoding Code

The function in Fig. 3-3 will decode one line of an IMG file. It assumes that the IMG file has been opened with the fopen function, although if you had the entire encoded file in memory you could replace the fp argument with a char pointer and simply fetch bytes from the source buffer. The buffer at p should be large enough to contain a complete scan line of the image.

Fig 3-3 A program to view IMG files

```
/* A program to look at IMG pictures */
#define EGACARD 1

#include "stdio.h"
#include "alloc.h"
#include "dos.h"
#if !EGACARD
#include "graphics.h"
#endif

char header[16];                /* where the header lives */

char linebuf[2048];             /* must be big enough to hold one line */

unsigned int width,depth;
unsigned int patternsize=1;
unsigned int bytes,repcount;
unsigned int pixels2bytes();

main(argc,argv)
        int argc;
        char *argv[];
{
        FILE *fp;
        char *p;

        if(argc > 1) {
                /* attempt to open the file */
```

Fig 3-3   continued

```
                if((fp=fopen(argv[1],"rb")) != NULL) {
                    /* read in the header */
                    if(fread(header,1,16,fp)==16) {
                        /* check to make sure it's a picture */
                        if(!memcmp("\x00\x01\x00\x08\x00\x01",
                            header,6)) {
                            /* allocate a big buffer */
                            patternsize = (header[7] & 0xff)+
                                ((header[6] & 0xff)<<8);
                            width = (header[13] & 0xff)+
                                ((header[12] & 0xff)<<8);
                            depth = (header[15] & 0xff)+
                                ((header[14] & 0xff)<<8);
                            bytes=pixels2bytes(width);

                            if((p=malloc(4+bytes*depth)) != NULL) {
                                /* unpack the file */
                                if(UnpackImgFile(p+4,fp)==
                                    bytes)
                                    /* show the picture */
                                    ShowImgPicture(p+4);
                                free(p);
                            }
                        } else printf("Not an IMG file.\n");
                    } else printf("Error reading %s.\n",argv[1]);
                    fclose(fp);
                } else printf("Error opening %s.\n",argv[1]);
    }
}
ShowImgPicture(p) /* display the top of the picture */
        char *p;
{
        unsigned int i;

        /* graphics on */
        init();

        #if EGACARD
        /* copy the graphics to the screen */
        for(i=0;i<350;++i)
                memcpy(MK_FP(0xa000,i*80),p+4+(i*bytes),bytes);

        #else
        p[0]=width-1;
        p[1]=((width-1) >> 8);
        p[2]=depth-1;
        p[3]=((depth-1) >> 8);
        putimage(0,0,p,COPY_PUT); /* show the picture      */
        #endif

        getch();
        deinit();
}
```

```
UnpackImgFile(p,fp)            /* open and print GEM/IMG image n */
        char *p;
        FILE *fp;
{
        int i,n;

        for(i=0;i<depth;) {
                if((n=ReadImgLine(linebuf,fp)) != bytes) break;
                while(repcount--) {
                        memcpy(p,linebuf,bytes);
                        ++i;
                        p+=bytes;
                }
        }
        return(n);
}


ReadImgLine(p,fp)              /* read and decode a GEM/IMG line into p */
        char *p;
        FILE *fp;
{
        char *pr;
        int j,k,n=0,c,i;

        memset(p,0,bytes);

        /* set the default replication count */
        repcount=1;
        /* loop 'tl the line's all decoded */
        do {
                c=fgetc(fp) & 0xff;

                if(c==0) {
                        /* it's a pattern or a rep */
                        c=fgetc(fp) & 0xff;
                        if(c==0) {
                                /*it's a rep count change*/
                                fgetc(fp);
                                /* throw away the ff */
                                repcount=fgetc(fp) & 0xff;
                        }
                        else {
                                i=c & 0xff;
                                pr=p+n;

                                j=patternsize;
                                while(j--) p[n++]=~fgetc(fp);

                                k=i-1;
                                while(k--) {
                                        memcpy(p+n,pr,patternsize);
                                        n+=patternsize;
                                }
                        }
                }
```

Fig 3-3   continued

```
                        }

                else if(c==0x80) {
                        /* it's a string of bytes */
                        i=fgetc(fp) & 0xff;
                        pr=p+n;
                        j=i;
                        while(j--) p[n++]=~fgetc(fp);
                }

                else if(c & 0x80) {
                        /* it's a solid white run - note that
                           it's artificially inverted here */
                        i = c & 0x7f;
                        pr=p+n;
                        j=i;
                        while(j--) p[n++]=~0xff;
                }
                else {
                        /* it's a solid black run */
                        i = c & 0x7f;
                        pr=p+n;
                        j=i;
                        while(j--) p[n++]=~0x00;
                }
        } while(n < bytes);

        /* this should be equal to bytes - it might not be if
           the line was corrupted */
        return(n);
}

#if EGACARD
init()                  /* turn on graphics mode */
{
        union REGS r;

        r.x.ax=0x0010;
        int86(0x10,&r,&r);
}

deinit()   /* turn off graphics card */
{
        union REGS r;

        r.x.ax=0x0003;
        int86(0x10,&r,&r);
}
#else

init()                  /* turn on graphics mode */
{
        int d,m,e=0;
```

```
        detectgraph(&d,&m);
        if(d<0) {
                puts("No graphics card");
                exit(1);
        }
        if(d==EGA) {
                d=CGA;
                m=CGAHI;
        }
        initgraph(&d,&m,"");
        e=graphresult();
        if(e<0) {
                printf("Graphics error %d: %s",e,grapherrormsg(e));
                exit(1);
        }
        setcolor(getmaxcolor());
}

deinit()   /* turn off graphics card */
{
        closegraph();
}
#endif

unsigned int pixels2bytes(n)
        unsigned int n;
{
        if(n & 0x0007) return((n >> 3) + 1);
        else return(n >> 3);
}
```

Despite its greater complexity compared to the function in the last chapter that decoded MacPaint lines, this code is fairly easy to follow. The main loop that decodes data from the source file starts by fetching a key byte to determine what sort of packet is coming next. It trickles through a decision tree, beginning with the zero case. A zero byte might indicate either a vertical replication packet or a pattern run packet. The function must fetch the next byte from the file to determine which it is. A replication packet is handled by simply setting the replication count. A pattern run entails fetching patternsize bytes and then duplicating them by the number of times defined in the index of the packet.

The patternsize variable is a global value, because it must be defined by whatever function calls this one.

The next case is for the key byte to be 0x80, indicating a string packet.

If both of these cases fail, the packet is a solid run, last two stops in the decision tree.

This function will return the number of bytes in a scan line of the image.

The next function to be discussed is the code that drives the previous one, something to decode a complete picture. This gets into a few complications, depending upon the nature of the pictures that are to be decoded and what your application has in mind for them. Because IMG files have no fixed image size, it's impossible to say that some of them won't result in decoded pictures that require more than 64k of memory. Handling large pictures requires some rather more involved code. Let's start with a simple, one segment decoder. The function in Fig. 3-3 will unpack a small IMG file into a single segment buffer.

Images that have been converted from MacPaint files into IMG files are good test pictures in this respect. Inasmuch as MacPaint pictures always fit into one segment, such an IMG file can be assumed to do so as well.

Once again, this assumes that the file has been opened by fopen and that the file pointer is pointing to the first byte of the first packet of image data, that is, that the file header has been read and processed before this code is called. This function will return the depth of the file and store the image in the buffer at p.

The program in Fig. 3-4 is a complete application to look at the top portion of a small IMG file, just like the ones discussed in chapter 2 that dealt with MacPaint files. In chapter 2 the problem of displaying monochrome bitmaps on an EGA screen was handled with a bit of a cheat using a second version of the program. To keep things simple—because you should understand how the cheat worked by now—the equivalent program for IMG files embodies both versions of the display code. It can be compiled either into a version for color cards and Hercules displays, in which case it uses the Turbo C putimage function to drive the screen, or into an EGA version that uses the direct screen access approach discussed previously.

Fig 3-4   A program to view IMG files which unpack to images larger than 64 kilobytes

```
/* A program to look at big IMG pictures */
#define EGACARD 1

#include "stdio.h"
#include "alloc.h"
#include "dos.h"
#if !EGACARD
#include "graphics.h"
#endif

char header[16];                 /* where the header lives */
char linebuf[8192];
unsigned int width,depth;
unsigned int patternsize=1;
unsigned int bytes,repcount;
unsigned int pixels2bytes();
char *farPtr();

main(argc,argv)
        int argc;
        char *argv[];
{
```

```
        FILE *fp;
        char *p;

        if(argc > 1) {
                /* attempt to open the file */
                if((fp=fopen(argv[1],"rb")) != NULL) {
                        /* read in the header */
                        if(fread(header,1,16,fp)==16) {
                                /* check to make sure it's a picture */
                                if(!memcmp("\x00\x01\x00\x08\x00\x01",
                                    header,6)) {
                                        /* allocate a big buffer */
                                        patternsize = (header[7] & 0xff)+
                                            ((header[6] & 0xff)<<8);
                                        width = (header[13] & 0xff)+
                                            ((header[12] & 0xff)<<8);
                                        depth = (header[15] & 0xff)+
                                            ((header[14] & 0xff)<<8);
                                        bytes = pixels2bytes(width);

                                        if((p=farmalloc(4L+((long)bytes*
                                            (long)depth))) != NULL) {
                                                /* unpack the file */
                                                if(UnpackImgFile(farPtr(p,
                                                    4L),fp)==bytes)
                                                    /* show the picture */
                                                    ShowImgPicture(farPtr(p,
                                                        4L));
                                                farfree(p);
                                        } else puts("Error allocating memory");
                                } else printf("Not an IMG file.\n");
                        } else printf("Error reading %s.\n",argv[1]);
                        fclose(fp);
                } else printf("Error opening %s.\n",argv[1]);
        }
}
ShowImgPicture(p) /* display the top of the picture */
        char *p;
{
        unsigned int i;

        /* graphics on */
        init();

        #if EGACARD
        /* copy the graphics to the screen */
        for(i=0;i<350;++i)
                memcpy(MK_FP(0xa000,i*80),
                        farPtr(p,4L+((long)i*(long)bytes)),bytes);
        #else
        p[0]=width-1;
        p[1]=((width-1) >> 8);
        p[2]=depth-1;
        p[3]=((depth-1) >> 8);
```

Fig 3-4   continued

```
        putimage(0,0,p,COPY_PUT); /* show the picture      */
        #endif

        /* wait for a key press */
        getch();
        /* graphics off */
        deinit();
}

UnpackImgFile(p,fp)
        char *p;
        FILE *fp;
{

        int i,n;

        for(i=0;i<depth;) {
                if((n=ReadImgLine(linebuf,fp)) != bytes) break;
                while(repcount--) {
                        memcpy(p,linebuf,bytes);
                        ++i;
                        p=farPtr(p,(long)bytes);
                }
        }
        return(n);
}

ReadImgLine(p,fp)              /* read and decode a GEM/IMG line into p */
        char *p;
        FILE *fp;
{

        char *pr;
        int j,k,n=0,c,i;

        memset(p,0,bytes);

        /* set the default replication count */
        repcount=1;

        /* loop 'tl the line's all decoded */
        do {
                c=fgetc(fp) & 0xff;
                if(c==0) {
                        /* it's a pattern or a rep */
                        c=fgetc(fp) & 0xff;
                        if(c==0) {
                                /*it's a rep count change*/
                                fgetc(fp);
                                /* throw away the ff */
                                repcount=fgetc(fp) & 0xff;
                        }
                        else {
                                i=c & 0xff;
                                pr=p+n;
```

```
                                   j=patternsize;
                                   while(j--) p[n++]=~fgetc(fp);

                                   k=i-1;
                                   while(k--) {
                                           memcpy(p+n,pr,patternsize);
                                           n+=patternsize;
                                   }
                           }
                   }

           else if(c==0x80) {
                   /* it's a string of bytes */
                   i=fgetc(fp) & 0xff;
                   pr=p+n;
                   j=i;
                   while(j--) p[n++]=~fgetc(fp);
           }

           else if(c & 0x80) {
                   /* it's a solid white run - note that
                      it's artificially inverted here */
                   i = c & 0x7f;
                   pr=p+n;
                   j=i;
                   while(j--) p[n++]=~0xff;
           }
           else {
                   /* it's a solid black run */
                   i = c & 0x7f;
                   pr=p+n;
                   j=i;
                   while(j--) p[n++]=~0x00;
           }
   } while(n < bytes);
   return(n);
}

#if EGACARD
init()              /* turn on graphics mode */
{
       union REGS r;

       r.x.ax=0x0010;
       int86(0x10,&r,&r);
}

deinit()   /* turn off graphics card */
{
       union REGS r;

       r.x.ax=0x0003;
       int86(0x10,&r,&r);
}
```

Fig 3-4   continued

```
#else
init()              /* turn on graphics mode */
{
        int  d,m,e=0;

        detectgraph(&d,&m);
        if(d<0) {
                puts("No graphics card");
                exit(1);
        }
        if(d==EGA) {
                d=CGA;
                m=CGAHI;
        }
        initgraph(&d,&m,"");
        e=graphresult();
        if(e<0) {
                printf("Graphics error %d: %s",e,grapherrormsg(e));
                exit(1);
        }
        setcolor(getmaxcolor());
}

deinit()  /* turn off graphics card */
{
        closegraph();
}
#endif

unsigned int pixels2bytes(n)
        unsigned int n;
{
        if(n & 0x0007) return((n >> 3) + 1);
        else return(n >> 3);
}

char *farPtr(p,l) /* return a far pointer p + l */
        char *p;
        long l;
{
        unsigned int seg,off;

        seg = FP_SEG(p);
        off = FP_OFF(p);
        seg += (off / 16);
        off &= 0x000f;
        off += (unsigned int)(l & 0x000fL);
        seg += (l / 16L);
        p = MK_FP(seg,off);
        return(p);
}
```

The EGACARD equate at the top of the program determines which version of the program will be compiled. If it's true, the program will use direct EGA graphics.

There are a few trivial variations on the functions just discussed as they appear in this program. To begin with, this code is still confronted with the problem of a PC's screen being inverted black to white from the way the image is naturally stored. It's easiest to simply invert the bytes being written to each line being decoded. To make it obvious how this is handled, the ReadImgLine function simply NOTs each data byte being read or generated. The tilde character handles NOTing a byte under C. In those parts of the function that deal with solid runs, you will encounter the rather questionable structures ~0xff and ~0x00. The value of ~0xff is ~0x00, and vice versa. There is actually no extra code generated by this—the compiler evaluates constant expressions at compile time—so it's acceptable to leave these as they are in the interest of more easily understood code.

As discussed in chapter 2, the first 4 bytes of an image buffer must continue the dimensions of the image if the buffer is to be used with put-image. This is not the case if the buffer is simply to be stuffed into an EGA screen. However, to avoid an excessive number of #if directives, this code allows that the buffer will be 4 bytes bigger than necessary for both versions of the program, admittedly wasting the 4 bytes in the EGA card manifestation.

Bigger Pictures

The only real limitation of the previous program is that it can't cope with big images, ones that will occupy more than one memory segment when they're unpacked. In fact, there's a good chance that it will crash if it's confronted with a big image because it's not smart enough to detect when the size argument to malloc has wrapped around past zero. Handling large images presents a file viewer program with a new set of problems.

The fortunate thing about dealing with large pictures is that they break down nicely into small chunks of data, their individual scan lines, none of which will be anything like the size of a whole memory segment. As you might recall from chapter 1, there is a simple function, farPtr, which will allow you to address any 64k block within a large buffer. This works nicely when you have to place decoded scan lines in a big image.

Figure 3-4 is the IMG file reader program modified to allow for a big image buffer and full 32-bit addressing of the data in it.

Not a great deal has changed in this program as compared to the first one in this chapter, except that farPtr crops up fairly frequently. You might well ask why, for example, one requires farPtr just to add 4 bytes to a pointer—as happens up in the main function—when 4 bytes is a long way from filling a whole segment. This is actually a case of being very careful.

It's very unlikely that adding 4 bytes to a pointer would cause it to wrap around back through zero, but it could happen if the pointer's offset value was within 4 bytes of 0xffff. As such, it's a good idea to always use farPtr when you can't be sure that there's room for whatever you're planning to add to a pointer.

If you look carefully at the code for farPtr you'll notice that it always adjusts the pointers it returns so that their offsets are as low as possible—within 16 bytes of zero—shuffling the difference into the segment component of the pointer. For this reason, it's safe to increment p in ReadImgLine in the conventional way because you can be sure that p will have been adjusted so as to have a safe margin.

This would only fall apart in pictures having more than half a million pixels per line. One encounters fairly few of these.

Note that this version of the program allocates its image buffer with farmalloc rather than with straight malloc, as was seen in the first IMG file viewer. The farmalloc function accepts a long integer for a size argument and calls the DOS INT 21H memory allocation function on your behalf. This is actually very useful to know because when INT 21H allocates memory for you, it returns a 32-bit pointer in which the offset component is always zero.

If you attempt to view a large picture with this program while it's still under development and running from within the Turbo C integrated environment, you'll probably find that it can't allocate enough memory for an image buffer. Bear in mind that Turbo C will probably be tying up about half the available memory. In this case you'll have to exit from Turbo C, try the program, and get back into Turbo C if you have to make any changes to it.

As a rule, it's best to get the bugs out of this sort of code using a small IMG file first and then try it out with a large one.

Panning Over a Large Picture

Figure 3-5 illustrates a large image scanned from an Escher print. The area in the box represents the part of it that can be seen when it's displayed on an EGA card using the preceding program. This is a fairly small area—one problem with the simple viewers that have been discussed thus far is that they don't allow for access to a whole image if the image is bigger than the screen.

Making the "window" of your monitor pan over a large virtual page is a great deal less complex than it might seem. All you really have to do is to start displaying the picture from somewhere other than the upper left corner of the image area. The window can be made to appear to move if it's updated from different parts of the buffer. As paging over a virtual screen is a commonly found facility in many graphics programs, let's have a look at how it's done with a big IMG file, a fairly simple example.

Fig 3-5   A very large IMG image illustrating the area visible on an EGA screen at one time. This picture was downloaded from Rose Media (416) 226-9260

Consider the picture in Fig. 3-6. The area in the box again represents the visible part of the picture as seen through an EGA monitor. The upper left corner of the visible part of the picture—the zero'th pixel of the monitor screen—will be defined as having the location (x,y) in the picture as a whole. This happens to be point (220,140) in this picture. Furthermore,

(220,140)

Fig 3-6   Moving the screen to look at a different part of the picture

the variable bytes will contain the width of a scan line of the picture in bytes, as with the previous versions of the IMG file viewer. The picture is in a large buffer called p.

The first byte of the visible part of the picture can be located with the following expression.

farPtr(p,(long)bytes*(long)y + (long)(x > >3));

If you copy 80 bytes starting with the one that the pointer returned by the above expression points to into the first 80 bytes of an EGA card's buffer you'll have displayed the first scan line correctly no matter where it actually originated in the image. If you then increase y by one and repeat the process you'll be able to see the second scan line, and so on.

The only obvious catch to this is that x and y must be constrained not to exceed the edges of the image minus the dimensions of the screen.

The program in Fig. 3-7 illustrates the large IMG viewer adapted so as to support a screen that can be panned over a big picture. Having loaded up a picture, the arrow keys will move the window, the home and end keys will place it in the upper left and lower right corners of the image, respectively, and the escape key will end the program and return to DOS.

Fig 3-7   A program to pan over large IMG files using virtual screen paging

```
/* A program to pan over big IMG pictures */
#define EGACARD 1

#include "stdio.h"
#include "alloc.h"
#include "dos.h"
#if !EGACARD
#include "graphics.h"
#endif

#define HOME            0x4700
#define CURSOR_UP       0x4800
#define CURSOR_LEFT     0x4b00
#define CURSOR_RIGHT    0x4d00
#define END             0x4f00
#define CURSOR_DOWN     0x5000

#define step            32

char linebuf[8192];

char header[16];                /* where the header lives */
unsigned int width,depth;
unsigned int patternsize=1;
unsigned int bytes,repcount;
unsigned int pixels2bytes();
unsigned int screenWide=640;
unsigned int screenDeep=350;
```

```
char *farPtr();
#if !EGACARD
char *ibuf;
#endif

main(argc,argv)
        int argc;
        char *argv[];
{

        FILE *fp;
        char *p;

        if(argc > 1) {
                /* attempt to open the file */
                if((fp=fopen(argv[1],"rb")) != NULL) {
                        /* read in the header */
                        if(fread(header,1,16,fp)==16) {
                                /* check to make sure it's a picture */
                                if(!memcmp("\x00\x01\x00\x08\x00\x01",
                                    header,6)) {
                                        /* allocate a big buffer */
                                        patternsize = (header[7] & 0xff)+
                                            ((header[6] & 0xff)<<8);
                                        width = (header[13] & 0xff)+
                                            ((header[12] & 0xff)<<8);
                                        depth = (header[15] & 0xff)+
                                            ((header[14] & 0xff)<<8);
                                        bytes = pixels2bytes(width);

                                        if((p=farmalloc((long)bytes*
                                            (long)depth)) != NULL) {
                                                /* unpack the file */
                                                if(UnpackImgFile(p,fp)==bytes)
                                                    /* show the picture */
                                                    PanImgPicture(p);
                                                farfree(p);
                                        } else puts("Error allocating memory");
                                } else printf("Not an IMG file.\n");
                        } else printf("Error reading %s.\n",argv[1]);
                        fclose(fp);
                } else printf("Error opening %s.\n",argv[1]);
        }
}

PanImgPicture(p)
        char *p;
{
        int c,x=0,y=0;

        init();
        do {
                ShowImgPicture(farPtr(p,((long)y*(long)bytes)+(long)(x>>3)));
                switch(c=GetKey()) {
                case CURSOR_LEFT:
```

Fig 3-7 continued

```
                        if((x-step) > 0) x-=step;
                        else x=0;
                        break;
            case CURSOR_RIGHT:
                        if((x+step+screenWide) < width) x+=step;
                        else if(width > screenWide) x=width-screenWide;
                        else x=0;
                        break;
            case CURSOR_UP:
                        if((y-step) > 0) y-=step;
                        else y=0;
                        break;
            case CURSOR_DOWN:
                        if((y+step+screenDeep) < depth) y+=step;
                        else if(depth > screenDeep) y=depth-screenDeep;
                        else y=0;
                        break;
            case HOME:
                        x=y=0;
                        break;
            case END:
                        if(width > screenWide) x=width-screenWide;
                        else x=0;
                        if(depth > screenDeep) y=depth-screenDeep;
                        else y=0;
                        break;
            }
        } while(c != 27);
        deinit();
}

ShowImgPicture(p) /* display the top of the picture */
        char *p;
{
        unsigned int i,w;
        if(width > screenWide) w=pixels2bytes(screenWide);
        else w=bytes;

        #if EGACARD
        for(i=0;i<350;++i)
                memcpy(MK_FP(0xa000,i*80),
                        farPtr(p,((long)i*(long)bytes)),w);
        #else
        ibuf[0]=screenWide-1;
        ibuf[1]=((screenWide-1) >> 8);
        ibuf[2]=screenDeep-1;
        ibuf[3]=((screenDeep-1) >> 8);

        for(i=0;i<screenDeep;++i) {
                memset(ibuf+4+(i*(screenWide >> 3)),0,screenWide >> 3);
                memcpy(ibuf+4+(i*(screenWide >> 3)),
                        farPtr(p,(long)i*(long)bytes),w);
        }
```

```
                putimage(0,0,ibuf,COPY_PUT);        /* show the picture    */
                #endif
        }

        UnpackImgFile(p,fp)
                char *p;
                FILE *fp;
        {
                int i,n;

                for(i=0;i<depth;) {
                        if((n=ReadImgLine(linebuf,fp)) != bytes) break;

                        while(repcount--) {
                                memcpy(p,linebuf,bytes);
                                ++i;
                                p=farPtr(p,(long)bytes);
                        }

                }
                return(n);
        }

        ReadImgLine(p,fp)            /* read and decode a GEM/IMG line into p */
                char *p;
                FILE *fp;
        {
                char *pr;
                int j,k,n=0,c,i;

                memset(p,0,bytes);

                /* set the default replication count */
                repcount=1;

                /* loop 'tl the line's all decoded */
                do {
                        c=fgetc(fp) & 0xff;

                        if(c==0) {
                                /* it's a pattern or a rep */
                                c=fgetc(fp) & 0xff;
                                if(c==0) {
                                        /*it's a rep count change*/
                                        fgetc(fp);
                                        /* throw away the ff */
                                        repcount=fgetc(fp) & 0xff;
                                }
                                else {
                                        i=c & 0xff;
                                        pr=p+n;

                                        j=patternsize;
                                        while(j--) p[n++]=~fgetc(fp);
```

Fig 3-7   continued

```
                                        k=i-1;
                                        while(k--) {
                                                memcpy(p+n,pr,patternsize);
                                                n+=patternsize;
                                        }
                                }
                        }

                        else if(c==0x80) {
                                /* it's a string of bytes */
                                i=fgetc(fp) & 0xff;
                                pr=p+n;
                                j=i;
                                while(j--) p[n++]=~fgetc(fp);
                        }

                        else if(c & 0x80) {
                                /* it's a solid white run - note that
                                   it's artificially inverted here */
                                i = c & 0x7f;
                                pr=p+n;
                                j=i;
                                while(j--) p[n++]=~0xff;
                        }
                        else {
                                /* it's a solid black run */
                                i = c & 0x7f;
                                pr=p+n;
                                j=i;
                                while(j--) p[n++]=~0x00;
                        }
                } while(n < bytes);

                /* this should be equal to bytes - it might not be if
                   the line was corrupted */
                return(n);
}


#if EGACARD
init()               /* turn on graphics mode */
{
        union REGS r;

        r.x.ax=0x0010;
        int86(0x10,&r,&r);
}

deinit()   /* turn off graphics card */
{
        union REGS r;

        r.x.ax=0x0003;
        int86(0x10,&r,&r);
```

```
}

#else

init()             /* turn on graphics mode */
{
        int  d,m,e=0;

        detectgraph(&d,&m);
        if(d<0) {
                puts("No graphics card");
                exit(1);
        }
        if(d==EGA) {
                d=CGA;
                m=CGAHI;
        }
        initgraph(&d,&m,"");
        e=graphresult();
        if(e<0) {
                printf("Graphics error %d: %s",e,grapherrormsg(e));
                exit(1);
        }
        screenWide=getmaxx()+1;
        screenDeep=getmaxy()+1;
        if((ibuf=malloc(4+((screenWide >> 3) * screenDeep))) == NULL) {
                deinit();
                puts("Error allocating screen buffer");
                exit(1);
        }
        setcolor(getmaxcolor());
}

deinit()  /* turn off graphics card */
{
        closegraph();
        if(ibuf != NULL) free(ibuf);
}
#endif

unsigned int pixels2bytes(n)
        unsigned int n;
{
        if(n & 0x0007) return((n >> 3) + 1);
        else return(n >> 3);
}

char *farPtr(p,l) /* return a far pointer p + l */
        char *p;
        long l;
{
        unsigned int seg,off;

        seg = FP_SEG(p);
```

Fig 3-7 continued

```
        off = FP_OFF(p);
        seg += (off / 16);
        off &= 0x000f;
        off += (unsigned int)(l & 0x000fL);
        seg += (l / 16L);
        p = MK_FP(seg,off);
        return(p);
}

GetKey()
{
        int c;

        c = getch();
        if(!(c & 0x00ff)) c = getch() << 8;
        return(c);
}
```

There are quite a few things happening in this program, most of them having to do with the way the display is updated. As with previous IMG viewers, the program can be compiled either to drive an EGA card directly, or to drive monochrome displays through the Turbo C screen drivers. The EGA implementation is pretty easy to follow. The screen driver approach requires some cunning.

Notice that the four byte offset into the image buffer is gone. It's no longer practical to use the putimage function directly from the image buffer, for reasons that will be discussed in a moment.

The EGA card display code is very nearly untouched from that of the previous program. The only extra features it has involve calculating the offset into the image buffer based on the location of the window in relation to the image a whole. The monochrome graphics routine, on the other hand, has become quite a bit more complex. The init function now allocates a buffer the size of the screen for use by the display routine when the program is compiled with the EGACARD define set false.

To make the putimage function work properly, it's necessary to extract a screen size fragment from the image buffer, store the fragment in a separate buffer, and then use putimage to copy that to the screen. The buffer is called ibuf here. Because it's possible that the image actually might be narrower than the screen—as in the case of a MacPaint picture, for example—each line of ibuf must be cleared to zero before a line is copied to it. The final buffer, with its two dimension integers in the first 4 bytes, again looks like a real image fragment to putimage, and can be copied to any monochrome graphics screen without difficulty.

This approach is dreadfully slow, even in comparison to the C language EGA screen driver in this program. If you're using an XT compatible machine, the time it takes to copy an image fragment to ibuf and then to invoke putimage for the entire screen in interminable. In fact, this approach to updating the screen is so slow it causes problems with the keyboard input. Even on a fast 386 machine, holding down one of the arrow keys so the key repeats will quickly overflow the keyboard buffer and cause the machine to beep insanely as the screen update can't keep up with the repeat rate.

The high speed machine language screen drivers (to be discussed later in this book) will start to make a great deal more sense once you've watched this program work for a while.

There's a new function in this program, too. Instead of calling Show-ImgPicture directly, main calls PanImgPicture which, in turn, makes multiple calls to ShowImgPicture to update the screen. The pointer passed to Show-ImgPicture points to different areas in the image buffer based on where the screen window has been placed with the arrow keys.

The code that drives the keyboard should be pretty easy to under-stand. The GetKey function is used to return the scan codes of the PC's extended keys when they turn up, so they can be used in a simple switch statement. The scan codes for the keys of interest to this program are defined at the top of the listing. If you look at the switch statement, you can see how the values of x and y are manipulated to change to origin of the screen window.

You can apply the techniques discussed here to any of the image file formats. You might want to go back to the MacPaint decoder program to see if you can get that to scroll, so that you can view an entire image. Pan-ning will turn up again later on in the chapters that pertain to machine language graphics drivers and GIF images. GIF images frequently exceed the dimensions of all but the highest end display hardware.

PACKING IT UP AGAIN

Encoding an IMG file will involve the discussion of a lot less code than unpacking one did. However, the way in which you approach encoding might be a matter of some consideration. The IMG format has a lot of flexi-bility built into it—there's a decided tradeoff between the speed at which you can pack a file and the amount of compression you can achieve.

To really get an image squeezed into an IMG file as tightly as possible, you would have to do some pretty lengthy analysis of the raw image data to determine how the various parameters of the compression process should be set. For example, the optimum length of pattern fields varies from image to image. In effect, though, you would have to compress the image several times with a variety of pattern sizes to determine the best value for the image in question.

Despite its improvement over MacPaint compression, IMG format run length encoding is still pretty crude. The most efficient compression—after exhaustive analysis—is rarely all that much better than just running with some well thought out defaults. The IMG files so created always can be compressed substantially further by simply running them through an

LZW compression program, such as PKARC or PKZIP. Chapter 5 will get into LZW compression in greater detail.

It's usually the case that the speed at which you can store and view images is a lot more important than getting an extra five percent size reduction in the final file. As such, the compression code in this chapter has been optimized for speed. It does almost no complex data analysis, and it ignores several of the features of the IMG format. You might want to add variable pattern sizes and vertical replication to it once you get the basic encoding function working. Be warned, though—neither enhancement is trivial to write and the results are rarely worth the effort.

The code for the following example assumes that there is a raw, unpacked image in the buffer pointed to by p. It further assumes that this is a small image, one that occupies less than 64k of memory in its unpacked state. However, you can easily modify this code for use with a large image by simply applying farPtr to handle the pointer calculations.

The principle behind encoding the scan lines of an image into an IMG file is exactly the same as it was for MacPaint files. All that really changes here is the way in which the various packets are represented.

The function in Fig. 3-8 will pack a single line of image data into a file opened for writing. This is the heart of the compression process. Beginning with the start of each line, the function checks for a run of bytes. If a run is found, it gets written to the file in a suitable packet. There are three possible packet types, one each for a black run, a white run, or a run of some byte representing a pattern. This function assumes that the pattern size will be one byte.

Fig 3-8 A function to pack one line of image data into an IMG file

```
writeImgLine(p,fp)              /* IMG encode and write the line in p to fp */
        char *p;
        FILE *fp;
{
        char b[0x0080];
        unsigned int bdex=0,i=0,j=0,t=0;

        do {
                i=0;
                /* begin by counting bytes which are the same. we
                   must check to see that we don't write too long a
                   line, as the start of the next line might have the
                   same bit pattern as the end of this one. */

                while((p[t+i]==p[t+i+1]) &&
                    ((t+i) < (bytes-1)) && i < 0x7e) ++i;

                /* if there's a run or the output buffer is full,
                   we must write the data to the file. */
                if(i>0 || bdex >= 0x7e) {
```

```
                    /* if bdex is true, there's a string in the
                       buffer... it's left from the last pass. */
                    if(bdex) {
                            /* strings are written as litteral
                               data... just a field key and data.*/
                            fputc(0x80,fp);
                            fputc(bdex,fp);
                            j+=2;
                            fwrite(b,1,bdex,fp);
                            j+=bdex;
                            bdex=0;
                    }

                    /* if i is true, the current field is a string.*/
                    if(i) {

                            /* IMG has various ways to compress
                               strings, with emphasis on solid
                               black or white runs */
                            if(p[t+i]==0xff) {
                                    fputc(0x80+i+1,fp);
                                    j+=1;
                            }
                            else if(p[t+i]==0x00) {
                                    fputc(i+1,fp);
                                    j+=1;
                            }
                            else {

                                    /* runs of something other than
                                       black or white must be written
                                       as three byte fields */
                                    fputc(0x00,fp);
                                    fputc(i+1,fp);
                                    fputc(p[t+i],fp);
                                    j+=3;
                            }
                            t+=(i+1);
                    }

            /* if there's no run, add the byte to the current string
               and loop again to see if the next byte is the start
               of a run */

            } else b[bdex++]=p[t++];
    } while(t<bytes);

/* we have now dealt with all the source data in the line.
   there may be a string still waiting in the buffer, however,
   so we must check bdex one last time */

if(bdex) {
        fputc(0x80,fp);
```

Fig 3-8   continued

```
                fputc(bdex,fp);
                j+=2;
                fwrite(b,1,bdex,fp);
                j+=bdex;
        }

        return(ferror(fp));
}
```

If a run is not found, all the bytes that don't constitute a run are added to a string buffer until either a run begins or the end of the line is encountered. When the next run begins, or the end of the line is reached, the string buffer is emptied by writing its contents to a string packet.

This process will be repeated as often as necessary to pack the whole line.

The program in Fig. 3-9 uses the WriteImgLine function. It reads in a binary file that contains a monochrome image fragment and packs it into an IMG file. The binary files it reads in can be created with the Turbo C getimage function by copying part of a graphics screen into a buffer and then writing the buffer to a file. The screen must be in a monochrome graphics mode—either CGA or Hercules—for this to work. The resulting file should have the extension BIN.

Fig 3-9   A program to pack a getimage fragment into an IMG file

```
/* a program to pack a getimage fragment into an IMG file */

#include "stdio.h"
#include "alloc.h"

#define size      (wide * pixels2bytes(deep))

char bin_file[80];        /* buffers for file names */
char img_file[80];
char IMGheader[16] = {
        0x00,0x01,0x00,0x08,0x00,0x01,0x00,0x01,
        0x00,0x55,0x00,0x55,0x00,0x00,0x00,0x00
                };        /* IMG header */

int wide,deep,bytes;      /* global size values */

main(argc,argv)
        int argc;
        char *argv[];
{
        FILE *source,*dest;
        char *p,b[4];

        if(argc > 1) {
```

```
                    /* make file names */
                    strmfe(bin_file,argv[1],"BIN");
                    strmfe(img_file,argv[1],"IMG");

                    /* open the source file */
                    if((source=fopen(bin_file,"rb")) != NULL) {
                            /* create the destination file */
                            if((dest=fopen(img_file,"wb")) != NULL) {
                                    /* read in the size */
                                    if(fread(b,1,4,source)==4) {
                                            /* and get it from the buffer */
                                            wide = b[0]+(b[1]<<8)+1;
                                            deep = b[2]+(b[3]<<8)+1;
                                            bytes = pixels2bytes(wide);
                                            /* allocate an image buffer */
                                            if((p=malloc(size)) != NULL) {
                                                    /* read in the image */
                                                    if(fread(p,1,size,source)
                                                        == size) {
                                                            printf("Packing image "
                                                                "%d by %d pixels\n",
                                                                wide,deep);
                                                            /* pack the image */
                                                            PackImgFile(dest,p);
                                                    } else
                                                        printf("Error reading %s\n",
                                                        bin_file);
                                                    free(p);
                                            } else puts("Error allocating memory");
                                    } else puts("Error reading header");
                                    fclose(dest);
                            } else printf("Error creating %s\n",img_file);
                            fclose(source);
                    } else printf("Error opening %s\n",bin_file);
            } else puts("I need an argument");
}

/* pack in image into an IMG file */
PackImgFile(fp,p)
        FILE *fp;
        char *p;
{
        int i;

        /* write the header */
        WriteImgHeader(fp);
        /* pack the lines */
        for(i=0;i<deep;++i) WriteImgLine(p+(i*bytes),fp);
}

/* write an IMG header */
WriteImgHeader(fp)
        FILE *fp;
{
```

Fig 3-9   continued

```
        IMGheader[12]=wide >> 8;
        IMGheader[13]=wide;
        IMGheader[14]=deep >> 8;
        IMGheader[15]=deep;
        return(fwrite(IMGheader,1,16,fp));
}


writeImgLine(p,fp)              /* IMG encode and write the line in p to fp */
        char *p;
        FILE *fp;
{
        char b[0x0080];
        unsigned int bdex=0,i=0,j=0,t=0;

        do {
                i=0;
                /* begin by counting bytes which are the same. we
                   must check to see that we don't write too long a
                   line, as the start of the next line might have the
                   same bit pattern as the end of this one. */
                while((p[t+i]==p[t+i+1]) &&
                    ((t+i) < (bytes-1)) && i < 0x7e) ++i;
                /* if there's a run or the output buffer is full,
                   we must write the data to the file. */
                if(i>0 || bdex >= 0x7e) {

                        /* if bdex is true, there's a string in the
                           buffer... it's left from the last pass. */
                        if(bdex) {
                                /* strings are written as litteral
                                   data... just a field key and data.*/
                                fputc(0x80,fp);
                                fputc(bdex,fp);
                                j+=2;
                                fwrite(b,1,bdex,fp);
                                j+=bdex;
                                bdex=0;
                        }
                        /* if i is true, the current field is a string.*/
                        if(i) {

                                /* IMG has various ways to compress
                                   strings, with emphasis on solid
                                   black or white runs */
                                if(p[t+i]==0xff) {
                                        fputc(0x80+i+1,fp);
                                        j+=1;
                                }
                                else if(p[t+i]==0x00) {
                                        fputc(i+1,fp);
                                        j+=1;
```

```
                             }
                             else {

                                     /* runs of something other than
                                        black or white must be written
                                        as three byte fields */
                                     fputc(0x00,fp);
                                     fputc(i+1,fp);
                                     fputc(p[t+i],fp);
                                     j+=3;
                             }
                             t+=(i+1);
                     }

             /* if there's no run, add the byte to the current string
                and loop again to see if the next byte is the start
                of a run */

             } else b[bdex++]=p[t++];
        } while(t<bytes);

        /* we have now dealt with all the source data in the line.
           there may be a string still waiting in the buffer, however,
           so we must check bdex one last time */

        if(bdex) {
                fputc(0x80,fp);
                fputc(bdex,fp);
                j+=2;
                fwrite(b,1,bdex,fp);
                j+=bdex;
        }

        return(ferror(fp));
}

/* make a new file name with a fixed extension */
strmfe(new,old,ext)
        char *new,*old,*ext;
{
        while(*old != 0 && *old != '.') *new++=*old++;
        *new++='.';
        while(*ext) *new++=*ext++;
        *new=0;
}
/* return number of bytes in number of pixels */
pixels2bytes(n)
        int n;
{
        if(n & 0x0007) return((n >> 3) + 1);
        else return(n >> 3);
}
```

A binary image file like this will simply be two integers representing the dimensions of the picture—minus one in both cases—followed by the raw image data. If you don't want to create a binary image file by capturing it from the screen—which will be the case if you have an EGA card—you can arrive at a suitable test file to try out the file compression code. You can do this by modifying one of the viewer programs discussed earlier in this chapter so that it writes the contents of its image buffer to a file—preceded by four bytes representing the size.

If the original file was 576 by 720 pixels, for example, the first four bytes of the BIN file would be:

```
0x3f,0x02,0xCf,0x02
```

The program itself should be fairly easy to follow. The function strmfe creates a file name with a defined extension. If the program passes a file name with any BIN extension, or no extension, it will load its first argument with the original file name, but having the extension "BIN." This function will crop up from time to time throughout this book.

If you call this program PACKIMG, you would invoke it to compress TESTFILE.BIN into TESTFILE.IMG like this:

```
PACKIMG TESTFILE
```

The strmfe function is used to create the proper name of the source file, TESTFILE.BIN, and the output file, TESTFILE.IMG, from this one argument.

The main function opens the source binary file and creates a destination IMG file. It reads in the first four bytes of the binary image file to determine the image dimensions. Having worked this out, it can calculate the number of bytes that will be required to contain the image.

If you decide to modify this code so it will accept big images, make sure you change the buffer allocation from malloc to farmalloc.

The actual image packing should be pretty straight forward by now. The WriteImgHeader function loads the last two fields of the header with the dimensions of the image and writes it to the dest file. This compression code assumes that the pattern size will be one and the pixels will be 85 microns across. The header is set up to reflect these defaults, so none of the other fields need be filled in.

The actual packing process simply involves calling WriteImgLine once for each line in the picture.

ONWARD TO COLOR

The IMG format probably will be of intense interest to you if you're involved with Ventura Publisher, or one of the GEM applications, and of no interest at all otherwise. However, many of the ideas from this chapter will turn up later in this book.

One of the things that you'll see in chapter 12 is format conversion or swabbing, that is, changing an image file packed in one format into a file in a different format. For example, there are lots of applications for a program that would convert MacPaint files into IMG files.

One obvious way to do this is to unpack the MacPaint file into a buffer using the code from chapter 2 and pack it into an IMG file using the routines in this chapter. There is another way, however, which is faster and requires no meaningful amount of memory. If you've really got a handle on how simple image compression works you'll probably be able to figure it out before you read about it in chapter 12.

4
CHAPTER

PC Paintbrush
Files—Color at Last

If architects built buildings the way programmers write programs the first
woodpecker that came along would destroy civilization.
—Murphy's Laws of Computers

The PC Paintbrush file format was, perhaps not surprisingly, developed for use with the PC Paintbrush package, a commercial paint program by ZSoft. Originally a bit grisly to work with, PC Paintbrush has gotten a lot better of late. The current version, PC Paintbrush IV, is quite respectable and pretty powerful. A Microsoft Windows compatible version of PC Paintbrush also exists and is a reasonable bit of work, although it suffers a lot of limitations at the hands of Microsoft Windows.

The PC Paintbrush file format is the first one to be discussed that supports color. It's also a good example of what happens when one does not build some future into one's present plans. You can almost hear the original designers of the format saying "go on . . . there'll never be a video card that can display more than 16 colors." These guys ought to be bronzed, right along with the IBM engineers who decided that no one would ever need more than 640k of memory.

As you'll see, the PC Paintbrush format—also called PCX after its file extension—actually is several formats in one, with lots of hacks and patches tacked onto it to drag it kicking and screaming into the nineties.

In this section you'll see several ways to arrive at color images in a bit-mapped picture file. This will include an introduction to palettes.

Because the PCX format is rather intimate with the specific hardware on which its images are intended to be displayed, you also will learn a bit more about the workings of EGA and VGA cards, although their complete unveiling will really come later in this book.

Figure 4-1 illustrates a typical 16-color PC Paintbrush image.

Fig 4-1   A 16-color PCX file, halftoned here for reproduction. This picture was downloaded from Canada Remote Systems (416) 629-0136

MONOCHROME PCX FILES

As with the previous two image formats already discussed, the PCX format uses run length encoding to compress its image data, although the format is a bit strange. In fact, PCX encoding is the least efficient of the three formats seen thus far. If you compress the same picture as a MacPaint, IMG and PCX file, the PCX file usually will be larger by a sizable margin.

As you'll see shortly, 16-color PCX files are really just an extension of monochrome ones, and 256-color images a further extension, although they work in a fundamentally different way.

All PCX files carry around a 128-byte header that defines things such as the size of the image, the color palette if the image isn't monochrome—sometimes—and several other bits of information. It also has quite a bit of dead space, much as the MacBinary header did. In this case, though, it's not obvious why all that extra room was left there.

The PCX file header can be defined in C language terms as shown in Fig. 4-2. Unlike the IMG file header, the integer values are stored as proper integers, and once they're stashed in a buffer that your program will regard as a suitable struct, they're painless to access.

It's pretty easy to read the first 128 bytes of a PCX file into a PCX-HEAD structure from C. You can either just load them into a buffer and

Fig 4-2   The structure of a PCX file header

```
typedef struct  {
        char    manufacturer;           /* always 0xa0 */
        char    version;                /* version number */
        char    encoding;               /* always 1 */
        char    bits_per_pixel;         /* color bits */
        int     xmin,ymin;              /* image origin */
        int     xmax,ymax;              /* image dimensions */
        int     hres;                   /* resolution values */
        int     vres;
        char    palette[48];            /* color palette */
        char    reserved;
        char    colour_planes;          /* color planes */
        int     bytes_per_line;         /* line buffer size */
        int     palette_type;           /* grey or color palette */
        char    filler[58];
} PCXHEAD;
```

cast a PCXHEAD pointer to point to the base of the buffer, or you can do this:

```
PCXHEAD h;

if((fread((char *)&h,1,sizeof(PCXHEAD),fp) = =
        sizeof(PCXHEAD)) {
            /* some code goes here */
} else puts("Error reading header");
```

This assumes that the PCX file whose header is being read has been opened for reading with the file pointer fp.

The fields of the PCXHEAD struct all relate to the image that comprises the rest of the file—sort of. In fact, they frequently tell you things that would have to be calculated under other formats. Some of the information isn't relevant to monochrome files.

The manufacturer byte of the PCX header always will be 0x0a. This is really the only check that the format provides for software that reads a PCX file. If the first byte isn't 0x0a, the file isn't a PCX file despite what its extension might imply.

The version byte tells you which version of PC Paintbrush created the file. This also offers a programmer wishing to decode the file some clues as to what the file might contain. This byte can contain one of four values as of this writing.

If the version byte is zero, the file has come from version 2.5 of PC Paintbrush, the earliest incarnation. If it's two, the file has come from version 2.8 of PC Paintbrush and it contains valid palette information. Palettes and how they affect PC Paintbrush files will be discussed shortly. If this byte is three, the picture has come from version 2.8 of PC Paintbrush, but it contains no palette information, that is, it's either monochrome or it intends to use the default palette of whatever display card it's shown on. If it's five, this file has come from version 3.0 or better. This byte will become more important in dealing with 256-color PCX files.

The encoding byte should always contain the value one. This indicates that the file has been compressed using the PCX run length encoding scheme. Presumably ZSoft could introduce a second, more efficient encoding scheme some time in the future and make this byte a flag that determines which of the two compression techniques is in use.

The bits_per_pixel value has to do with color images, and will be explained later on.

The xmin, ymin, xmax, and ymax values define the dimensions of the image in the file in question. The actual dimensions in pixels can be determined by subtracting the min from the max values. In most cases, the min values will be zero. In fact, the values in these fields are a bit misleading— by one bit. If the horizontal dimension of a PCX file is defined as being 639, this means that the pixels will run from pixel 0 through pixel 639, for a total of 640 pixels. As such, you must keep in mind that the dimension values found in a PCX file header are always one smaller than the actual dimensions of the picture in the file.

The hres and vres members define the resolution of the device that created the image, and are of no real use.

The palette buffer contains the color palette if the image has 16 or fewer colors. It's 48 bytes long. The structure of the palette of a PCX file will be discussed shortly.

The color_planes value also will be discussed later in this chapter.

The bytes_per_line value is extremely useful, because it obviates the need to use the pixels2bytes function (discussed in the last chapter) to find out how many bytes are required to contain each line of image data in the file. This is an int value, not a char.

The palette_type field is a fairly new one—it only has significance with the advent of VGA cards, which can do meaningful grey scales. It tells you whether the image is intended to be displayed as a grey scale or in color. This field will contain one for grey scales and two for full color.

If some of the information in these fields doesn't make complete sense just yet, don't worry. It will all turn up in the source code you'll encounter later in this chapter.

Unpacking the Image Data

The first byte immediately after the header of a PCX file is the beginning of the compressed image data. The run length encoding scheme for PCX file data is weird, and one must imagine that it has been structured in this way because it's fast to decode. It certainly isn't a terribly effective way to squeeze pictures.

Figure 4-3 illustrates the basic decoding procedure for a PCX file.

Ø   2.5
2   2.8
3   2.8 no palette
5   3.Ø

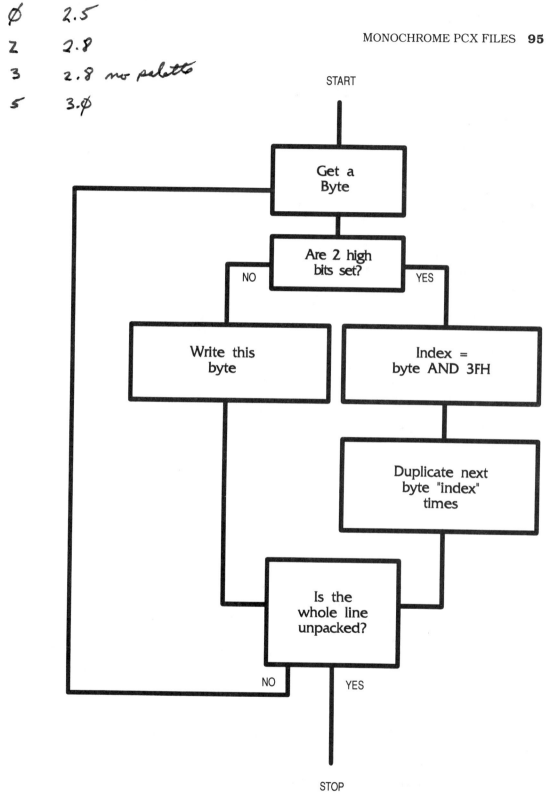

Fig 4-3   The procedure for unpacking one line of a PCX file

As with the previous two run length encoding systems discussed thus far, the data in a PCX file can be thought of as being a series of packets containing key bytes and data bytes. There are only two types of fields, as with MacPaint files, the string fields and run of byte fields.

If the upper two bits of a key byte are set, then the index of the current image packet can be found in the lower six bits. The next byte in the file is to be repeated for as many times as is specified in the index. Because the index can only use six bits, a run of bytes field in a PCX file can be only a maximum of 63 bytes long. Longer fields would require two packets.

If the upper two bits aren't set, the byte is written to the image "as is." In other words, string bytes require no key byte so long as the image data in all the bytes of the string can fit in the lower six bits of each byte.

You might well be wondering how string data with the occasional high order bits set might be stored. Each such byte would be stored as a run of bytes packet with a length of one. As such, if you had a line of data that consisted entirely of random data, all of which had its two high order bits set, that line would require twice as many bytes to store in its compressed form than it did in its raw form.

This is, to be sure, a pathological case, and one that doesn't crop up all that often in quite so extreme a fashion. However, this most peculiar run length encoding scheme does frequently create some very large files.

If you consider the PCX encoding system carefully, you'll realize that it's heavily weighted for efficient run of bytes encoding. This is actually in keeping with the nature of PCX files as created by PC Paintbrush. Because PC Paintbrush is a paint program which was, at least initially, intended solely for use as a drawing tool, its file format doesn't make particular provisions for those sorts of images that might have a lot of uncompressable string data, primarily scanned pictures. Scanners were by no means common when PC Paintbrush was first released back in the dawn of time.

Decoding a PCX file is extremely simple. The function in Fig. 4-4 illustrates how it's done.

The ReadPcxLine function will return the length of the line in bytes. It assumes that the file pointer fp is pointing to the compressed data representing the start of a line when it's called, and that the global variable bytes represents the width of the line in bytes, as found in the bytes per line member of a PCXHEAD struct.

As with the previous two formats discussed, the data in a PCX file is constrained to be compressed one line at a time, such that you always can be certain of reaching the end of a line at the end of a packet.

The exact nature of the data returned in the p buffer passed to ReadPcxLine will vary depending upon the number of colors in the original image. In a monochrome image it will be bitmap data, just as has been the case for IMG and MacPaint files.

Having worked out how to decode one line of PCX image information, it's pretty simple to write a program that will display an entire PCX image.

Fig 4-4   A function to decode one line of a PCX file

```
ReadPcxLine(p,fp)      /* read and decode a PCX line into p */
        char *p;
        FILE *fp;
{
        int n=0,c,i;

        /* null the buffer */
        memset(p,0,bytes);
        do {
                /* get a key byte */
                c=fgetc(fp) & 0xff;
                /* if it's a run of bytes field */
                if((c & 0xc0) == 0xc0) {
                        /* and off the high bits */
                        i=c & 0x3f;
                        /* get the run byte */
                        c=fgetc(fp);
                        /* run the byte */
                        while(i--) p[n++]=~c;
                }
                /* else just store it */
                else p[n++]=~c;
        } while(n < bytes);
        return(n);
}
```

run

string char

At least, it's easy to handle a monochrome PCX image. The program in Fig. 4-5 will be recognizable as being one of the IMG viewers from the previous chapter with the IMG specific code replaced by equivalent functions having to do with PCX files.

This viewer will work only with monochrome images that will fit in a single memory segment when they're unpacked. Once again, MacPaint files converted into PCX format make excellent test images in this case. There's little to be said about the workings of this program that wasn't discussed in Chapter 3.

Fig 4-5   A program to view monochrome PCX files

```
/* A program to look at PCX pictures */
#define EGACARD 1

#include "stdio.h"
#include "alloc.h"
#include "dos.h"
#if !EGACARD
#include "graphics.h"
#endif
```

Fig 4-5   continued

```
typedef struct   {
        char     manufacturer;
        char     version;
        char     encoding;
        char     bits_per_pixel;
        int      xmin,ymin;
        int      xmax,ymax;
        int      hres;
        int      vres;
        char     palette[48];
        char     reserved;
        char     colour_planes;
        int      bytes_per_line;
        int      palette_type;
        char     filler[58];
                 } PCXHEAD;

PCXHEAD header;                     /* where the header lives */
unsigned int width,depth;
unsigned int bytes;

main(argc,argv)
        int argc;
        char *argv[];
{
        FILE *fp;
        char *p;

        if(argc > 1) {
                /* attempt to open the file */
                if((fp=fopen(argv[1],"rb")) != NULL) {
                        /* read in the header */
                        if(fread((char *)&header,1,sizeof(PCXHEAD),fp)
                            == sizeof(PCXHEAD)) {
                                /* check to make sure it's a picture */
                                if(header.manufacturer==0x0a) {
                                        /* allocate a big buffer */
                                        width = (header.xmax-header.xmin)+1;
                                        depth = (header.ymax-header.ymin)+1;
                                        bytes=header.bytes_per_line;

                                        if((p=malloc(4+bytes*depth)) != NULL) {
                                                /* unpack the file */
                                                if(UnpackPcxFile(p+4,fp)
                                                  ==bytes)
                                                    /* show the picture */
                                                    ShowPcxPicture(p+4);
                                                free(p);
                                        }
                                } else printf("Not a PCX file.\n");
                        } else printf("Error reading %s.\n",argv[1]);
                        fclose(fp);
                } else printf("Error opening %s.\n",argv[1]);
```

```
        }
}

ShowPcxPicture(p) /* display the top of the picture */
        char *p;
{
        unsigned int i;

        /* graphics on */
        init();

        #if EGACARD
        /* copy the graphics to the screen */
        for(i=0;i<350;++i)
                memcpy(MK_FP(0xa000,i*80),p+4+(i*bytes),bytes);

        #else
        p[0]=width-1;
        p[1]=((width-1) >> 8);
        p[2]=depth-1;
        p[3]=((depth-1) >> 8);
        putimage(0,0,p,COPY_PUT); /* show the picture      */
        #endif

        /* wait for a key press */
        getch();
        /* graphics off */
        deinit();
}

UnpackPcxFile(p,fp)             /* open and print GEM/IMG image n */
        char *p;
        FILE *fp;
{
        int i,n;

        for(i=0;i<depth;++i) {
                n=ReadPcxLine(p,fp);
                p+=bytes;
        }
        return(n);
}

ReadPcxLine(p,fp)    /* read and decode a PCX line into p */
        char *p;
        FILE *fp;
{
        int n=0,c,i;

        /* null the buffer */
        memset(p,0,bytes);
        do {
                /* get a key byte */
                c=fgetc(fp) & 0xff;
```

Fig 4-5   continued

```
                /* if it's a run of bytes field */
                if((c & 0xc0) == 0xc0) {
                        /* and off the high bits */
                        i=c & 0x3f;
                        /* get the run byte */
                        c=fgetc(fp);
                        /* run the byte */
                        while(i--) p[n++]=c;
                }
                /* else just store it */
                else p[n++]=c;
        } while(n < bytes);
        return(n);
}


#if EGACARD
init()              /* turn on graphics mode */
{
        union REGS r;

        r.x.ax=0x0010;
        int86(0x10,&r,&r);
}


deinit()   /* turn off graphics card */
{
        union REGS r;

        r.x.ax=0x0003;
        int86(0x10,&r,&r);
}
#else
init()              /* turn on graphics mode */
{
        int d,m,e=0;

        detectgraph(&d,&m);
        if(d<0) {
                puts("No graphics card");
                exit(1);
        }
        if(d==EGA) {
                d=CGA;
                m=CGAHI;
        }
        initgraph(&d,&m,"");
        e=graphresult();
        if(e<0) {
                printf("Graphics error %d: %s",e,grapherrormsg(e));
                exit(1);
        }
        setcolor(getmaxcolor());
```

```
}

deinit()  /* turn off graphics card */
{
        closegraph();
}
#endif
```

Packing the Image Data

Packing PCX data also is similar to packing monochrome IMG information. The function in Fig. 4-6, which will handle monochrome PCX lines in
the example to be discussed here, is exactly the same code that would be
used to deal with color pictures.

The process of compressing picture data in the PCX format is similar
to that of doing it under the previous two formats discussed in this book,
except that PCX files require that string data be handled peculiarly for reasons that were dealt with earlier in this chapter. A function to pack PCX
lines must look for runs of bytes, encoding them where they're found, and
deal with any bytes that do not lend themselves to run of byte encoding as

Fig 4-6   A function to pack one line of image data into a PCX file

```
WritePcxLine(p,fp)
        char *p;
        FILE *fp;
{
        char b[64];
        unsigned int i=0,j=0,t=0;

        do {
                i=0;
                while((p[t+i]==p[t+i+1]) && ((t+i) < bytes) && (i<63))++i;
                if(i>0) {
                        fputc(i | 0xc0,fp);
                        fputc(~p[t],fp);
                        t+=i;
                        j+=2;
                }
                else {
                        if(((~p[t]) & 0xc0)==0xc0) {
                                fputc(0xc1,fp);
                                ++j;
                        }
                        fputc(~p[t++],fp);
                        ++j;
                }
        } while(t<bytes);
        return(j);
}
```

strings. Of course, many of these will be handled as run of byte packets too, but as very small ones.

The function in Fig. 4-6 will pack a single line of data into the file pointed to by fp.

The file header for a PCX file being created is fairly elaborate, and it's worth having a special function to manage it. A suitable function is illustrated in Fig. 4-7. This version is for a monochrome image. As you become more familiar with the PCX format extensions that deal with color images you will be able to modify this to handle them.

Fig 4-7   A function to write a PCX file header

```
WritePcxHeader(fp)
        FILE *fp;
{
        memset((char *)&header,0,sizeof(PCXHEAD));
        header.manufacturer=0x0a;
        header.version=0;
        header.encoding=1;

/* bits per pixel:      1 for monochrome
                        4 for 16 colors
                        8 for 256 colors */

        header.bits_per_pixel=1;
        header.xmin=header.ymin=0;
        header.xmax=wide-1;
        header.ymax=deep-1;
        header.colour_planes=1;
        header.bytes_per_line=bytes;
        header.palette_type=2;
        return(fwrite((char *)&header,1,sizeof(PCXHEAD),fp));
}
```

With everything that's been discussed thus far, it should be easy to modify the image compression example from Chapter 3 so it will work with PCX files. The code that handles binary image fragments can be left as it is—all you'll really have to do is to substitute the previous two functions for their IMG counterparts and do a bit of cosmetic surgery around the source file.

The resulting program is illustrated in Fig. 4-8.

The binary image fragment that was used to develop the monochrome packing programs is illustrated in Fig. 4-9. This is obviously a drawn image, rather than a scanned one. It represents few of the pathological cases that plague the PCX packing format. Even still, the PCX version of this image was about 10 percent bigger than the IMG version. PCX compression still managed a 50 percent reduction in size over the original binary image.

Fig 4-8   A program to pack a monochrome getimage fragment into a PCX file

```
/* a program to pack a getimage fragment into a PCX file */

#include "stdio.h"
#include "alloc.h"

#define size      (wide * pixels2bytes(deep))

char bin_file[80];        /* buffers for file names */
char pcx_file[80];

typedef struct  {
        char    manufacturer;
        char    version;
        char    encoding;
        char    bits_per_pixel;
        int     xmin,ymin;
        int     xmax,ymax;
        int     hres;
        int     vres;
        char    palette[48];
        char    reserved;
        char    colour_planes;
        int     bytes_per_line;
        int     palette_type;
        char    filler[58];
                } PCXHEAD;

PCXHEAD header;                     /* where the header lives */

int wide,deep,bytes;      /* global size values */

main(argc,argv)
        int argc;
        char *argv[];
{
        FILE *source,*dest;
        char *p,b[4];

        if(argc > 1) {
                /* make file names */
                strmfe(bin_file,argv[1],"BIN");
                strmfe(pcx_file,argv[1],"PCX");

                /* open the source file */
                if((source=fopen(bin_file,"rb")) != NULL) {
                        /* create the destination file */
                        if((dest=fopen(pcx_file,"wb")) != NULL) {
                                /* read in the size */
                                if(fread(b,1,4,source)==4) {
                                        /* and get it from the buffer */
                                        wide = b[0]+(b[1]<<8)+1;
                                        deep = b[2]+(b[3]<<8)+1;
```

Fig 4-8   continued

```
                                        bytes = pixels2bytes(wide);
                                        /* allocate an image buffer */
                                        if((p=malloc(size)) != NULL) {
                                          /* read in the image */
                                          if(fread(p,1,size,source) == size) {
                                            printf("Packing image %d by "
                                                    "%d pixels\n",
                                                    wide,deep);
                                            /* pack the image */
                                            PackPcxFile(dest,p);
                                          } else printf("Error reading %s\n",
                                              bin_file);
                                          free(p);
                                        } else puts("Error allocating memory");
                                } else puts("Error reading header");
                                fclose(dest);
                        } else printf("Error creating %s\n",pcx_file);
                        fclose(source);
                } else printf("Error opening %s\n",bin_file);
        } else puts("I need an argument");
}


WritePcxLine(p,fp)
        char *p;
        FILE *fp;
{
        char b[64];
        unsigned int i=0,j=0,t=0;

        do {
                i=0;
                while((p[t+i]==p[t+i+1]) && ((t+i) < bytes) && (i<63))++i;
                if(i>0) {
                        fputc(i | 0xc0,fp);
                        fputc(~p[t],fp);
                        t+=i;
                        j+=2;
                }
                else {
                        if(((~p[t]) & 0xc0)==0xc0) {
                                fputc(0xc1,fp);
                                ++j;
                        }
                        fputc(~p[t++],fp);
                        ++j;
                }
        } while(t<bytes);
        return(j);
}


/* pack an image into a PCX file */
PackPcxFile(fp,p)
```

```
        FILE *fp;
        char *p;
{
        int i;

        /* write the header */
        WritePcxHeader(fp);
        /* pack the lines */
        for(i=0;i<deep;++i) WritePcxLine(p+(i*bytes),fp);
}

/* write a PCX header */
WritePcxHeader(fp)
        FILE *fp;
{
        memset((char *)&header,0,sizeof(PCXHEAD));
        header.manufacturer=0x0a;
        header.version=0;
        header.encoding=1;
        header.bits_per_pixel=8;
        header.xmin=header.ymin=0;
        header.xmax=wide-1;
        header.ymax=deep-1;
        header.colour_planes=1;
        header.bytes_per_line=bytes;
        header.palette_type=2;
        return(fwrite((char *)&header,1,sizeof(PCXHEAD),fp));
}

/* make a new file name with a fixed extension */
strmfe(new,old,ext)
        char *new,*old,*ext;
{
        while(*old != 0 && *old != '.') *new++=*old++;
        *new++='.';
        while(*ext) *new++=*ext++;
        *new=0;
}

/* return number of bytes in number of pixels */
pixels2bytes(n)
        int n;
{
        if(n & 0x0007) return((n >> 3) + 1);
        else return(n >> 3);
}
```

If the image in Fig. 2-5 is stored in PCX and IMG formats, the difference in size between the two widens to about 25 percent. This image is a scanned photograph and doesn't take as kindly to the PCX encoding system.

It's worth noting that big monochrome PCX images, ones that will not fit in a single memory segment, are not at all uncommon. They turn up in

Fig 4-9   The getimage fragment used to test the packing programs so far. This picture was downloaded from Rose Media (416) 226-9260

the public domain quite frequently, because PCX is probably the most widely accepted image file format among desktop publishing programs for the PC. As such, you might be interested in modifying one of the large image viewers from Chapter 3 for use with PCX files.

SIXTEEN-COLOR IMAGES

Once you know the basic mechanics of dealing with the PCX image encoding scheme, monochrome PCX images aren't much of a problem. Color pictures get a bit more interesting because they involve a whole new area of image handling.

For reasons that will become a bit more apparent when you see how 256-color images work, PCX files can be thought of as falling into three groups. The first contains monochrome files, which you will now know how to work with about as well as anyone ever needs to. The second contains color images with 16 or fewer colors. The third contains 256-color images.

Because of the way a color palette is structured, the maximum number of colors an image file can support always will be an even power of two. Thus, a PCX file in the second group can have 2, 4, 8, or 16 colors. There is no way to represent color palettes of between 32 and 128 colors except for promoting them to 256-color palettes and leaving some of the color entries unused.

To properly understand how a color PCX file works, it's important to know what a color display card is really doing. The process probably will not turn out to be as you'd imagine it if you haven't done much programming for color displays.

This discussion will deal primarily with EGA cards, which, as you'll see, is what 16-color PCX files are really intended for use with. It's true that CGA cards have a color graphics mode of sorts, but it's not really of much use for bit-mapped graphics.

VGA cards will turn up in conjunction with 256-color PCX files. In the mean time, you should be aware that VGA cards encompass EGA cards as well. If you have a VGA card in your system, all of these EGA specific examples will work with it. In addition, the basic workings of color palettes is the same for both EGA and VGA cards, except that a VGA card has more colors.

Color and Color Displays

Color can be represented in one of two basic ways, depending upon the medium being used to reproduce it. The easiest color representation system to understand is the one you probably experienced when you bought this book, although it's not the one that you will being using once you get inside it.

When color pictures are printed on paper, they are done so using what is often called CMY printing. This stands for cyan, magenta, and yellow. In fact, it's properly called CMYK, where the K stands for black, because printing with ink requires that black areas be printed with real black ink even though in theory this should not be necessary. For the sake of clarity, however, let's deal with the simplified three-color model.

Before the pressmen got hold of it, the cover of this book was white. As you'll probably recall from high school physics—if you didn't cut that particular class—white light is a mixture of all colors of light. As such, a white sheet of paper can be said to reflect all colors of light equally well.

If you print an area of red ink on white paper, the light being reflected from the paper will have been filtered so that the paper is still a reasonably good reflector of red light and a poor reflector of other colors of light.

This is called *subtractive color synthesis*. The original light, containing all the colors, has subtracted from it those colors that are not required, leaving those that are.

The three primary colors of subtractive color synthesis are cyan, a medium blue color; magenta, a rather vulgar red color; and pure yellow. You might have encountered swatches of these on the glue flaps of cereal boxes, on improperly trimmed magazine pages and so on. Printers often include them with the alignment marks and other objects that are used to set up printing presses.

Laser printers that can print color use subtractive color, and their color is expressed in these terms.

This model will not work on a video display because, as you will note if you look at one, video displays are not naturally white. They're black, which is to say that in their quiescent state they emit no light at all. Any light that does emerge from a picture tube is added to this basic blackness. As such, the process of creating color on a computer screen is exactly the opposite of doing so on paper. It's called *additive color synthesis*. Its primary colors are red, green, and blue.

Additive color synthesis is often referred to as RGB color for this reason. Figure 4-10 illustrates the relationship between CMY and RGB color—in black and white.

In essence, a color graphic being displayed on a computer screen involves some mechanism where every pixel can determine what percentage of red, green, and blue light will be displayed when the scanning beams of the picture tube go to illuminate it.

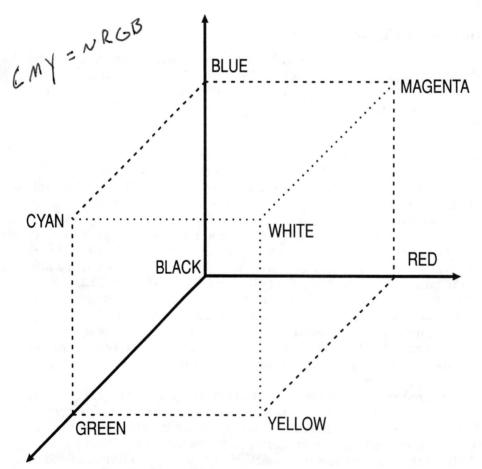

Fig 4-10   The relationship between additive and subtractive color

The most obvious way to do this would be to have three bytes of information associated with each pixel, one for each of the percentages of the primary additive colors. There are a few drawbacks to this, not the least of which being that such a screen with the dimensions of an EGA graphics mode screen would require something on the order of three quarters of a megabyte of memory. The disk files for such an image, even with the most sophisticated string based compression techniques, would be comparably immense. Such a screen would be very slow to update.

This is a pity, because a video display structured like this would be capable of reproducing a picture with something on the order of 16 million different colors all displayed at once.

Palettes

Color palettes represent a step closer to reality from the ideal—but somewhat impractical color graphics display described above. A color palette can be thought of as being a big lookup table in which each entry consists of three numbers representing the percentages of red, green, and blue light required to form a specific color on the screen.

Every pixel on the screen of a color display can be thought of as having a number behind it. This number does not specify the color directly, but rather specifies a palette entry. As such, if palette entry number nine specified blue light and pixel (6,40) was to be blue, its value would be nine.

In displaying graphics, an EGA card is "loaded" with the red, green, and blue palette values for each of its 16 colors. It then knows, for example, when it sees a pixel with the value nine, how much red, green, and blue light to use to generate the particular sort of blue that the originator of the picture had in mind.

In fact, this is something of an oversimplification, but the true nature of it won't become important until Chapter 10. In the mean time, it's worth noting that in fact the color values passed to an EGA card as RGB percentages are actually compressed into a single byte.

An EGA card doesn't have that many shades of blue to choose from—it has a color palette of 16 colors chosen from a maximum of 64. Things get a bit more interesting when you start looking at VGA cards. However, the principal is easiest to understand on an EGA card.

Figure 4-11 illustrates what an EGA card really does to display a pixel. If it's not completely clear yet, read on.

Color Planes

An EGA card's color graphics mode utilizes its display memory in a very odd way. You have seen it behave as a monochrome display in the examples discussed thus far, but, in fact, it was really being a color display all the time. However, without knowing how to coerce it into revealing itself as such, the only two colors it will display are black and white.

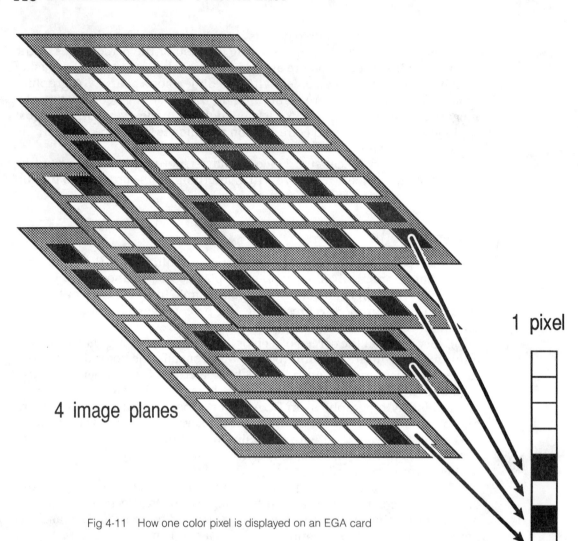

Fig 4-11   How one color pixel is displayed on an EGA card

The EGA graphics buffer lives at segment 0xa000. It has four 32k memory pages, or layers, any one of which can appear at this address. There are registers in the card that can be tickled to define which one is addressable at the moment. By sequentially making each layer appear and updating it, a complete 16-color image can be created.

Each layer can be thought of as a monochrome screen. However, the EGA card itself deals with them slightly differently. You can update them as you would a monochrome display card's buffer—as the monochrome EGA programs discussed previously did, for example—but the EGA card itself derives palette numbers from the individual planes to display colors.

The process is simple once you understand it—the tricky part is in figuring out why it was done this way to begin with.

If all the bytes in all the layers are set to zero, all the pixels on the screen will be displayed in palette color zero, which is black in the default palette. If you were to write a monochrome bitmap to the upper layer, as has been done by many of the EGA specific programs discussed thus far, the "on" pixels in the bitmap would be displayed in palette color eight, which is white in the default EGA palette.

The bits in the first plane correspond to the forth bit in the color palette indices for each pixel.

Both of these colors could be changed by simply changing the color information in their respective palettes. This means that you can change the colors of whole areas of the screen instantly by just writing new values to the appropriate palette registers.

If you were to make the second layer of the EGA card appear on the memory bus—by as yet mysterious means—and write the same bitmap to it, all the "on" pixels would be displayed in color 12. This is the number that results from the combination of 0x08 and 0x04, that is, having the third and forth bits in a byte set. The bits in the second plane represent the third bit in the color palette indices for each pixel.

You could repeat this process for the other two layers, which would cause all the on bits to be displayed in color 15.

Figure 4-12 illustrates a 16-color PCX picture broken down into its four EGA planes. These four bitmaps, when loaded into the corresponding planes of an EGA card, will result in a complete, 16-color picture.

The process of updating a complete EGA image is quite timeconsuming in C, so much so that it's never really done this way. A machine language driver is required, something that will not be dealt with until Chapter 10. In the mean time, the 16-color PCX viewer to be discussed here will get by with Turbo C's putimage function, which is fairly interesting in its own right in this application.

The following discussion, and the program which accompanies it, will only work with EGA and VGA cards.

If you capture part of an EGA graphics screen using the Turbo C getimage function, the first 4 bytes of the buffer will contain the image dimensions, but the rest of it will make no immediate sense. In fact, it's not completely mysterious, but you have to understand how an EGA card works to fully appreciate its structure.

It also helps to know how programmers think.

Whoever wrote the Turbo C graphics functions obviously would have wanted to structure the getimage image fragment buffers so as to make their contents as fast as possible to move on and off the screen. Inasmuch as there was no need to have these buffers compatible with anything else, their creator was free to make them wholly dedicated to the EGA screen structure. Thus, it's reasonable to suppose that they might be structured a lot like an EGA screen itself.

A bit of experimentation proves this to be so. If you were to compare a monochrome getimage fragment with a getimage fragment of the same size

Original image

Fig 4-12   The four planes of a 16-color PCX file

captured from an EGA screen, you would discover that the EGA fragment had four times as many lines, but that each line represented legitimate monochrome bitmap scan lines. The four monochrome bitmaps are inter-leaved, so that the first line belongs to the first image, the second line to the second image, and so on. If you were to copy every forth line out of an image fragment taken from an EGA screen, you would have a mono-chrome bit-mapped image representing one of the four color components.

This process can be reversed, of course. Once you understand how the image fragment buffers are structured, you can easily synthesize image fragment buffers that will display properly with putimage on an EGA card. The function in Fig. 4-13, for example, will return a pointer to a buffer that is suitable for use with putimage running under an EGA card when it's

Fig 4-13   A function to convert a monochrome getimage fragment to an EGA getimage fragment

```
/* return an EGA version of a monochrome bitmap */
char *mono2ega(source)
        char *source;
{
        char *p;
        int x,y,i,j,ls,sz;

        x=1+source[0]+(source[1] << 8);
        y=1+source[2]+(source[3] << 8);
        if((sz=imagesize(0,0,x,y)) != -1) {
                if((p=malloc(sz)) != NULL) {
                        memset(p,0,sz);
                        memcpy(p,source,4);
                        ls=pixels2bytes(x);
                        for(j=0;j<y;++j) {
                                memcpy(p+4+((j*4)*ls),
                                    source+4+(j*ls),ls);
                                memcpy(p+4+ls+((j*4)*ls),
                                    source+4+(j*ls),ls);
                                memcpy(p+4+(ls*2)+((j*4)*ls),
                                    source+4+(j*ls),ls);
                                memcpy(p+4+(ls*3)+((j*4)*ls),
                                    source+4+(j*ls),ls);
                        }
                        return(p);
                }
        } else return(NULL);
}
```

passed a monochrome buffer returned—and presumably saved in a disk file—by getimage. It also will work with synthetic putimage buffers, as have been described earlier in this book.

The function in Fig. 4-13 should illustrate the structure of an EGA putimage buffer pretty clearly.

There is a catch to this process. The buffers passed to putimage can't be larger than 64k. An EGA screen requires four 32k buffers for a total of 128k of memory. Clearly, even if you know how to translate a color PCX image into a putimage buffer, you can't copy the whole picture to the screen. At least, you can't do so all at once.

Color PCX Files

Nothing has been said thus far about how color PCX files are structured. However, you might well have deduced how they're handled from the foregoing discussion of EGA cards. Bear in mind that, like the author of the Turbo C graphics routines, the creator of the PCX 16-color file format clearly wanted to be able to update an EGA screen as quickly as possible.

A 16-color PCX file consists of four interleaved images, each one perfect for stuffing into one of the pages of an EGA card. You could unpack a
PCX file directly into an EGA card's display pages. The first line read from
the file would go into the first line of the first layer. The next line would go
into the first line of the second layer, and so on. The fifth line read would go
into the second line of the first layer. Although this process would be
rather slow and ugly to watch, it illustrates how well the 16-color PCX format matches the data structure of an EGA card's video buffer.

To do this, however, you would have to know how to tell the EGA card
to change pages, something that will not crop up until Chapter 10. In this
example, then, putimage will do all the work.

The next viewer program to be discussed will display a 640-by-350-
pixel, 16-color PCX file. Because a putimage buffer can't hold all the data in
a full screen PCX file at once, it will do so 50 lines at a time. That is, it will
unpack 50 lines—actually 200 monochrome lines—and display them,
repeating the process seven times until the whole picture has been
unpacked and displayed.

The complete program is illustrated in Fig. 4-14. This really is another
variation on the earlier viewer programs, although this time the changes
have been quite substantial.

Fig 4-14   A program to view 640-by-350 pixel, 16-color PCX files on an EGA or VGA card

```
/* A program to look at 16 colour PCX pictures */

#include "stdio.h"
#include "alloc.h"
#include "dos.h"
#include "graphics.h"

#define stripsize        50

typedef struct   {
        char    manufacturer;
        char    version;
        char    encoding;
        char    bits_per_pixel;
        int     xmin,ymin;
        int     xmax,ymax;
        int     hres;
        int     vres;
        char    palette[48];
        char    reserved;
        char    colour_planes;
        int     bytes_per_line;
        int     palette_type;
        char    filler[58];
                } PCXHEAD;

PCXHEAD header;                   /* where the header lives */
```

```
unsigned int width,depth;
unsigned int bytes;

main(argc,argv)
        int argc;
        char *argv[];
{
        FILE *fp;
        char *p;

        if(argc > 1) {
                /* attempt to open the file */
                if((fp=fopen(argv[1],"rb")) != NULL) {
                        /* read in the header */
                        if(fread((char *)&header,1,sizeof(PCXHEAD),fp)
                            == sizeof(PCXHEAD)) {
                                /* check to make sure it's a picture */
                                if(header.manufacturer==0x0a) {
                                        /* allocate a big buffer */
                                        width = (header.xmax-header.xmin)+1;
                                        depth = (header.ymax-header.ymin)+1;
                                        bytes=header.bytes_per_line;
                                        if((p=malloc(4+(stripsize*bytes*
                                            header.colour_planes))) != NULL) {
                                                /* unpack the file */
                                                UnpackPcxFile(p,fp);
                                                free(p);
                                        }
                                } else printf("Not a PCX file.\n");
                        } else printf("Error reading %s.\n",argv[1]);
                        fclose(fp);
                } else printf("Error opening %s.\n",argv[1]);
        }
}

UnpackPcxFile(p,fp)                /* open and print image */
        char *p;
        FILE *fp;
{
        int i,n=0,st=0,j;

        /* graphics on */
        init();
        /* set the palette */
        setEGApalette(header.palette,header.colour_planes);

        /* set the image size */
        p[0]=width-1;
        p[1]=((width-1) >> 8);
        p[2]=stripsize-1;
        p[3]=((stripsize-1) >> 8);

        for(i=0;i<depth;++i) {
                /* read lines in inverse order */
```

Fig 4-14   continued

```
                j=header.colour_planes;
                ReadPcxLine(p+4+(bytes*(n + --j)),fp);
                ReadPcxLine(p+4+(bytes*(n + --j)),fp);
                ReadPcxLine(p+4+(bytes*(n + --j)),fp);
                ReadPcxLine(p+4+(bytes*(n + --j)),fp);
                n+=header.colour_planes;

                /* if a whole strip is done, show it */
                if(n == (stripsize * header.colour_planes)) {
                        putimage(0,st*stripsize,p,COPY_PUT);
                        ++st;
                        n=0;
                }
        }
        getch();
        /* graphics off */
        deinit();
}

ReadPcxLine(p,fp)    /* read and decode a PCX line into p */
        char *p;
        FILE *fp;
{
        int n=0,c,i;

        /* null the buffer */
        memset(p,0,bytes);
        do {
                /* get a key byte */
                c=fgetc(fp) & 0xff;
                /* if it's a run of bytes field */
                if((c & 0xc0) == 0xc0) {
                        /* and off the high bits */
                        i=c & 0x3f;
                        /* get the run byte */
                        c=fgetc(fp);
                        /* run the byte */
                        while(i--) p[n++]=c;
                }
                /* else just store it */
                else p[n++]=c;
        } while(n < bytes);
        return(n);
}

init()             /* turn on graphics mode */
{
        int d,m,e=0;

        detectgraph(&d,&m);
        if(d<0) {
                puts("No graphics card");
```

```
                        exit(1);
                }
        if(d != EGA) {
                        puts("EGA card not found");
                        exit(1);
                }
        initgraph(&d,&m,"");
        e=graphresult();
        if(e<0) {
                        printf("Graphics error %d: %s",e,grapherrormsg(e));
                        exit(1);
                }
}

deinit()   /* turn off graphics card */
{
        closegraph();
}

setEGApalette(p,n)             /* set the EGA palette to RGB buffer p */
        char *p;
        int n;
{
        struct palettetype pt;

        /* translate it into colour numbers */
        rgb2ega_pal(pt.colors,p,1 << n);
        pt.size=(1 << n);
        /* and set it */
        setallpalette(&pt);
}

/* translate RGB values into an EGA colour number */
pbits(dest,source,l,h)
        char *dest,*source;
        int l,h;
{
        if(*source > 0x33) {
                *dest |=l;
                if(*source > 0x77) {
                        *dest &= ~l;
                        *dest |= h;
                        if(*source > 0xbb) *dest |= l+h;
                }
        }
}

/* translate a buffer of RGB values into EGA colour numbers */
rgb2ega_pal(dest,source,n)
        char *dest,*source;
        int n;
{
        int i;
```

Fig 4-14   continued

```
for(i=0;i<n;++i) {
        *dest=0;
        pbits(dest,source++,0x20,0x04);
        pbits(dest,source++,0x10,0x02);
        pbits(dest,source++,0x08,0x01);
        ++dest;
    }
}
```

Having allocated a buffer large enough to hold a putimage fragment 50 lines deep in EGA mode—something on the order of 16 kilobytes—the program starts unpacking lines into it. The first problem in this is that the lines come out of a PCX file in the wrong order. The first line read from the file is the forth line in the putimage buffer, the second line read is the third line in the buffer, and so on. As such, the program has to place the lines in nonsequential order to make everything look right on the screen.

The UnpackPcxPicture function does pretty well all the work. Its operation should be largely self-explanatory. This function is a bit naive, because it's hard wired into believing in 16-color images having vertical dimensions that are even multiples of 50. If either of these values is not what the code expects, it will misbehave to some extent. You might want to improve upon it once you fully understand what it's doing.

A great deal of this program is involved in setting the EGA card's palette. This is because of the palette structure of a PCX file. Oddly, while the image data is stored in a way completely in keeping with the workings of an EGA card, the palette is not. It wants to be loaded into a device such as the VGA card, which can define colors by true RGB percentages.

The EGA card defines its colors as single integers. The structure of an EGA "color number" is described in Chapter 9—it makes a bit more sense in machine language.

Turbo C kindly provides a function to set the palette from a color number, but nothing exists in its library to translate RGB values into color numbers. The function rgb2ega_pal does this. Once again, its workings will become clear once you've gotten through Chapter 10.

While this program manages to implement a 16-color PCX viewer without resorting to machine language, it does so with several penalties. The most obvious one is that the program relies on intimate knowledge of the internals of Turbo C, something that is not documented at all in Borland's manuals. This means that the program probably cannot be ported easily into other C language environments without some fairly radical changes—which will require still more undocumented inside information.

The second obvious penalty is that this program is slow and not very pretty to watch, because it paints the screen in chunks. It's particularly lethargic on early computers.

Replacing putimage with some dedicated machine language is, of course, the solution to both of these concerns. Because the structure of EGA cards remains constant no matter which C compiler you use, an assembly language module will regain much of the portability lost in this program, at least within a PC environment. Secondly, assembly language will get this program running at a reasonable speed.

THE 256-COLOR PCX FORMAT

mono

grey

color no palette

color 16

color 256

It's only quite recently that PC Paintbrush has supported a full palette of 256 colors. PC Paintbrush IV, the first version to do so, was only a few months old when this book was being written. This application exemplifies some of the problems involved in dealing with full color graphics, problems that will be discussed in greater detail later in this book. While PC Paintbrush IV has some phenomenal tools, first class hardware support and the like, the program itself ties up so much of the standard DOS memory that there's only enough room for a 320-by-200-pixel image in the 256-color mode.

As of this writing, PC Paintbrush IV did not support either extended or expanded memory to deal with larger pictures.

Your programs probably won't run into these sorts of problems—at least, not right away. However, color graphics occupy vast tracts of memory, even for pictures of fairly modest sizes. For example, a picture having the dimensions of a VGA card screen in its standard 256-color mode—320 by 200 pixels, or about a quarter of the area of an EGA card's graphic screen—requires almost 64k of memory.

Later on in this book you'll see how to display larger color images—and how to use extended and expanded memory to overcome the sorts of problems that obviously have befallen trusty old PC Paintbrush.

Large Color Palettes

If the color palette structure and bitmap arrangements of EGA cards forced you to read much of the preceding section several times, you'll probably enjoy the VGA card's graphics facilities. They're dead easy by comparison. This section will be dealing with the 13H MCGA mode of the VGA card.

As with the EGA card, the VGA's screen buffer begins at segment 0xa000. Because the dimensions of the mode 13H screen are quite a bit smaller than those of an EGA card, all the image data can fit in a single segment with no page swapping or other tricky manipulations.

A VGA card in this mode can display up to 256 unique colors drawn from a palette of about a quarter of a million. The colors are defined as percentages of red, green, and blue light this time. The actual percentage values are six bit numbers for a total of 18 bits of color information for each palette entry, which means that the card can handle pretty subtle variations in color.

The relationship of the screen information of a VGA card to its palette is essentially the same as that of an EGA card. Each pixel on the screen represents a number that tells the card which of its palette colors to display for that pixel. The difference is that on an EGA card the pixel numbers are derived by complex bitwise manipulation of multiple image planes. On a VGA card each pixel is represented by 1 byte.

The VGA graphics buffer is an area of memory with a one-to-one relationship of bytes to screen pixels. The first 320 bytes at segment 0A000H represent the first line of pixels on the screen. The next 320 bytes represent the second line, and so on.

It's hard to imagine a less complex way to display bit-mapped graphics.

Likewise, a VGA card's palette is extremely easy to set. In the case of 256-color PC Paintbrush files, the RGB color percentages are specified as eight bit values. In effect, they're fractions in which the denominator is 255. Because the VGA palette only uses six bit numbers, each of the PC Paintbrush palette values must be shifted right by two places, that is, divided by four.

Figure 4-15 illustrates a 256-color PC Paintbrush image as it would appear displayed on a VGA card.

Fig 4-15   A 256-color PCX file loaded into PC Paintbrush IV. This picture was converted from a GIF file that was downloaded from Rose Media (416) 226-9260

PCX 256-Color Extensions

A 256-color palette requires three bytes per color, for a total of 768 bytes. Despite their having left a bit of head room for expansion in the PCX header, the designers of the original file format clearly did not anticipate needing this much palette space. There is no way to put the color palette of a 256-color PCX file in that header.

As a result, it gets tacked onto the end of the file.

The procedure for locating the palette in a 256-color PCX file is a bit obscure. Any PCX file having the version member of its header loaded with the value five is a likely candidate for having a 256-color palette. If this is the case, the program reading the file should seek to the end of the file and count back 769 bytes. This can be done under C like this:

```
fseek(fp, - 769L,SEEK_END);
```

If your program reads a byte from this point in the file, it should see the value 0x0c, indicating that it has located the start of the palette. The next 768 bytes represent the palette itself. If you read them into a buffer, the first three bytes will be the red, green, and blue percentages, respectively, for the first color, the next three will be the percentages for the second color, and so on.

The actual image data that is stored after the PCX header is compressed using the same run length encoding scheme that earlier versions of the format used. However, the data is not compressed into monochrome image planes as the 16-color format used. It comes out of the unpacking function in exactly the same format in which the VGA card wants to see it, 1 byte per pixel. As such, one line of a 320-pixel-wide image would occupy 320 bytes.

The program in Fig. 4-16 is a simple 256-color PCX file viewer. This program is intended for use with images that are 320 by 200 pixels, the same size as the mode 13H screen. Although there is a 256-color VGA driver extant for Turbo C, it's not provided with the Turbo C package as of this writing. It turns up on bulletin boards from time to time. As such, this code doesn't use the putimage function, but rather accesses the VGA card's screen buffer directly. For reasons described previously, this is pretty easy to do.

Fig 4-16   A program to look at 256-color PCX files

```
/* A program to look at 256 colour PCX pictures */

#include "stdio.h"
#include "alloc.h"
#include "dos.h"
#include "graphics.h"
```

Fig 4-16   continued

```
typedef struct   {
        char    manufacturer;
        char    version;
        char    encoding;
        char    bits_per_pixel;
        int     xmin,ymin;
        int     xmax,ymax;
        int     hres;
        int     vres;
        char    palette[48];
        char    reserved;
        char    colour_planes;
        int     bytes_per_line;
        int     palette_type;
        char    filler[58];
                } PCXHEAD;

PCXHEAD header;                 /* where the header lives */
unsigned int width,depth;
unsigned int bytes;
char palette[768];              /* where the palette lives */

main(argc,argv)
        int argc;
        char *argv[];
{
        FILE *fp;

        if(argc > 1) {
                /* attempt to open the file */
                if((fp=fopen(argv[1],"rb")) != NULL) {
                        /* read in the header */
                        if(fread((char *)&header,1,sizeof(PCXHEAD),fp)
                            == sizeof(PCXHEAD)) {
                                /* check to make sure it's a picture */
                                if(header.manufacturer==0x0a &&
                                    header.version == 5) {
                                        /* find the palette */
                                        if(!fseek(fp,-769L,SEEK_END)) {
                                          if(fgetc(fp) == 0x0c &&
                                            fread(palette,1,768,fp) == 768) {
                                              fseek(fp,128L,SEEK_SET);
                                              /* allocate a big buffer */
                                              width = (header.xmax-
                                                  header.xmin)+1;
                                              depth = (header.ymax-
                                                  header.ymin)+1;
                                              bytes=header.bytes_per_line;
                                              /* unpack the file */
                                              UnpackPcxFile(fp);
                                              } else
                                                puts("Error reading palette");
```

```
                                    } else puts("Error seeking to palette");
                              } else printf("Not a 256 color PCX file.\n");
                        } else printf("Error reading %s.\n",argv[1]);
                        fclose(fp);
                } else printf("Error opening %s.\n",argv[1]);
        }
}

UnpackPcxFile(fp)     /* open and print image */
        FILE *fp;
{
        int i;

        /* graphics on */
        init();

        /* set the palette */
        setVGApalette(palette);

        /* unpack the file directly to the VGA buffer */
        for(i=0;i<depth;++i) ReadPcxLine(MK_FP(0xa000,i*320),fp);

        getch();
        /* graphics off */
        deinit();
}

ReadPcxLine(p,fp)     /* read and decode a PCX line into p */
        char *p;
        FILE *fp;
{
        int n=0,c,i;

        /* null the buffer */
        memset(p,0,bytes);
        do {
                /* get a key byte */
                c=fgetc(fp) & 0xff;
                /* if it's a run of bytes field */
                if((c & 0xc0) == 0xc0) {
                        /* and off the high bits */
                        i=c & 0x3f;
                        /* get the run byte */
                        c=fgetc(fp);
                        /* run the byte */
                        while(i--) p[n++]=c;
                }
                /* else just store it */
                else p[n++]=c;
        } while(n < bytes);
        return(n);
}

init()                /* turn on graphics mode */
```

Fig 4-16   continued

```
{
        union REGS r;

        r.x.ax=0x0013;
        int86(0x10,&r,&r);
}

deinit()   /* turn off graphics card */
{
        union REGS r;

        r.x.ax=0x0003;
        int86(0x10,&r,&r);
}

setVGApalette(p)    /* set the VGA palette to RGB buffer p */
        char *p;
{
        union REGS r;
        struct SREGS sr;
        int i;

        /* convert eight bits to six bits */
        for(i=0;i<768;++i) p[i]=p[i] >> 2;

        r.x.ax=0x1012;
        r.x.bx=0;
        r.x.cx=256;
        r.x.dx=FP_OFF(p);
        sr.es=FP_SEG(p);
        int86x(0x10,&r,&r,&sr);
}
```

In fact, because of the similar structure of the unpacked PCX image data and the video information stored in a VGA card's buffer, it's quite practical to unpack the PCX file directly into the screen buffer. There is no need to allocate an image buffer for this reason. The MK_FP function allows UnpackPcxImage in this version of the file viewer to create pointers into the VGA screen buffer on the fly.

The results of this program are quite stunning if you use a good 256-color image. The ROSE.PCX file provided with PC Paintbrush IV is a fine example of the art.

There are several potential drawbacks to this program, most of them involving size. The mode 13H screen is pretty small, allowing you to view only a limited image area. It's not difficult to arrange for a larger image to move around on a virtual screen behind the "window" of your monitor in this mode—the addressing is dead easy. However, as PC Paintbrush IV can't handle pictures bigger than 320 by 200; 256-color PCX files larger than this are a bit thin on the ground.

Another paint package, Deluxe Paint by Electronic Arts, is capable of reading and writing 256-color PCX files that are larger than this under some conditions. In addition, you can easily convert larger GIF files into PCX files using one of the programs discussed in Chapter 12.

You also can view more pixels—possibly. Most of the VGA compatible cards available support a superset of the original VGA modes—even fairly economical VGA cards offer higher resolution 256-color modes. You might be able to look at a complete 256-color picture with dimensions on the order of 640 by 480-pixels.

Figure 4-17 illustrates the area covered by graphics mode 13H and that of a 640-by-480 pixel "super" VGA screen.

There are some problems with this facility, however, not the least of which is that it's not in the slightest bit standardized from one manufacturer of VGA cards to the next. The problems of writing a super VGA driver will be covered in Chapter 10.

Super VGA
640 x 480
mode

Mode 13H
320 x 200

Fig 4-17   The relationship between a large 256-color image and the VGA mode 13H screen

PCX FILE PORTABILITY

The PCX format is a useful one because just about everything reads it to some extent. It's somewhat of a compromise in most cases—it does not store images efficiently and has numerous other quirks, as you will have seen in this chapter. The 256-color format is not widely supported as yet. However, it's very important to know how to use PCX files because they turn up so frequently.

No mention has been made in this chapter of PCC files. These are generated by versions of PC Paintbrush prior to PC Paintbrush IV to contain image fragments clipped from a larger image with the "Copy to..." function. They are, in fact, structured in exactly the same way that PCX files are, and can be unpacked with the same code.

PC Paintbrush IV seems to have dispensed with PCC files. It simply writes fragments of large PCX files into smaller PCX files.

5
CHAPTER

All the Colors of GIF—Decoding

Never try to teach a pig to sing. It wastes your time and annoys the pig.
—Murphy's Laws of Computers

Of all the image file formats we'll look at in this book, the CompuServe GIF format is the most complex and potentially the most interesting. While the format structure itself will be of interest primarily to programmers, the body of pictures that currently exist as GIF files—in its countless megabytes—is stunning. It's worth understanding the mechanism of the GIF file format just to be able to play with GIF images.

According to CompuServe, GIF is pronounced *jif*. GIF is an acronym for *Graphics Interchange Format*.

Unlike all the other file formats we've seen thus far, GIF was created to allow for the current expanding dimensions in video hardware. It's extremely open ended, with lots of hooks into it for growth. GIF files all but presuppose that anyone looking at them will have an EGA card. A VGA card would be better still, as will be discussed in this and several following chapters.

A picture with 256 colors available to it can look very nearly photographic, and many GIF images that have been scanned from photographs are all but indistinguishable from what those pictures would have looked like as normal, analog video on television.

Figure 5-1 illustrates a 16-color GIF file that has been halftoned to black and white.

Obviously, the visual splendor of 256-color GIF files is only meaningful if you have a display adapter that can reproduce 256 colors. The down side of GIF files is that while they're essentially device independent, and can be viewed on anything, a GIF file with more colors than your display can handle usually looks awful.

Fig 5-1 A 256-color GIF file. This picture was downloaded from Rose Media (416) 226-9260

There are other catches inherent in the workings of GIF, which will be discussed presently.

One important distinction between the GIF format and all of the other image file formats discussed in this book is that the GIF standard was devised wholly as a public domain entity. It was not the byproduct of any particular piece of software in the way, for example, that PCX files are inexorably linked to PC Paintbrush. While the odd commercial application has cropped up supporting GIF files—TerraVision's The Graphics Link package comes quickly to mind—most of the programs that utilize GIF files are shareware or public domain software. Likewise, virtually all of the extant GIF image files floating around also exist in the public domain.

It's reasonable to assume that at least some GIF files available contain images the rights to which are actually owned by someone. As such, you should exercise some caution about the copyright of ostensibly "public domain" GIF files. The files themselves might be free, but their contents could be a bit contentious.

BASIC COMPRESSION

Even moderate size GIF files are big. An EGA screen in its densest color mode has a resolution of 640 by 350 pixels for a total of almost a quarter of a million dots. At 16 colors per pixel each pixel requires four bits, or half a byte to hold it. This means that in its raw form an EGA image needs about a 128k to store it.

Pictures with more colors get correspondingly weightier.

Whereas in simple monochrome image file formats you can be more concerned about the speed of encoding and decoding pictures than about how big their compressed files actually get, the enormous size of color images makes this approach somewhat questionable. Especially as GIF files were expressly intended to be uploaded and downloaded amongst computer bulletin boards, the size of the resultant images was the most important consideration.

GIF files are not so much an exercise in imaging, then, as they are an application of data compression theory. This could be a book all by itself— the process of squeezing lots of data into a space obviously too small to contain it is one that has generated copious software.

Despite the digital nature of it, large amounts of data behave in a somewhat random manner. As such, one can talk about data compression from a theoretical perspective without having to worry about someone pinning down the issue and spoiling one's fun. Data compression, like quantum theory and political science, exists because it embraces uncertainty.

Before you can watch a GIF decoder do its stuff you probably should have a look at the terror of LZW compression. However, the code in this chapter that handles GIF file decoding is so modular and self-contained that if the thought of wading through all those string tables and code streams starts to wear you down you can quite comfortably skip over it. You can use the GIF decoder presented here without really understanding all the theory behind how it works.

The GIF Header

As with all the other image file formats discussed thus far, a GIF file contains a header before you get to the actual compressed image data. This fulfills all the functions of the headers you will have encountered in previous file formats plus a few others. It embodies the idea that the GIF file format is expandable, flexible, and looking brightly toward the future.

The future will be a very confusing place if it's anything like what GIF files think they're looking brightly towards.

The structure of a GIF file header varies with the image—or images— that the file contains. A GIF picture can be stored with several fairly subtle variations and the header reflects this. It also complicates the software that will unravel the file, but this sort of detail is rarely of concern to people who devise standards for things. The basic structure of a GIF file header is shown in Fig. 5-2.

The first thing that exists in a GIF file is the GIF *signature*, which is just a string to allow file decoders to know that they're actually looking at GIF files. This signature is, not surprisingly, the string "GIF."

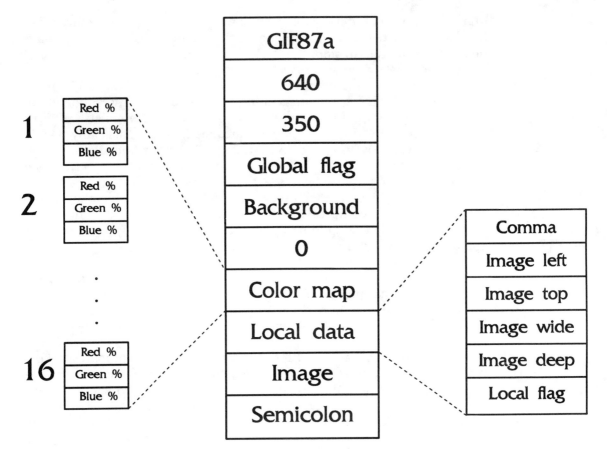

Fig 5-2   The structure of a GIF file

Actually, it's usually "GIF87a," with the latter three bytes being a revision number of sorts. Only the first three bytes should be tested for validity. If you want to be grindingly thorough, you might want to have your GIF decoder issue a warning if it finds a different revision number in the latter 3 bytes of the signature.

A GIF file can contain multiple images, although I've yet to encounter one that actually did. In theory, you could look at one and then have your decoding software encounter additional pictures later on in the file. As such, a GIF file header contains both global and local data. Global data refers to all the images in the file, although local data only pertains to the image it's associated with in a multiple image file.

Different GIF encoding programs handle this in different ways, making it essential that a GIF decoder be able to cope with all the variations even if you don't want to bother with multiple images in one file. In files with one picture per file—as is usually the case—much of the global and local data do the same things, and usually only one set is present.

The first thing one encounters in a GIF file after the GIF signature is the *screen descriptor*. This is the start of the global data. The nature of the screen that was used to view the GIF file at the time of its creation is part of the file. In practice you will rarely care about this, although you can dream up potential applications for this if you wish to.

It's worth pointing out that the screen dimensions, as stored in a GIF file, have little to do with the actual dimensions of the image that the file contains. Those numbers will be discussed in a moment. The screen descriptor just defines the screen of the computer that was used to create the file.

The following code fragment illustrates the basic structure of a GIF file header—at least in so far as it behaves consistently. As virtually all the low level GIF file handling in this chapter will be done in machine language, this might as well be too.

```
GIFHEADER    DB    'GIF87a'
             DW    SCREEN_WIDTH
             DW    SCREEN_DEPTH
             DB    GLOBAL_FLAG_BYTE
             DB    BACKGROUND_COLOR
             DB    0
```

Note that the width and depth of the screen are integers, not just bytes.

The background color can be a bit confusing. The GIF standard allows that you will, before the file is actually displayed, arrive at some understanding between the file and the computer about what the color palette will be. As you will recall from the discussion of the PC Paintbrush file format in the last chapter, it's possible for an image file to define the palette to be used to display itself, and virtually all of them do. It is actually possible to create a GIF file that does not contain palette information. This would—one might suppose—use the default palette information on the machine displaying it. This would not be in keeping with the portability designed into the GIF standard, as default palettes vary from system to system.

The background color value, as defined in the GIF header, is the number of the palette entry that will be used to define the background of the image. This means two things on a PC. First off, a GIF viewer program should clear the screen to this color before it displays an image in case the image is smaller than the screen. Secondly, on VGA cards there is an *over-scan* register that allows you to set the color of the border around the screen in graphics mode. It's usually black, and you might not even be aware of this facility. This, too, should be set to the background color.

Whether or not you implement the background color is kind of optional, but it's easy to do and worth getting together for the sake of completeness.

The global flag byte defines several things about the rest of the file—in particular, it tells your program what comes next. It also defines the number of colors, or palette size, for the pictures in the file. However, this is a default value: it can be overridden by local palettes for the actual images in the file, should they exist.

This is, once again, assuming that there are multiple pictures in the file. In many cases one finds that there is no local palette data and that these global numbers are what get used.

The global flag byte is a bit complex. Here's how to split it into meaningful parts:

The first thing you'll want to extract from the global flag byte is the number of colors to expect—assuming that there are any defined globally for this file. This is found by taking the first three bits of this byte, adding one to it and shifting one left by that many times. The maximum value of this part of the flag is eight, and one shifted left by eight is 256. This establishes the maximum number of colors a GIF image can contain.

For a file with 16 colors, the number in the first four bits of this byte would be three. The following code fragment illustrates how to deal with this part of the global flag byte.

```
MOV     CL,GLOBAL_FLAG_BYTE
AND     CL,07H
INC     CL
MOV     AX,1
SHL     AX,CL
```

The AX register would contain the global maximum number of colors for this file.

The 256-color upper limit also is the maximum number of colors that a VGA card can display. This refers to the number of simultaneous colors you can get on the screen. A VGA card can select those colors from something like a quarter of a million possible colors. This will be discussed in greater detail shortly. A GIF file can define its 256 colors from a palette of 16 million.

If the high order bit of the flag byte is set—if this bit of code:

```
TEST    GLOBAL_FLAG_BYTE,80H
```

results in the zero flag being false—then there is a global color map in the file. This is the GIF terminology for palette data.

The last byte in this part of the header is a zero. If it's not a zero in the file that your GIF decoder is decoding, there's something wrong with the file.

If the global flag byte indicated that there was a global color map in the file, it should get decoded next. Otherwise, the decoding program should just skip onto the next bit of the header—which is, in fact, the first bit of local data.

The color map consists of three bytes for each color defined by the file. The number of colors will have been by now worked out from the global flag byte. Because this process might have to be repeated if local color maps are found, the color decoding procedure usually is handled in a separate function or subroutine.

Colors in a GIF file are expressed just as they were in PC Paintbrush files. A color is defined as three bytes, one each for the percentage of red, green, and blue. Now, as with the PC Paintbrush format, these numbers actually represent fractions with the denominator being 255. As such, the value for 33 percent is 55H, or 85 decimal. This value, 85, divided by 255 is 0.33, or 33 percent.

This was handled fairly primitively under the basic PC Paintbrush format, wherein the programs involved were largely concerned with pictures having palettes of 16 colors. In the case of a 256-color GIF file to be displayed on a VGA card, you must express the palette information of the GIF file in a way that the VGA card will find acceptable.

While the details of VGA cards will be discussed in Chapter 9, suffice it to say for the moment that a VGA card expresses its color values as 6-bit numbers, ranging from 0 through 63, while the GIF standard allows for eight bits of color resolution, running from 0 through 255. To squeeze things down to values the VGA card will accept, all you need do is to shift every GIF color percentage number right by two, or to divide them by four.

If there are 16 colors in the global color map, there will be 48 bytes in it, that is, three bytes for each of the 16 colors. The first byte will be the red value for the first color. The next will be the green value, and the next will be the blue value. The next one will be the red value for the second color, and so it goes.

Usually a program decoding a GIF file will just store these bytes somewhere as it's reading through the file, to be converted into the appropriate palette values and used to program a display card closer to the time when the program is ready to actually display a picture. There's no sense in taking the time to convert the global palette data and load it into the display card at this point because it might well be superseded by a local color map later on.

The rest of the data in a GIF file is local. Once you've made it past the header, a GIF file can be thought of as being a collection of chunks. Each chunk can be one of three things, to wit, an image, an extension, or a file terminator.

A file terminator simply tells the decoder that the show's over. An image is pretty obvious. An extension is a bit of a mystery, as no one has as yet defined any extensions for GIF. The extensions are constrained to behave in a predictable way, however, so your programs can deal with them by ignoring them.

The first byte after you've dealt with the header will be one of three things, depending upon the nature of the chunk it defines. A comma indicates that the chunk is an image. An exclamation point tells you that it's an extension. A semicolon defines it as a terminator and tells you that the entire file has been dealt with. Any other value for this byte signifies a corrupted file.

Usually you'll encounter a comma here.

If a program deals with the contents of the chunk as it's supposed to, the next byte after the chunk will be one of the 3 bytes we've just discussed, indicating the start of the next chunk.

In this discussion let's assume that the GIF file being decoded consists of a header, one image chunk, as denoted by a comma, and then one terminator, denoted by a semicolon. This is the usual state of GIF files at the moment.

An image chunk is comprised of a local header followed by the compressed image itself. This is the structure of the local header:

```
LOCAL_HEADER:    DB     ','
                 DW     IMAGE_LEFT
                 DW     IMAGE_TOP
                 DW     IMAGE_WIDE
                 DW     IMAGE_DEEP
                 DW     LOCAL_FLAG_BYTE
```

These numbers actually refer to the image dimensions, not to the screen as did the global size values. The top and left values represent the position of the upper left corner of the image in relation to the upper left corner of the screen. They can be ignored if you want your image to always appear starting in the upper left corner of your tube, which is usually the case. The width and depth values are the dimensions of the image in pixels.

As you'll see in just a second, one pixel is represented by one byte in the GIF format, so multiplying the width by the depth will give you the number of bytes required to contain the image. In most cases you will do well to use long integers for this calculation—the numbers involved will be unpleasantly huge.

The local flag byte behaves in somewhat the same way as did the global one, with a few extra fields. The lowest three bits represent the number of colors in the local color map if there is one. Again, the number of colors is one shifted left by this number plus one. If there is no local map, the number of colors defined by the global flag byte prevails.

The seventh bit of this byte is something of a pig. If it's set, the image to follow is stored with its lines interlaced, such that the first line in the unpacked image is the first line on the screen, the second line is the eighth line on the screen, the third line is the twenty-fourth line on the screen and so on—for the first pass. The next pass repeats this process starting with the fifth row. The third pass writes every fourth row, starting with the third. The last pass writes every other row, starting with the second. If the image is not interlaced, the order of the lines in the file is the same as the order of the lines on the screen.

Figure 5-3 illustrates an interlaced image being unpacked.

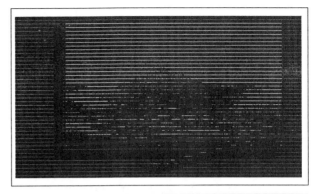

Fig 5-3   An interlaced GIF file while it's unpacking

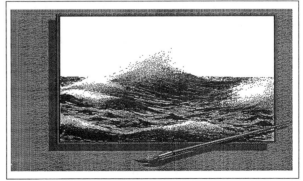

One of the things that the designers of the GIF format clearly had in mind was that GIF images could be viewed directly over a modem using suitable software. Several public domain programs have appeared to handle this. One imagines that the interlacing process has something to do with it, because it allows you to see what the image is roughly like before the whole thing has been transmitted.

As you'll observe later in this book, the possibility of interlaced GIF images presents programmers trying to work with the GIF format with no end of problems.

If the eighth, or high order, bit of the local flag byte is set, the file contains a local color map that begins with the next byte in the file. If it is not set, the global color map should be used.

The local color map, if it exists, has the number of colors specified in the local flag byte and is structured just like the global one was.

The next byte of the file is the first byte of the compressed image—which brings one back around to the tender mercies of LZW compression.

As with the color images stored in the newer of the two PC Paintbrush file formats, the color data in a GIF file always is stored as numbers, not as bit planes. In the GIF file format, each pixel is represented by one byte. The number in the byte corresponds to one of the colors in the display card's palette, presumably as set by one of the color maps discussed previously.

One line of a 320-byte wide image—the width of a VGA card's screen in its basic 256-color mode—would require 320 bytes. One screen of 200 lines would require about 60k.

This system seems very inefficient if you want to store images of less than 256 colors. If you encode a picture with 16 colors as a GIF file, the upper four bits of every byte will be wasted. In fact, you pick this space up again when you compress the data, because LZW compression handles variable sized characters.

It's interesting to note that the basic PC Paintbrush format, with its color information arranged in image planes, is ideally suited to the EGA card. As you might recall from the last chapter, the bit-mapped planes of a PC Paintbrush file slide nicely into the image planes of an EGA display. The byte-oriented display of a GIF file is exactly the same as the byte oriented display of the 256-color mode of a VGA card. Displaying GIF files on an EGA card requires a certain amount of bitwise juggling to convert the byte representation of its pixels into multiple bit planes.

LZW COMPRESSION

Basic compression theory has it that any data that exhibits some sort of predictability can be reduced in size by representing the predictable parts with tokens of some sort. This idea goes back a long way because computer types have always been confronted by less time, memory, disk space or printer paper than they'd have ideally liked to have had.

Early users of Microsoft's BASIC interpreters will recall that these programs tokenized their text. As such, a question mark could be used as a "PRINT" statement, for example, as one simply skipped the tokenization process and inserted the token to begin with. For less devious users, the tokenization process was largely transparent. If you typed "PRINT," BASIC would translate this into a question mark, thus saving four bytes of memory. When you subsequently listed your program, BASIC would expand each instance of a question mark token into the work "PRINT," such that one never actually saw the tokenization happening.

The C language occasionally has been described by its detractors as a tokenization process in which the code that expands the tokens got lost.

There have been a lot of squeezing and compressing techniques around, of which LZW compression is the most recent and the most sophisticated. In a basic sense, it behaves not unlike some of the dedicated image file compression techniques we've seen in simpler formats. However, it works with much less predictable data and it usually results in the smallest possible file formats.

Usually. As it's more complex than most other compression techniques, LZW compression also gives rise to the largest potential for "pathological" cases that compress into files larger than their uncompressed source images. The other commonly found application of LZW data compression, the popular public domain ARC, PKARC, and PKZIP programs, analyze their data with multiple file compression techniques to get around this problem. They store pathological data in an uncompressed form if it happens to be more economical of space to do so. This is why the authors of these programs have come up with words like *squeezing*, *scrunching*, *squashing*, *crunching* and, most recently, *imploding* to describe the various compression techniques being used.

The GIF format doesn't allow for this.

The LZW compression process—it's named for Lempel-Ziv and Welch, by the way—will squeeze and unsqueeze any sort of data. It's modified very slightly for use in GIF files because the data in a bit-mapped image exists in convenient little packets, that is, the image lines. As you'll see, however, while convenient for the encoding process these are not necessarily convenient for anything else. Because of the possibility of interlaced images, the lines don't necessarily come out of the LZW decompression code in the order that one might like to put them on the screen.

What differentiates LZW compression from other compression techniques is its ability to devise its tokens on the fly. It builds up a "table" of tokens as it encodes data, so that if it identifies one chunk of data and then encounters it again, it will have the token for it already stashed in its table from its first brush with that chunk.

For the moment, let's discuss the basic implementation of LZW compression for GIF image lines. In fact, there are two variations on the theme that can be added later on. The process of LZW data compression is illustrated in Fig. 5-4.

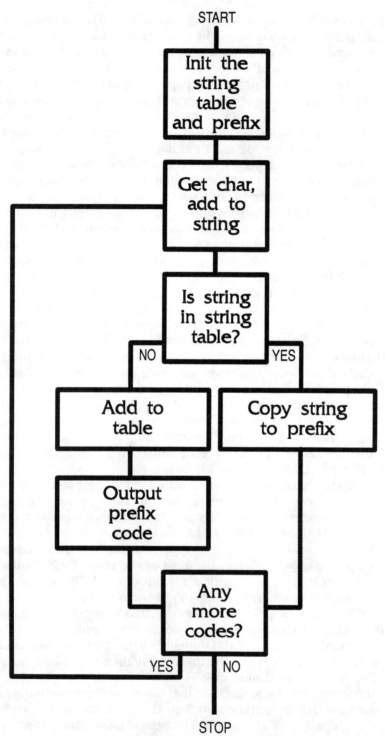

Fig 5-4   The procedure for packing a GIF file. Unpacking one works in exactly the opposite way

In reducing the size of data, LZW compression converts the raw bytes into a series of tokens, or *codes*, which can subsequently be turned back into data. If all goes well, the codes will occupy less space than the raw data did.

A hypothetical LZW compression program handles three things while it's working. The data coming in is called the *character* stream. The codes going out are called the *code* stream—you'd probably already guessed that. In the middle there's a string *table*, which is what the program uses to do its magic.

A GIF file is encoded with up to 12 bits of compression. Twelve bits allows the compression algorithm to represent numbers from 0 through 4096—as such, the string table will contain a maximum of this many entries. Don't ponder on why just now—all will become clear, or at least less murky, in a moment.

Let's assume that the compression program is compressing a 256-color picture. It will start off the compression process by initializing the first 256 entries of the table with the numbers from 0 through 255. In mathemagical terms, this means that the first 256 entries in the table map to a root. They represent unique, indivisible entries and the value of each entry also will be its location in the table. None of the subsequent table entries will be able to claim this property.

With this set up, the program can look at the first byte in the character stream, the input. It will deal with two buffers, which are the *current prefix* and the *current string*. Both are empty when it starts. The current string is defined as always being the current prefix plus the next character in the character stream.

When the program gets the first character from the character stream, the current string is equal to the prefix, which is empty, plus the character. In simpler terms, the current string would be the character just input and nothing more. The program then will look through the initialized string table to see if it can find this string.

By definition, this byte will exist somewhere in the table because the table has an entry for every possible byte, or code. Because the current string exists in the table, the program will copy the current string into the current prefix and repeat the process, adding the next character from the character stream to the current string. The current string is now two bytes long.

The program now will search through the initialized string table to see if it can find this string. Not surprisingly, it will not be able to because, among other things, there are no two byte strings in the table. At this point, it will create a new entry in the string table that contains the two bytes it has input thus far. This will be entry number 256, because entries zero through 255 are spoken for. It will send the number 256 to the code stream, the output.

The program then will repeat the process again, and keep doing so until it runs out of data to compress.

There are two additions to this for GIF files. First off, from time to time, a special *clear* code is output. This tells the decoding software to re-initialize its string table. In practice, this happens whenever the encoding software decides that the table is full. This tells the decoding software to trash its table and start over. This code is defined as being the maximum number of colors for the image—256 in this case—one more than the values in the character stream could possibly be.

The second addition is an *end of image* code. This is defined as being one more than the clear code. If it's encountered, the decoding software knows to pack up and go home—the image has been completely unpacked. This keeps the decoding software from having to count the decoded bytes to see when it's done. If an image has 200 actual lines, the encoding program will output line 201 when it's done compressing the actual image, this line starting with the EOI code and containing no data.

Because of these two extra codes, adding new codes to the table actually takes place two entries beyond the last initialized code.

LZW DECOMPRESSION

Decoding a GIF image is, quite elegantly, pretty well the encoding process done backward. The character stream becomes the output and the code stream becomes the input. Once again, the program starts by initializing the string table. This represents all the possible root code values. It also has to define the current code and the old code. The current code starts off being the first code input from the code stream, that is, from the GIF file being decoded.

The program starts things off by looking up the first code in the table. It will be there, of course—consider how it was created in the encoding process. It outputs the string in the string table of this code to the character stream, and copies this code into the old code.

At this point, the string is just the root of the code.

The program will now take the first character of the string it has output and add it to the current prefix. The first time around the current prefix will contain just this character. It will add this string to the string table and copy the old code into the current code.

It will then repeat the process.

Sooner or later the decoder will get a code from the code stream that is not in the table, just as the encoder eventually got a string that was not in the table during the encoding process. Now, if you think about it, you will realize that this code must be the next code in the table after all the known ones, as the compression program would have put it in its table this way. Because the first character of the string must have mapped to a root in the compression process, the decoder program can work out the contents of the mystery string represented by this code as being the string represented by the root of the first character in that string plus one new character.

In practice, it's not really all that necessary to understand how LZW compression works. Chances are your interests will not lie in writing a better LZW algorithm, but in doing something with GIF images. Some pretty tight code for handling GIF files exists in this book, and you can put it in whatever applications for GIF files you dream up. You might want to check out the reference at the end of this chapter if you seek to further understand the deeper inner mysteries of LZW compression.

THE GIF FILE DECODER

Although the previous image file decoders in this book have been handled in C for the most part, the working part of the GIF decoder is entirely an assembler. It would have been a lot easier to understand what it was up to if it had been handled in C, but it takes so incredibly long to actually run a C language GIF decoder that it's hardly worth the effort. The machine language routine in this chapter is among the fastest ones going and it will handle files of virtually any size. It's also extremely flexible, allowing it to be attached to all sorts of different applications.

Writing image handling routines usually gets down to a tradeoff between size and speed. This code has been entirely stripped down for speed, letting the memory fall where it might. In fact, it's a memory pig of the worst sort, allocating huge static buffers at every turn. When it's linked into a C language program—which is how it's intended to be used—it gobbles up something approaching 30k of the data segment with its buffers.

While sloppy in concept, this allows the beast to be very fast. Were it to use dynamically allocated buffers for this space, it would be obliged to switch the values of its segment registers around a lot, which would slow down the decoder.

Let's start with the basic structure of the program. The assembly language module that does the actual work is intended to be linked to a C language "front end," which calls its functions. In practice, it can be linked to anything—a Pascal program, BASIC, or even more assembly language. However, it's probably easiest to see it work in C. Figure 5-5 illustrates the GIF decoder shell program.

Fig 5-5   The C language part of a GIF file viewer

```
/*
        An example C language GIF decoder.
        Links to assembly language module.
*/

#include "stdio.h"
#include "dos.h"
#include "alloc.h"

extern char PALETTE[256][4],OUTROW[1024],COPYRIGHT[];
```

Fig 5-5   continued

```
extern int INTERLACED,IMAGEWIDE,IMAGEDEEP;
extern int IMAGEX,IMAGEY,XLOC,YLOC;
extern int VERSION,SUBVERSION;

char *pbf=NULL;            /* pointer to line work space */

main(argc,argv)
        int argc;
        char *argv[];
{
        char filename[65];
        int i,e,ShowIt(),Colourize();
        int ImageDone(),BadError(),BGround();

        SetShow(ShowIt);
        SetPalette(Colourize);
        SetImage(ImageDone);
        SetError(BadError);
        SetBackground(BGround);
        if(argc > 1) {
                if((pbf=malloc(4096)) != NULL) {
                        EGAgraphics();
                        for(i=1;i<argc;++i) {
                                strmfe(filename,argv[i],"GIF");
                                if((e=UnpackGIF(filename)) == 0)
                                        if(getch()==27) break;
                                else break;
                        }
                        Text();
                        if(e) printf("Error code %d",e);
                        free(pbf);
                } else puts("Error allocating memory");
        }
        ShowCopyright();
}

/* This function should do whatever is to be done when the
   image has been fully unpacked. The simplest thing is to
   do nothing, if the image was being displayed as it was
   unpacked. In this case, we'll beep. */
ImageDone()
{
        nosound();
        sound(660);
        delay(100);
        sound(880);
        delay(50);
        sound(440);
        delay(75);
        nosound();
}
/* This function should do whatever is needed to set the palette
   of the display card to the colour map in the palette buffer
```

```
at palette. The n value is the number of valid colours. */
Colourize(n,palette)
        int n;
        char *palette;
{
        char b[256];

        Gif2EgaPALETTE(b,palette,n);
        PaletteEGA(b,n);
}

/* This function is called after each line has been unpacked. It
   should show the line in the gloabl buffer OUTROW on the screen
   starting at line _YLOC. To be really proper about it, it should
   add IMAGEX pixels to the left and IMAGEY pixels to the top. */
ShowIt()
{
        Gif2Ega(pbf,OUTROW,IMAGEWIDE);
        ShowEGA(pbf,IMAGEWIDE>>3,YLOC);
}

/* This function is called to set the background colour. The colour
   number will be found in n. This can be ignored if you like. */
BGround(n)
        int n;
{
        int i;

        memset(OUTROW,n,80);
        Gif2Ega(pbf,OUTROW,IMAGEWIDE);
        for(i=0;i<350;++i) ShowEGA(pbf,IMAGEWIDE>>3,i);
}

/* This function will be called if something bad happens in the process
   of unpacking a GIF file, such that the process really should not
   continue. It's passed the address of a string which describes the
   nature of the problem. It's not adviseable to return from this
   function. */
BadError(s)
        char *s;
{
        Text();
        printf("\007\007\007Fatal error - %s.\n",s);
        exit(1);
}

/* This function will access and print the copyright notice. Some version
   of this should exist in your program because CompuServe gripes if they
   aren't mentioned in GIF programs. You have been warned. */
ShowCopyright()
{
        char *p;

        p = COPYRIGHT;
        while(*p) {
```

Fig 5-5   continued

```
                p += printf(p)+1;
                puts("");
        }
}

strmfe(new,old,ext)                     /* make file name with specific extension */
        char *new,*old,*ext;
{
        while(*old != 0 && *old != '.') *new++=*old++;
        *new++='.';
        while(*ext) *new++=*ext++;
        *new=0;
}
```

When it's compiled and linked to the assembly language routine (to be discussed in a moment), this code will produce a program that will display all the GIF files passed to it as command line arguments in up to 16 colors on an EGA card. A VGA implementation of it will be discussed later on once the decoder itself has been beaten into submission.

This module presupposes the existence of some EGA specific graphics routines, such as Gif2Ega, ShowEGA, and so on. These are detailed in Chapter 9.

When one is decoding a GIF file one cannot know in what order the lines are going to come out of the file before hand because they might or might not be interlaced. It is awkward to write a decoder with a function that you just call multiple times to get the lines. Furthermore, there are things such as the color palette to be set. If the decoder is to be device independent, it must allow the code that it's linked to the privilege of setting the color palette, displaying or otherwise dealing with the decoded lines and so on.

There are a number of ways to handle this, but the most elegant one is to allow the code calling the GIF decoder to set "process pointers" for the various hardware dependent functions that the GIF decoder might want to access. This has a number of very real advantages if you want to write a GIF decoder to handle multiple types of display cards or modes, because the hardware dependent stuff need not decide amongst multiple options every time it's called.

Process pointers are a little obscure, but fairly easy to understand. Consider that there is a two word buffer in the as yet unseen assembly language GIF decoder, as shown here:

```
PROCESS LABEL   WORD
PROCOFF DW      OFFSET PROCEDURE
PROCSEG DW      _CODE
```

where PROCEDURE is the start of the routine that will display a line of decoded GIF information on the screen. Let's ignore for the moment where the actual screen buffer is. The code at PROCEDURE can be assumed to know this, as well as what it's to do with a line of decoded image data.

This line will call PROCEDURE indirectly by calling it through the label at PROCESS:

```
CALL    CS:[PROCESS]
```

The thing that's useful about this obtuse bit of coding is that the values for PROCOFF and PROCSEG can be changed and the actual code that gets called by whatever wants to call our line display routine will be entirely at the discretion of whatever defines where this pointer points. If you look at the assembly language listing for the GIF decoder itself, you'll find that there are five process pointers to handle displaying a line of graphic information on the screen, setting the current palette, manipulating a completely decoded image, setting the background color, and handling a critical error in decoding resulting from a corrupted file.

The GIF decoder itself can do none of these things, because the exact nature of what they are will vary depending on what the GIF data being decoded is going to be used for. For example, it would be displayed on the screen by a GIF viewer but it would be re-encoded and written to a different file if you were creating a program to translate GIF images into PC Paintbrush files.

The generic assembly language GIF decoder calls process pointers whenever it wants to have one of these functions performed for it. It assumes that they, in turn, will have been set up by the calling code. They default to dummy return values if this hasn't been done, so that your machine won't crash if you forget to provide a process to point to.

You can see the initialization of the process pointers at the top of the main function. Most of the rest of the program consists of the rudimentary handlers for each of these functions. Obviously, you can call the functions anything you like in your GIF programs—this is just an example of how they're called.

The ShowIt function will be called by the GIF decoder every time it has successfully decoded a line of graphic information. This should handle the line. Normally, you'd show it on the screen, but if you wanted to write a GIF decoder that allowed for paging over a big GIF image, this might just store the line in a buffer.

This function requires that the C program know three things, that is, the place where the line data is stored, how many bytes of it there is, and what line in the image it represents. It would have been rather more elegant to have passed this information to the ShowIt function on the stack when the GIF decoder called it—as has been done with other process handlers here—but this function should work as quickly as possible and it's a bit less time-consuming to allow it to read this information from the global variables of the GIF decoder. The line data lives in OUTROW, the line number in YLOC and the number of bytes in IMAGEWIDE.

The two functions called by ShowIt in this example GIF viewer are both contained in the assembly language module that does EGA specific screen handling, as explained in detail in Chapter 9. The Gif2Ega function converts a line of GIF picture information into four lines of bit-map data to pour into the four color planes of an EGA card. This is handled in assembly language for the same reason that the GIF decoder itself is—it's a fairly involved process, and you'll want it to happen as quickly as possible.

The ShowEGA function displays the converted data on the screen at the line in YLOC.

The conversion of GIF data to EGA style bit planes uses the buffer pbf. This is allocated when the program starts. In this program it has been defined as being big enough to handle any reasonable sized GIF image. It would have been better to have allocated it based on the dimensions of the actual GIF file in question. The program can't know this when it starts running, but it is known by the time the GIF decoder calls the Colourize function in this code. To be really proper about things, then, the program should wait to allocate it until this function is invoked.

If you want to write a GIF program that stores the entire decoded image in memory, you can allocate the buffer to hold this from within the Colourize function too. It can be calculated by casting the values of IMAGEWIDE and IMAGEDEEP to *long* and multiplying them together. Both buffers can be deallocated from within the ImageDone function, which is called after the GIF decoder has completely unpacked the image. If you're unpacking the image into a buffer you should only deallocate this buffer when you no longer want the image data.

The ImageDone function should be used to do anything you want to get together with the completed image. In the case of this simple decoder, which only shows one screenful of the image no matter what size it is, this function doesn't really have any purpose. It just beeps to tell whoever's using the program that the decoding is complete. In a more complex GIF decoder this would handle paging through an image that's larger than the screen by refreshing the screen from different parts of the image buffer. This will be discussed in Chapter 9.

If you elect to write a GIF file viewer it's worth noting that the apparent speed of your decoder will be judged by most people not by how long they have to wait to see something, but rather by how quickly the screen updates. The screen update procedures outlined in this book are very fast, much more so than is the GIF decoder. If you want your GIF viewer program to be regarded as being snappy and quick, unpack the whole file into a buffer and then display it, rather than displaying it as it's unpacked, as this example program does.

The Colourize function is passed a pointer to the raw palette data and an integer representing the number of colors in it. This function is responsible for setting the palette of the current display card to resemble the GIF palette as closely as possible. You can see how this is done in Chapter 9.

One of the drawbacks to GIF files is that an image with more colors than the card it's being shown on can display looks uniquely dreadful. This program simply ignores the extra color map entries if they exist. You might want to devise a more sophisticated approach, one that maps similar colors into a single color entry to reduce the size of the palette. Figure 5-6 illustrates the same 256 color image being viewed on an EGA and a VGA card.

The BGround function sets the background color. This merely paints the screen with the color value passed to it in this example—in the VGA viewer it also sets the overscan register.

Fig 5-6   A 16-color view (above) of a 256-color image

Finally, the BadError function is called by the GIF decoder if something really nasty turns up in the decoding process, usually because of a corrupted file. The decoder passes this function a string that describes the error. The BadError function should print the string, clean up the graphics mode and crash out to DOS. If it returns to the decoder the decoder will probably just call it again presently. Data that has been LZW compressed does not exhibit much of an error recovery rate.

There are a few other things you'll want to know about this program. The Graphics and Text functions also are part of the EGA display code in Chapter 9, and merely switch modes and do some light housekeeping for the graphics display routines. The ShowCopyright function displays a copyright notice built into the GIF decoder. It returns a series of strings, which can be printed any way you see fit. It's not a bad idea to display this thing somewhere—CompuServe makes frequent reference to its being essential for any software that uses GIF files.

The Assembly Language Module

If the C part of this effort looked a bit troublesome, the assembly language stuff will certainly make you cringe noticeably. It's rather large and unpleasant, and I think it uses just about every addressing mode that the 8088 has to offer at least once somewhere within its workings. The whole module is illustrated in Fig. 5-7. Unlike most of the machine language modules in this book, this one is shown with everything required to assemble it down to an object file.

Fig 5-7 The assembly language GIF decoder module. This code will be used in many places throughout this book

```
;
;                GIF Decoder
;

VERSION          EQU      1              ;VERSION
SUBVERSION       EQU      1              ;SUBVERSION

_AOFF            EQU      6              ;FAR STACK OFFSET

BSIZE            EQU      4096           ;SIZE OF INTERNAL FILE BUFFER
EOF              EQU      0FFFFH         ;END OF FILE MARKER

;THIS MACRO FETCHES THE DATA SEGEMENT
DATASEG          MACRO
                 PUSH     AX
                 MOV      AX,_DATA
                 MOV      DS,AX
                 POP      AX
                 ENDM

GIF_TEXT         SEGMENT BYTE PUBLIC 'CODE'
                 ASSUME  CS:GIF_TEXT,DS:_DATA
```

```
;THIS ROUTINE OPENS A (GIF) FILE - DS:DX = PATH TO FILE
;RETURNS ZERO IF OK OR EOF IF NOT FOUND
OPENFILE        PROC    NEAR
                MOV     AX,3D00H                ;DOS OPEN FILE FUNCTION
                INT     21H
                JNC     OG1                     ;IF NO CARRY, IT'S OPEN
                MOV     AX,EOF
                JMP     OG2

OG1:            DATASEG                         ;GET THE DATA SEGMENT
                MOV     HANDLE,AX               ;SAVE THE HANDLE
                MOV     AX,0                    ;SET THE RETURN CODE
                MOV     BUFFER_INDEX,0          ;SET UP THE BUFFER
                MOV     BUFFER_POINT,OFFSET BUFFER
OG2:            RET
OPENFILE        ENDP

;THIS ROUTINE CLOSES A (GIF) FILE
CLOSEFILE       PROC    NEAR
                MOV     AX,3E00H                ;DOS CLOSE FILE FUNCTION
                MOV     BX,HANDLE
                INT     21H
                RET
CLOSEFILE       ENDP

;THIS FUNCTION GETS THE NEXT BYTE FROM A FILE
FGETC           PROC    NEAR
                PUSH    SI

                CMP     BUFFER_INDEX,0          ;ARE THERE BYTES TO READ?
                JNE     FGETC2                  ;IF SO, JUST GO GET ONE

                PUSH    BX                      ;OTHERWISE, WE MUST DO A
                PUSH    CX                      ;DOS CALL TO GET SOME
                PUSH    DX                      ;MORE BYTES INTO THE
                MOV     AX,3F00H                ;BUFFER. THIS TRASHES SOME
                MOV     BX,HANDLE               ;EXTRA REGISTERS, WHICH
                MOV     CX,BSIZE                ;WE SHOULD PRESERVE.
                MOV     DX,OFFSET BUFFER
                INT     21H
                POP     DX
                POP     CX
                POP     BX
                JNC     FGETC1                  ;IF NO ERROR, GO ON
                MOV     AX,EOF                  ;OTHERWISE, SAY IT'S OVER
                JMP     FGETCX

FGETC1:         MOV     BUFFER_INDEX,AX         ;HOW MANY BYTES WERE READ
                MOV     BUFFER_POINT,OFFSET BUFFER

FGETC2:         PUSH    SI                      ;NOW, GET THE NEXT BYTE
                MOV     SI,BUFFER_POINT         ;FROM THE BUFFER
                LODSB
                POP     SI
```

Fig 5-7   continued

```
                INC     BUFFER_POINT            ;POINT TO SUBSEQUENT BYTE
                DEC     BUFFER_INDEX
                MOV     AH,00H                  ;NULL THE HIGH ORDER BYTE
FGETCX:         POP     SI
                RET
FGETC           ENDP

;THIS FUNCTION GETS THE NEXT WORD FROM A FILE
FGETW           PROC    NEAR
                CALL    FGETC                   ;GET LOW ORDER BYTE
                MOV     BX,AX                   ;SAVE IT
                CALL    FGETC                   ;GET HIGH ORDER BYTE
                MOV     BH,AL                   ;COMBINE THEM
                MOV     AX,BX                   ;AND RETURN THEM
                RET
FGETW           ENDP

;THIS FUNCTION GETS THE COLOURS FROM A GIF FILE - PSIZE IN CX
GETCOLOURS      PROC    NEAR
                MOV     AX,1                    ;SHIFT RIGHT BY PSIZE
                SHL     AX,CL
                MOV     CX,AX                   ;AX IS NUMBER OF COLOURS
                SUB     BX,BX

GETCOLOUR1:     PUSH    CX                      ;LOAD UP THE PALETTE
                CALL    FGETC
                MOV     BYTE PTR [_PALETTE + BX + 0],AL
                CALL    FGETC
                MOV     BYTE PTR [_PALETTE + BX + 1],AL
                CALL    FGETC
                MOV     BYTE PTR [_PALETTE + BX + 2],AL
                ADD     BX,3
                POP     CX
                LOOP    GETCOLOUR1

                RET
GETCOLOURS      ENDP

;THIS ROUTINE INITIALIZES THE CODE TABLE - CLEARCODE IN CX
INIT_CODETABLE  PROC    NEAR
                SUB     BX,BX                   ;START WITH A ZERO CODE
                MOV     AX,CX                   ;THE NEXT CODE WILL BE THE
                ADD     AX,2                    ;CLEAR CODE PLUS TWO
                MOV     _NEXTCODE,AX

                MOV     AX,CX                   ;NEXT LIMIT WILL BE
                SHL     AX,1                    ;CLEAR CODE TIMES TWO
                MOV     _NEXTLIM,AX

INITTABLE1:     CMP     BX,CX
                JGE     INITTABLE2              ;WHILE CODE < CC
```

```
            MOV     [_CTFIRST + BX ],BL     ;CTFIRST[CODE]=CODE
            MOV     [_CTLAST + BX],BL       ;CTLAST[CODE]=CODE
            SHL     BX,1
            MOV     [_CTLINK + BX],-1       ;CTLINK[CODE]=-1
            SHR     BX,1
            INC     BX
            JMP     INITTABLE1

INITTABLE2: CMP     BX,4096                 ;WHILE CODE < 4096
            JGE     INITTABLE3              ;CTLINK[CODE++]= -2
            SHL     BX,1
            MOV     [_CTLINK+BX],-2
            SHR     BX,1
            INC     BX
            JMP     INITTABLE2

INITTABLE3: RET
INIT_CODETABLE ENDP

;THIS ROUTINE GETS THE BUFFER LENGTH
GETGB           PROC    NEAR
                CMP     _BUFCT,0            ;IF BUFCT == 0
                JNE     GETGB2

                CALL    FGETC
                MOV     _BUFCT,AX           ;SAVE THE SIZE

                CMP     _BUFCT,EOF          ;IF IT'S EOF
                JE      GETGB1
                CMP     _BUFCT,0            ;OR ZERO LENGTH
                JE      GETGB1              ;GO HANDLE THE ERROR
                JMP     GETGB2              ;OTHERWISE, CARRY ON

GETGB1:         MOV     AX,_DATA
                PUSH    AX
                MOV     AX,OFFSET GETGB_ERR
                PUSH    AX
                CALL    CS:[ERRORHANDLER]
                ADD     SP,4

GETGB2:         CALL    FGETC               ;GET THE BYTE
                CMP     AX,EOF              ;IF IT'S EOF
                JNE     GETGB3

                MOV     AX,_DATA
                PUSH    AX
                MOV     AX,OFFSET GETGB_ERR
                PUSH    AX
                CALL    CS:[ERRORHANDLER]
                ADD     SP,4

GETGB3:         DEC     _BUFCT              ;SAY WE GOT THIS BYTE
```

Fig 5-7   continued

```
                    RET
GETGB               ENDP

;THIS ROUTINE GETS A BCODE - REQCT IS IN DX
GETBCODE            PROC    NEAR
                    CMP     _REMCT,0                ;IF REMCT == 0
                    JNE     GETBCODE1

                    CALL    GETGB                   ;REM = GetGB
                    MOV     _REM,AX
                    MOV     _REMCT,8                ;REMCT = 8

GETBCODE1:          MOV     AX,DX
                    CMP     _REMCT,AX               ;IF REMCT < REQCT
                    JNL     GETBCODE2

                    CALL    GETGB                   ;REM |= GetGB << REMCT
                    MOV     CX,_REMCT
                    SHL     AX,CL
                    OR      _REM,AX

                    ADD     _REMCT,8                ;REMCT +=8

GETBCODE2:          MOV     BX,DX                   ;RETCODE = REM & CMASK[REQCT]
                    MOV     AL,[_CMASK + BX]
                    AND     AX,00FFH
                    MOV     BX,_REM
                    AND     BX,AX
                    PUSH    BX

                    SUB     _REMCT,DX               ;REMCT -= REQCT

                    MOV     CX,DX
                    SHR     _REM,CL                 ;REM = REM >> REQCT

                    POP     AX                      ;GET THE RETURN CODE BACK
                    RET
GETBCODE            ENDP

;THIS ROUTINE GETS A CODE - REQCT IS IN DX
GETCODE             PROC    NEAR

                    CMP     DX,8                    ;IF REQCT <= 8
                    JG      GETCODE1

                    PUSH    DX
                    CALL    GETBCODE                ;RETURN GETBCODE(REQCT)
                    POP     DX
                    JMP     GETCODE2

GETCODE1:           PUSH    DX
                    MOV     DX,8                    ;TEMP = GETBCODE(8)
```

```
                CALL    GETBCODE
                POP     DX                      ;RESTORE REQCT
                PUSH    AX                      ;SAVE TEMP

                PUSH    DX
                SUB     DX,8                    ;MINUS 8
                CALL    GETBCODE                ;GETBCODE
                POP     DX
                MOV     CX,8
                SHL     AX,CL                   ;<< 8
                POP     BX                      ;GET TEMP BACK
                OR      AX,BX                   ;| TEMP
GETCODE2:       RET
GETCODE         ENDP

;THIS ROUTINE HANDLES FLUSHING THE INPUT - NO ARGUMENTS
FLUSHIN PROC    NEAR
FLUSHIN1:       CMP     _BUFCT,0
                JE      FLUSHIN2
                CALL    FGETC
                DEC     _BUFCT
                JMP     FLUSHIN1

FLUSHIN2:       CALL    FGETC
                MOV     _BUFCT,AX
                CMP     _BUFCT,0
                JNE     FLUSHIN1
                RET
FLUSHIN ENDP

;THIS ROUTINE INSERTS A CODE INTO THE TABLE
;CODE IN BX, OLDCODE IN CX, CSIZEPTR IN ES:DI
INSERTCODE      PROC    NEAR
                PUSH    BX
                MOV     BX,_NEXTCODE
                SHL     BX,1
                MOV     [_CTLINK + BX],CX       ;CTLINK[NEXTCODE]=OLDCODE
                POP     BX

                PUSH    BX
                MOV     AL,[_CTFIRST + BX]      ;CTFIRST[CODE]
                MOV     BX,_NEXTCODE
                MOV     [_CTLAST + BX],AL       ;CTLAST[NEXTCODE]

                MOV     BX,CX                   ;OLDCODE
                MOV     AL,[_CTFIRST + BX]
                MOV     BX,_NEXTCODE
                MOV     [_CTFIRST + BX],AL      ;CTFIRST[NEXTCODE]
                POP     BX                      ;...=CTFIRST[OLDCODE]

                INC     _NEXTCODE
                MOV     AX,_NEXTCODE
                CMP     AX,_NEXTLIM
                JNE     INSERTCODE2             ;IF ++NEXTCODE == NEXTLIM
```

Fig 5-7   continued

```
                CMP     WORD PTR ES:[DI],12     ;IF * CSIZEPTR < 12
                JNL     INSERTCODE2

                INC     WORD PTR ES:[DI]
                SHL     _NEXTLIM,1
INSERTCODE2:    RET
INSERTCODE      ENDP

;THIS ROUTINE HANDLES ONE PIXEL - VALUE IN AX
DOPIXEL         PROC    NEAR
                MOV     BX,_XLOC                ;GET X POSITION
                MOV     [_OUTROW + BX],AL       ;SAVE THE CHARACTER
                INC     _XLOC                   ;BUMP IT

                DEC     _ROWCNT                 ;LINE DONE?
                CMP     _ROWCNT,0000H
                JNE     DOPIXEL3

                CALL    CS:[SHOWHANDLER]        ;SHOW THE LINE

                MOV     _XLOC,0                 ;ZERO THE X COUNT
                MOV     AX,_IMAGEWIDE           ;SET UP NEXT LINE
                MOV     _ROWCNT,AX

                CMP     _INTERLACED,0           ;ARE WE INTERLACED?
                JE      DOPIXEL2                ;THANK THE GODDESS, NO...

                MOV     BX,_PASS                ;WELL, IF SO, HANDLE IT
                SHL     BX,1
                MOV     AX,[INCTABLE + BX]      ;GET NEXT LINE FROM TABLE
                ADD     _YLOC,AX

                MOV     AX,_YLOC
                CMP     AX,_IMAGEDEEP
                JL      DOPIXEL1

                INC     _PASS
                MOV     BX,_PASS
                SHL     BX,1
                MOV     AX,[STARTABLE + BX]
                MOV     _YLOC,AX

DOPIXEL1:       JMP     DOPIXEL3

DOPIXEL2:       INC     _YLOC                   ;BUMP LINE NUMBER
                MOV     AX,_YLOC
                CMP     AX,_IMAGEDEEP
                JL      DOPIXEL3

                MOV     _YLOC,0

DOPIXEL3:       RET
DOPIXEL         ENDP
```

```
;THIS ROUTINE PUTS A CODE INTO THE TABLE - CODE IN BX, PSIZE IN DX
PUTX            PROC      NEAR
                SUB       CX,CX
                MOV       SI,OFFSET _OSTACK

PUTX1:          MOV       AL,[_CTLAST + BX]
                MOV       [SI],AL
                INC       SI                      ;[SI] = CTLAST[CODE]

                INC       CX
                SHL       BX,1
                MOV       BX,[_CTLINK + BX]
                CMP       BX,-1
                JNE       PUTX1

                CMP       DX,0001H
                JNE       PUTX3

PUTX2:          DEC       SI
                MOV       AL,[SI]
                AND       AX,0001;
                PUSH      CX
                PUSH      SI
                CALL      DOPIXEL
                POP       SI
                MOV       AL,[SI]
                AND       AX,00FFH
                SHR       AX,1
                PUSH      SI
                CALL      DOPIXEL
                POP       SI
                POP       CX
                LOOP      PUTX2
                JMP       PUTX4

PUTX3:          DEC       SI
                MOV       AL,[SI]
                AND       AX,00FFH
                PUSH      CX
                PUSH      SI
                CALL      DOPIXEL
                POP       SI
                POP       CX
                LOOP      PUTX3

PUTX4:          RET
PUTX            ENDP

;THIS FUNCTION EXTRACTS A GIF IMAGE  - CODE START IN CX, PIXELSIZE IN DX
UNPACK_IMAGE    PROC      NEAR
                PUSH      CX
                PUSH      DX

                MOV       AX,1
```

Fig 5-7   continued

```
                SHL     AX,CL
                MOV     _CLEARCODE,AX            ;CLEARCODE = 1 << CODESTART

                INC     AX
                MOV     _EOI,AX                  ;EOI = CLEARCODE + 1

                INC     CX
                MOV     _REQCT,CX                ;REQCT = CODESTART + 1

                MOV     CX,_CLEARCODE
                CALL    INIT_CODETABLE           ;INIT TABLE WITH CLEAR CODE

                MOV     _OLDCODE,0FFFFH
                MOV     _DONE,0000H
                MOV     _PASS,0000H
                MOV     AX,_IMAGEWIDE
                MOV     _ROWCNT,AX               ;ROWCNT = IMAGEWIDE

                MOV     _XLOC,0000H
                MOV     _YLOC,0000H              ;INITIALIZE SCREEN POSITION

                POP     DX
                POP     CX

EXTIMG1:        PUSH    CX
                PUSH    DX
                MOV     DX,_REQCT
                CALL    GETCODE                  ;CODE = GETCODE(REQCT)
                MOV     _CODE,AX
                POP     DX
                POP     CX

                CMP     AX,_CLEARCODE            ;IF CLEARCODE, CLEAR LINE
                JNE     EXTIMG2

                PUSH    CX
                PUSH    DX
                MOV     CX,_CLEARCODE
                CALL    INIT_CODETABLE           ;INIT CODETABLE WITH CLEARCODE
                POP     DX
                POP     CX

                MOV     AX,CX
                INC     AX
                MOV     _REQCT,AX                ;REQCT = CODESTART + 1

                MOV     _OLDCODE,0FFFFH          ;OLDCODE = -1
                JMP     EXTIMG7

EXTIMG2:        CMP     AX,_EOI                  ;IF CODE = EO1
                JNE     EXTIMG3
```

```
                CALL    FLUSHIN                 ;FLUSH THE INPUT
                MOV     _DONE,0FFFFH            ;SAY WE'RE DONE
                JMP     EXTIMG7

EXTIMG3:        MOV     BX,_CODE                ;DEFAULT CONDITION
                SHL     BX,1
                CMP     [_CTLINK + BX],0FFFEH   ;IF CTLINK[CODE] != -2
                JE      EXTIMG5

                CMP     _OLDCODE,0FFFFH         ;IF OLDCODE != -1
                JE      EXTIMG4

                PUSH    CX
                PUSH    DX
                MOV     BX,_CODE
                MOV     CX,_OLDCODE
                MOV     AX,_DATA
                MOV     ES,AX
                MOV     DI,OFFSET _REQCT
                CALL    INSERTCODE
                POP     DX
                POP     CX
EXTIMG4:        JMP     EXTIMG6

EXTIMG5:        PUSH    CX
                PUSH    DX
                MOV     BX,_OLDCODE
                MOV     CX,_OLDCODE
                MOV     AX,_DATA
                MOV     ES,AX
                MOV     DI,OFFSET _REQCT
                CALL    INSERTCODE
                POP     DX
                POP     CX

EXTIMG6:        PUSH    CX
                PUSH    DX
                MOV     BX,_CODE
                CALL    PUTX                    ;PUTX(CODE,PIXELSIZE)
                POP     DX
                POP     CX

                MOV     AX,_CODE                ;OLDCODE=CODE
                MOV     _OLDCODE,AX

EXTIMG7:        CMP     _DONE,0
                JNE     EXTIMG8
                JMP     EXTIMG1

EXTIMG8:        RET
UNPACK_IMAGE    ENDP

;THIS FUNCTION UNPACKS A GIF FILE
```

Fig 5-7   continued

```
;                   CALLED AS
;                   UnpackGIF(path);
;                   char *path;
;
;                   returns 0 if ok or code
;                           0 = file unpacked
;                           1 = file not found
;                           2 = file not GIF
;                           3 = file corrupted

UPG_SFLAGS      EQU     2
UPG_GPIX        EQU     4
UPG_PIXELSIZE   EQU     6
UPG_ALLDONE     EQU     8
UPG_WORK        EQU     10
UPG_IFLAGS      EQU     12
UPG_ADJUST      EQU     14


                PUBLIC  _UnpackGIF
_UnpackGIF      PROC    FAR
                PUSH    BP
                MOV     BP,SP
                SUB     SP,UPG_ADJUST               ;ADJUST FOR LOCAL VARIABLES

                MOV     DI,OFFSET STARTINIT         ;ZERO OUT ALL THE BYTES
                MOV     AX,_DATA                    ;IN THE INITIALIZED DATA
                MOV     ES,AX                       ;AREA. THIS IS A LOT FASTER
                MOV     CX,ENDINIT - STARTINIT      ;THAN RE-INITIALIZING
                CLD                                 ;THE PERTINENT BUFFERS ONE
                MOV     AL,0                        ;AT A TIME IF THE CODE IS
        REPNE   STOSB                               ;CALLED MULTIPLE TIMES.

                MOV     DS,[BP + _AOFF + 2]         ;SEGMENT OF SOURCE
                MOV     DX,[BP + _AOFF + 0]         ;OFFSET OF SOURCE
                CALL    OPENFILE                    ;OPEN THE FILE

                DATASEG

                CMP     AX,0
                JE      UPG1
                MOV     AX,0001H                    ;ERROR CODE FOR FILE NOT FOUND
                JMP     UPGX                        ;GO TELL IT

UPG1:           CALL    FGETC
                CMP     AL,'G'                      ;SEE IF IT'S A GIF FILE
                JE      UPG2
                CALL    CLOSEFILE
                MOV     AX,0002H                    ;ERROR CODE FOR FILE NOT GIF
                JMP     UPGX

UPG2:           MOV     CX,5
UPG3:           PUSH    CX
                CALL    FGETC
```

```
                POP     CX
                LOOP    UPG3                    ;THROW AWAY REST OF HEADER

                CALL    FGETW
                MOV     _SCREENWIDTH,AX         ;GET SCREEN WIDTH

                CALL    FGETW
                MOV     _SCREENHEIGHT,AX        ;GET SCREEN HEIGHT

                CALL    FGETC
                MOV     [BP - UPG_SFLAGS],AX    ;GET GLOBAL FLAGS

                AND     AX,0007H
                INC     AX
                MOV     [BP - UPG_GPIX],AX      ;CALCULATE GLOBAL PIXEL SIZE

                CALL    FGETC
                MOV     _BACKGROUND,AX

                CALL    FGETC
                CMP     AL,0
                JE      UPG4
                CALL    CLOSEFILE
                MOV     AX,0003                 ;ERROR CODE FOR FILE CORRUPTED
                JMP     UPGX

UPG4:           TEST    WORD PTR [BP - UPG_SFLAGS],0080H
                JZ      UPG5                    ;TEST FOR GLOBAL COLOUR PALETTE

                MOV     CX,[BP - UPG_GPIX]      ;GET THE GLOBAL PIXEL SIZE
                CALL    GETCOLOURS              ;GET THE PALETTE

                MOV     AX,_DATA                ;GET THE LOCATION OF
                PUSH    AX                      ;THE PALETTE BUFFER
                MOV     AX,OFFSET _PALETTE
                PUSH    AX

                MOV     CX,[BP - UPG_GPIX]      ;GET THE NUMBER OF VALID
                MOV     AX,1
                SHL     AX,CL                   ;...COLOURS AND SAVE
                PUSH    AX                      ;THEM ON THE STACK
                CALL    CS:[PALTHANDLER]        ;MAKE THE PALETTE ACTIVE
                ADD     SP,6

UPG5:           MOV     WORD PTR [BP - UPG_ALLDONE],0000H

                ; MAIN LOOP FOR EXTRACTING GIF COMPONENTS
UPG6:           CMP     WORD PTR [BP - UPG_ALLDONE],0000H
                JE      UPG7
                CALL    CLOSEFILE
                MOV     AX,0
                JMP     UPGX

UPG7:           CALL    FGETC                   ;GET THE NEXT DELIMINATOR
```

Fig 5-7 continued

```
                MOV     [BP - UPG_WORK],AX
                CMP     AX,EOF                      ;IF IT'S EOF, WE'RE DONE
                JNE     UPG8
                CALL    CLOSEFILE
                MOV     AX,0                        ;NO ERROR
                JMP     UPGX

UPG8:           CMP     AL,','                      ;IS IT AN IMAGE?
                JE      UPG9
                JMP     UPG11                       ;TRY AN EXTENSION

UPG9:           CALL    FGETW                       ;PROCESS THE IMAGE
                MOV     _IMAGEX,AX                  ;GET IMAGE LEFT

                CALL    FGETW
                MOV     _IMAGEY,AX                  ;GET IMAGE TOP

                CALL    FGETW
                MOV     _IMAGEWIDE,AX               ;GET IMAGE WIDTH

                CALL    FGETW
                MOV     _IMAGEDEEP,AX               ;GET IMAGE DEPTH

                CALL    FGETC                       ;GET LOCAL FLAGS
                MOV     [BP - UPG_IFLAGS],AX
                AND     AX,0040H
                MOV     _INTERLACED,AX              ;SEE IF IMAGE IS INTERLACED

                MOV     AX,[BP - UPG_GPIX]          ;SET DEFAULT PIXEL SIZE
                MOV     [BP - UPG_PIXELSIZE],AX ;... FROM GLOBAL VALUE

                TEST    WORD PTR [BP - UPG_IFLAGS],0080H
                JZ      UPG10                       ;CHECK FOR LOCAL COLOUR MAP

                MOV     AX,[BP - UPG_IFLAGS]        ;IF SO, GET LOCAL PIXEL SIZE
                AND     AX,0007H
                INC     AX
                MOV     [BP - UPG_PIXELSIZE],AX
                MOV     CX,AX
                PUSH    CX
                CALL    GETCOLOURS                  ;GET THE LOCAL PALETTE
                POP     CX
                MOV     AX,1                        ;GET THE NUMBER OF
                SHL     AX,CL                       ;...COLOURS AND SAVE
                PUSH    AX                          ;THEM ON THE STACK

                CALL    CS:[PALTHANDLER]            ;MAKE THE LOCAL PALETTE ACTIVE

UPG10:          MOV     AX,_BACKGROUND              ;GET THE BACKGROUND
                PUSH    AX                          ;ON THE STACK
                CALL    CS:[BACKHANDLER]            ;SET THE BACKGROUND
                ADD     SP,2                        ;ADJUST THE STACK
```

```
                MOV     _BUFCT,0000H
                CALL    FGETC                        ;GET CODE START

                MOV     CX,AX
                MOV     DX,[BP - UPG_PIXELSIZE]
                CALL    UNPACK_IMAGE
                CALL    CS:[IMAGEHANDLER]            ;DO SOMETHING WITH IMAGE
                JMP     UPG6                         ;AND GO LOOP

UPG11:          CMP     AL,'!'                       ;IS IT AN EXTENSION?
                JE      UPG12
                JMP     UPG16                        ;IF NOT, TRY END OF FILE

UPG12:          CALL    FGETC                        ;THROW AWAY NEXT BYTE

UPG13:          CALL    FGETC                        ;THROW AWAY EXTENSIONS
                MOV     CX,AX
                CMP     AX,0
                JE      UPG15
UPG14:          PUSH    CX                           ;THROW AWAY FIELD
                CALL    FGETC
                POP     CX
                LOOP    UPG14
                JMP     UPG13                        ;AND CHECK FOR THE NEXT ONE
UPG15:          JMP     UPG6                         ;GO TRY FOR NEXT ITEM

UPG16:          CMP     AL,3BH                       ;CHECK FOR ALL DONE (SEMICOLON)
                JNE     UPG17
                MOV     WORD PTR [BP - UPG_ALLDONE],0FFFFH
                JMP     UPG6

UPG17:          CALL    CLOSEFILE
                MOV     AX,0003                      ;BAD FILE ERROR

UPGX:           ADD     SP,UPG_ADJUST
                POP     BP
                RET
_UnpackGIF      ENDP

;THIS FUNCTION SETS THE LINE SHOW PROCEDURE
;               CALLED AS
;               SetShow(proc);
;               (int)()proc;
;
                PUBLIC  _SetShow
_SetShow        PROC    FAR
                PUSH    BP
                MOV     BP,SP

                MOV     AX,[BP + _AOFF + 0]          ;OFFSET OF SOURCE
                MOV     BX,[BP + _AOFF + 2]          ;SEGMENT OF SOURCE

                MOV     CS:[_SHOWOFF],AX
                MOV     CS:[_SHOWSEG],BX
```

Fig 5-7   continued

```
                DATASEG
                POP     BP
                RET
_SetShow        ENDP

;THIS FUNCTION SETS THE PALETTE PROCEDURE
;               CALLED AS
;               SetPalette(proc);
;               (int)()proc;
;
;               The palette procedure should make the current GIF
;               palette, as passed to it, current for the display
;               adapter. It is called with two arguments, the number
;               of colours and the palette buffer.

                PUBLIC  _SetPalette
_SetPalette     PROC    FAR
                PUSH    BP
                MOV     BP,SP

                MOV     AX,[BP + _AOFF + 0]     ;OFFSET OF SOURCE
                MOV     BX,[BP + _AOFF + 2]     ;SEGMENT OF SOURCE

                MOV     CS:[_PALTOFF],AX
                MOV     CS:[_PALTSEG],BX

                DATASEG
                POP     BP
                RET
_SetPalette     ENDP

;THIS FUNCTION SETS THE ERROR PROCEDURE
;               CALLED AS
;               SetError(proc);
;               (int)()proc;
;
                PUBLIC  _SetError
_SetError       PROC    FAR
                PUSH    BP
                MOV     BP,SP

                MOV     AX,[BP + _AOFF + 0]     ;OFFSET OF SOURCE
                MOV     BX,[BP + _AOFF + 2]     ;SEGMENT OF SOURCE

                MOV     CS:[_ERROROFF],AX
                MOV     CS:[_ERRORSEG],BX
                DATASEG
                POP     BP
                RET
_SetError       ENDP

;THIS FUNCTION SETS THE IMAGE PROCEDURE
;               CALLED AS
```

```
;               SetImage(proc);
;               (int)()proc;
;
                PUBLIC  _SetImage
_SetImage       PROC    FAR
                PUSH    BP
                MOV     BP,SP

                MOV     AX,[BP + _AOFF + 0]     ;OFFSET OF SOURCE
                MOV     BX,[BP + _AOFF + 2]     ;SEGMENT OF SOURCE

                MOV     CS:[_IMAGOFF],AX
                MOV     CS:[_IMAGSEG],BX

                DATASEG
                POP     BP
                RET
_SetImage       ENDP

;THIS FUNCTION SETS THE BACKGROUND PROCEDURE
;               CALLED AS
;               SetBackground(proc);
;               (int)()proc;
;
;               The background procedure should set the background
;               colour to the value passed to it.

                PUBLIC  _SetBackground
_SetBackground  PROC    FAR
                PUSH    BP
                MOV     BP,SP

                MOV     AX,[BP + _AOFF + 0]     ;OFFSET OF SOURCE
                MOV     BX,[BP + _AOFF + 2]     ;SEGMENT OF SOURCE

                MOV     CS:[_BACKOFF],AX
                MOV     CS:[_BACKSEG],BX

                DATASEG
                POP     BP
                RET
_SetBackground  ENDP

;THIS FUNCTION IS A DUMMY RETURN FOR UNSET PROCEDURES
_DUMMY          PROC    FAR
                RET
_DUMMY          ENDP

SHOWHANDLER     LABEL   DWORD
_SHOWOFF        DW      _DUMMY
_SHOWSEG        DW      GIF_TEXT
PALTHANDLER     LABEL   DWORD
_PALTOFF        DW      _DUMMY
_PALTSEG        DW      GIF_TEXT
```

Fig 5-7   continued

```
ERRORHANDLER     LABEL    DWORD
_ERROROFF        DW       _DUMMY
_ERRORSEG        DW       GIF_TEXT

IMAGEHANDLER     LABEL    DWORD
_IMAGOFF         DW       _DUMMY
_IMAGSEG         DW       GIF_TEXT

BACKHANDLER      LABEL    DWORD
_BACKOFF         DW       _DUMMY
_BACKSEG         DW       GIF_TEXT

GIF_TEXT         ENDS

;
;                THE DATA AND OTHER GROTTY BITS
;

DGROUP           GROUP    _DATA,_BSS
_DATA            SEGMENT WORD PUBLIC 'DATA'

                 PUBLIC _VERSION,_SUBVERSION
                 PUBLIC _PALETTE,_OUTROW,_INTERLACED
                 PUBLIC _XLOC,_YLOC, _COPYRIGHT
                 PUBLIC _IMAGEWIDE,_IMAGEDEEP,_IMAGEX,_IMAGEY
                 PUBLIC _SCREENWIDTH,_SCREENHEIGHT,_BACKGROUND

_VERSION         DW       VERSION              ;VERSION AND SUBVERSION -
_SUBVERSION      DW       SUBVERSION           ;CONSTRAINED TO START OF DATA

STARTINIT        LABEL    BYTE                 ;START OF INITIALIZED AREA

_INTERLACED      DW       0                    ;FLAG FOR INTERLACED MODE
_IMAGEWIDE       DW       0                    ;WIDTH OF IMAGE
_IMAGEDEEP       DW       0                    ;DEPTH OF IMAGE
_IMAGEX          DW       0                    ;LEFT OF IMAGE
_IMAGEY          DW       0                    ;TOP OF IMAGE
_XLOC            DW       0                    ;PIXEL HORIZONTAL POSITION
_YLOC            DW       0                    ;PIXEL VERTICAL POSITION
_SCREENWIDTH     DW       0                    ;GLOBAL SCREEN WIDTH
_SCREENHEIGHT    DW       0                    ;GLOBAL SCREEN DEPTH
_BACKGROUND      DW       0                    ;GLOBAL BACKGROUND COLOUR
_PALETTE         DB       768 DUP(0)           ;WHERE THE PALETTE WILL GO

;MAKE THIS BUFFER BIGGER IF YOU ENCOUNTER GIF FILES WHICH
;HAVE HORIZONTAL DIMENSIONS BIGGER THAN 2048 PIXELS
_OUTROW          DB       2048 DUP(0)          ;BUFFER FOR DECODED LINES

BUFFER_POINT     DW       0                    ;NEXT BYTE TO READ IN BUFFER
BUFFER_INDEX     DW       0                    ;NUMBER OF BYTES IN BUFFER
BUFFER           DB       BSIZE DUP(0)         ;FILE INPUT BUFFER
HANDLE           DW       0                    ;FILE HANDLE
```

```
_EOI            DW      0                           ;LZW EOI VALUE
_REM            DW      0
_REMCT          DW      0
_BUFCT          DW      0
_NEXTLIM        DW      0
_NEXTCODE       DW      0
_ROWCNT         DW      0                           ;ROW COUNTER FOR OUTPUT
_PASS           DW      0
_CLEARCODE      DW      0                           ;LZW CLEAR CODE
_REQCT          DW      0                           ;REQUEST COUNT
_DONE           DW      0                           ;FLAG FOR DONE'NESS
_CODE           DW      0                           ;THIS LZW UNCOMPRESSION CODE
_OLDCODE        DW      0                           ;LAST LZW UNCOMPRESSION CODE

_OSTACK         DB      4096 DUP(0)                  ;TEMPORARY OUTPUT STACK
_CTFIRST        DB      4096 DUP(0)                  ;TABLE OF FIRST CODES
_CTLAST         DB      4096 DUP(0)                  ;TABLE OF LAST CODES
_CTLINK         DW      4096 DUP(0)                  ;TABLE OF TABLE LINKS

ENDINIT         LABEL   BYTE                         ;END OF INITIALIZED AREA

_CMASK          DB      00H,01H,03H,07H,0FH,1FH,3FH,7FH,0FFH

INCTABLE        DW      8,8,4,2,0                    ;INTERLACED BUMP TABLE
STARTABLE       DW      0,4,2,1,0                    ;INTERLACED START TABLE

GETGB_ERR       DB      'Error reading data',0  ;GETGB ERROR MESSAGE

_COPYRIGHT      DB      'GIF and "Graphics Interchange Format" ',0
                DB      'are trademarks (tm) of CompuServe ',0
                DB      'Incorporated, an H&R Block Company.',0
                DB      0

_DATA           ENDS

_BSS            SEGMENT WORD PUBLIC 'BSS'
_BSS            ENDS
                END
```

Ready?

Despite all its incredible complexity, the callable parts of this program are few. The functions that set process pointers already have been discussed at length—you can see how they work here, although their operation should have been fairly obvious even at the C level. All they do is to store the process pointers as they're passed in buffers.

The rest of this code is all there to provide a single externally callable function, to wit, DecodeGIF. Assuming that all the process pointers have been set up in some useful way, passing this thing a path to a valid GIF file will uncompress it and do something useful with its contents.

Obviously, a lot is going on in this function and in the code that it calls.

The file handling for the GIF decoder is done through a synthetic buffered file system that's part of this module. As you'll probably have realize by now, DOS does not provide a way to get a single byte from a file, at least, not efficiently. It wants to read in whole blocks of files and let the code that called it sort through the mess. That's essentially what the file handler here does. It's a greatly simplified implementation of the streamed file functions that C provides. Amongst its simplifications is that it can open but a single file at a time, and that only for reading.

It does, however, actually do buffered input. It reads in a block of data from the file and hands it out one byte at a time with each successive call to FGETC, which you'll find near the top of the code. When the current block of data is all used up it gets some more.

You might want to check out the first part of DecodeGIF. This is the code for magic, self-initializing data. It's a good trick to use if you have any sort of function that requires that multiple buffers and variables be initialized to a constant value—usually zero. Anything placed between the labels STARTINIT and ENDINIT down in the _DATA segment will be cleared every time this function is called. There's no need to initialize them individually, which would be considerably more time-consuming, and no chance of accidentally forgetting to initialize something that might cause the rest of the program to misbehave later on.

Obviously this initialization only matters for multiple calls to Decode-GIF. Everything's set up properly for the first time.

If you walk through the rest of the code in this function you'll see the inputting and stashing away of all the variables and flags discussed earlier in this chapter.

The UNPACK_IMAGE routine is the primary internal bit of code that does all the work. Assuming that it has had the image width, and the flag values set up for it by UnpackGIF, it can go to work on the file itself. It assumes that the file pointer of the open GIF file will be pointing to the start of the compressed image data—which it will be if UnpackGIF has done its stuff correctly.

Working through this code, UNPACK_IMAGE calculates the clear code and the end of image code. It initializes the code table—theoretically not necessary, because the first code in the GIF file should do this—and sets up a few useful defaults. Then it starts decoding.

There are three cases for the codes that the principle loop of this routine will process. These are the clear code, the end of image code, and everything else. If it finds a clear code it reinitializes the table and continues. If it finds an end of image code it flushes any data left in the character stream and belts out of the loop by setting the _DONE flag true.

The rest of the codes are processed as straight LZW compressed data. The _CTLINK part of the current table will be − 2, or OFFFEH, if the current code doesn't exist in it. Because this part of the table consists of a list of words, rather than of bytes, the program must do a bit of a dance with the BX register to address it, as you can see at EXTIMG3. If the code does exist, its contents are fetched from the table by PUTX and output to wherever the uncompressed GIF image is going. The mechanism for this will be discussed in a moment. The loop goes around again to get the next code from the file.

If the code doesn't exist it's inserted into the appropriate blank spot in the table by INSERTCODE and then its contents are output with PUTX—so that when the same code comes by again it will be in the table.

The PUTX routine is pretty simple. Given an index into the table in BX, it fetches the data at that location in the table and outputs it by calling DOPIXEL. It's actually in DOPIXEL that things start getting a bit peculiar, because this is one of the places where the assembly language program makes a call back to the C program that originally called it.

The DOPIXEL routine stores the pixels that are passed to it in the buffer OUTROW. When the size of the row equals the width of the image being decompressed it calls SHOWHANDLER to do something with the data. As was discussed, this "something" is up to the calling program. The most obvious thing would be to display the data on the screen.

Note that DOPIXEL also calculates the next line number. This might simply be one more than the last line number or it might not. If the picture is interlaced this routine might have to calculate the next line using the interlace tables at INCTABLE and STARTABLE.

The INSERTCODE routine is equally simple. It just places the code passed it in BX into the table at the location of the code, which is also in BX, of course.

I called this module GIF1.ASM, which assembled down to GIF1.OBJ. This links to GIF.OBJ, from GIF.C, and EGASCR.OBJ, from EGASCR.ASM in Chapter 9, to form GIF.EXE.

To look at the GIF file BODE1.GIF you would type the following:

```
GIF BODE1.GIF
```

VGA Decoder

Being restricted to driving an EGA card, the previous decoder also was restricted to displaying a maximum of 16 colors. If you have a VGA card, you can look at pictures with up to 256. The program in Fig. 5-8 is a simple variation on the first C program that will support a VGA card in mode 13H. This module must link to GIF1.OBJ and VGASCR.OBJ from Chapter 9. The GIF decoder in GIF1.ASM remains unchanged.

There are a few things to note about this code. First of all, the line display stuff in Showlt is a great deal simpler, owing to the essentially identical formats of decoded GIF information and the screen data for the VGA card's mode 13H. Also note that the overscan register is set in BGround using a BIOS call.

Fig 5-8   A 256-color GIF viewer to drive a VGA card

```
/*
        An example C language VGA GIF decoder.
        Links to assembly language module.
        Copyright (c) 1989 Alchemy Mindworks
*/

#include "stdio.h"
#include "dos.h"
#include "alloc.h"

extern char PALETTE[256][4],OUTROW[1024],COPYRIGHT[];
extern int INTERLACED,IMAGEWIDE,IMAGEDEEP;
extern int IMAGEX,IMAGEY,XLOC,YLOC;
extern int VERSION,SUBVERSION;

char *pbf=NULL;          /* pointer to line work space */

main(argc,argv)
        int argc;
        char *argv[];
{
        char filename[65];
        int i,e,ShowIt(),Colourize();
        int ImageDone(),BadError(),BGround();

        SetShow(ShowIt);
        SetPalette(Colourize);
        SetImage(ImageDone);
        SetError(BadError);
        SetBackground(BGround);
        if(argc > 1) {
                if((pbf=malloc(4096)) != NULL) {
                        VGAgraphics();
                        for(i=1;i<argc;++i) {
                                strmfe(filename,argv[i],"GIF");
                                if((e=UnpackGIF(filename)) == 0) {
                                        if(getch()==27) break;
                                }
                                else break;
                        }
                        VGAText();
                        if(e) printf("Error code %d",e);
                        free(pbf);
                } else puts("Error allocating memory");
        }
        ShowCopyright();
}

/* This function should do whatever is to be done when the
   image has been fully unpacked. The simplest thing is to
   do nothing, if the image was being displayed as it was
   unpacked. In this case, we'll beep. */
ImageDone()
```

```
{
        nosound();
        sound(660);
        delay(100);
        sound(880);
        delay(50);
        sound(440);
        delay(75);
        nosound();
}
/* This function should do whatever is needed to set the palette
   of the display card to the colour map in the palette buffer
   at palette. The n value is the number of valid colours. */
Colourize(n,palette)
        int n;
        char *palette;
{
        SetVgaPalette(palette,n);
}


/* This function is called after each line has been unpacked. It
   should show the line in the gloabl buffer OUTROW on the screen
   starting at line YLOC. To be really proper about it, it should
   add IMAGEX pixels to the left and IMAGEY pixels to the top. */
ShowIt()
{
        ShowVGA(OUTROW,IMAGEWIDE,YLOC);
}


/* This function is called to set the background colour. The colour
   number will be found in n. This can be ignored if you like. */
BGround(n)
        int n;
{
        union REGS r;
        int i;

        memset(pbf,n,320);
        for(i=0;i<200;++i) ShowVGA(pbf,IMAGEWIDE,i);

        r.x.ax=0x1001;
        r.x.bx=n << 8;
        int86(0x10,&r,&r);                          /* set overscan */
}


/* This function will be called if something bad happens in the process
   of unpacking a GIF file, such that the process really should not
   continue. It's passed the address of a string which describes the
   nature of the problem. It's not adviseable to return from this
   function. */
BadError(s)
        char *s;
{
        VGAText();
```

Fig 5-8   continued

```
        printf("\007\007\007Fatal error - %s.\n",s);
        exit(1);
}


/* This function will access and print the copyright notice. Some version
   of this should exist in your program because CompuServe gripes if they
   aren't mentioned in GIF programs. You have been warned. */
ShowCopyright()
{
        char *p;
        p = COPYRIGHT;
        while(*p) {
                p += printf(p)+1;
                puts("");
        }
}

strmfe(new,old,ext)                     /* make file name with specific extension */
        char *new,*old,*ext;
{
        while(*old != 0 && *old != '.') *new++=*old++;
        *new++='.';
        while(*ext) *new++=*ext++;
        *new=0;
}
```

You can, of course, write similar C language functions for the GIF decoder module to drive any sort of card you like. If you have something that is essentially monochrome, such as a Hercules card or perhaps a full page desktop publishing display, it might be interesting to write a variation on this program that uses the dithering techniques in Chapter 11 to display color images directly in black and white.

Perhaps more interesting will be some of the specialized modes available on enhanced VGA cards. Some cards allow for 800-by-600-line pictures. If you have such a card—and can pry the details of driving it in its extended modes from its manufacturer—writing a version of this program to show GIF files on it should be an interesting hack. You'll also have to write a corresponding version of VGASCR.ASM, as found in Chapter 9.

Finally, you also might want to see if you can implement virtual screen paging, as was done in Chapter 3, to look at GIF files that are larger than your screen is.

REFERENCES

Welch, T.A. "A Technique for High Performance Data Compression," *IEEE Computer*, volume 17 number six, June 1984.

6

CHAPTER

All the Colors of GIF—Encoding

The first rule of intelligent tinkering is to save all the parts.
—Murphy's Laws of Computers

Having looked at the process of decoding GIF files in Chapter 5—along with enough of the attendant theory behind LZW compression to make the whole exercise seem at least nominally analytical—reversing the process shouldn't be quite as weighty. In fact, a GIF encoder takes about the same amount of code to write, although the workings are a great deal less complex. Assuming that you enjoy tracing your way through assembly language listings, you'll find the encoder a lot easier to fathom.

Once again, the GIF encoder is more an exercise in data compression than in imaging. As was touched on in the last chapter—and will be discussed in greater detail here—encoding a GIF file involves a modified version of the LZW compression techniques used in straight file crunching, such as are found in the popular ARC and ZIP programs.

By the way, one of the things that devotees of the public domain will have noticed about the GIF files found on bulletin boards and other download facilities is that they don't ARC. Unlike virtually all other sorts of files, using the ARC, PKARC, and PKZIP programs to pack one or more GIF files into an archive does not reduce their sizes—on a good day, you'll achieve a one percent space savings, which is hardly worth the bother.

There's a very obvious reason for this, of course. An encoded GIF file is image data that has been LZW compressed. Although ARC programs have a variety of compression techniques at their disposal, they usually use LZW compression as well. Compressing data that has been compressed once before does not further reduce its size. The one percent space savings one does encounter is the result of the ARC program compressing the color maps of the GIF files it's given to squeeze.

BINARY IMAGES

The first problem that you will encounter in developing a GIF encoder is the same one that has cropped up in previous chapters of this book. You will need an image to encode. Short of capturing the image on your screen—which really does require resident code and a lot of tricky interrupt trapping that's beyond the scope of this chapter—you will be left with encoding a binary file again. In the case of a GIF file, this gets a bit complicated, because you will have not only the image data but also the color map data to deal with.

As with the GIF decoder, this chapter will work up to a generic assembly language encoder that will *bolt* onto a C language driver program. As such, although this chapter will outline a fairly artificial situation—encoding a raw binary file from the disk—it will be pretty easy for you to bolt the assembly language module onto whatever GIF programs you decide to write.

Chapter 12 features a more practical application of the code in this chapter, a PCX to GIF converter.

Once again, the working parts are in assembly language because a C version of the encoder just takes too long to run. Referring to the ARC and PKARC programs, it's worth observing that the relatively slow ARC package is written in C, but the much faster PKARC and PKZIP programs were done in assembler.

Before you can try out the encoder, you will need something to encode. Therefore, the first program to be discussed in this chapter is another decoder application, this one called GIF2BIN. This is a variation on the C language driver for the GIF decoder in Chapter 5. Given a GIF file, it will create two new files from it. The first, a PAL file, contains the raw color map information. The second, a BIN file, contains the raw image information packed with 1 byte per pixel just as it would come out of the GIF decoder. The latter file will be very large—a 640-by-350-pixel GIF file will produce a 224,000-byte BIN file and a PAL file with three times the number of bytes as there are colors in the GIF file, typically 768 bytes for a 256-color image.

The GIF2BIN program is shown in Fig. 6-1.

Fig 6-1   A GIF decoder to create a test file for the encoder

```
/*

        An example C language GIF decoder.
        Creates a binary and palette file.
```

```
*/

#include "stdio.h"
#include "dos.h"
#include "alloc.h"

extern char PALETTE[768],OUTROW[1024],COPYRIGHT[];
extern int INTERLACED,IMAGEWIDE,IMAGEDEEP;
extern int IMAGEX,IMAGEY,XLOC,YLOC;
extern int VERSION,SUBVERSION;

char *pbf=NULL;         /* pointer to line work space */

unsigned int colours=0;
char filename[65];
FILE *fp=NULL;

main(argc,argv)
        int argc;
        char *argv[];
{
        int i,e,ShowIt(),Colourize();
        int ImageDone(),BadError(),BGround();

        SetShow(ShowIt);
        SetPalette(Colourize);
        SetImage(ImageDone);
        SetError(BadError);
        SetBackground(BGround);
        if(argc > 1) {
                if((pbf=malloc(4096)) != NULL) {
                        EGAgraphics();
                        for(i=1;i<argc;++i) {
                                strmfe(filename,argv[i],"GIF");
                                if((e=UnpackGIF(filename)) == 0) {
                                        if(getch()==27) break;
                                }
                                else break;
                        }
                        Text();
                        printf("The image was packed with %u colours.\n",
                            colours);
                        printf("It's %u wide by %u deep.\n",
                            IMAGEWIDE,IMAGEDEEP);
                        if(e) printf("Error code %d",e);
                        free(pbf);
                } else puts("Error allocating memory");
        }
}

ImageDone()
{
```

Fig 6-1   continued

```
            fclose(fp);
            nosound();
            sound(660);
            delay(100);
            sound(880);
            delay(50);
            sound(440);
            delay(75);
            nosound();
}

Colourize(n,palette)
            int n;
            char *palette;
{
            char s[65],b[256];
            int i;

            colours=n;
            Gif2EgaPALETTE(b,palette,n);
            PaletteEGA(b,n);
            strmfe(s,filename,"PAL");
            if((fp=fopen(s,"wb")) != NULL) {
                    for(i=0;i<n;++i) {
                            fputc(palette[0],fp);
                            fputc(palette[1],fp);
                            fputc(palette[2],fp);
                            palette+=3;
                    }
                    fclose(fp);
            }
            else {
                    Text();
                    puts("Error writing palette");
                    exit(1);
            }
            strmfe(s,filename,"BIN");
            if((fp=fopen(s,"wb")) == NULL) {
                    Text();
                    puts("Error opening binary file");
                    exit(1);
            }
}

ShowIt()
{
            if(fwrite(OUTROW,1,IMAGEWIDE,fp) != IMAGEWIDE) {
                    Text();
                    printf("Error writing line %d\n",YLOC);
                    exit(1);
```

```
        }
        Gif2Ega(pbf,OUTROW,IMAGEWIDE);
        ShowEGA(pbf,IMAGEWIDE>>3,YLOC);
}


BGround(n)
        int n;
{
        int i;

        memset(OUTROW,n,80);
        Gif2Ega(pbf,OUTROW,IMAGEWIDE);
        for(i=0;i<350;++i) ShowEGA(pbf,IMAGEWIDE>>3,i);
}


BadError(s)
        char *s;
{
        Text();
        printf("\007\007\007Fatal error - %s.\n",s);
        exit(1);
}

strmfe(new,old,ext)                      /* make file name with specific extension */
        char *new,*old,*ext;
{
        while(*old != 0 && *old != '.') *new++=*old++;
        *new++='.';
        while(*ext) *new++=*ext++;
        *new=0;
}
```

There's nothing terribly new going on in this program. It must be linked to the object file created by the assembly language GIF decoder module from Chapter 5 and to EGASCR.OBJ. If you run it like this:

GIF2BIN LIPS.GIF

it will create LIPS.BIN, writing the image data to it from the ShowIt function, and LIPS.PAL, which will fill up from the Colourize function. It will show you the image and, when you hit a key, it will tell you the important statistics about the decoded picture.

These numbers will be hard coded into the example encoder—you'll want to make note of them when you run this thing on a GIF file.

It's worth pointing out that this program will not work if the example GIF file passed to it is interlaced. There are various ways of making it compatible with interlaced source files, but as its real purpose is merely as a quick lash up to try out the encoder program, it isn't really worth getting into the complexities here. You might want to see if you can modify GIF-2BIN to handle interlaced files.

If you've obtained the source disk for this book, you'll find a READ.ME file on it that specifies which of the example GIF images are interlaced.

Having run GIF2BIN, you're ready to actually look at the encoder.

Forming the Header

Writing the GIF file header should be pretty unadventurous by now. In fact, because in compressing a file you will know which of the various options of the header you'll need and which aren't applicable to your code, it's a lot easier to write one of these things than it is to read it.

There are a few observations that will get you through most of the complexities of the header. The first thing that goes into a new GIF file is the signature string, "GIF87a." The screen size words can be anything you like, but the most obvious values to put here are the dimensions of the GIF image you'll be encoding. Alternately, you could pick the size of an EGA or VGA graphics screen with a color resolution equivalent to the file being encoded. It hardly matters either way, actually—these numbers are rarely used by GIF decoders.

In forming the global flag byte, you will have two chunks of information to attend to. The first is the maximum number of bits of color information that the encoded image in the file will contain—minus one. As this is represented by the lowest three bits of the byte, you need only OR any other bits onto this number.

This number is represented as being one smaller than its actual value so it will fit into three bits. Because there will never be an image encoded into zero bits of data—at least, not without some sort of programming error—you can get away with this.

The second thing to consider is whether to have a global or a local color map. Because you'll be packing a single image into a single file in this example, it hardly matters where you put the color map. In this example it has been made a global map, but you can change this if you want to. To indicate the presence of the global map, you would OR the flag byte with 80H.

The next byte is the background color. To be more precise, it specifies which of the colors defined by whatever color map you'll eventually be using will fill the background and possibly the overscan of the screen. In this example it has arbitrarily been made the first color in the palette.

The next byte written to the file should be a zero.

Because this example has a global color map, its data comes next. It's encoded as three bytes of color information for each color in the image, so a 16-color image would have a 48-byte color map. Each byte represents the percentage of its respective color with a number from zero to 255. If a byte is set to 255 it indicates that the corresponding color is fully turned on.

The first byte in a 3-byte color map entry is the red percentage, the second is the green percentage, and the third is the blue percentage.

By rights, the file header should involve only the global data. However, in a one image per file encoder it's convenient to write the local part of the data while you're at it. As such, you can put the image block start marker—a comma—into the file next, followed by the left and top values of the image. In this case, these numbers will be zero too—note that these are words, not bytes.

The next two words are the actual width and depth of the image you'll be encoding. Finally, you will need a local flag. The flag tells the decoder, which will eventually try to make sense of the GIF file you're creating, whether there'll be a local color map and whether the image is interlaced or not. Actually, it includes several other things pertaining to local color, but because you won't be having any you can ignore them.

In this example, the program won't be interlacing the image, either, because there's no obvious reason for making the code additionally complex to get it together.

The next byte will be the first byte of the actual compressed data.

Image Compression

In straight LZW compression, one normally starts with the first byte of the data to be compressed and keeps going until the source of the raw data—usually a file—is exhausted. This is not the way it's done in encoding GIF image data. Because one of the criteria in designing the GIF standard was to make GIF images amenable to being viewed through a modem, with the receiving software doing the decoding on line, there was no obvious way to be sure that the receiving decoder would know when the end of an image had been reached.

Fortunately, you won't encounter too many applications that involve watching a quarter megabyte GIF file crawl onto your screen over a 1200-baud modem. However, the structure of the images remains. GIF files use a modified form of LZW compression to chop up the picture data into small packets, each one of a specified size. The end of an image is indicated by a packet with zero bytes of encoded data in it.

Each packet of data in a GIF file consists of an index byte followed by up to 255 bytes of LZW-encoded data. If you've ever done any Pascal programming you'll recognize this as being equivalent to the Pascal Str255 data type. The index byte tells you how many bytes there actually are in the packet. The next byte along after the packet is the index byte of the next packet. If the index of a particular packet is 0FFH, or 255, that packet will be 256 bytes long—the data size plus one byte for the index.

You can write a program to check a GIF file for integrity by "walking" through the packet indices. This process would read the first index and seek that many bytes further along in the file. Then it would read the next byte, treat it as an index and seek that many bytes further along. If it could do this and eventually encounter a zero byte—an empty packet—before it encountered the end of the file, the GIF image would have been properly packed.

Writing an efficient GIF encoder involved the creation of several sorts of file walkers along this line.

It's inefficient to write each byte to the disk as it's generated by the GIF encoder, because DOS does not provide a way to read or write single bytes. It's a lot more sensible to save each encoded byte in a buffer and write the buffer to the disk now and again when it gets full. If you make the buffer 255 bytes long, that plus its index constitutes a proper GIF image packet. Thus, you can just write it whenever the buffer approaches being full and the image will fall naturally into the GIF encoding scheme.

For practical reasons, you must "flush" the buffer when it gets to be within 4 bytes of being full.

The actual LZW compression takes place using the techniques that were discussed in Chapter 5. It maintains a string table—this time in a slightly different form—that it deals with in the same way as did the GIF decoder. It uses the same clear and end of image codes—the encoder will output a clear code whenever its table is full, telling the decoder to throw away its table and start over. This happens three or four times in an average screen size image.

As with the decoder, the assembly language module that handles the encoding does all its own file handling through DOS. As such, all it needs be passed is a pointer to the file name to be created, pointers to the image and its color maps and the pertinent details of the picture to be compressed. The mechanics of this will be discussed in just a moment. First, however, Fig. 6-2 is the assembly language code for the GIF encoder.

Fig 6-2   A GIF encoder module

```
;
;               GIF encoder
;               With reference to LZCOMP.ASM by Tom Pfau
;
;

VERSION         EQU     1                       ;VERSION
SUBVERSION      EQU     0                       ;SUBVERSION

BUFFERSIZE      EQU     255
MAXMAX          EQU     4096                    ;MAX CODE + 1

STRUCTSIZE      EQU     32
```

```
HASHFIRST        EQU      0                              ;OFFSETS INTO HASH TABLE
HASHNEXT         EQU      2                              ;...ENTRY
HASHCHAR         EQU      4

_AOFF            EQU      6                              ;FAR STACK OFFSET

;THIS MACRO FETCHES THE DATA SEGEMENT
DATASEG          MACRO
                 PUSH     AX
                 MOV      AX,_DATA
                 MOV      DS,AX
                 POP      AX
                 ENDM

;THIS MACRO FETCHES THE EXTRA SEGMENT
EXTRASEG         MACRO
                 PUSH     AX
                 MOV      AX,_DATA
                 MOV      ES,AX
                 POP      AX
                 ENDM


GIFENC_TEXT      SEGMENT BYTE PUBLIC 'CODE'
                 ASSUME  CS:GIFENC_TEXT,DS:_DATA


;THIS FUNCTION PACKS A RAW IMAGE FILE INTO A GIF FILE
;                CALLED AS
;                PackGIF(gd);
;                GIFDATA *gd
;
;                return codes    0 ok
;                                1 error creating file
;                                2 error writing header
;                                3 error writing data/footer
;                                4 error closing file

                 PUBLIC   _PackGIF
_PackGIF         PROC     FAR
                 PUSH     BP
                 MOV      BP,SP

                 MOV      DI,OFFSET STARTINIT     ;ZERO OUT ALL THE BYTES
                 MOV      AX,_DATA                ;IN THE INITIALIZED DATA
                 MOV      ES,AX                   ;AREA. THIS IS A LOT FASTER
                 MOV      CX,ENDINIT - STARTINIT  ;THAN RE-INITIALIZING
                 CLD                              ;THE PERTINENT BUFFERS ONE
                 MOV      AL,0                     ;AT A TIME IF THE CODE IS
          REPNE  STOSB                            ;CALLED MULTIPLE TIMES.

                 MOV      SI,[BP + _AOFF + 0]     ;OFFSET OF STRUCT
                 MOV      DS,[BP + _AOFF + 2]     ;SEGMENT OF STRUCT
```

Fig 6-2   continued

```
                EXTRASEG                        ;POINT TO LOCAL
                MOV     DI,OFFSET GIFSTRUCT      ;STRUCT BUFFER
                MOV     CX,STRUCTSIZE
                CLD
        REPNE   MOVSB                           ;MOVE THE STRUCT

                DATASEG

                MOV     CX,BITS                  ;GET NUMBER OF BITS
                MOV     AX,1                     ;AND WORK OUT
                SHL     AX,CL                    ;NUMBER OF COLOURS

                MOV     CLEAR,AX                 ;WHICH IS CLEAR CODE
                INC     AX                       ;PLUS ONE
                MOV     EOI,AX                   ;IS GET EOI CODE
                INC     AX                       ;PLUS ONE
                MOV     FIRSTFREE,AX             ;IS FIRST FREE POSITION

                CALL    FCREATE                  ;CREATE THE FILE
                JNC     PACK1                    ;CHECK FOR ERROR
                MOV     AX,0001H                 ;ERROR CODE
                JMP     PACKX                    ;AND LEAVE

PACK1:          CALL    HEADER                   ;WRITE THE GIF HEADER
                JNC     PACK2                    ;CHECK FOR ERROR
                CALL    FCLOSE                   ;CLOSE FILE
                MOV     AX,0002H                 ;ERROR CODE
                JMP     PACKX                    ;SCOOT

PACK2:          CALL    COMPRESS                 ;WRITE THE GIF DATA
                CALL    FOOTER                   ;CLEAN UP
                JNC     PACK3                    ;CHECK FOR ERROR
                CALL    FCLOSE                   ;CLOSE FILE
                MOV     AX,0003H                 ;ERROR CODE
                JMP     PACKX

PACK3:          CALL    FCLOSE                   ;CLOSE THE FILE
                JNC     PACK4                    ;CHECK FOR ERROR
                MOV     AX,0004H                 ;ERROR CODE
                JMP     PACKX                    ;SCOOT

PACK4:          MOV     AX,0                     ;NO ERROR - WE'RE LAUGHING

PACKX:          POP     BP
                RET
_PackGIF        ENDP

;WRITE THE GIF HEADER
HEADER          PROC    NEAR

                MOV     DX,OFFSET GIFHEAD
```

```
            MOV     CX,6
            CALL    FWRITE                  ;WRITE 'GIF87a'
            MOV     AX,SCREENWIDE
            CALL    FPUTW                   ;WRITE SCREEN WIDE
            MOV     AX,SCREENDEEP
            CALL    FPUTW                   ;WRITE SCREEN DEEP
            MOV     AX,BITS
            DEC     AX
            OR      AL,90H
            CALL    FPUTC                   ;WRITE GLOBAL FLAG
            MOV     AX,BACKGROUND
            CALL    FPUTC                   ;WRITE BACKGROUND
            MOV     AL,00H
            CALL    FPUTC                   ;WRITE DUMMY BYTE

            MOV     AX,1                    ;SIZE OF GLOBAL
            MOV     CX,BITS                 ;...COLOUR MAP IS
            SHL     AX,CL                   ;...2^BITS
            MOV     CX,3                    ;...TIMES THREE
            MUL     CX

            MOV     CX,AX
            MOV     DX,PALETTEOFF
            PUSH    DS
            MOV     DS,PALETTESEG
            CALL    FWRITE                  ;WRITE GLOBAL PALETTE
            POP     DS
            MOV     AL,','
            CALL    FPUTC                   ;WRITE IMAGE BLOCK
            MOV     AX,IMAGELEFT
            CALL    FPUTW                   ;WRITE UPPER X
            MOV     AX,IMAGETOP
            CALL    FPUTW                   ;WRITE UPPER Y
            MOV     AX,IMAGEWIDE
            CALL    FPUTW                   ;WRITE IMAGE WIDTH
            MOV     AX,IMAGEDEEP
            CALL    FPUTW                   ;WRITE IMAGE DEPTH

            MOV     AX,BITS
            DEC     AX
            CALL    FPUTC                   ;WRITE GLOBAL FLAG

            MOV     AX,BITS                 ;WRITE INITIAL CODE SIZE
            CALL    FPUTC
            RET
HEADER      ENDP

;TIDY UP AFTER THE GIF FILE DATA HAS BEEN WRITTEN
FOOTER      PROC    NEAR
            MOV     AL,0
            CALL    FPUTC                   ;WRITE ZERO LENGTH BLOCK
            MOV     AL,3BH
```

Fig 6-2 continued

```
                CALL    FPUTC                   ;WRITE END OF FILE MARKER
                RET
FOOTER          ENDP

;COMPRESS THE FILE POINTED TO BY IMAGESEG:IMAGEOFF
COMPRESS        PROC    NEAR
                CALL    INIT_TABLE              ;INITIALIZE THE TABLE
                MOV     AX,CLEAR                ;WRITE A CLEAR CODE
                CALL    WRITE_CODE
                CALL    FGETCH                  ;READ FIRST CHAR
L4:             XOR     AH,AH                   ;TURN CHAR INTO CODE
L4A:            MOV     PREFIXCODE,AX           ;SET PREFIX CODE
                CALL    FGETCH                  ;READ NEXT CHAR
                JC      L17                     ;CARRY MEANS NO MORE BYTES
                MOV     THISBYTE,AL             ;SAVE CHAR IN K
                MOV     BX,PREFIXCODE           ;GET PREFIX CODE
                CALL    LOOKUP_CODE             ;SEE IF THIS PAIR IN TABLE
                JNC     L4A                     ;NC MEANS YES, NEW CODE IN AX
                CALL    ADD_CODE                ;ADD PAIR TO TABLE
                PUSH    BX                      ;SAVE NEW CODE
                MOV     AX,PREFIXCODE           ;WRITE OLD PREFIX CODE
                CALL    WRITE_CODE
                POP     BX
                MOV     AL,THISBYTE             ;GET LAST CHAR
                CMP     BX,MAXCODE              ;EXCEED CODE SIZE?
                JL      L4                      ;LESS MEANS NO
                CMP     NBITS,12                ;CURRENTLY LESS THAN 12 BITS?
                JL      L14                     ;YES
                MOV     AX,CLEAR                ;WRITE A CLEAR CODE
                CALL    WRITE_CODE
                CALL    INIT_TABLE              ;REINIT TABLE
                MOV     AL,THISBYTE             ;GET LAST CHAR
                JMP     L4                      ;START OVER

L14:            INC     NBITS                   ;INCREASE NUMBER OF BITS
                SHL     MAXCODE,1               ;DOUBLE MAX CODE SIZE
                JMP     L4                      ;GET NEXT CHAR

L17:            MOV     AX,PREFIXCODE           ;WRITE LAST CODE
                CALL    WRITE_CODE
                MOV     AX,EOI                  ;WRITE EOI CODE
                CALL    WRITE_CODE
                MOV     AX,BITOFFSET            ;MAKE SURE BUFFER IS FLUSHED
                CMP     AX,0                    ;TO THE FILE
                JE      L18
                MOV     CX,8                    ;CONVERT BITS TO BYTES
                XOR     DX,DX
                DIV     CX
                OR      DX,DX                   ;IF EXTRA BITS, MAKE SURE THEY
                JE      L17A                    ;GET WRITTEN
                INC     AX
```

```
L17A:           CALL    FLUSH
L18:            RET
COMPRESS        ENDP

;INITIALIZE THE TABLE
INIT_TABLE      PROC    NEAR

                MOV     AX,BITS                 ;INITIAL NUMBER OF BITS IS
                INC     AX                      ;THE CODE SIZE PLUS ONE
                MOV     NBITS,AX

                MOV     AX,CLEAR                ;THE INITIAL MAXIMUM CODE IS
                SHL     AX,1                    ;TWICE THE MAXIMUM NUMBER
                MOV     MAXCODE,AX              ;OF COLOURS

                MOV     AX,CLEAR                ;CLEAR FIRST ENTRIES
                PUSH    ES                      ;SAVE SEG REG
                EXTRASEG
                MOV     CX,5                    ;SIZE OF HASH STRUCT
                MUL     CX
                MOV     CX,AX
                MOV     AX,-1                   ;UNUSED ENTRY FLAG
                MOV     DI,OFFSET HASH          ;POINT TO FIRST ENTRY
        REP     STOSW                           ;CLEAR IT OUT
                POP     ES
                MOV     AX,FIRSTFREE
                MOV     FREECODE,AX
                RET
INIT_TABLE      ENDP

;WRITE ONE CODE
WRITE_CODE      PROC    NEAR
                PUSH    AX                      ;SAVE CODE
                MOV     AX,BITOFFSET            ;GET BIT OFFSET
                MOV     CX,NBITS                ;ADJUST BIT OFFSET BY CODE SIZE
                ADD     BITOFFSET,CX
                MOV     CX,8                    ; BIT OFFSET TO BYTE OFFSET
                XOR     DX,DX
                DIV     CX
                CMP     AX,BUFFERSIZE-4         ;APPROACHING END OF BUFFER?
                JL      WC1                     ;LESS MEANS NO
                CALL    FLUSH                   ;OTHERWISE WRITE THE BUFFER
                PUSH    DX                      ;DX CONTAINS OFFSET WITHIN BYTE
                ADD     DX,NBITS                ;ADJUST BY CODE SIZE
                MOV     BITOFFSET,DX            ;NEW BIT OFFSET
                POP     DX                      ;RESTORE DX
                ADD     AX,OFFSET OUTPUTDATA    ;POINT TO LAST BYTE
                MOV     SI,AX                   ;PUT IN SI
                MOV     AL,BYTE PTR [SI]        ;MOVE BYTE TO FIRST POSITION
                MOV     OUTPUTDATA,AL
                XOR     AX,AX                   ;BYTE OFFSET OF ZERO
WC1:            ADD     AX,OFFSET OUTPUTDATA    ;POINT INTO BUFFER
                MOV     DI,AX                   ;DESTINATION
```

Fig 6-2   continued

```
                POP     AX              ;RESTORE CODE
                MOV     CX,DX           ;OFFSET WITHIN BYTE
                XOR     DX,DX           ;DX WILL CATCH BITS ROTATED OUT
                JCXZ    WC3             ;IF OFFSET IS ZERO, SKIP SHIFT
WC2:            SHL     AX,1            ;ROTATE CODE
                RCL     DX,1
                LOOP    WC2
                OR      AL,BYTE PTR [DI]    ;GRAB BITS CURRENTLY IN BUFFER
WC3:            PUSH    ES
                EXTRASEG
                STOSW                   ;SAVE DATA
                MOV     AL,DL           ;GRAB EXTRA BITS
                STOSB                   ;AND SAVE
                POP     ES
                RET
WRITE_CODE      ENDP

FLUSH           PROC    NEAR
                PUSH    AX              ;SAVE ALL REGISTERS
                PUSH    BX              ;AX CONTAINS NUMBER
                PUSH    CX              ;OF BYTES TO WRITE
                PUSH    DX
                MOV     ONEBYTE,AL      ;SAVE INDEX

                MOV     BX,HANDLE       ;WRITE THE BUFFER PLUS
                MOV     DX,OFFSET ONEBYTE   ;THE INDEX BYTE... THE
                MOV     CX,AX           ;GIF STANDARD LIKES
                INC     CX              ;LITTLE CHUNKS OF DATA
                MOV     AX,4000H        ;STORED LIKE PASCAL
                INT     21H             ;STRINGS

                POP     DX
                POP     CX
                POP     BX
                POP     AX
                RET
FLUSH           ENDP

;READ ONE BYTE FROM THE RAW DATA
FGETCH          PROC    NEAR

                CMP     SIZEMSB,0       ;IF THE COUNTER IS ZERO
                JNE     FGETCH0         ;WE'RE DONE
                CMP     SIZELSB,0
                JNE     FGETCH0

                STC                     ;END OF IMAGE - GO HOME
                RET

FGETCH0:        PUSH    ES              ;OTHERWISE
```

```
                PUSH    SI
                MOV     ES,IMAGESEG         ;POINT TO THE NEXT BYTE
                MOV     SI,IMAGEOFF
                MOV     AL,ES:[SI]          ;FETCH IT
                POP     SI
                POP     ES
                INC     IMAGEOFF            ;DO 32 BIT INCREMENT
                JNZ     FGETCH1             ;... IF OFFSET WRAPS,
                ADD     IMAGESEG,4096       ;... INCREMENT SEGMENT

FGETCH1:        CMP     SIZELSB,0           ;DO 32 BIT DECREMENT OF
                JE      FGETCH2             ;... SIZE COUNTER FOR
                DEC     SIZELSB             ;... THE NEXT CALL
                JMP     FGETCH3

FGETCH2:        DEC     SIZEMSB
                DEC     SIZELSB

FGETCH3:        CLC                         ;SIGNAL THIS BYTE IS GOOD
                RET
FGETCH          ENDP

;FIND THE CODE IN THE TABLE
LOOKUP_CODE     PROC    NEAR
                CALL    INDEX               ;CONVERT CODE TO ADDRESS
                MOV     DI,0                ;FLAG
                CMP     BYTE PTR [SI + HASHFIRST],-1 ;IN USE?
                JE      GC4                 ;EQUAL MEANS NO
                INC     DI                  ;SET FLAG
                MOV     BX,[SI + HASHFIRST] ;GET FIRST ENTRY
GC2:            CALL    INDEX               ;CONVERT CODE TO ADDRESS
                CMP     [SI + HASHCHAR],AL  ;IS CHAR THE SAME?
                JNE     GC3                 ;NE MEANS NO
                CLC                         ;SUCCESS
                MOV     AX,BX               ;PUT FOUND CODE IN AX
                RET                         ;DONE
GC3:            CMP     WORD PTR [SI + HASHNEXT],-1 ;MORE LEFT WITH THIS PREFIX
                JE      GC4                 ;EQUAL MEANS NO
                MOV     BX,[SI + HASHNEXT]  ;GET NEXT CODE
                JMP     GC2                 ;TRY AGAIN
GC4:            STC                         ;NOT FOUND
                RET                         ;DONE
LOOKUP_CODE     ENDP

;CONVERT INDEX TO ADDRESS - QUICKLY
INDEX           PROC    NEAR
                MOV     SI,BX               ;SI = BX * 5 (5 BYTE STRUCT)
                SHL     SI,1                ;SI = BX * 2 * 2 + BX
                SHL     SI,1
                ADD     SI,BX
                ADD     SI,OFFSET HASH      ;PLUS START OF TABLE
                RET
```

Fig 6-2   continued

```
INDEX           ENDP

;ADD A CODE TO THE TABLE
ADD_CODE        PROC    NEAR
                MOV     BX,FREECODE             ;GET CODE TO USE
                CMP     DI,0                    ;FIRST USE OF THIS PREFIX?
                JE      AC1                     ;EQUAL MEANS YES
                MOV     [SI + HASHNEXT],BX      ;POINT LAST USE TO NEW ENTRY
                JMP     AC2
AC1:            MOV     [SI + HASHFIRST],BX     ;POINT FIRST USE TO NEW ENTRY
AC2:            CMP     BX,MAXMAX               ;HAVE WE REACHED CODE LIMIT?
                JE      AC3                     ;EQUAL MEANS YES, JUST RETURN
                CALL    INDEX                   ;GET ADDRESS OF NEW ENTRY
                MOV     WORD PTR [SI + HASHFIRST],-1 ;INITIALIZE POINTERS
                MOV     WORD PTR [SI + HASHNEXT],-1
                MOV     [SI + HASHCHAR],AL      ;SAVE SUFFIX CHAR
                INC     FREECODE                ;ADJUST NEXT CODE
AC3:            RET
ADD_CODE        ENDP

;THIS ROUTINE CREATES AN EMPTY GIF FILE BASED ON PATH - CARRY=0 IF OK
FCREATE         PROC    NEAR
                PUSH    DS
                MOV     DX,PATHOFF
                MOV     DS,PATHSEG

                MOV     AX,3C00H                ;DOS OPEN FILE FUNCTION
                MOV     CX,0000H
                INT     21H
                POP     DS
                MOV     HANDLE,AX
                RET
FCREATE         ENDP

;THIS ROUTINE WRITES CX BYTES AT DS:DX TO THE FILE
FWRITE          PROC    NEAR
                PUSH    DS
                DATASEG
                MOV     BX,HANDLE
                POP     DS
                MOV     AX,4000H
                INT     21H
                RET
FWRITE          ENDP

;THIS ROUTINE WRITES ONE BYTE IN AL TO THE FILE
FPUTC           PROC    NEAR
                MOV     ONEBYTE,AL
                MOV     AX,4000H
                MOV     BX,HANDLE
                MOV     CX,0001H
```

```
                MOV     DX,OFFSET ONEBYTE
                INT     21H
                RET
FPUTC           ENDP

;THIS ROUTINE WRITES ONE WORD IN AX TO THE FILE
FPUTW           PROC    NEAR
                PUSH    AX
                CALL    FPUTC
                POP     AX
                MOV     AL,AH
                CALL    FPUTC
                RET
FPUTW           ENDP

;THIS ROUTINE CLOSES THE GIF FILE
FCLOSE          PROC    NEAR
                MOV     AX,3E00H              ;DOS CLOSE FILE FUNCTION
                MOV     BX,HANDLE
                INT     21H
                RET
FCLOSE          ENDP


GIFENC_TEXT     ENDS

DGROUP          GROUP   _DATA,_BSS
_DATA           SEGMENT WORD PUBLIC 'DATA'

GIFHEAD         DB      'GIF87a'              ;HEADER FOR A GIF FILE

STARTINIT       LABEL   BYTE                  ;START OF INITIALIZED AREA
GIFSTRUCT       LABEL   BYTE                  ;THIS IS WHERE THE STRUCT
SCREENWIDE      DW      ?                     ;...PASSED TO PackGIF GETS
SCREENDEEP      DW      ?                     ;...STORED... EVERYTHING
IMAGELEFT       DW      ?                     ;...WINDS UP ASSOCIATED
IMAGETOP        DW      ?                     ;...WITH CONVENIENT LABELS
IMAGEWIDE       DW      ?
IMAGEDEEP       DW      ?
BACKGROUND      DW      ?
BITS            DW      ?
SIZELSB         DW      ?
SIZEMSB         DW      ?
PALETTEOFF      DW      ?
PALETTESEG      DW      ?
IMAGEOFF        DW      ?
IMAGESEG        DW      ?
PATHOFF         DW      ?
PATHSEG         DW      ?

CLEAR           DW      0
EOI             DW      0
FIRSTFREE       DW      0
```

Fig 6-2 continued

```
PREFIXCODE       DW        0
FREECODE         DW        0
MAXCODE          DW        0
NBITS            DW        0
THISBYTE         DB        0
BITOFFSET        DW        0
HANDLE           DW        0

ONEBYTE          DB        0                      ;OUTPUT INDEX
OUTPUTDATA       DB        BUFFERSIZE DUP (0)       ;OUTPUT BUFFER

HASH             DB        20480 DUP (0)           ;HASHING TABLE
ENDINIT          LABEL     BYTE                   ;END OF INITIALIZED AREA

_DATA            ENDS

_BSS             SEGMENT WORD PUBLIC 'BSS'
_BSS             ENDS
                 END
```

The only callable function in this thing is PackGIF. This is passed a pointer to a structure of the type GIFDATA, which contains all the bits and pieces it needs to assemble a GIF file. This includes pointers to the file name, the image and so on, plus the image dimensions, the background color, and the screen size. All these things could have been passed to Pack-GIF from C as individual arguments. However, aside from being messy in C, and requiring a lot of stack space, they would have been exceedingly awkward to have dealt with in assembly language. By passing a single struct, you can copy all the relevant numbers into local memory and not have to bother with juggling segments or pointers to pointers.

As with the encoder, this thing ties up quite a bit of static memory for its string table. If you eventually write a program that uses both this module and the decoder module in the last chapter, you can overlay the string tables for them so that there's only one huge buffer, rather than two. This assumes, of course, that you will not be encoding and decoding a GIF image at the same time.

Alternately, you can dynamically allocate the string table as a buffer, as was discussed in the last chapter. This does tend to slow down the code a bit, though, as you'll have to keep track of the segment of your table as well as those of the code and data.

This routine is designed to be called from a C language driver. The listing in Fig. 6-3 is a simple program that reads in the BIN and PAL files created by GIF2BIN, stores them in buffers, and calls PackGIF to turn them into a proper GIF file again.

Fig 6-3   An example GIF file encoder

```
/*
                An example GIF encoder
                links to assembly language module
*/

#include "stdio.h"
#include "alloc.h"
#include "dos.h"

/* struct of information for assembly language function */
typedef struct {          unsigned int screenwide;
                          unsigned int screendeep;
                          unsigned int imageleft;
                          unsigned int imagetop;
                          unsigned int imagewide;
                          unsigned int imagedeep;
                          unsigned int background;
                          unsigned int bits;
                          unsigned long imagesize;
                          char *palette;
                          char *image;
                          char *path;
                } GIFDATA;

main(argc,argv)
        int argc;
        char *argv[];
{
        GIFDATA gd;
        FILE *BIN,*PAL;
        char binFile[65],palFile[65],gifFile[65];
        unsigned long size;
        char *p,*farPtr();
        unsigned int n;
        if(argc > 1) {
                /* make file names */
                strmfe(binFile,argv[1],"BIN");
                strmfe(palFile,argv[1],"PAL");
                strmfe(gifFile,argv[1],"GIF");

                /* fill in struct */
                gd.screenwide=640;
                gd.screendeep=350;
                gd.imageleft=0;
                gd.imagetop=0;
                gd.imagewide=640;
                gd.imagedeep=350;
                gd.background=0;
                gd.bits=4;
                gd.path=gifFile;
```

Fig 6-3 continued

```
if((BIN=fopen(binFile,"rb")) != NULL) {
        fseek(BIN,0L,SEEK_END);
        size=gd.imagesize=ftell(BIN);
        rewind(BIN);

        /* load binary image */
        if((gd.image=farmalloc(size)) == NULL) {
                puts("Error allocating image memory");
                exit(1);
        }
        p=gd.image;

        /* get one 64K block at a gulp */
        do {
                if(size > 0xff00L) n= 0xff00;
                else n=(unsigned int)size;
                fread(p,n,1,BIN);
                p=farPtr(p,(long)n);
                size -= (long)n;
        } while(size > 0L);
        fclose(BIN);
        puts("Image loaded");
}
else {
        puts("Error opening binary file");
        exit(1);
}

/* load the palette file */
if((PAL=fopen(palFile,"rb")) != NULL) {
        fseek(PAL,0L,SEEK_END);
        size=ftell(PAL);
        rewind(PAL);
        if((gd.palette=malloc((unsigned int)size)) == NULL) {
                puts("Error allocating palette memory");
                exit(1);
        }
        fread(gd.palette,1,(unsigned int)size,PAL);
        fclose(PAL);
        puts("Palette loaded");
}
else {
        puts("Error opening palette file");
        exit(1);
}

/* pack the beast */
if((n=PackGIF(&gd)) != 0)
    printf("Error %d writing GIF file",n);
farfree(gd.image);
```

```
                free(gd.palette);
        }
}

strmfe(new,old,ext)                    /* make file name with specific extension */
        char *new,*old,*ext;
{
        while(*old != 0 && *old != '.') *new++=*old++;
        *new++='.';
        while(*ext) *new++=*ext++;
        *new=0;
}

char *farPtr(p,l) /* return a far pointer p + l */
        char *p;
        long l;
{
        unsigned int seg,off;

        seg=FP_SEG(p);
        off=FP_OFF(p);
        seg+=(off / 16);
        off += (unsigned int)(l & 0x000fL);
        seg += (l / 16L);
        p=MK_FP(seg,off);
        return(p);
}
```

This program illustrates the structure of the GIFDATA struct—as well as why all those values weren't passed as separate arguments. Assuming that you have LIPS.BIN and LIPS.PAL on a disk, as created by GIF2BIN, and that you compile and link this code and the assembly language code above to form ENGIF.EXE . . . you would run this program as:

ENGIF LIPS

to read in the palette and image data and recreate the original GIF file. There are a few things to note here, though.

To begin with, when you wrote the original PAL and BIN files with GIF-2BIN, you did not write the image dimensions nor the color palette size anywhere except to the screen. As such, this program has no way of finding these things unless you tell it what they are. Because this is simply a demonstration program to illustrate how the GIF encoder is called, you can be lazy and write them directly into the program. You can see them up in main where the program loads up the gd struct members. In this case, the image is 640-by-350 pixels with 16 colors. You might want to change this if your source GIF file dimensions—as deciphered by GIF2BIN—are different.

You really only have to change gd.imagewide and gd.imagedeep.

The next important point is that no GIF image worth looking at will fit in 64k in its uncompressed form. As such, you must allocate the image buffer with farmalloc. This will present you with the difficulty that C does not provide a convenient way to read more than 64k from a file into a buffer. The problems associated with far pointers, as seen earlier in this book, are also present here. The solution, to use farPtr, is also the same.

In the real world—beyond the comforts of higher level languages—all large model pointers are created equally, because they are all comprised of segment and offset values. As such, when you pass the small palette buffer and the large image buffer to PackGIF, you don't have to differentiate between them. They'll both wind up as 32-bit numbers.

There are various things that can go wrong in the image encoding process—most of them having to do with the disk file that PackGIF wants to write its GIF data into. As such, the function will return zero if all is well or an error code. The error codes are detailed in the assembly language source code should you have need of them.

NO MORE GIFS

By now, you should have a pretty good grip on the albeit slippery concepts of LZW compression, large color palettes, and the peculiarities of the GIF standard.

References

Most programs are derivations of earlier programs, and the GIF decoder and encoder programs presented in Chapters 5 and 6 of this book are no exception. They're based on various public domain programs that have been released as source. The encoder is a fusion of the concepts found in GIF85.C by Kyle Powell, ARC, by Thom Henderson and in the article by Terry Welch mentioned at the end of Chapter 5. The former program is a C language GIF decoder designed to drive the IBM 8514 display. The latter is the basic public domain file achieving program, which incorporates LZW decompression. The source code for this was available in the public domain as of this writing.

The GIF encoder is based on an elegantly simple LZW file compression program by Tom Pfau called LZCOMP.ASM. This is not equivalent to the family of ARC and ZIP programs, although it uses much the same process. This is often found on bulletin boards in a file called LZW.ARC or LIMPEL.ARC, should you be interested in having a look at it. This application has added the GIF specific parts of the code and made it into a C language callable module.

7
CHAPTER

TIFF Files—The
Variable Standard

If it isn't broken don't fix it.
—Murphy's Laws of Computers

The last of the five formats to be dealt with in detail in this book also will be the most difficult. While TIFF files need not involve the level of programming complexity that you'll have experienced in looking at GIF files, they amply compensate for it with organizational complexities.

The *tagged image file format* is something of a misnomer. It's not so much a format as a loosely woven collection of suggestions about how images might be stored in a file. TIFF is extremely flexible. However, like other notably flexible objects—rubber screwdrivers and Styrofoam broadswords among them—the TIFF format sacrifices a bit of utility in trying to be all things to all applications.

Despite the problems that beset programmers attempting to write software to deal with TIFF files, there are several very powerful aspects to TIFF files. They can support images of any size, in monochrome or in up to 24 bits of color. TIFF files travel easily between architectures, meaning that they can be ported between a PC and a Macintosh, for example, without undue perturbations. They have grey scaling features. Perhaps still more important, TIFF files are not proprietary to anything—they did not start life attached to a specific piece of software—and, as such, they are being supported by a wide variety of applications.

This chapter will deal with monochrome images based on the TIFF 4.0 standard.

Figure 7-1 illustrates a typical TIFF file. There's a lot that is characteristically TIFF about this image. It has obviously been scanned from a hard copy original, and it is very detailed, that is, the image file was very large. This is the sort of work that good scanners can do, and the better scanners usually export TIFF files.

Fig 7-1   An example TIFF file. This picture came from Page 1 Publications, P.O. Box 33097, Austin, TX 78764

TIFF files—notably smaller ones—also appear as the preview images for encapsulated PostScript files, something that will be discussed later in this chapter and in greater detail in Chapter 10.

The only negative aspect to TIFF files is that they are exceedingly complex to unpack because of their particularly variable structure. Perhaps it would be more accurate to say that writing a program that would unpack all TIFF files would be exceedingly complex, and few applications that use TIFF files do so. Working with a subset of the TIFF standard is considerably easier.

This chapter will examine a number of TIFF tools and example applications to deal with TIFF files—some TIFF files. You might well have to rearrange the tools provided here to cope with your requirements of TIFF.

Unlike the other formats in this book, this chapter is by no means a complete discussion of TIFF. To have done so could have easily doubled the size of this book and made for a really impenetrable document. Instead, this chapter will provide you with a basic understanding of TIFF and some code to work with the majority of TIFF files.

TIFF gurus will unquestionably object to this.

TAGS

The thing that separates TIFF from all the other formats we've looked at thus far is its tags. A TIFF file consists of a header followed by any number of tagged *fields*. A field can be practically anything in a TIFF file, but it's probably easiest to think of one as being one part in the jigsaw puzzle of recreating the picture stored in the file.

Because later versions of the TIFF standard can add more tags to the definition of TIFF, the whole effort is very open ended.

A field can specify the width or height of the image. It might tell the decoder which of the several packing schemes that TIFF supports has been used to compress the image. It might specify all or part of the image itself.

In unpacking a TIFF file, then, the basic task of the decoding software is to read through each tagged field, extract the information in the field—retaining what is relevant—and build up the picture as it goes. The exact nature of the fields will become a bit clearer shortly.

Every field starts with an integer, or *tag*, which tells the decoder what to make of the rest of the field. For example, this is a typical field, one that must be present in every TIFF file:

```
DW    0100H
DW    0003H
DD    00000000H
DD    00000240H
```

The first word is the tag. The tag 0100H is called ImageWidth. The next word defines the nature of the data in the rest of the tag. If this word is three, as it is here, the remaining two fields are to be regarded as integers. Obviously, they're not integers—they're longs. In this case, the upper word of each is to be ignored.

The TIFF standard refers to integers as *shorts* in some cases.

The first of the two long integers is irrelevant to the ImageWidth tag—it defines the length of the data associated with those tags where this information would be meaningful. The second long integer is the actual data that this tag carries. This number is referred to as the offset, although this is frequently misleading. If the information that the tag carries will fit in a single 32-bit number it's stored in the offset element directly. If it will not, this number actually contains the offset in the file where the information is stored.

In this case, the width of the image is an integer, 0240H, which will fit in 32 bits with room to spare.

There are five types of data that can be conveyed by a tag, or six if you include raw data such as image information. They are specified by the contents of the second word in the tag, which can range from one through five. The value of this word can be interpreted as follows:

1. The offset contains a byte, that is, only the least significant byte is meaningful.
2. The offset contains an offset into the file that points to where a null terminated ASCII string is stored.
3. The offset contains an integer, that is, only the lower two bytes are meaningful.
4. The offset contains a long integer.
5. The offset contains an offset into the file that points to two long integers. The first represents the numerator of a fraction, the second the denominator. This is called a *rational* number.

If a tag points to image data it will have either three or four in the second integer.

As will become apparent in the course of this chapter, you need only write those parts of a TIFF decoder that might be needed to handle the TIFF files that you anticipate running into. As such, for example, if none of the tags that interest you involve rational numbers, you can ignore those tags that do and not bother to write a rational number handler into your decoder.

Rational numbers are unusual in TIFF files. The example programs in this chapter follow this strategy and ignore their existence.

Having gotten through this field the decoder would move along to the next one. Regrettably, this example is one of the simple fields—some of them are very weird.

Ignoring things is very much a part of using TIFF files. Many TIFF files, especially those that come from scanner drivers, are frequently loaded with tags, many of which provide no useful information. For example, the Make tag records the manufacturer of the equipment that created the TIFF file if it's present. You can successfully decode a TIFF file without knowing this. A TIFF reader is free to use as much or as little of the information in a TIFF file as it requires to decode the TIFF image and use it.

In keeping with the spirit of short, understandable programs the example TIFF code in this chapter ignores a lot of the tags that a TIFF file could contain. If you're interested in doing so you can fill in some of the blank tag handlers once you fully understand what the tags themselves are there for.

Header and Directory

Nothing has been said, as yet, about where in a TIFF file the aforementioned tags reside. Despite the rather sophisticated structure of a TIFF file, most of the phenomena of image files that have thus far appeared in other formats—file headers and the like—also occur in TIFF files.

The first thing you'll encounter in a TIFF file will be its header. The structure of a TIFF header is extremely simple—it's illustrated in Fig. 7-2.

The first 2 bytes in a TIFF header are very important because they define the data structure for the rest of the file. They will either be "II" or "MM." The I stands for Intel and the M for Motorola.

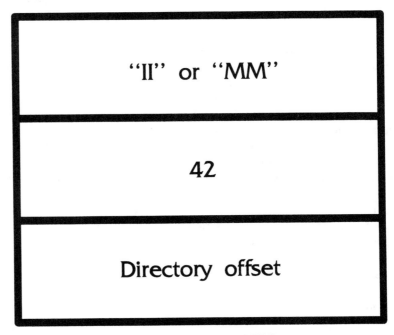

Fig 7-2 The header of a TIFF file

To make the TIFF standard equally easy—or difficult—to interpret on Macintosh and PC compatible computers, its designers allowed that the structure of integers and long integers in the fields of a TIFF file can be stored in whatever format is native to the machine that created the file. This serves to confuse things if a TIFF file makes its way from a Macintosh to a PC, for example, but this is a minor concern. As such, the setting of the first two bytes in a TIFF file must be saved somewhere in a program that decodes TIFF files so that the numbers in the rest of the file will be readable.

You will recall from Chapter 2 that Intel and Motorola microprocessors store their multiple byte numerical objects with different byte orders. What this really means is that a TIFF file reader on a PC compatible computer must be able to handle both Intel and Motorola style numbers.

The next 2 bytes in a TIFF file represent the version of the TIFF standard under which the image was created. This will be 42 decimal for the current version of TIFF as of this writing. Of course, that's 42 stored in an integer, so which of the 2 bytes of the integer holds the number 42 will depend on whether the first 2 bytes were "MM" or "II."

The next 4 bytes represent a long integer that specifies where in the file, relative to the beginning, the first *image file directory* begins. An image file directory is a list of the aforementioned tags that define all the parameters of the image in the file. This long integer is the number of bytes from the start of the file to the start of the image file directory.

Actually, it points to the first image file directory—in theory, there could be more than one. The examples in this chapter assume that there will only be one.

If you've been following this discussion, you will probably guess that the offset value would be 8L, that is, 2 bytes for the "II" or "MM" at the front, 2 bytes for the version number, and 4 bytes for the long integer. In fact, this is frequently the case, although it doesn't have to be. Depending on how you contrive to store TIFF data, it's often easiest to put the image data in first and then to add the descriptive tags about it at the end of the file, something that the TIFF specification certainly allows for. In this case, the offset value could be quite enormous.

The example TIFF packing program in this chapter places the image file directory at the end of the file.

An image file directory begins with an integer specifying how many tagged fields are in the directory. A field is always 12 bytes long. Each field can be defined in C language terms as follows:

```
typedef struct {
        int tag_type;
        int number_size;
        long length;
        long offset;
        } TIF_FIELD;
```

This is very misleading for any number of reasons. To begin with, if you were to read a field of a TIFF file into this struct on a PC compatible machine, as was done with the PCX file header, for example, the data would be correct only if the TIFF file had been stored in Intel format, that is, if the first two bytes of the file were "II." Otherwise all the numbers would be backward. Second, the two long integers aren't always long integers. Depending upon the value that turns up in the number size field, they might be bytes, integers, or pointers.

Although this struct illustrates the structure of a tagged field, it's not practical to treat fields this way unless you know you'll only be working with files that conform to these limitations. In practice, tags are read in one number at a time.

The TIFF standard constrains the tags in an image file directory to be sorted in ascending order by their tag numbers, although most decoders function well enough if this is not the case.

TIFF Data Considerations

The first thing to do in decoding a TIFF file is to read the first 2 bytes into an int variable. This can be used to determine how to read the rest of the multiple byte numbers in the file. The function in Fig. 7-3 can be used to get 16-bit and 32-bit number numbers.

Fig 7-3   Functions to fetch integers and long integers from a TIFF file

```
fgetWord(fp)        /* fetch an integer from a TIF file */
        FILE *fp;
{
        if(numberType == 'II')
            return((fgetc(fp) & 0xff) +
            ((fgetc(fp) & 0xff) << 8));
        else
            return(((fgetc(fp) & 0xff) << 8) +
            (fgetc(fp) & 0xff));
}
unsigned long fgetLong(fp)            /* fetch a long from a TIF file */
        FILE *fp;
{
        if(numberType == 'II')
            return((unsigned long)(fgetc(fp) & 0xff) +
                ((unsigned long)(fgetc(fp) & 0xff) << 8) +
                ((unsigned long)(fgetc(fp) & 0xff) << 16) +
                ((unsigned long)(fgetc(fp) & 0xff) << 24));
        else
            return(((unsigned long)(fgetc(fp) & 0xff) << 24) +
                ((unsigned long)(fgetc(fp) & 0xff) << 16) +
                ((unsigned long)(fgetc(fp) & 0xff) << 8) +
                (unsigned long)(fgetc(fp) & 0xff));
}
```

The variable numberType is used to store the first 2 bytes in the TIFF file. Even though numberType is undefined when the TIFF file is first opened, you can use fgetWord to set it. Inasmuch as the first 2 bytes will be the same, it doesn't matter which order they're read in.

If you use these two functions to get numbers from a TIFF file you can ignore their potentially inverse byte orders. At least, you can unless you run into problems. This peculiar arrangement can lead to all sorts of difficulties when you start trying to actually write a TIFF decoder.

Many TIFF tags can have variable length elements. For example, there's a tag called RowsPerStrip. It doesn't matter what it actually does, only that the offset value could be an int or it could be a long depending on whether the number size element was three or four. If it's an int in a particular TIFF file, you would call fgetWord twice for each long integer, once to get the number and once to throw away the extra word. If it's a long you would call fgetLong to get the long integer.

If you just call fgetLong and cast the resulting long integer to int when only the first 2 bytes are meaningful, the results will be workable for an Intel format file but not for a Motorola format file, because the int you want will be in the high order word.

A lot of these little inconveniences crop up in TIFF files.

What's in the Tags

To keep this chapter down to a manageable level of complexity, a complete listing of the TIFF file tags and their real meanings appears in Appendix B of this book. It's not an easy read, to be sure. However, the fortunate part of it is that you really needn't read it most of the time. Few TIFF files include more than a handful of rudimentary tags needed to define an image.

For practical purposes, you can get by with four tags to store a monochrome image. These represent things that must be defined under the TIFF format if there's to be enough information to work out how to locate and handle the image data. The four tags are ImageWidth, ImageLength, StripOffsets, and BitsPerSample.

The ImageWidth and ImageLength tags tell the decoder what the dimension of the image in the file is. Their values are specified in pixels. As of this writing, the TIFF standard defined these fields as being integers, that is, that the dimension values specified by these two tags are stored as integers in the offset elements of these tags.

The length elements of these two tags are undefined.

The BitsPerSample tag defines how many bits of data represent a single pixel in the final image. In a monochrome TIFF image this tag would contain one in the offset element. If this was a color TIFF file—something which will be discussed briefly later on in this chapter—it would require more than one bit per pixel.

The value in the offset element of this tag always is treated as an integer value.

Having told the decoder software what the vital statistics of the image are, the only important thing left to do is to define where the image data lives. This is handled by the StripOffsets tag. The offset element of this tag can be treated as an integer for small files or as a long integer for large ones, although there's no advantage to making it an integer. It specifies where in the file relative to the start the first byte of image data lives. The decoder is then left with the task of extracting it.

Image Encoding and Storage

The exact nature of the image data located by the StripOffsets tag is not necessarily the same from one TIFF file to the next. In the four essential tags just discussed, no mention was made of a tag that defined the method used to compress the image data. There actually is such a tag—it's called Compression, and its offset element contains one of several codes that tell the decoding software how to interpret the stored image data. This tag is not an essential one because the TIFF standard allows that, in its absence, the compression defaults to what it calls *type one storage*.

Type one storage means that the raw image data is stored in the file with no compression at all. Allowing for the TIFF file header and the other things that have thus far been discussed, a TIFF file that uses type one storage always will be just a bit bigger than it would have been if you'd simply written the raw image data to disk.

There actually are several good reasons for using this simple storage technique in creating TIFF files, especially fairly small ones. Uncompressed image data can be stored and extracted more rapidly than even lightly compressed image information. Secondly, inasmuch as TIFF files are intended for use with a very wide range of decoding software—not all of which can be assumed to support the entire standard—using type one storage means that the image should be readable by just about any software that reads TIFF images. Type one storage is so easy to implement that virtually all applications that will import TIFF files can handle it.

Obviously, storing big images this way has its drawbacks.

If the Compression tag is present it can define one of several other forms of image storage. The values in its offset field can be one of the following:

If the Compression tag has a value of 32771 the data is stored with no compression, just like under storage type one. The only difference is that if a line of the compressed image is of a length that normally would require an odd number of bytes to contain, an extra dummy byte is added to the end of each row to make the byte count even. In other words, each row starts on an even word boundary.

This is useful, at least in theory, for processors that can do more efficient data transfers when they're allowed to work with data that always starts on a word boundary. The 8086 has this characteristic. It's a subtle refinement, to be sure.

Storage types two, three, and four are variations of CCITT modified Huffman encoding. This is a form of run length encoding in some ways similar to techniques that have been discussed earlier. It's a moderately efficient way to compress image data, especially for complex scanned and dithered images, but it has a serious drawback in terms of this book. A CCITT compression decoder requires a pretty enormous chunk of source code to implement, much of which consists of vast decoding tables. Because CCITT compression almost never actually is used in creating TIFF files in real world applications, it won't be discussed here.

Finally, if the Compression tag has a value of 32773 the data pointed to by the offset value of the StripOffsets tag will be compressed using the by now familiar MacPaint run length encoding scheme. This is precisely identical to the system described in Chapter 2 except that the dimensions of the stored image are not constrained to be 576 by 720 pixels, as is the case with real MacPaint images.

In practice, most simple monochrome TIFF images are either stored with no compression at all or with MacPaint compression. The latter case is actually a very effective way to store even heavily dithered image information. The example programs in this chapter will use MacPaint compression.

If you wanted to write a universal TIFF decoder you would have to implement all the decompression schemes that TIFF currently supports. Unfortunately, the documentation for the TIFF standard strongly suggests that TIFF probably will support several more in the immediate future to better allow for color and grey scale images.

You might be wondering why the tag that defined where the image data lives in a TIFF file is called StripOffsets rather than something like ImageOffset. The reason is equally as nettlesome as much of the other obscurae of the TIFF standard. In the discussion thus far, it has been assumed that the data that this tag located in a TIFF file would be an entire image—in other words, that there would be only one StripOffsets tag in each TIFF file and that it would handle the entire picture. In fact, the TIFF standard makes no such stipulation.

The StripOffsets tag is so named because a TIFF file allows images to be chopped up into strips, with a separate tag for each one. There are good reasons why the creator of a file might want to do this—for example, the driving software for scanners that generate large images often produce TIFF files with multiple strips so that each strip will require less than 64k of memory to store. Such image chunks are faster to work with than a huge image buffer requiring the constant use of 32-bit pointers, as has been done throughout this book.

Bearing in mind that some scanners can produce images that will occupy three quarters of a megabyte or more, contiguous image memory isn't always possible anyway.

For most moderate size TIFF files there will be only one strip of image data—the whole image—and hence only one StripOffsets tag. The sample programs to be discussed shortly will make this assumption, but you might not want to in the TIFF decoder applications you eventually write.

As you will have ascertained by now, you probably will have to tailor your TIFF related code to the source of the TIFF files you plan to work with. A program that will make sense of all the permutations of TIFF files, although wholly possible to write, would be a substantial undertaking.

A *TIFF* FILE VIEWER

The example program in Fig. 7-4 is a TIFF file viewer that allows you to look at many sorts of TIFF files. Among the ones with which it was tested successfully were TIFF files generated by TGL Plus, the TIFF images that came with Adobe Streamline for the Macintosh and several public domain TIFF files. It also read the TIFF previews of all the encapsulated PostScript files it could find.

Fig 7-4 A program to display monochrome TIFF files

```
/* A program to pan over big TIFF pictures */
#define EGACARD 1
#define PREVIEW 0
#define DEBUG   0

#include "stdio.h"
#include "alloc.h"
#include "dos.h"
#include "tiff.h"

#if !EGACARD
#include "graphics.h"
#endif

#define HOME            0x4700
#define CURSOR_UP       0x4800
#define CURSOR_LEFT     0x4b00
#define CURSOR_RIGHT    0x4d00
#define END             0x4f00
#define CURSOR_DOWN     0x5000

#define step            32

char header[16];                /* where the header lives */
unsigned int width,depth,bytes; /* the trusty image dimensions */
unsigned int screenWide=640;    /* screen dimensions... maybe */
unsigned int screenDeep=350;
unsigned int numberType=0;      /* number storage format */
unsigned int TIFFversion=0;     /* TIFF version */
unsigned int TIFFentries=0;     /* number of IFD entries */
unsigned int TIFFsubfile=0;     /* subfile type */
unsigned int TIFFsamples=0;     /* number of samples */
```

Fig 7-4   continued

```c
unsigned int TIFFplancfg=0;      /* planar configuration */
unsigned int TIFFcompres=1;      /* compression type */
unsigned int TIFFphotmet=0;      /* photometric interpretaton */

unsigned long TIFFoffset=0L;     /* TIFF offset */
unsigned long TIFFrowstrip=0L;
unsigned long TIFFstripoff=0L;   /* where the first one is */
unsigned long TIFFstripcnt=0L;   /* how many there are */
unsigned long TIFFbytecnt=0L;

unsigned long imageSize=0L;      /* buffer size for image */
unsigned long imageStart=0L;     /* first byte of image */

typedef struct {                 /* EPSF header */
        char epsf[4];
        long ps_start;
        long ps_size;
        long meta_start;
        long meta_size;
        long tiff_start;
        long tiff_size;
        int checksum;
        } EPSFHEAD;

char *farPtr();
unsigned long fgetLong();
unsigned int pixels2bytes();
#if !EGACARD
char *ibuf;
#endif

char *buffer=NULL;

main(argc,argv)
        int argc;
        char *argv[];
{
        FILE *fp;
        char *p;
        int i;

        if(argc > 1) {
                /* attempt to open the file */
                if((fp=fopen(argv[1],"rb")) != NULL) {
                        #if PREVIEW
                        FindPreview(fp);
                        #endif
                        /* read in the header */
                        numberType=fgetWord(fp);
                        if(numberType == 'MM' || numberType == 'II') {
                                if((TIFFversion=fgetWord(fp)) == 42) {
                                        TIFFoffset=fgetLong(fp);
```

```
                                fseek(fp,imageStart+
                                    TIFFoffset,SEEK_SET);
                                TIFFentries=fgetWord(fp);
                                for(i=0;i<TIFFentries;++i)
                                    DecodeTag(fp);
                                #if DEBUG
                                puts("Hit any key");
                                getch();
                                #endif
                                /* fool screen */
                                TIFFphotmet ^=1;

                                if(width != 0 && depth != 0 &&
                                    TIFFstripoff != 0L) {
                                        imageSize=(long)bytes * (long)depth;
                                        if((buffer=farmalloc(imageSize)) != NULL)
                                          UnpackTifPicture(buffer,fp);
                                          PanTifPicture(buffer);
                                          farfree(buffer);
                                        } else
                                          puts("Error allocating "
                                                "memory");
                                } else puts("Illegal size values");
                        } else
                            printf("Version %d of TIFF not supported\n");
                } else printf("Not a TIFF file.\n");
                fclose(fp);
        } else printf("Error opening %s.\n",argv[1]);
    }
}

#if PREVIEW
FindPreview(fp)                 /* locate the EPSF preview */
        FILE *fp;
{
        EPSFHEAD e;

        if(fread((char *)&e,1,sizeof(EPSFHEAD),fp) == sizeof(EPSFHEAD)) {
                if(!memcmp(e.epsf,"\xc5\xd0\xd3\xc6",4)) {
                        if(e.tiff_start > 0L) {
                                imageStart=e.tiff_start;
                                fseek(fp,e.tiff_start,SEEK_SET);
                        }
                        else {
                                puts("No TIFF preview");
                                exit(1);
                        }
                }
                else {
                        puts("No EPSF header");
                        exit(1);
                }
        }
        else {
```

Fig 7-4   continued

```
                puts("Error reading EPSF header");
                exit(1);
        }
}
#endif

UnpackTifPicture(p,fp)        /* unpack a TIFF image */
        char *p;
        FILE *fp;
{
        long l,t;
        int i,n;

        if(TIFFstripcnt==1L) {
        /* if there is only one strip, the offset points to it */
                fseek(fp,imageStart+TIFFstripoff,SEEK_SET);

                for(i=0;i<depth;++i) {
                        n=ReadTifLine(p,fp);
                        p=farPtr(p,(long)bytes);
                }
        }
        else {
        /* if there is more than one strip, the offset points to
           the offset of the first strip - convoluted, you say? */
                for(l=0L;l<TIFFstripcnt;++l) {
                        fseek(fp,imageStart+TIFFstripoff+(l*sizeof(long)),
                            SEEK_SET);
                        t=fgetLong(fp);
                        fseek(fp,t,SEEK_SET);
                        n=ReadTifLine(p,fp);
                        p=farPtr(p,(long)bytes);
                }
        }
        return(n);
}

ReadTifLine(p,fp) /* read and decode a line into p */
        char *p;
        FILE *fp;
{
        unsigned long offs,strip;
        int n=0,c,i;

        memset(p,0,bytes);
        if(TIFFcompres == COMPnone) {
                n=fread(p,1,bytes,fp);
                if(TIFFphotmet==1) for(i=0;i<bytes;++i) p[i]=~p[i];
        }
        else if(TIFFcompres == COMPmpnt) {
                do {
                        c=fgetc(fp) & 0xff;
                        if(c & 0x80) {
```

```
                              if(c != 0x80) {
                                       i = ((~c) & 0xff)+2;
                                       c=fgetc(fp);
                                       if(TIFFphotmet==1)
                                           while(i--) p[n++] = ~c;
                                       else while(i--) p[n++] = c;
                              }
                      else {
                              i=(c & 0xff)+1;
                              if(TIFFphotmet==1) while(i--)
                                  p[n++] = ~fgetc(fp);
                              else while(i--) p[n++] = fgetc(fp);
                      }
              } while(n < bytes);
        }
        else {
                printf("Undefined compression method %d\n",TIFFcompres);
                exit(1);
        }
        return(n);
}

DecodeTag(fp)
        FILE *fp;
{
        long length,offset;
        int tag,type;

        tag=fgetWord(fp);
        type=fgetWord(fp);

        if(type == TIFFlong) {
                length=fgetLong(fp);
                offset=fgetLong(fp);
        }
        else {
                length=(unsigned long)fgetWord(fp);
                fgetWord(fp);
                offset=(unsigned long)fgetWord(fp);
                fgetWord(fp);
        }

        #if DEBUG
printf("tag:%-20.20s  type:%u  length:%lu  offset:%lu (%lXH)\n",
    tag_name(tag),type,length,offset,offset);
#endif
switch(tag) {
        case SubfileType:
                TIFFsubfile=(unsigned int)offset;
                break;
        case ImageWidth:
                width=(unsigned int)offset;
```

Fig 7-4   continued

```
                        bytes=pixels2bytes(width);
                        break;
        case ImageLength:
                        depth=(unsigned int)offset;
                        break;
        case RowsPerStrip:
                        if(type==TIFFlong) TIFFrowstrip=offset;
                        else TIFFrowstrip=offset & 0xffffL;
                        break;
        case StripOffsets:
                        if(type==TIFFlong) {
                                TIFFstripoff=offset;
                                TIFFstripcnt=length;
                        }
                        else {
                                TIFFstripoff= offset & 0xffffL;
                                TIFFstripcnt= length & 0xffffL;
                        }
                        break;
        case StripByteCounts:
                        if(type==TIFFlong) TIFFbytecnt=offset;
                        else TIFFbytecnt= offset & 0xffffL;
                        break;
        case SamplesPerPixel:
                        TIFFsamples=(unsigned int)offset;
                        break;
        case BitsPerSample:
                        break;
        case PlanarConfiguration:
                        TIFFplancfg=(unsigned int)offset;
                        break;
        case Compression:
                        TIFFcompres=(unsigned int)offset;
                        break;
        case Group3Options:
                        break;
        case Group4Options:
                        break;
        case FillOrder:
                        break;
        case Threshholding:
                        break;
        case CellWidth:
                        break;
        case CellLength:
                        break;
        case MinSampleValue:
                        break;
        case MaxSampleValue:
                        break;
        case PhotometricInterp:
                        TIFFphotmet=(unsigned int)offset;
                        break;
```

```
                case GrayResponseUnit:
                        break;
                case GrayResponseCurve:
                        break;
                case ColorResponseUnit:
                        break;
                case ColorResponseCurves:
                        break;
                case XResolution:
                        break;
                case YResolution:
                        break;
                case ResolutionUnit:
                        break;
                case Orientation:
                        break;
                case DocumentName:
                        break;
                case PageName:
                        break;
                case XPosition:
                        break;
                case YPosition:
                        break;
                case PageNumber:
                        break;
                case ImageDescription:
                        break;
                case Make:
                        break;
                case Model:
                        break;
                case FreeOffsets:
                        break;
                case FreeByteCounts:
                        break;
                default:
                        printf("Unrecognized tag %d\n",tag);
                        exit(1);
                        break;
        }
        return(length);
}

PanTifPicture(p)
        char *p;
{
        int c,x=0,y=0;

        init();
        do {
                ShowTifPicture(farPtr(p,
                    ((long)y*(long)bytes)+(long)(x>>3)));
                switch(c=GetKey()) {
```

Fig 7-4   continued

```
            case CURSOR_LEFT:
                    if((x-step) > 0) x-=step;
                    else x=0;
                    break;
            case CURSOR_RIGHT:
                    if((x+step+screenWide) < width) x+=step;
                    else if(width > screenWide) x=width-screenWide;
                    else x=0;
                    break;
            case CURSOR_UP:
                    if((y-step) > 0) y-=step;
                    else y=0;
                    break;
            case CURSOR_DOWN:
                    if((y+step+screenDeep) < depth) y+=step;
                    else if(depth > screenDeep) y=depth-screenDeep;
                    else y=0;
                    break;
            case HOME:
                    x=y=0;
                    break;
            case END:
                    if(width > screenWide) x=width-screenWide;
                    else x=0;
                    if(depth > screenDeep) y=depth-screenDeep;
                    else y=0;
                    break;
            }
    } while(c != 27);
    deinit();
}

ShowTifPicture(p) /* display the top of the picture */
    char *p;
{

    unsigned int i,w,d;

    if(width > screenWide) w=pixels2bytes(screenWide);
    else w=bytes;

    if(depth > screenDeep) d=screenDeep;
    else d=depth;

    #if EGACARD
    for(i=0;i<d;++i)
            memcpy(MK_FP(0xa000,i*80),
                farPtr(p,((long)i*(long)bytes)),w);
    #else

    ibuf[0]=screenWide-1;
    ibuf[1]=((screenWide-1) >> 8);
    ibuf[2]=screenDeep-1;
    ibuf[3]=((screenDeep-1) >> 8);
```

```
for(i=0;i<screenDeep;++i) {
        memset(ibuf+4+(i*(screenWide >> 3)),0,screenWide >> 3);
        memcpy(ibuf+4+(i*(screenWide >> 3)),
            farPtr(p,(long)i*(long)bytes),w);
}
putimage(0,0,ibuf,COPY_PUT);        /* show the picture     */
#endif
}

#if EGACARD
init()              /* turn on graphics mode */
{
        union REGS r;

        r.x.ax=0x0010;
        int86(0x10,&r,&r);
}

deinit()   /* turn off graphics card */
{
        union REGS r;

        r.x.ax=0x0003;
        int86(0x10,&r,&r);
}
#else
init()              /* turn on graphics mode */
{
        int d,m,e=0;

        detectgraph(&d,&m);
        if(d<0) {
                puts("No graphics card");
                exit(1);
        }
        if(d==EGA) {
                d=CGA;
                m=CGAHI;
        }
        initgraph(&d,&m,"");
        e=graphresult();
        if(e<0) {
                printf("Graphics error %d: %s",e,grapherrormsg(e));
                exit(1);
        }
        screenWide=getmaxx()+1;
        screenDeep=getmaxy()+1;
        if((ibuf=malloc(4+((screenWide >> 3) * screenDeep))) == NULL) {
                deinit();
                puts("Error allocating screen buffer");
                exit(1);
        }
        setcolor(getmaxcolor());
}
```

Fig 7-4   continued

```
deinit()   /* turn off graphics card */
{
        closegraph();
        if(ibuf != NULL) free(ibuf);
}
#endif

unsigned int pixels2bytes(n)
        unsigned int n;
{
        if(n & 0x0007) return((n >> 3) + 1);
        else return(n >> 3);
}

char *farPtr(p,l) /* return a far pointer p + l */
        char *p;
        long l;
{
        unsigned int seg,off;

        seg = FP_SEG(p);
        off = FP_OFF(p);
        seg += (off / 16);
        off &= 0x000f;
        off += (unsigned int)(l & 0x000fL);
        seg += (l / 16L);
        p = MK_FP(seg,off);
        return(p);
}

GetKey()
{
        int c;

        c = getch();
        if(!(c & 0x00ff)) c = getch() << 8;
        return(c);
}

fgetWord(fp)
        FILE *fp;
{
        if(numberType == 'II')
            return((fgetc(fp) & 0xff) + ((fgetc(fp) & 0xff) << 8));
        else return(((fgetc(fp) & 0xff) << 8) + (fgetc(fp) & 0xff));
}

unsigned long fgetLong(fp)
        FILE *fp;
{

        if(numberType == 'II')
            return((unsigned long)(fgetc(fp) & 0xff) +
```

```
                   ((unsigned long)(fgetc(fp) & 0xff) << 8) +
                   ((unsigned long)(fgetc(fp) & 0xff) << 16) +
                   ((unsigned long)(fgetc(fp) & 0xff) << 24));
      else
           return(((unsigned long)(fgetc(fp) & 0xff) << 24) +
                   ((unsigned long)(fgetc(fp) & 0xff) << 16) +
                   ((unsigned long)(fgetc(fp) & 0xff) << 8) +
                   (unsigned long)(fgetc(fp) & 0xff));
}
```

This program is yet another variation on one of the IMG file viewers described in Chapter 3. This one allows for both large images and virtual screen panning to allow you to look at a picture larger than the "window" of your monitor. Because large scanned images are really a hallmark of the TIFF format, these features are most desirable in any program that purports to handle the TIFF format.

To compile the program in Fig. 7-4 you will also need the TIFF.H file in Fig. 7-5. This file defines the various constants associated with the TIFF format.

Fig 7-5   The TIFF.H header file

```
/* TIFF tag names */
#define SubfileType           255    /* 0xFF  */
#define ImageWidth            256    /* 0x100 */
#define ImageLength           257    /* 0x101 */
#define RowsPerStrip          278    /* 0x116 */
#define StripOffsets          273    /* 0x111 */
#define StripByteCounts       279    /* 0x117 */
#define SamplesPerPixel       277    /* 0x115 */
#define BitsPerSample         258    /* 0x102 */
#define PlanarConfiguration   284    /* 0x11C */
#define Compression           259    /* 0x103 */
#define Group3Options         292    /* 0x124 */
#define Group4Options         293    /* 0x125 */
#define FillOrder             266    /* 0x10A */
#define Threshholding         263    /* 0x107 */
#define CellWidth             264    /* 0x108 */
#define CellLength            265    /* 0x109 */
#define MinSampleValue        280    /* 0x118 */
#define MaxSampleValue        281    /* 0x119 */
#define PhotometricInterp     262    /* 0x106 */
#define GrayResponseUnit      290    /* 0x122 */
#define GrayResponseCurve     291    /* 0x123 */
#define ColorResponseUnit     300    /* 0x12C */
#define ColorResponseCurves   301    /* 0x12D */
#define XResolution           282    /* 0x11A */
#define YResolution           283    /* 0x11B */
#define ResolutionUnit        296    /* 0x128 */
#define Orientation           274    /* 0x112 */
```

Fig 7-5   continued

```
#define DocumentName            269   /* 0x10D */
#define PageName                285   /* 0x11D */
#define XPosition               286   /* 0x11E */
#define YPosition               287   /* 0x11F */
#define PageNumber              297   /* 0x129 */
#define ImageDescription        270   /* 0x10E */
#define Make                    271   /* 0x10F */
#define Model                   272   /* 0x110 */
#define FreeOffsets             288   /* 0x120 */
#define FreeByteCounts          289   /* 0x121 */

/* TIFF sizes */
#define TIFFbyte                1
#define TIFFascii               2
#define TIFFshort               3
#define TIFFlong                4
#define TIFFrational            5

/* TIFF compression types */
#define COMPnone                1
#define COMPhuff                2
#define COMPfax3                3
#define COMPfax4                4
#define COMPwrd1                0x8003
#define COMPmpnt                0x8005

#if DEBUG
#define tag_count               37

typedef struct {
        int number;
        char name[20];
        } TAGNAME;

static TAGNAME tag_names[tag_count] = {
{ 255,"SubfileType"}, { 256,"ImageWidth"},
{ 257,"ImageLength"}, { 278,"RowsPerStrip"},
{ 273,"StripOffsets"}, { 279,"StripByteCounts"},
{ 277,"SamplesPerPixel"}, { 258,"BitsPerSample"},
{ 284,"PlanarConfiguration"}, { 259,"Compression"},
{ 292,"Group3Options"}, { 293,"Group4Options"},
{ 266,"FillOrder"}, { 263,"Threshholding"},
{ 264,"CellWidth"}, { 265,"CellLength"},
{ 280,"MinSampleValue"}, { 281,"MaxSampleValue"},
{ 262,"PhotometricInterp"}, { 290,"GrayResponseUnit"},
{ 291,"GrayResponseCurve"}, { 300,"ColorResponseUnit"},
{ 301,"ColorResponseCurves"}, { 282,"XResolution"},
{ 283,"YResolution"}, { 296,"ResolutionUnit"},
{ 274,"Orientation"}, { 269,"DocumentName"},
{ 285,"PageName"}, { 286,"XPosition"},
{ 287,"YPosition"}, { 297,"PageNumber"},
{ 270,"ImageDescription"}, { 271,"Make"},
```

```
{ 272,"Model"}, { 288,"FreeOffsets"},
{ 289,"FreeByteCounts"},
};

char *tag_name(n)
        int n;
{
        int i;

        for(i=0;i<tag_count;++i) {
                if(n==tag_names[i].number)
                    return(tag_names[i].name);
        }
        return("BadTag");
}

#endif
```

This viewer is quite full of holes as far as the complete TIFF standard is concerned, but then so are most other programs that deal with TIFF files to some extent. If you allow yourself 15 minutes with the tag list in Appendix B you should be able to come up with at least half a dozen tag permutations that will cause this program to misbehave or, if you really understand the TIFF standard well, to crash.

This little viewer will handle most TIFF files because very few applications that generate TIFF files use many of the format's more exotic tags and facilities.

The operation of the basic TIFF viewer is pretty easy to follow, especially because all the panning and image display code hasn't changed from the original IMG viewer. The main function handles checking out the header and locating the image file directory. It figures out how many tags are in the directory and calls DecodeTag for each one.

The DecodeTag function fetches the two integers and two long integers of a tag and then uses a big switch statement to deal with each tag. Note that it only deals with length values that are integers or long integers correctly. None of the tags that are provided for in this example use anything else.

The switch in DecodeTag contains a case for every possible tag currently defined in the TIFF format even though most of them don't do anything. If you develop a TIFF reader for particular sorts of TIFF files you probably will want to fill in some of these blank cases.

One of the as yet unmentioned tags that does make a difference to this reader is one called PhotometricInterpretation, which defines whether the set pixels in a monochrome image will be white or black. In other words, a TIFF file can instruct the software decoding it whether to invert the image or not.

For reasons that have been discussed earlier in this book, the screen on a PC prefers to display bit-mapped graphics inverted. While there are lots of ways around this, for the sake of this simple viewer program you can just lie to the decoder about the setting of the photometric interpretation. The value returned by this tag will be either one or zero. There's a line in the main function that simply inverts this value, flipping black to white for the image.

You will want to remove this line if you incorporate this code into an application that requires real photometric interpretation of TIFF images.

Actually reading the TIFF image data, once it has been located in a file by a StripOffsets tag, is easy. For the most part the ReadTifLine function is just a MacPaint uncompressor. The only important difference is that the photometric interpretation setting is used to decide whether to invert the decompressed data.

Debugs and Previews

If you look up at the top of the program in Fig. 7-4 you'll notice that there are two new defines, PREVIEW and DEBUG. These are set false in the program as it's shown here, but you might want to experiment with them.

Setting the DEBUG define true doesn't do all that much. It causes the program to compile into a version that lists all the tags in a TIFF file before it attempts to display the image. Because TIFF files can have such a wide variety of tags, it's often handy to be able to see what a specific file is throwing at your decoder when you're trying to ascertain why things aren't working.

The PREVIEW define is a bit more interesting. Many encapsulated PostScript—or EPS—files include TIFF files tacked onto the end of the PostScript code so that applications that import the PostScript files—Ventura Publisher, for example—can display a facsimile of the PostScript image on their screens even if they lack the smarts to actually read and interpret PostScript. Chapter 10 digs into PostScript previews in greater detail.

The important thing about previews, as far as this chapter is concerned, is that there are viewable TIFF files to be found in many encapsulated PostScript files. These are completely standard TIFF images except that they're tacked onto the ends of long text files, the text being the PostScript code.

It's extremely easy to tell if an EPS file has a TIFF preview. The first thing to check for is an EPSF binary header. If this is present, the EPS file will have some binary trash before the first line of text. Figure 7-6 illustrates the start of an EPS file with a TIFF preview as seen in DEBUG.

The first 4 bytes of the header are always the letters EPSF with their high order bits set. The complete structure of the header is defined in Fig. 7-7. Assuming that the member epsf actually contains the start of the header, you would check for the existence of a TIFF preview by looking at the value of the tiff_start member. This will be 0L if there's no TIFF preview.

Fig 7-6   An EPS file with its binary header, indicating the presence of a TIFF preview

```
2F7C:0100   C5 D0 D3 C6 1E 00 00 00-BB AA 00 00 00 00 00 00    EPSF....;*......
2F7C:0110   00 00 00 00 D9 AA 00 00-F1 CA 00 00 FF FF 25 21    ....Y*..qJ....%!
2F7C:0120   50 53 2D 41 64 6F 62 65-2D 32 2E 30 20 45 50 53    PS-Adobe-2.0 EPS
2F7C:0130   46 2D 31 2E 32 0D 25 25-43 72 65 61 74 6F 72 3A    F-1.2.%%Creator:
2F7C:0140   20 41 64 6F 62 65 20 49-6C 6C 75 73 74 72 61 74     Adobe Illustrat
2F7C:0150   6F 72 20 38 38 28 54 4D-29 20 31 2E 36 0D 25 25    or 88(TM) 1.6.%%
2F7C:0160   46 6F 72 3A 20 28 44 72-65 61 64 4C 6F 72 64 29    For: (DreadLord)
2F7C:0170   20 28 4E 65 74 68 65 72-73 75 63 68 29 0D 25 25     (Nethersuch).%%
```

Fig 7-7   The EPSF header

```
typedef struct {
        char epsf[4];
        long ps_start;
        long ps_size;
        long meta_start;
        long meta_size;
        long tiff_start;
        long tiff_size;
        int checksum;
} EPSFHEAD;
```

Otherwise it will contain the number of bytes between the start of the file and the first byte of the TIFF image.

To read the TIFF preview, then, all the reader has to do is to read in the EPSF header and seek to the start of the TIFF file. However, because a TIFF file has a number of things in it that are placed relative to the start of the image file, it's necessary to add the offset found in the EPSF header to any values used with fseek when the TIFF file is being decoded. This value is stored in imageStart in the program—it remains 0L if the TIFF viewer is compiled with PREVIEW set false, that is, to view normal TIFF files.

Figure 7-8 illustrates an Adobe Illustrator image being created on a Macintosh. Illustrator on the Mac is kind enough to create EPS files complete with TIFF previews for PC applications if you ask it to.

If this picture is printed out, it looks like the one in Fig. 7-9. The zebra actually started life as a TIFF file that was traced with Adobe Streamline on the Macintosh to make it into a PostScript graphic.

Finally, Fig. 7-10 is the TIFF preview that Illustrator added to the EPS file it exported for use with PC applications. The EPS file itself had previously found its way to a PC over a local area network. This is what you'd see if you viewed the EPS file with the TIFF viewer in Fig. 7-4 with the PREVIEW define set true.

Encapsulated PostScript files with previews suitable for peeking at with the program in Fig. 7-4 need not come from a Macintosh. All sorts of PC-based applications can create them, including Micrographix Designer, Adobe Illustrator for Windows, and Corel Draw. In Chapter 10 you'll see how to create EPS files with previews for yourself.

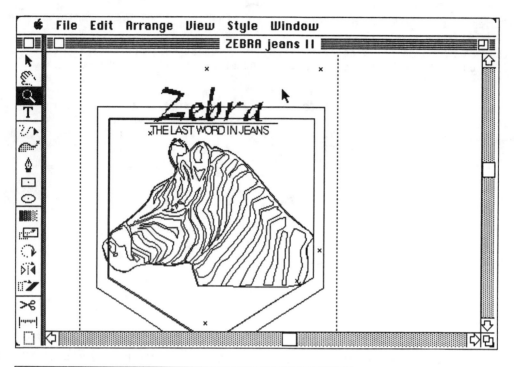

Fig 7-8 ABOVE
An EPS file being created in Adobe
Illustrator on a Macintosh

Fig 7-9 RIGHT
The actual EPS image

Fig 7-10 LEFT
The TIFF preview from the EPS file

If you use an application such as Corel Draw and frequently export EPS files for use in desktop publishing, you might want to compile a version of the TIFF viewer with PREVIEW set true and keep it handy. It's a great deal easier to use the TIFF viewer to see what's in a mystery EPS file than it is to boot up Windows and, in turn, Corel Draw.

COLOR *TIFF* FILES

If you peek ahead you'll notice that this discussion of color TIFF files is short to the point of nonexistence. TIFF files can do first rate color, but it's almost useless in a PC environment as of this writing. The TIFF format attempts to describe color in a manner similar to the idealized color display that was described and discarded in Chapter 4 as being impractical.

The current version of TIFF offers no way to define a color palette. Instead, it lets you create a color image with a red, green, and blue percentage value for each pixel. By using the BitsPerSample tag you can even define what resolution you want for the color percentages.

This is the best way to handle color, of course. Regrettably, the affordable display cards available for a PC—VGA cards—require the use of palettes and no more than 256 unique colors per image. There are lots of ways to interpret a color TIFF image for use on a VGA card, but these are beyond the scope of this book. Software that can group similar colors together to derive a 256-color palette from a complex picture is extremely sophisticated.

Color TIFF files are largely a Macintosh phenomenon. Color display boards are available for the Macintosh II that can handle 24-bit color, making the high end color capabilities of TIFF files useful in this context.

PACKING *TIFF* FILES

Creating a TIFF file from scratch is infinitely easier than trying to read TIFF images generated by another application. In writing a TIFF file you get to hold all the cards. You can decide on the number format, which tags to use, how to compress the image, and so on.

Most of the complexities of the TIFF format are ignored easily when you're writing a TIFF file encoder. In fact, the flexibility of the format that is a bit frustrating in decoding TIFF files is a positive asset in writing them. There are lots of ways to handle most functions and you're free to pick the ones that best suit you.

Writing a TIFF file usually will involve a certain amount of seeking around in the file to fill in fields that could not have been known earlier. In devising a strategy for creating a TIFF file, one good criteria is to minimize this as much as possible. Seeking around in a file is relatively slow.

The example program to be discussed illustrates one way of creating a TIFF file. You probably can come up with all sorts of good reasons for ing some of the elements differently. The TIFF format gives you the flexibility to do this.

The program in Fig. 7-11 is a variation on the image fragment packing program that appeared in Chapter 3. It takes the same getimage fragment, but creates a TIFF file rather than an IMG file.

Fig 7-11   A program to pack a monochrome getimage fragment into a TIFF file

```c
/* a program to pack a getimage fragment into a TIFF file */
#include "stdio.h"
#include "alloc.h"
#include "tiff.h"

#define size        (wide * pixels2bytes(deep))

char bin_file[80];      /* buffers for file names */
char tif_file[80];

int wide,deep,bytes;    /* global size values */

main(argc,argv)
        int argc;
        char *argv[];
{
        FILE *source,*dest;
        char *p,b[4];

        if(argc > 1) {
                /* make file names */
                strmfe(bin_file,argv[1],"BIN");
                strmfe(tif_file,argv[1],"TIF");

                /* open the source file */
                if((source=fopen(bin_file,"rb")) != NULL) {

                        /* create the destination file */
                        if((dest=fopen(tif_file,"wb")) != NULL) {

                                /* read in the size */
                                if(fread(b,1,4,source)==4) {

                                        /* and get it from the buffer */
                                        wide = b[0]+(b[1]<<8)+1;
                                        deep = b[2]+(b[3]<<8)+1;
                                        bytes = pixels2bytes(wide);

                                        /* allocate an image buffer */
                                        if((p=malloc(size)) != NULL) {

                                                /* read in the image */
                                                if(fread(p,1,size,source)
                                                    == size) {
                                                        invert(p,size);
```

Fig 7-11   continued

```
                                                  printf("Packing image"
                                                      " %d by %d "
                                                      "pixels\n",
                                                     wide,deep);

                                                  /* pack the image */
                                                  PackTifFile(dest,p);
                                     } else
                                         printf("Error reading %s\n"
                                             ,bin_file);
                                     free(p);
                                 } else puts("Error allocating memory");
                     } else puts("Error reading header");
                     fclose(dest);
                     } else printf("Error creating %s\n",tif_file);
                     fclose(source);
                 } else printf("Error opening %s\n",bin_file);
         } else puts("I need an argument");
     }

     /* pack in image into a TIFF file */
     PackTifFile(fp,p)
         FILE *fp;
         char *p;
     {
         int i;

         /* write the header */
         WriteTifHeader(fp);
         /* pack the lines */
         for(i=0;i<deep;++i) WriteTifLine(p+(i*bytes),fp,bytes);
         /* write the dictionary */
         WriteTifDict(fp);
     }

     /* write a TIFF header */
     WriteTifHeader(fp)
         FILE *fp;
     {
         fputWord(fp,'II');              /* intel packing */
         fputWord(fp,42);           /* version 42 */
         fputLong(fp,0L);           /* filler for offset */
     }

     /* write a TIFF IFD */
     WriteTifDict(fp)
         FILE *fp;
     {
         long l;

         /* remember where we parked */
         l=ftell(fp);
```

```
        /* there will be six tags */
        fputWord(fp,6);

        /* write the tags */
        WriteTifTag(fp,ImageWidth,TIFFshort,0L,(long)wide);
        WriteTifTag(fp,ImageLength,TIFFshort,0L,(long)deep);
        WriteTifTag(fp,BitsPerSample,TIFFshort,0L,1L);
        WriteTifTag(fp,Compression,TIFFshort,0L,(long)COMPmpnt);
        WriteTifTag(fp,PhotometricInterp,TIFFshort,0L,1L);
        WriteTifTag(fp,StripOffsets,TIFFlong,1L,8L);
        /* you might want to add some more tags - consider
           including your name, birthday or Compu$erve
           ID in your TIFF files */

        /* point to offset field of header */
        fseek(fp,4L,SEEK_SET);

        /* point to the start of the IFD */
        fputWord(fp,1);
}
/* write one TIFF tag to the IFD */
WriteTifTag(fp,tag,type,length,offset)
        FILE *fp;
        int tag,type;
        long length,offset;
{
        fputWord(fp,tag);
        fputWord(fp,type);
        fputLong(fp,length);
        fputLong(fp,offset);
}

/* write a TIFF line - MacPaint compression */
writeTifLine(p,fp,n)
        char *p;
        FILE *fp;
        int n;
{
        char b[72];
        unsigned int bdex=0,i=0,j=0,t=0;

        do {
                i=0;
                while((p[t+i]==p[t+i+1]) && i < (n-1) && ((t+i) < 71)) ++i;
                if(i > 0 || bdex >= 71) {

                        /* check for a previous string */
                        if(bdex) {
                                fputc(((bdex-1) & 0x7f),fp);
                                j+=1;
                                fwrite(b,1,bdex,fp);
                                j+=bdex;
                                bdex=0;
                        }
```

Fig 7-11   continued

```
                        if(i) {

                                   /*...and then write the run */
                                   fputc((~i+1),fp);
                                   fputc(p[t+i],fp);
                                   j+=2;
                                   t+=(i+1);
                        }
                   } else b[bdex++]=p[t++];
          } while(t<n);

          /* check for any pending strings */
          if(bdex) {
                  fputc(((bdex-1) & 0x7f),fp);
                  j+=1;
                  fwrite(b,1,bdex,fp);
                  j+=bdex;
                  bdex=0;
          }

          /* now this is a bit questionable. in theory it shouldn't
             matter whether the lines end on even word boundaries,
             but quite a few TIFF readers complain if they don't. */
          if(j & 1) fputc(0x80,fp);
          return(ferror(fp));
}

/* make a new file name with a fixed extension */
strmfe(new,old,ext)
       char *new,*old,*ext;
{
       while(*old != 0 && *old != '.') *new++=*old++;
       *new++='.';
       while(*ext) *new++=*ext++;
       *new=0;
}

/* return number of bytes in number of pixels */
pixels2bytes(n)
       int n;
{
       if(n & 0x0007) return((n >> 3) + 1);
       else return(n >> 3);
}

fputWord(fp,n)                    /* write one word to the file */
       FILE *fp;
       int n;
{
       fputc(n,fp);
       fputc((n >> 8),fp);
}
```

```
fputLong(fp,n)                 /* write one long to the file */
        FILE *fp;
        long n;
{
        fputc(n,fp);
        fputc((n >> 8),fp);
        fputc((n >> 16),fp);
        fputc((n >> 24),fp);
}

invert(p,n)
        char *p;
        unsigned int n;
{
        int i;

        for(i=0;i<n;++i) p[i]=~p[i];
}
```

The file that this program creates will have a very simple structure. The first thing in it will be a TIFF header. This file uses the Intel number format, so the first two bytes of the header will be "II."

The long integer in the header that points to the image file directory is left blank at first. A long zero is written to it to keep its place. At the moment the eventual position of the image file directory can't be known.

It's questionable whether it's best to put the image or the image file directory immediately after the header. In this case, the image data won the toss. More complex TIFF files might have several chunks of data to contend with—perhaps a few ASCII strings as well as the compressed picture—in which case placing the data before the image file directory that will address it saves a considerable amount of seeking around in the file.

The image data is compressed using the WriteTifLine function, which is simply the MacPaint compression routine lifted from Chapter 2.

You will note that the image is inverted up in the main function. This makes it display correctly in TIFF readers that ignore the photometric interpretation tag. You probably will want to dispense with this in most serious TIFF programs.

Writing the image file directory actually is simple. It's handled by the WriteTifDict function. The first thing it does is to use ftell to record where the file pointer is so the offset field of the file header eventually can be filled in. It then writes the number of tags to be placed in the directory, six in this case, and finally handles the tags themselves.

The tags shown here are the basic ones needed to create an image. There are quite a few others that you could add if you felt like it. For example, you might want to figure out what would be involved in modifying this program to include the data and a tag for an imaginary scanner manufacturer.

The StripOffsets tag defines the offset as being 8L, that is, it says that the image data starts eight bytes into the file. It knows this because the image data was written immediately after the TIFF header, which is 8 bytes long. If the image file directory had come first the value for this tag would have depended on the current file position as well as the number of remaining tags, if any.

The last thing this function does is to seek back to the long integer in the header—four bytes into the file—and write the offset value that will point to the image file directory.

This example program has created its TIFF file by writing all the elements directly to the disk. If your application calls for generating moderate size TIFF files you might be able to work entirely in memory, only writing the file out to disk when it's complete. This is a great deal easier and faster, although it places considerable restrictions on the size of the TIFF files you can work with.

FAREWELL TO *TIFF*

TIFF files will again rear their heads in Chapter 10 when encapsulated PostScript previews turn up. The TIFF file viewer discussed here actually is a very useful tool in debugging programs that create EPS files, because it lets you see if the preview part of an EPS file has been properly assembled.

TIFF files offer considerable room for experimentation.

8
CHAPTER

High-Speed Monochrome Sreen Drivers

Never allow a computer to know you're in a hurry.
—Murphy's Laws of Computers

The problem of unpacking bit-mapped images is in many ways analogous to that of displaying them. In both cases, one is confronted not so much with a lack of programming as with poor documentation—or documentation written in Sanskrit, which amounts to the same thing. The functions that have been discussed in conjunction with unpacking images consisted of some rather esoteric code at times, but there was fairly little of it. The code to drive a graphics screen is even more sparse—and perhaps still more esoteric.

Until now, fairly little has been said about how the various display cards used in PC compatible computers work. The only one that has come up has been the EGA card, and that only because it's exceedingly simple. In most of the examples thus far, the work has been done either by higher level language code—the trusty putimage function—or by object modules borrowed from the next chapter.

There are several good reasons for wanting to do away with putimage in writing programs that work with large bit-mapped images. To begin with, it's slow. One of the features of putimage is its ability to place bit-mapped fragments anywhere on the screen, ignoring the byte boundaries that actually comprise a screen image. As such, it does a lot of figuring every time it goes to modify the screen buffer, figuring which is unnecessary for the applications in this book.

In addition to this, putimage requires that the image data to be displayed be converted into its image fragment format, which is both time and memory consuming. It imposes limitations on the amount of data that can be written to the screen at once, 64k in this case. Finally, putimage is nonportable—it only exists in Turbo C. Many other compilers have equivalent functions, but with at least minor lexical differences. Translating a Turbo C program that incorporates it into a program for another C compiler—Microsoft C, for example—would require at least some "retouching."

The putimage function really wasn't written to do the tasks it has been pressed into service for thus far. Compilers call for dedicated screen drivers that have been optimized for the single function of updating the entire screen from an image buffer very quickly.

This chapter will look at high speed monochrome screen drivers, with color drivers being left until the next chapter. Many of the concepts that are easy to understand in looking at monochrome screen driver code carry over—in rather more complex forms—into color.

The primary consideration in writing graphics screen drivers is that they be fast. As such, the primary functions in the next two chapters will be written largely in assembly language to be interfaced to C code. Some of the ancillary functions can be handled in either language, and will be presented here in both.

The screen driver function in this chapter is listed here as a complete assembly language program, all ready to assemble and link to a C language application. This file is called MONOSCR.ASM, producing MONOSCR.OBJ. Later assembly language functions in the chapter are listed only as functions—you will want to add them to the MONOSCR.ASM file as you go.

MONOCHROME DISPLAY CARDS

One of the primary difficulties in writing a monochrome screen driver is that it has to drive a number of cards, many of which are uncomfortably peculiar internally. The first generation cards for the PC are very strange, which manages to complicate the strategy for driving them in their graphics modes considerably. In addition, just about every meaningful parameter varies from card to card.

This discussion will encompass four popular display cards that support monochrome graphics. These are the CGA card (or color card), the Hercules card, the EGA card, and the VGA card. In fact, each of these has a few addenda associated with it.

The CGA card was the first PC display card to have any sort of graphics facilities at all. It actually supports two graphics modes. Its medium resolution mode features a 320-by-200-pixel screen in four colors. The colors are selected from two possible palettes, both of which are startlingly ugly. Medium resolution color card graphics are both difficult to code and so unpleasant to use as to prompt no further discussion of them.

The high resolution mode of the color card is arguably a bit more useful. It manages 640 by 200 pixels in two colors. This still isn't much of a display by contemporary standards, and most of the applications that still support this mode claim to do so for the sake of backward compatibility.

Hercules cards are a bit more useful, and in fact, the Hercules graphics display originally was designed because the graphics offered by CGA cards were so dreadful. A Hercules card offers 720 by 348 pixels in two colors. However, there's a bit more happening in a Herc card than there appears to be, inasmuch as there are actually two "pages" of graphic information in a Hercules card's video buffer. Either page can be made visible. As such, you can store two distinct screens in a Hercules card and flip between them in hardware. This will be discussed later in this chapter.

The EGA card isn't a monochrome card at all—it's a 16-color display card that is structured to allow one to easily ignore 14 of those colors. It lends itself to being used as a high-speed monochrome display for this reason.

The quick 'n nasty C language EGA drivers that appeared in the earlier programs in this book make a fairly elegant formal driver when they're transliterated into assembly language.

Finally, VGA cards usually are associated with 256 color images, but they actually have a variety of modes. One of these is a seldom used 640-by-480-pixel two color mode, making a VGA card capable of displaying the highest resolution of any of the cards to be discussed here. This mode turns out to be easy to access and very simple to drive.

Most super VGA cards have enhanced monochrome modes as well as enhanced color ones. This chapter will discuss the 800-by-600-pixel mode of the Paradise Plus card as an example of how these are handled.

The problem in writing a driver for monochrome graphics is that it must not only be able to drive each of these cards effectively, but that it must handle them all. The ideal driver would be *device independent*. You should be able to hand it a bitmap and have it figure out which sort of screen it's driving and what to do with the data. In fact, this turns out to be fairly easy to accomplish.

This sort of device independence also makes it relatively easy to add other display types to the above list. If you have one of the more esoteric display systems—a full page desktop publishing monitor, for example—you will find that modifying the driver to be discussed here to accommodate it will be pretty easy.

The only catch to the preceding rather bold statement is that getting the working details of such displays out of their respective manufacturers is often a lot more work than is actually writing the requisite code.

Where the Lines Go

The way in which the various display cards function is basically the same. They are all *memory mapped devices*, that is, they appear to your

PC as addressable memory just like normal program memory does. You could—at least in theory—load a program into the screen buffer of your display card and execute it there. This is not a very good idea in practice.

The difference between program memory and display memory is that display memory has some extra hardware that watches it and makes things happen on your monitor as a result of the contents of this memory. The nature of these "things" varies with the mode your card is in at the time. If it's in text mode, the hardware watches about 4k of display memory and puts text on your screen. If it's in a graphics mode, it watches a lot more memory and interprets what it finds there as bit-mapped graphics.

In most cases, the text memory and the graphics memory are actually the same memory.

Each of the cards to be discussed keeps its display memory at a particular memory segment and, of course, each one uses a different segment. There is no particularly good reason for this, but it's the way things are and programmers who write code to drive these cards are stuck with it.

Changing the data in a card's display buffer causes the hardware watching it to change the display on the screen.

To begin with, let's discuss the problem of writing a driver for the most elderly of the monochrome cards, the CGA and Hercules displays. These two cards are the crankiest of the lot, and ultimately will help explain the best way to write a high speed screen driver.

At the time the CGA and Hercules cards were designed, there was very little large scale integration around. Just about everything was done with discrete logic—this included both display cards and the computers that drove them. The motherboards of early PC's were rippling seas of small chips.

Restricted to simple logic devices, the designers of these cards were unable to implement particularly elegant memory decoding for the graphics buffers of their displays. Consider that neither 80 or 90—the number of bytes in one line of graphics information for a CGA and a Herc card, respectively—is a nice round number for a computer.

Hardware designers have no idea why the sky is blue—the color of the sky is a software problem. Likewise, the way the graphics got written to these early display cards was left to the people who developed code.

If you use an EGA or VGA card and want to see if the following rather obtuse examples really work, you can force your card into CGA emulation mode to try them out.

A CGA card behaves rather peculiarly in its monochrome graphics mode. Its screen buffer lives at segment 0B800H, just like its text buffer. Each line is 640 pixels—or 80 bytes—long. If you were to execute the following line of code with the card in its monochrome graphics mode, a white line would appear at the top of the screen.

```
memset(MK_FP(0xb800,0),0xff,80);
```

This bit of code simply creates a pointer to the base of the graphics buffer using the MK_FP function and then sets the first 80 bytes to 0xff, that is, so that all their pixels are all on.

This version sets the following eighty bytes on.

```
memset(MK_FP(0xb800,80),0xff,80);
```

If you guess that this second line will not result in the second line on your screen turning white, you have the making of a first class programmer. In fact, it will result in a line part way down the screen lighting up.

Because of the limited hardware available to them at the time, the designers of the CGA card were unable to arrive at a linear memory arrangement for the graphic buffer. The lines of memory in the buffer do not have a one-to-one relationship with the lines as they appear on your screen. This is often referred to as *interleaving* the lines. Describing the process thus makes it sound like it was intentional, rather than just a byproduct.

Needless to say, the relationship of the screen memory to the screen display does follow a logic of sorts, if not a terribly convenient one. In the case of the color card, this works as follows: If the line number is even, the start of the line is 8192 bytes further into the graphics buffer than it would be if the line number was odd.

If p is a pointer to a bit-mapped image and bytes is the width of the image in bytes, the following bit of code will copy 200 lines of the image to a CGA card, albeit rather slowly.

```
int i;
for(i = 0;i < 200; + + i)
     memcpy(MK_FP(0xb800,(0x2000 * (i%2)) + (80*(i/2))),p + (i*bytes),bytes);
```

The rather nasty looking calculation in the memcpy function works out the offset for each line based on the real line number in i. This is the major reason that this program is so slow. Multiplication—even integer multiplication—is one of the most time-consuming operations a PC can do.

The Hercules card has a similar interleaved memory arrangement, although it doesn't work in quite the same way. The lines are 90 bytes long, rather than 80, the screen memory starts at segment 0B000H—at least, some of the time—and the interleave itself is different. In this case, the screen buffer is interleaved four times, rather than twice.

The following bit of code will copy the first 348 lines of a bitmap at p into a Hercules card's graphics buffer. This assumes that page zero of the graphics buffer is active at the moment. The card defaults to this state—graphics pages will be discussed at greater length in a while.

```
int i;

for(i = 0;i < 200; + + i)
     memcpy(MK_FP(0xb000,(0x2000 * (i%4)) + (90*(i/4))),p + (i*bytes),bytes);
```

The ideal driver would be one that would drive each of these display cards and could do so without having to perform these complicated calculations for each line. In fact, this can be arrived at, if in a rather obtuse way.

Line Start Tables

There are only 200 possible values that can be returned by the calculation involved in locating the line starts for the CGA card—there being only 200 legal line numbers. Likewise, there are only 348 possible values for the Hercules card calculation.

Each of the numbers returned by these calculations is, in fact, the number of bytes from the beginning of the buffer and the start of the memory in question that holds the line data, that is, the buffer offset. Because neither of these buffers is larger than 64k, unsigned integers will suffice to hold these offset, or *line start*, values.

Assuming that the application that ultimately will be updating the screen intends to do so several times, you could save considerable time by performing these calculations once and then storing their results in a table.

The table would work like this:

```
int i,table[200];

for(i=0;i<200;++i) table[i] = (0x2000 * (i%2)) + (80*(i/2));
```

In order to update the screen, then, you could do this:

```
int i;

for(i=0;i<200;++i)
    memcpy(MK_FP(0xb800,table[i],p+(i*bytes),bytes);
```

Using this system, virtually all of the complex calculations are done first and saved in the table. The second code fragment, the one that actually updates the screen, does little more than extract entries from the table.

If the object of this chapter had been to write a driver in C, rather than in assembly language, this could have been improved upon by using a table of pointers rather than integers. However, the approach illustrated here is more in keeping with the way the eventual machine language driver will work.

Consider that the only things that make this example dependent on a CGA card are the table, the screen segment, and the screen dimensions. Let's rewrite it slightly with variables for these values:

```
for(i=0;i<SCREENDEEP;++i)
    memcpy(MK_FP(SCREENSEG,table[i],p+(i*bytes),bytes);
```

This code fragment will drive either a CGA or a Hercules card, depending upon how the table and the other variables are set up. In fact, it also will drive an EGA card and virtually any other monochrome graphics display.

The line start table, or *lookup table*, is a powerful tool in trading code size for speed. It unquestionably takes more room—to accommodate the 640-by-480-line display of a VGA card in its monochrome mode, 960 bytes must be tied up in the table—but it allows for almost instantaneous screen updates.

Linear Display Memory

The EGA and VGA cards feature linear display memory, that is, the order of the lines on the screen correspond to the order of the lines in the display memory. This makes designing a driver for them a lot simpler. However, such a driver would still require some calculations for each line, so it's desirable to make it table driven even if you don't care about supporting the CGA and Hercules cards.

Pretty well all present generation graphics display cards use linear memory addressing, and working out how to drive them in the absence of any more concrete documentation is pretty easy if you assume this. The monochrome VGA driver to be discussed in a moment was "deduced" in this way.

The area of the PC address bus available for video memory begins at segment 0A000H, and all of the more recent cards have started their buffers at this point. You can calculate the amount of memory each line will take by dividing the number of pixels in a line by eight. This will allow you to work out the calculations necessary to create a suitable table.

In the case of an EGA card, the code would work like this:

```
for (i = 0;i < 350; + +i) table[i] = i*80;
```

The table for 640-by-480-pixel monochrome VGA display would be the same, except that it would be calculated to 480 entries rather than to 350.

If you have one of the many "super" VGA cards, you might be able to write a driver to see even more pixels on your screen at once. The aforementioned Paradise Plus card, for example, has an 800-by-600-pixel monochrome mode when it's used with a multisync monitor. Super VGA drivers, however, represent a rather exotic and oftentimes frustrating area of programming. These modes are often wholly undocumented in the manual that comes with a VGA card—on the assumption that the users of the card would only be confused by hex numbers—and more detailed information is not always easy to pry out of hardware manufacturers.

Writing a Monochrome Super VGA Driver

The Paradise Plus card is better than most for hardware level documentation, in that Western Digital, its manufacturer, will send you some documentation if you write to the company. The sheets you'll get probably will be very nearly incomprehensible, but the information you need to program the card is in there if you dig deep enough.

It's actually possible to work out a monochrome super VGA driver in many cases without any documentation for the card in question. Monochrome graphics tend to function in pretty well the same way on all the super VGA boards. Super VGA color graphics are very much more problematic, as will be discussed in the next chapter.

In working through the logic for a monochrome driver for the Paradise Plus, you should be able to figure out the approach required for almost any other sort of monochrome display. The following bit of guessing and assumption was done without the assistance of anything beyond the users' manual that came with the card.

The only really important piece of information required to write a monochrome driver for the 800-by-600 mode of the Paradise Plus card is the procedure for putting it into the right mode. Because this is a specialized card, the Turbo C initgraph function does not support it. As such, your program will have to explicitly turn on the 800-by-600 mode if you want to use it.

This requires the use of a BIOS call, whether using the INT 10H instruction from assembly language or the int86 function under C. To switch modes using this interrupt, the AH register must contain zero and the AL register the number of the mode you want to use.

The Paradise documentation refers to the mode in question as "mode 59" in several places. It seems a reasonable guess that this refers to the BIOS function number that is used to switch the display into this mode. It's unclear whether this means 59 hex or 59 decimal. However, as the same manual refers to other mode numbers using letters—that is, in hex notation—you might start off with the assumption that it's in hex.

This does actually prove to be the case. If you run the following bit of C code with a Paradise Plus card in your computer, the screen will clear and the card will switch into its 800-by-600-pixel monochrome graphics mode:

```
union REGS r;

r.h.ah = 0;
r.h.al = 0x59;
int86(0x10,&r,&r);
```

Because the Paradise Plus card is a VGA display at heart, and as VGA cards place their graphics buffers at segment 0A000H for normal modes, it seems reasonable to assume that the graphics buffer for this mode will appear there too. Let's further assume that this uses linear memory addressing, rather than some unpleasant form of interleaving.

The number of bytes in a line is easy to work out. Because there are 800 pixels, one line must occupy 100 bytes. There are 600 such lines in the buffer, meaning that the memory buffer only occupies 60,000 bytes, that is, it fits in a single memory segment. This is quite important, because were it to require more than one segment the card probably would have to page memory on and off the bus. Without knowing how it does this, any attempt to write a driver deductively would be stumped.

This problem will come up for real in the next chapter.

With this information it's possible to write an experimental routine to drive the card. It's a lot easier to experiment in C, and because speed is not really important in this case, the trial code can be written using calculations for each line. The pointer p is assumed to point to a bitmap bytes wide:

```
int i;

for(i = 0;i < 600; + + i)
     memcpy(MK_FP(0xa000,i * 100)
          p + (i * bytes),bytes);
```

Needless to say this does actually work. If you have a different super VGA card with an 800-by-600-pixel monochrome mode, you'll probably find that it works for you as well. The only thing that probably will need changing is the mode number for switching into this mode.

Depending on your application, writing a driver for one of these super VGA modes can be well worth the effort. One rarely sees this much of a picture on a screen at once, and the results of doing so can look very slick indeed. Figure 8-1 illustrates the varying screen dimensions of the cards that have been discussed thus far.

Supporting Multiple Display Types

It's more or less practical to write a monochrome screen driver that can detect which sort of card it's expected to drive when the choices are fairly few. For example, you easily can write a function to determine the type of card being used when you know that it must be either a CGA, EGA, or Hercules card. With some slightly more clever programming, you can add stock VGA cards to this list.

As will be discussed later in this chapter, the computer that your program runs on will tell you a fair bit about the card it supports. For example, the text mode that the machine defaults to will be mode seven if the text screen is running with a Hercules card and something else if it's a CGA or EGA card. A bit of memory bashing will differentiate between a CGA and an EGA card, and so on.

Super VGA cards are not constrained to offer a program any clues as to their origin, although some do. The Paradise Plus card can be identified by looking for the string "VGA=" at memory location C000:007DH, for example. Even at that, however, many of the super VGA modes that the card can provide are dependent upon the sort of monitor that it's attached to, something the card itself does not know and, as such, can't tell programs that attempt to drive it.

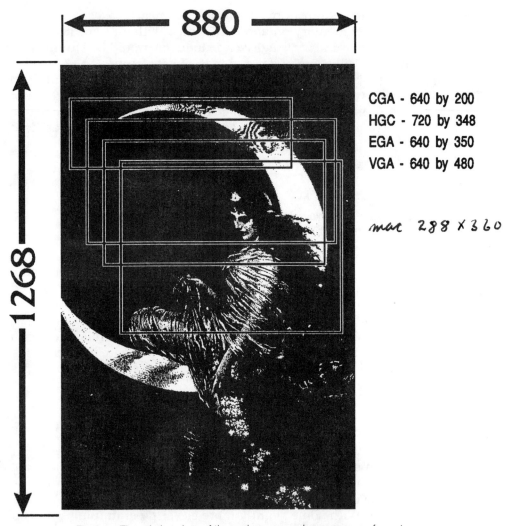

CGA - 640 by 200
HGC - 720 by 348
EGA - 640 by 350
VGA - 640 by 480

mac 288 X 360

Fig 8-1   The relative sizes of the various monochrome screen formats

It's not really practical to write a driver that can figure out which brand of super VGA card is being used and set itself up accordingly. If nothing else, it would entail your buying a lot of VGA cards. In practice, large applications that will drive multiple sorts of cards usually involve user definable options that allow the user of the program to specify which sort of display he or she owns.

WRITING THE DRIVER

In writing an assembly language function to update a graphics screen, the primary consideration is in making it fast. A few secondary things also apply. For example, it should be suitable for use with bitmaps of different sizes. As you will see in a moment, there are several potential catches in using images that are wider than the screen, ones that must be allowed for in the design of the code.

As you will realize by now, the machine language driver that does the actual screen updates never need know what sort of card it's driving. All of the hardware specific information is determined by the function that creates the line start table and loads the dependent variables, that is, the screen segment, the line width, and so on.

The table setup function could be written in C, with the address of the table and the other values passed to the assembly language function. However, it's just as easy to handle it in assembly language, and probably more elegant.

The variables in question can be declared PUBLIC in the assembly language module, and as extern in the C program that will link to it. As such, they can be accessed by both.

Figure 8-2 illustrates the complete assembly language module for driving the monochrome displays discussed thus far. This includes the Paradise Plus card, which you might or might not wish to use.

Fig 8-2   An assembly language screen driver for monochrome screens

```
                COMMENT +

                High speed monochrome screen driver
                Supports CGA, Hercules, EGA and MCGA
                in monocrome modes

                        +

_AOFF           EQU     6           ;STACK OFFSET TO FIRST ARG

CGA             EQU     1           ;THESE EQUATES ARE EQUIVALENT TO
MCGA            EQU     2           ;THE VALUES RETURNED BY THE
EGA             EQU     3           ;TURBO C DetectGraph FUNCTION
HERCMONO        EQU     7

PARADISE        EQU     59H         ;FAKE VALUE FOR PARADISE CARD

LARGEPIX        EQU     1           ;SET TRUE FOR SOURCE IMAGES > 64K

;THIS MACRO FETCHES THE DATA SEGEMENT
DATASEG         MACRO
                PUSH    AX
                MOV     AX,_DATA
                MOV     DS,AX
                POP     AX
                ENDM

MONOSCR_TEXT    SEGMENT BYTE PUBLIC 'CODE'
                ASSUME  CS:MONOSCR_TEXT,DS:_DATA
```

Fig 8-2   continued

```
;---------------------------------------------------------
;
;                 Display a bitmap
;                 Update(p,w,l);
;
;                 char *p;        /* pointer to bitmap */
;                 int w;          /* width in bytes    */
;                 int l;          /* number of lines   */

UPDATE_MOVE      EQU      2
UPDATE_PAD       EQU      4
UPDATE_ADJUST    EQU      6

                 PUBLIC  _Update
_Update          PROC     FAR
                 PUSH     BP
                 MOV      BP,SP
                 SUB      SP,UPDATE_ADJUST

                 DATASEG
                 MOV      ES,_SCREENSEG         ;POINT TO THE SCREEN

                 MOV      AX,[BP + _AOFF + 4]   ;GET THE WIDTH OF MOVE
                 MOV      [BP - UPDATE_MOVE],AX ;SAVE IT LOCALLY

                 MOV      WORD PTR [BP - UPDATE_PAD],0    ;SET ADJUSTMENT

                 CMP      AX,_SCREENBYTES       ;IF THE MOVE IS LESS THAN
                 JL       UPDATE0               ;SCREEN WIDTH, GO FOR IT
                 SUB      AX,_SCREENBYTES       ;ELSE, SET MOVE WIDTH
                 MOV      [BP - UPDATE_PAD],AX  ;...AND THE AMOUNT TO

                 MOV      AX,_SCREENBYTES       ;...ADJUST THE POINTER
                 MOV      [BP - UPDATE_MOVE],AX ;...AFTER EACH LINE

UPDATE0:         MOV      SI,[BP + _AOFF + 0]   ;OFFSET OF BITMAP
                 MOV      DS,[BP + _AOFF + 2]   ;SEGMENT OF BITMAP
                 MOV      CX,[BP + _AOFF + 6]   ;NUMBER OF LINES

                 CLD                            ;CLEAR DIRECTION FLAG
                 SUB      BX,BX                  ;ZERO THE COUNTER

UPDATE1:         PUSH     CX                     ;SAVE COUNT (LINE NUMBER)

                 PUSH     DS                     ;SAVE THE DATA SEGMENT
                 MOV      AX,_DATA
                 MOV      DS,AX                  ;POINT TO THE LOCAL DATA
                 MOV      DI,DS:[_SCREENTBL + BX]
                 ADD      BX,2                   ;POINT TO NEXT LINE
                 POP      DS

                 MOV      CX,[BP - UPDATE_MOVE]  ;GET THE MOVE SIZE
         REPNE   MOVSB                           ;DO THE MOVE
```

```
                ADD       SI,[BP - UPDATE_PAD]      ;ADJUST THE POINTER

                IF        LARGEPIX
                CMP       SI,0F800H                 ;ARE WE WITHIN 2K OF TOP?
                JL        UPDATE2                   ;IF NOT, CARRY ON

                MOV       AX,SI                     ;SEE HOW MANY SEGMENTS ARE
                MOV       CL,4                      ;...IN SI (SI DIV 4)
                SHR       AX,CL

                MOV       CX,DS                     ;ADD THEM TO THE DATA SEGMENT
                ADD       CX,AX                     ;...(YOU CAN'T JUST ADD DS,AX)
                MOV       DS,CX
                AND       SI,000FH                  ;ADJUST SI (SI MOD 16)
                ENDIF     ;LARGEPIX

UPDATE2:        POP       CX                        ;GET COUNT BACK
                LOOP      UPDATE1                   ;DECREMENT AND LOOP

                DATASEG

                ADD       SP,UPDATE_ADJUST
                POP       BP
                RET

_Update         ENDP

;-------------------------------------------------------
;
;               Set up the screen table
;               DoTable(n);
;               int n;          /* card number */
;
                PUBLIC    _DoTable
_DoTable        PROC      FAR
                PUSH      BP
                MOV       BP,SP

                DATASEG

                CMP       WORD PTR [BP + _AOFF + 0],CGA
                JNE       NOT_CGA                   ;CHECK CARD TYPE

                ;IT'S A CGA CARD
                MOV       _SCREENSEG,0B800H
                MOV       _SCREENBYTES,80
                MOV       _SCREENWIDE,640
                MOV       _SCREENDEEP,200

                MOV       CX,_SCREENDEEP
                SUB       DX,DX
                MOV       SI,OFFSET _SCREENTBL

CTB0:           PUSH      CX
```

Fig 8-2   continued

```
                PUSH    DX
                MOV     AX,_SCREENBYTES ;AX = WIDTH OF TUBE
                MOV     BX,DX           ;BX =
                MOV     CL,1            ;
                SHR     BX,CL           ; ... LINE NUMBER DIV 4
                PUSH    DX
                MUL     BX              ;MUL WIDTH OF SCREEN
                MOV     DI,AX           ;DI IS NOW THE PARTIAL OFFSET
                POP     DX

                SUB     DH,DH           ;
                MOV     AX,2000H        ;MULTIPLY DX MOD 4 BY 2000H
                AND     DX,1
                MUL     DX
                ADD     DI,AX           ;ADD TO THE OFFSET
                POP     DX
                POP     CX

                MOV     BX,DX           ;AND PUT IT IN THE TABLE
                SHL     BX,1
                MOV     [SI+BX],DI
                INC     DX
                LOOP    CTB0
                SUB     AX,AX           ;EVERYTHING'S FINE
                JMP     TABLE_OK

NOT_CGA:        CMP     WORD PTR [BP + _AOFF + 0],EGA
                JNE     NOT_EGA

                ;IT'S AN EGA CARD
                MOV     _SCREENSEG,0A000H
                MOV     _SCREENBYTES,80
                MOV     _SCREENWIDE,640
                MOV     _SCREENDEEP,350

                MOV     CX,_SCREENDEEP
                SUB     DX,DX
                MOV     SI,OFFSET _SCREENTBL

ETB0:           PUSH    DX
                MOV     AX,_SCREENBYTES
                MUL     DX
                MOV     [SI],AX
                ADD     SI,2
                POP     DX
                INC     DX
                LOOP    ETB0
                SUB     AX,AX           ;EVERYTHING'S FINE
                JMP     TABLE_OK

NOT_EGA:        CMP     WORD PTR [BP + _AOFF + 0],MCGA
                JNE     NOT_MCGA
```

```
                    ;IT'S AN MCGA CARD
                    MOV     _SCREENSEG,0A000H
                    MOV     _SCREENBYTES,80
                    MOV     _SCREENWIDE,640
                    MOV     _SCREENDEEP,480

                    MOV     CX,_SCREENDEEP
                    SUB     DX,DX
                    MOV     SI,OFFSET _SCREENTBL

MTB0:               PUSH    DX
                    MOV     AX,_SCREENBYTES
                    MUL     DX
                    MOV     [SI],AX
                    ADD     SI,2
                    POP     DX
                    INC     DX
                    LOOP    MTB0
                    SUB     AX,AX             ;EVERYTHING'S FINE
                    JMP     TABLE_OK

NOT_MCGA:           CMP     WORD PTR [BP + _AOFF + 0],HERCMONO
                    JNE     NOT_HERCMONO

                    ;IT'S A HERCULES CARD
                    MOV     _SCREENSEG,0B000H
                    MOV     _SCREENBYTES,90
                    MOV     _SCREENWIDE,720
                    MOV     _SCREENDEEP,348

                    MOV     CX,_SCREENDEEP
                    SUB     DX,DX
                    MOV     SI,OFFSET _SCREENTBL

HTB0:               PUSH    CX
                    PUSH    DX
                    MOV     AX,_SCREENBYTES ;AX = WIDTH OF TUBE
                    MOV     BX,DX           ;BX =
                    MOV     CL,2            ;
                    SHR     BX,CL           ; ... LINE NUMBER DIV 4
                    PUSH    DX
                    MUL     BX              ;MUL WIDTH OF SCREEN
                    MOV     DI,AX           ;DI IS NOW THE PARTIAL OFFSET
                    POP     DX
                    SUB     DH,DH           ;
                    MOV     AX,2000H        ;MULTIPLY DX MOD 4 BY 2000H
                    AND     DX,3
                    MUL     DX
                    ADD     DI,AX           ;ADD TO THE OFFSET
                    POP     DX
                    POP     CX

                    MOV     SI,OFFSET _SCREENTBL
                    MOV     BX,DX
```

Fig 8-2   continued

```
                SHL     BX,1
                MOV     [SI+BX],DI
                INC     DX
                LOOP    HTB0
                SUB     AX,AX             ;EVERYTHING'S FINE
                JMP     TABLE_OK

NOT_HERCMONO:   CMP     WORD PTR [BP + _AOFF + 0],PARADISE
                JNE     NOT_PARADISE

                ;IT'S A PARADISE CARD
                MOV     _SCREENSEG,0A000H
                MOV     _SCREENBYTES,100
                MOV     _SCREENWIDE,800
                MOV     _SCREENDEEP,600

                MOV     CX,_SCREENDEEP
                SUB     DX,DX
                MOV     SI,OFFSET _SCREENTBL

PTB0:           PUSH    DX
                MOV     AX,_SCREENBYTES
                MUL     DX
                MOV     [SI],AX
                ADD     SI,2
                POP     DX
                INC     DX
                LOOP    PTB0
                SUB     AX,AX             ;EVERYTHING'S FINE
                JMP     TABLE_OK

NOT_PARADISE:   MOV     AX,-1

TABLE_OK:       POP     BP
                RET
_DoTable        ENDP

MONOSCR_TEXT    ENDS

DGROUP          GROUP   _DATA,_BSS
_DATA           SEGMENT WORD PUBLIC 'DATA'

                PUBLIC  _SCREENTBL
                PUBLIC  _SCREENSEG,_SCREENBYTES
                PUBLIC  _SCREENWIDE,_SCREENDEEP

;BUFFER FOR SCREEN POSITION TABLE
_SCREENTBL      DW      600 DUP(?)        ;MAXIMUM LINE COUNT
_SCREENSEG      DW      ?                 ;POINTER TO SCREEN
_SCREENBYTES    DW      ?                 ;WIDTH OF SCREEN IN BYTES
_SCREENWIDE     DW      ?                 ;WIDTH OF SCREEN IN PIXELS
_SCREENDEEP     DW      ?                 ;DEPTH OF SCREEN IN PIXELS
```

```
_DATA          ENDS

_BSS           SEGMENT WORD PUBLIC 'BSS'

_BSS           ENDS

               END
```

This module provides two functions for a C program linked to it. The first is DoTable, which creates the line start table and sets up a few other important values. The second, Update, updates the screen with a bit-mapped image passed to it.

The DoTable function is incapable of figuring out which sort of card to create a table for. It must be told what to do. Later in this chapter we'll see how to let some software work this out, but for now it's convenient to use the mode values returned by the Turbo C detectgraph function. These are defined at the top of the file, and correspond to the constants in the Turbo C "graphics.h" header file. There is no detectgraph constant for the Paradise card's 800-by-600-pixel mode, so this program uses the mode number. In fact, all of these numbers are arbitrary—any values would have worked, so long as they were all different.

If you look at the code for DoTable you can see what this function is up to. It implements the machine language equivalent of a case statement, comparing the value passed to it from the calling C program with each of the card types defined at the top of the program. When it figures out which sort of card it's suppose to be working with, it sets the four global variables _SCREENSEG, _SCREENBYTES, _SCREENWIDE, and _SCREENDEEP appropriately. Obviously, _SCREENBYTES is just _SCREENWIDE divided by eight. It's quicker to do this calculation once and save it somewhere than it is to perform it each time the length of the screen line in bytes is needed.

The calculations for the line start tables are somewhat involved for the CGA and Hercules cards. They're quite simple for the others, because no interleaving is involved.

The really useful part of this code, Update, is a very simple routine. In fact, this is an essential element in its design—it does very little and as such does it very fast.

Passing a pointer to a bitmap, the loop in Update fetches each line, finds out where in the screen buffer it's to go based on the contents of the current line start table, and finally copies the line into the buffer using the string move instruction MOVSB.

If the bitmap passed to Update could be assumed to be the same size as the screen, much of the complexity of the Update code could be omitted. There are two potential catches in its design.

The MOVSB instruction increments both the SI and DI registers. The SI register points into the source bitmap, and the DI register into the screen buffer. If the code copies the entire bitmap to the screen, SI never need be adjusted, because the end of one line of the source image would leave off where the next line starts. In fact, simply allowing the code to copy each line to the buffer, regardless of its length, does work. If a source line is too long, it simply wraps to the next screen line and is subsequently overwritten.

This, however, entails copying more data to the screen buffer than is necessary, slowing down the routine somewhat. It also looks funny, because the screen flashes a lot if the ends of lines happen to have any white pixels in them.

The way around this is to only copy as many bytes as will fit on one line, and then to adjust SI to skip over the rest of the line. It would be unnecessarily time-consuming to do this calculation for each line, especially as the results would always be the same. As such, the two numbers are stored in stack variables—UPDATE_MOVE contains the number of bytes to move and UPDATE_PAD the number of bytes to add to SI at the end of each line. If the bitmap is narrower than the screen, UPDATE_PAD will contain zero and SI will not be adjusted.

You can see how these values are used down around the label UPDATE1.

This routine also can run into some very troubling pointer problems, especially when it's asked to deal with large images. Consider the following situation. In the Paradise 800-by-600-pixel mode, the screen requires 60,000 bytes of memory. This can be addressed by a single 16-bit pointer, if only just. However, if one were to use this routine to copy 600 lines of an image 2,000 pixels wide to the screen, the 600 lines of the image would occupy 150,000 bytes. Somewhere part way through the screen update, the SI register would wrap back to zero, and the bottom half of the screen would show a copy of the top half.

For this reason, it's necessary to adjust the DS:SI pointer to make sure that SI doesn't wrap. As you will recall from previous chapters, pointer adjustment isn't all that involved. If SI is greater than 16, the pointer can be adjusted by adding SI / 16 to DS and reducing SI to SI MOD 16, or SI AND 000FH.

It's not necessary to adjust the pointer each time it's used, but, rather, only when it gets to the point where it might wrap. In this routine, the pointer is adjusted when it gets within 2k, or 16,384 pixels, of the end of its range. This means that the routine will safely deal with images of up to 16,384 pixels across, which seems adequate.

THE C LANGUAGE CALLING PROGRAM

The machine language driver doesn't care about the original source of the bit-mapped images it updates the screen with, and you can apply it to any of the monochrome image formats discussed thus far. For this example, let's modify one of the earlier GEM/IMG file viewers to use this high-speed screen driver.

The program can be seen in Fig. 8-3. It looks a lot like the IMG file viewers discussed earlier in this book, except that the ShowImgPicture function is simply a call to the Update function provided by the assembly language screen driver.

Fig 8-3   An IMG viewer using the high-speed monochrome screen driver

```
/* A program to pan over big IMG pictures
   using an assembly language screen driver

   Must link to MONOSCR.OBJ

*/

#include "stdio.h"
#include "alloc.h"
#include "dos.h"
#include "graphics.h"

#define HOME            0x4700
#define CURSOR_UP       0x4800
#define CURSOR_LEFT     0x4b00
#define CURSOR_RIGHT    0x4d00
#define END             0x4f00
#define CURSOR_DOWN     0x5000

#define step            32
#define PARADISE        0x59

char header[16];                    /* where the header lives */
unsigned int width,depth;
unsigned int patternsize=1;
unsigned int bytes;
unsigned int pixels2bytes();
char *farPtr();

extern unsigned int SCREENTBL[];
extern unsigned int SCREENSEG,SCREENBYTES;      /* variables in */
extern unsigned int SCREENWIDE,SCREENDEEP;      /* MONOSCR.OBJ  */

main(argc,argv)
        int argc;
        char *argv[];
{
        FILE *fp;
        char *p;

        if(argc > 1) {
                /* attempt to open the file */
                if((fp=fopen(argv[1],"rb")) != NULL) {
                        /* read in the header */
                        if(fread(header,1,16,fp)==16) {
                                /* check to make sure it's a picture */
```

Fig 8-3   continued

```
                              if(!memcmp("\x00\x01\x00\x08\x00\x01",
                                   header,6)) {
                                   /* allocate a big buffer */
                                   patternsize = (header[7] & 0xff)+
                                        ((header[6] & 0xff)<<8);
                                   width = (header[13] & 0xff)+
                                        ((header[12] & 0xff)<<8);
                                   depth = (header[15] & 0xff)+
                                        ((header[14] & 0xff)<<8);
                                   bytes = pixels2bytes(width);

                                   if((p=farmalloc((long)bytes*
                                        (long)depth)) != NULL) {
                                        /* unpack the file */
                                        if(UnpackImgFile(p,fp)==bytes)
                                             /* show the picture */
                                             PanImgPicture(p);
                                        farfree(p);
                                   } else puts("Error allocating memory");
                              } else printf("Not an IMG file.\n");
                         } else printf("Error reading %s.\n",argv[1]);
                         fclose(fp);
                   } else printf("Error opening %s.\n",argv[1]);
         }
}

PanImgPicture(p)
         char *p;
{
         int c,x=0,y=0;

         /* graphics on */
         init();

         do {
                   ShowImgPicture(farPtr(p,((long)y*(long)bytes)+(long)(x>>3)));
                   switch(c=GetKey()) {
                   case CURSOR_LEFT:
                         if((x-step) > 0) x-=step;
                         else x=0;
                         break;
                   case CURSOR_RIGHT:
                         if((x+step+SCREENWIDE) < width) x+=step;
                         else if(width > SCREENWIDE) x=width-SCREENWIDE;
                         else x=0;
                         break;
                   case CURSOR_UP:
                         if((y-step) > 0) y-=step;
                         else y=0;
                         break;
                   case CURSOR_DOWN:
                         if((y+step+SCREENDEEP) < depth) y+=step;
                         else if(depth > SCREENDEEP) y=depth-SCREENDEEP;
```

```
                        else y=0;
                        break;
                case HOME:
                        x=y=0;
                        break;
                case END:
                        if(width > SCREENWIDE) x=width-SCREENWIDE;
                        else x=0;
                        if(depth > SCREENDEEP) y=depth-SCREENDEEP;
                        else y=0;
                        break;
                }
        } while(c != 27);
        /* graphics off */
        deinit();
}

ShowImgPicture(p) /* display the top of the picture */
        char *p;
{

        if(depth > SCREENDEEP) Update(p,bytes,SCREENDEEP);
        else Update(p,bytes,depth);
}

UnpackImgFile(p,fp)            /* open and print GEM/IMG image n */
        char *p;
        FILE *fp;
{

        int i,n;

        for(i=0;i<depth;++i) {
                n=ReadImgLine(p,fp);
                p=farPtr(p,(long)bytes);
        }
        return(n);
}

ReadImgLine(p,fp)          /* read and decode a GEM/IMG line into p */
        char *p;
        FILE *fp;
{

        char *pr;
        int r,j,k,n=0,c,i;

        memset(p,0,bytes);
        r=1;
        do {
                c=fgetc(fp) & 0xff;
                if(c==0) {                          /* it's a pattern or a rep */
                        c=fgetc(fp) & 0xff;
                        if(c==0) {               /*it's a rep count change*/
                                fgetc(fp);       /* throw away the ff */
                                r=fgetc(fp) & 0xff;
                        }
```

Fig 8-3   continued

```
            else {
                    i=c & 0xff;
                    pr=p+n;

                    j=patternsize;
                    while(j--) p[n++]=~fgetc(fp);

                    k=i-1;
                    while(k--) {
                            memcpy(p+n,pr,patternsize);
                            n+=patternsize;
                    }
                    j=r-1;
                    while(j--) {
                            k=i;
                            while(k--) {
                                    memcpy(p+n,pr,patternsize);
                                    n+=patternsize;
                            }
                    }
                    r=1;
            }
    }
    else if(c==0x80) {
            i=fgetc(fp) & 0xff;
            pr=p+n;
            j=i;
            while(j--) p[n++]=~fgetc(fp);
            j=r-1;
            while(j--) {
                    memcpy(p+n,pr,i);
                    n+=i;
            }
            r=1;
    }
    else if(c & 0x80) {
            i = c & 0x7f;
            pr=p+n;
            j=i;
            while(j--) p[n++]=~0xff;
            j=r-1;
            while(j--) {
                    memcpy(p+n,pr,i);
                    n+=i;
            }
            r=1;
    }
    else {
            i = c & 0x7f;
            pr=p+n;
            j=i;
            while(j--) p[n++]=~0x00;
            j=r-1;
```

```
                        while(j--) {
                                memcpy(p+n,pr,i);
                                n+=i;
                        }
                        r=1;
                }
        } while(n < bytes);
        return(n);
}

init()                  /* turn on graphics mode */
{
        int d,m,e=0;

        detectgraph(&d,&m);
        if(d<0) {
                puts("No graphics card");
                exit(1);
        }
        if(d==VGA) {                            /* if it's a VGA card, we */
                d=MCGA;                         /* really want the two color */
                m=MCGAHI;                       /* mode */
        }
        if(DoTable(d)) {                /* set up the table */
                puts("Error creating table");
                exit(1);
        }
        initgraph(&d,&m,"");
        e=graphresult();
        if(e<0) {
                printf("Graphics error %d: %s",e,grapherrormsg(e));
                exit(1);
        }
}

deinit()  /* turn off graphics card */
{
        closegraph();
}

unsigned int pixels2bytes(n)
        unsigned int n;
{
        if(n & 0x0007) return((n >> 3) + 1);
        else return(n >> 3);
}

char *farPtr(p,l) /* return a far pointer p + l */
        char *p;
        long l;
{
        unsigned int seg,off;

        seg = FP_SEG(p);
```

Fig 8-3   continued

```
        off = FP_OFF(p);
        seg += (off / 16);
        off &= 0x000f;
        off += (unsigned int)(1 & 0x000fL);
        seg += (1 / 16L);
        p = MK_FP(seg,off);
        return(p);
}

GetKey()
{
        int c;

        c = getch();
        if(!(c & 0x00ff)) c = getch() << 8;
        return(c);
}
```

To compile this program you would have to create a project file that contained the following lines. This assumes that the C language program is called FASTGEM.C and that you have called your screen driver MONOSCR.ASM, which was subsequently assembled to leave you with MONOSCR.OBJ. If you're using Turbo C version 2.0 or better, the project file would have these lines in it:

```
FASTGEM
MONOSCR.OBJ
```

If you're using version 1.5, you would have to include the graphics library in the project file too:

```
FASTGEM
MONOSCR.OBJ
GRAPHICS.LIB
```

This program uses the Turbo C graphics functions to switch display modes. This has some good features and a few drawbacks. The features include being able to use the high speed screen updates of the assembly language driver to update a whole screen and the Turbo C graphics facilities to draw text, move areas of the graphics around and so on. Figure 8-4 illustrates the two graphics techniques combined.

The drawbacks are that the Turbo C graphics library does not support super VGA cards in their higher resolution modes.

While the assembly language screen driver is able to support the Paradise card in its 800-by-600-pixel mode, the Turbo C initgraph function is not able to put the card in this mode. If you want to use it, you will have to forgo the Turbo C features and do everything "by hand."

In this case, you can replace the init and deinit functions in the C language program with one that is hard wired to use the Paradise 800-by-600-

Fig 8-4   An example of the high-speed monochrome screen driver combined with Turbo C's graphics

pixel mode—or any other super VGA mode you happen to have on tap. In the case of the Paradise card, these would be as shown in Fig. 8-5.

If you do this, none of the Turbo C graphics facilities will work, as Turbo C won't even know that your card is in graphics mode. This means, however, that you won't have the overhead of the Turbo C graphics library enlarging your programs, either.

Dedicated code to change the screen mode of your card without the use of initgraph will be discussed later in this chapter.

Fig 8-5   The init and deinit functions rewritten for use with the Paradise card's super VGA monochrome format

```
init()
{
        union REGS r;

        r.x.ax=0x0059;
        int86(0x10,&r,&r);
}

deinit()
{
        union REGS r;

        r.x.ax=0x0003;
        int86(0x10,&r,&r);
}
```

HERCULES CARD FEATURES

The Hercules card is a decidedly peculiar bit of hardware once you get into it. It's wholly unsupported by the PC BIOS, and things like changing its screen mode require considerable tracts of code. On other cards, such as the EGA and VGA cards, simple BIOS calls usually suffice.

The low cost and tight graphics of a Hercules card make it a worthwhile display card, however. In fact, it has a few tricks tucked away inside it that much more advanced cards can't manage. One of these is its ability flip pages.

Conventional display cards have a single "page" of display memory. When an EGA card is in its graphics mode, writing to the memory starting at segment 0A000H modifies the contents of the graphics screen. On a Hercules card, however, there are two screen buffers, referred to as page zero and page one. One starts at segment 0B000H and the other at 0B800H. Writing to the buffer at 0B000H will only modify the screen contents if page zero happens to be the currently active page.

The Hercules card provides facilities to make either of these pages visible. Because the mechanism for doing so works wholly in hardware, changing images on a Herc card by changing pages is infinitely faster than even the most carefully written software screen driver could ever hope to be.

It's easy to write programs that appear to manage stunningly fast graphics on a Hercules card. To have a picture pop onto the screen instantly, all you have to do is to write it to the currently inactive page and then flip pages.

The Hercules text screen uses the first 4k of the first screen buffer. Unlike as with the other cards discussed here, changing modes need not destroy the contents of the video buffers unless you specifically fill the buffers with zero bytes. As such, if you want to switch to text mode for a while without corrupting your graphics, simply store the first 4k of memory at segment 0B000H somewhere, change the card to text mode, change it back to graphics mode, and restore the afflicted memory.

The Turbo C initgraph function does, in fact, erase both of the Herc buffers when it changes modes. If you want to preserve the graphics buffers through a mode change you'll have to look at the custom mode change functions discussed later in this chapter.

The program in Fig. 8-6 illustrates how to use the page exchange feature of a Hercules card. It loads up the first 348 lines of two IMG files and swaps pages each time you hit Enter. The Esc key will get you back to DOS.

Note that this code does not use the assembly language screen driver. The two images are unpacked directly into the two screen buffers. You would want to do something a little more sophisticated than this for a real world application.

Fig 8-6   A program to flip between two IMG files on a Hercules card

```
/* A program to look at two IMG pictures on a Herc card

        invoke as HERCPAGE FILE1.IMG FILE2.IMG

*/

#include "stdio.h"
#include "alloc.h"
#include "dos.h"
#include "graphics.h"

char header[2][16];                 /* where the headers live */
unsigned int width[2],depth[2];
unsigned int patternsize[2]={1,1};
unsigned int bytes[2];

unsigned int pixels2bytes();

main(argc,argv)
        int argc;
        char *argv[];
{
        FILE *fp[2];
        int c,page=0;

        if(argc > 2) {
                /* attempt to open the files */
                if((fp[0]=fopen(argv[1],"rb")) != NULL &&
                   (fp[1]=fopen(argv[2],"rb")) != NULL ) {
                        /* read in the header */
                        if(fread(header[0],1,16,fp[0])==16 &&
                           fread(header[1],1,16,fp[1])==16 ) {
                                /* check to make sure it's a picture */
                                if(!memcmp("\x00\x01\x00\x08\x00\x01",
                                    header[0],6) &&
                                   !memcmp("\x00\x01\x00\x08\x00\x01",
                                    header[0],6)) {
                                        patternsize[0]=(header[0][7] & 0xff)+
                                          ((header[0][6] & 0xff)<<8);
                                        width[0]=(header[0][13] & 0xff)+
                                          ((header[0][12] & 0xff)<<8);
                                        depth[0]=(header[0][15] & 0xff)+
                                          ((header[0][14] & 0xff)<<8);
                                        bytes[0]=pixels2bytes(width[0]);

                                        patternsize[1]=(header[1][7] & 0xff)+
                                          ((header[1][6] & 0xff)<<8);
                                        width[1]=(header[1][13] & 0xff)+
                                          ((header[1][12] & 0xff)<<8);
                                        depth[1]=(header[1][15] & 0xff)+
                                          ((header[1][14] & 0xff)<<8);
                                        bytes[1]=pixels2bytes(width[1]);
```

Fig 8-6   continued

```
                                                init();
                                                UnpackImgFile(0,fp[0]);
                                                UnpackImgFile(1,fp[1]);
                                                do {
                                                if((c=getch()) == 13) {
                                                        page=page ^ 1;
                                                        HercPage(page);
                                                }
                                        } while(c != 27);
                                        deinit();
                                } else printf("Not an IMG file.\n");
                        } else printf("Error reading files\n");
                        fclose(fp[0]);
                        fclose(fp[1]);
                } else printf("Error opening files\n");
        }
}

UnpackImgFile(page,fp)          /* open and print GEM/IMG image n */
        int page;
        FILE *fp;
{
        char *p;
        unsigned int i,seg;

        /* see which segment to use */
        if(page==0) seg=0xb000;
        else seg=0xb800;

        /* read the lines directly into the screen buffer */
        for(i=0;i<depth[page];++i) {
                if(i >= 348) break;
                p=MK_FP(seg,(0x2000 * (i%4))+(90*(i/4)));
                ReadImgLine(p,fp,page);
        }
}

ReadImgLine(p,fp,page)                  /* read and decode a GEM/IMG line into p */
        char *p;
        FILE *fp;
        int page;
{
        char *pr;
        int r,j,k,n=0,c,i;

        r=1;
        do {
                c=fgetc(fp) & 0xff;
                if(c==0) {                              /* it's a pattern or a rep */
                        c=fgetc(fp) & 0xff;
                        if(c==0) {                      /*it's a rep count change*/
                                fgetc(fp);      /* throw away the ff */
                                r=fgetc(fp) & 0xff;
```

page 0 = 6000
1 = b800
out = 4 cd 90

```
        }
        else {
                i=c & 0xff;
                pr=p+n;

                j=patternsize[page];
                while(j--) p[n++]=~fgetc(fp);

                k=i-1;
                while(k--) {
                        memcpy(p+n,pr,patternsize[page]);
                        n+=patternsize[page];
                }
                j=r-1;
                while(j--) {
                        k=i;
                        while(k--) {
                                memcpy(p+n,pr,
                                    patternsize[page]);
                                n+=patternsize[page];
                        }
                }
                r=1;
        }
}
else if(c==0x80) {
        i=fgetc(fp) & 0xff;
        pr=p+n;
        j=i;
        while(j--) p[n++]=~fgetc(fp);
        j=r-1;
        while(j--) {
                memcpy(p+n,pr,i);
                n+=i;
        }
        r=1;
}
else if(c & 0x80) {
        i = c & 0x7f;
        pr=p+n;
        j=i;
        while(j--) p[n++]=~0xff;
        j=r-1;
        while(j--) {
                memcpy(p+n,pr,i);
                n+=i;
        }
        r=1;
}
else {
        i = c & 0x7f;
        pr=p+n;
        j=i;
        while(j--) p[n++]=~0x00;
```

Fig 8-6   continued

```
                         j=r-1;
                         while(j--) {
                                 memcpy(p+n,pr,i);
                                 n+=i;
                         }
                         r=1;
                 }
        } while(n < bytes[page]);
        return(n);
}

init()              /* turn on Hercules graphics mode */
{
        int d,m,e=0;
        detectgraph(&d,&m);
        if(d<0) {
                puts("No graphics card");
                exit(1);
        }
        if(d != HERCMONO) {
                puts("This program requires a Hercules card");
                exit(1);
        }
        m=HERCMONOHI;
        initgraph(&d,&m,"");
        e=graphresult();
        if(e<0) {
                printf("Graphics error %d: %s",e,grapherrormsg(e));
                exit(1);
        }
}

deinit()  /* turn off graphics card */
{
        closegraph();
}

unsigned int pixels2bytes(n)
        unsigned int n;
{
        if(n & 0x0007) return((n >> 3) + 1);
        else return(n >> 3);
}

HercPage(n)         /* set the hercules card to page number n */
        int n;
{
        if(n==0) outp(0x03b8,0x0a);
        else outp(0x03b8,0x8a);
}
```

The interesting part of this program is the HercPage function at the bottom of the listing. This code does some low level register manipulations with the Hercules card's CRT controller chip, this being the only way to instruct the card to change pages. The register usage of the Hercules card—and the tickling thereof—is a subject of deep and arcane mystery, and one that will not be discussed in detail here. A whole book could be devoted to it and, in fact, several have.

One of the legendary nasties of Herc cards is the ability of the card to physically damage the monitor attached to it if the card is programmed incorrectly. You really have to want to do this—it's all but impossible to make it happen by accident. One way to arrange it, however, is to run Herc-Page when the card is not in its graphics mode. Be warned.

The C language version of HercPage is suitably fast, but it does suffer from one noticeable drawback. Because the instruction to switch pages could come in the middle of the scanning of one frame of the monitor, a momentary hiccup in the card's display might accompany some page flips. This is more noticeable on real Herc cards than on cards that emulate the Hercules graphics mode—the Paradise Plus, for example.

You can avoid this by making the routine that flips pages wait for the monitor "retrace" before changing pages. The retrace is the period during which the beam of the cathode ray tube of your monitor switches off and travels between the lower right corner of the screen and the upper left corner to begin to scan another frame. Because the Hercules card actually tells the beam when to scan each line of the monitor, it knows when the retrace period happens. You can check the state of the retrace in software.

Unfortunately, to switch pages at just the right moment, there can be no delay between the instant at which your program decides that the retrace is occurring and the instruction to change pages. As such, a Herc-Page routine that waits for the retrace must be written in assembly language. Figure 8-7 illustrates the code to do this.

You can use this with the program in Fig. 8-6 by adding this function to MONOSCR.ASM and reassembling it. Delete the C language HercPage function from the end of the listing and create a project file to link MONOSCR.OBJ and your C program.

There is a final condition to making the Hercules card flip pages for you. The Hercules card can be set up in one of two modes, these being full and half. In the former mode, both pages are accessible and the page flipping feature of the card should work. In the half mode, however, the buffer for page one is held off line, and cannot be accessed. This was originally done to allow a Hercules card to coexist with a CGA card.

The Hercules card defaults to full mode. The Turbo C initgraph function places it in full mode, as will the assembly language mode switching routines to be discussed shortly. However, if you're using a multimode card that emulates the Hercules graphics mode, you might find that it starts up in half mode. Check this, if the page flipping program doesn't work.

Fig 8-7   An assembly language function to perform clean page changes on a Hercules card

```
;------------------------------------------------------------
;
;              Set the Hercules card page
;              HercPage(n);
;              int n;              /* page number */
;
              PUBLIC   _HercPage
_HercPage     PROC     FAR
              PUSH     BP
              MOV      BP,SP

              DATASEG

              MOV      DX,03BAH        ;WAIT FOR VERTICAL RETRACE
HP1:          IN       AL,DX
              SHL      AL,1
              JNC      HP1

HP2:          IN       AL,DX
              SHL      AL,1
              JC       HP2

              MOV      DX,03B8H
              MOV      CL,7
              MOV      AX,[BP + _AOFF + 0]
              SHL      AL,CL
              ADD      AL,0AH
              OUT      DX,AL

              POP      BP
              RET
_HercPage     ENDP
```

CHANGING MODES

While it's convenient to use the Turbo C initgraph function to switch into a graphics mode, this has several drawbacks. Some of them will be apparent by now. Among the less obvious ones are the notable increase in size experienced by programs that make use of the Turbo C graphics library. Another consideration is that of portability—having written a program that depends on Turbo C specific functions, you might find it cumbersome to port it to another compiler if this becomes necessary one day.

If the only thing you need the Turbo C graphics library for is to switch modes, you can save some space and simplify your code by writing the mode switching functions yourself. In most cases they're simple. In the one that is not—predictably that of the Hercules card—the code is certainly understandable if you really insist on knowing what it's up to.

There are no compelling reasons for writing the mode switching routines in either C or assembly language—meaningful sounding arguments can be had for both approaches. If you're writing a small program in C, you probably won't want to go to the trouble of creating a project file to link in an assembly language module. On the other hand, these functions are so simple and so unlikely to be modified that one can safely plot them in an assembly language file and forget about them, linking them in as needs be. They occupy considerably less space in their assembly language form.

Practical mode switching involves a function to change modes, of course. It also involves a second function to know which mode to select, that is, to decide what sort of card is in the computer your program finds itself running on. Because each card requires at least slightly different tickling to get it into a graphics mode, the identity of the card to be tickled must be worked out before the fact. This can prove to be a bit difficult.

Let's begin with the problem of changing modes.

C Language Mode Switching

The PC BIOS supports all the graphics modes any of the popular video cards can get into with the notable exception of the Hercules graphics mode. In all cases except for this one, a few lines of code can select any graphics mode you please. If you can be certain that no one using your programs will want to do so with a Herc card, your mode switching functions can be exceedingly simple.

This is probably not a very good assumption. Herc cards remain very popular low cost video displays.

The INT 10H function, subfunction zero, will select any screen mode your video card supports. In addition to the ones defined in a standard BIOS, EGA and VGA cards extend the number of valid modes to encompass the ones supported by these cards. For example, a standard BIOS suddenly will find itself capable of selecting mode 59H if the computer it's running in has a Paradise Plus VGA card installed in it.

To select a different screen mode, you must load the AH register with zero, the AL register with the number of the mode you want and execute an INT 10H instruction. In C, this can be handled like this:

```
union REGS r;

r.h.ah = 0;
r.h.al = mode_number;
int86(0x10,&r,&r);
```

Because it's usually the case that you'll want to hard code in a specific mode for an int86 call, it's often more convenient to write the above bit of code like this:

```
union REGS r;
```

```
r.x.ax = 0x0003;
int86(0x10,&r,&r);
```

In this case, this code will select screen mode three, which is the standard text mode for everything but a Hercules card. Likewise, this call will select the EGA graphics mode:

```
union REGS r;

r.x.ax = 0x0010;
int86(0x10,&r,&r);
```

The Hercules card has no BIOS support, and cannot have its mode changed by the BIOS. In fact, insofar as the BIOS is concerned, the Hercules card has no graphics mode. As you'll see in a moment, you won't even need a BIOS call to restore the Hercules text mode when your graphics are done with. As far as the BIOS is concerned, the card was displaying text the whole time.

This has a number of unfortunate consequences beyond simply needing more elaborate code to handle graphics mode switching for the Hercules card. Because the BIOS does not recognize the Hercules graphics mode, its graphics text printing functions don't work for a Herc card. You can't use DEBUG in the Hercules graphics mode, as discussed at the beginning of this book, and if your program does something to offend your computer and provoke an unexpected interrupt, the message that tells you so will be rendered as a meaningless clutter of dots on a Herc screen.

After a while you'll get to recognize that particular dot pattern, but this is not exactly the height of user friendliness.

To select the Hercules graphics mode, you must reprogram the 6845 CRT controller that forms the basic of the Hercules display. This is an exceedingly arcane bit of work, because it involves fiddling with hardware registers. It's certainly beyond the scope of this book to discuss how this chip works and, fortunately, beyond the requirements of most programmers.

Because the Hercules card has but a single graphics mode with no meaningful variations, you can simply program it and forget about it. The two tables in the following code, t_table and g_table hold the values to be programmed into the 6845's registers.

Switching a Hercules card back into its text mode is equally as complex, requiring a similar assault on the 6845's registers. Everything about the procedure, including clearing the screen of the data left over from whatever graphics operations were performed, must be handled by your code. You can see how this works in the code in Fig. 8-8—the text screen buffer is filled with the word 0x0720. This works out to filling it with character 0x20, or 32 decimal—that is, a space character—and setting all the spaces to attribute 0x07, normal text.

The code in Fig. 8-8 illustrates a pair of functions that will select any of the monochrome graphics modes discussed in this chapter and then

Fig 8-8 Functions to change modes on the monochrome display cards discussed in this chapter

```
#define CGA                 1
#define MCGA                2
#define EGA                 3
#define HERCMONO            7
#define PARADISE            0x59

int _gmode=-1;

TextMode()                      /* set text mode */
{
        union REGS r;
        static char t_table[12] = { 0x61,0x50,0x52,0x0f,
                                     0x19,0x06,0x19,0x19,
                                     0x02,0x0d,0x0b,0x0c };

        switch(_gmode) {
            case CGA:
                    r.x.ax=0x0003;
                    int86(0x10,&r,&r);
                    break;
            case MCGA:
                    r.x.ax=0x0003;
                    int86(0x10,&r,&r);
                    break;
            case EGA:
                    r.x.ax=0x0003;
                    int86(0x10,&r,&r);
                    break;
            case HERCMONO:
                    outp(0x3bf,0);
                    HercMode(t_table,32,0x0720,0x2000);
                    break;
            case PARADISE:
                    r.x.ax=0x0003;
                    int86(0x10,&r,&r);
                    break;
        }
}

GraphicsMode(n)                 /* set graphics mode to n */
        int n;
{
        union REGS r;
        static char g_table[12] = { 0x35,0x2d,0x2e,0x07,
                                     0x5b,0x02,0x57,0x57,
                                     0x02,0x03,0x00,0x00 };

        switch(n) {
            case CGA:
                    r.x.ax=0x0006;
                    int86(0x10,&r,&r);
                    break;
```

Fig 8-8   continued

```
                case MCGA:
                        r.x.ax=0x0011;
                        int86(0x10,&r,&r);
                        break;
                case EGA:
                        r.x.ax=0x0010;
                        int86(0x10,&r,&r);
                        break;
                case HERCMONO:
                        outp(0x3bf,1);
                        HercMode(g_table,2,0,0x4000);
                        break;
                case PARADISE:
                        r.x.ax=0x0059;
                        int86(0x10,&r,&r);
                        break;
                default:
                        n=-1;
                        break;
        }
        _gmode=n;
        return(n);
}


HercMode(table,n,fill,fillsize)
        char *table;
        unsigned int n,fill,fillsize;
{
        char *p;
        int i;

        outp(0x3b8,2);
        for(i=0;i<12;++i) {
                outp(0x3b4,i);
                outp(0x3b5,table[i]);
        }
        p=MK_FP(0xb000,0);
        for(i=0;i<fillsize;++i) {
                *p++=fill;
                *p++=fill>>8;
        }
        outp(0x3b8,n+8);
}
```

return your screen to the appropriate text mode. The modes are selected by passing the GraphicsMode function one of the mode constants that Turbo C defines for its graphics library. Note that as these functions obviate the need for the graphics library entirely for full screen bit-map operations, these values are used purely for the sake of consistency. You can change them if you like.

The mode constants are usually defined in the Turbo C "graphics.h" header file, which is no longer needed. As such, you should define those of them that are applicable yourself, as has been done in the previous example.

Because the Hercules graphics mode cannot be "undone" with a BIOS call, it's important for the TextMode function to know which graphics mode was initially selected. The value used by GraphicsMode is stored in _gmode for this reason. There are other ways of handling this—for example, if you've run DoTable after running GraphicsMode, the external global variable SCREENSEG will be 0xb000 if the card is in Hercules graphics mode and something else if it's not. You could use this to allow TextMode to figure out how to do its stuff.

It's also possible to work out the current mode entirely by reading the state of the computer at the moment. If you execute INT 10H, function 0x0f, the AL register will return with the current video mode number in it. In the case of a Hercules card, this will be seven. Recall that the BIOS remains unaware of any mode changes for a Herc card—mode seven is the monochrome text mode.

You can determine whether a Hercules card is in its text or graphics mode through a very convoluted bit of low level code. It's illustrated in Fig. 8-9. While the design of the Hercules card omits a direct way of reading the current video mode, you can work it out by reading the amount of memory the light pen scans. Because this value changes between the text and graphics modes, it provides a reliable indicator of the current mode of the card.

The IsHercGraf function will return a true value if the card is in graphics mode. It works by reading the scan length of the light pen and comparing it to the average of the text mode and graphics mode scans, that is, 2957. It will hang if you execute it with something other than a Hercules card in place, as it will wait for a vertical retrace that never happens. Make sure that you're dealing with a Hercules board—either by reading the video mode or by checking the graphics screen segment—before using IsHercGraf.

Fig 8-9   A function to decide whether a Hercules card is in its graphics mode

```
;---------------------------------------------------------
;
;               Return true if HGC graphics
;               IsHercGraf();
;
                PUBLIC  _IsHercGraf
_IsHercGraf     PROC    FAR
                CLI                             ;TURN OFF THE INTERUPTS FOR A WHILE
                MOV     DX,03BAH                ;WAIT FOR VERTICAL RETRACE
ISHERC1:        IN      AL,DX
                SHL     AL,1
                JNC     ISHERC1
ISHERC2:        IN      AL,DX
```

Fig 8-9   continued

```
                SHL     AL,1
                JC      ISHERC2

                XOR     AL,AL
                MOV     DX,03BBH        ;RESET THE LIGHT PEN
                OUT     DX,AL
                MOV     DX,03B9H
                OUT     DX,AL
                MOV     AL,16
                MOV     DX,03B4H        ;SELECT LIGHT PEN REGISTER
                OUT     DX,AL

                INC     DX
                IN      AL,DX           ;GET THE LOW ORDER BYTE
                MOV     AH,AL           ;AND SAVE IT
                MOV     AL,17           ;GET THE HIGH ORDER
                DEC     DX              ;...BYTE IN AL
                OUT     DX,AL
                INC     DX
                IN      AL,DX

                CMP     AX,2957         ;CHECK THE TIMING THRESHOLD
                JB      ISHERC3
                MOV     AX,-1
                JMP     ISHERC4
ISHERC3:        MOV     AX,0
ISHERC4:        STI
                RET
_IsHercGraf     ENDP
```

Assembly Language Mode Switching

There are several good reasons for using an assembly language function to change screen modes. Aside from being smaller, doing so facilitates waiting for the vertical retrace period on a Hercules card, allowing the mode to change without making the screen burp.

Figure 8-10 illustrates the assembly language counterparts for Text-Mode and GraphicsMode. They work in exactly the same way as the C functions did, and you can simply comment out the appropriate C code and link these functions in their place. They also work in the same way: the only addition is the retrace wait in HERC_MODE, starting with label HERC_MODE2.

The two Hercules register tables must be placed in the _DATA segment of your source file to be addressable.

Fig 8-10   An assembly language function to change screen modes

```
;-------------------------------------------------------
;
;               Switch to graphics mode
;               GraphicsMode(n);
;               int n;          /* card number */
;
                PUBLIC  _GraphicsMode
_GraphicsMode   PROC    FAR
                PUSH    BP
                MOV     BP,SP

                DATASEG

                MOV     AX,[BP + _AOFF + 0]
                MOV     GMODE,AX

                CMP     GMODE,CGA
                JNE     NOT_GCGA

                MOV     AX,0006H
                INT     10H
                JMP     GRAF_OK

NOT_GCGA:       CMP     GMODE,EGA
                JNE     NOT_GEGA

                MOV     AX,0010H
                INT     10H
                JMP     GRAF_OK

NOT_GEGA:       CMP     GMODE,MCGA
                JNE     NOT_GMCGA

                MOV     AX,0011H
                INT     10H
                JMP     GRAF_OK

NOT_GMCGA:      CMP     GMODE,PARADISE
                JNE     NOT_GPARADISE

                MOV     AX,0059H
                INT     10H
                JMP     GRAF_OK

NOT_GPARADISE:  MOV     DX,03BFH
                MOV     AL,1
                OUT     DX,AL

                MOV     AL,2
                MOV     SI,OFFSET GTABLE
```

Fig 8-10   continued

```
                MOV     BX,0
                MOV     CX,4000H
                CALL    HERC_MODE
GRAF_OK:        POP     BP
                RET
_GraphicsMode   ENDP


;-----------------------------------------------------------
;
;               Switch to text mode
;               TextMode();
;
                PUBLIC  _TextMode
_TextMode       PROC    FAR
                PUSH    BP
                MOV     BP,SP

                DATASEG

                CMP     GMODE,HERCMONO
                JE      TEXT_HERC

                MOV     AX,0003H
                INT     10H
                JMP     TEXT_OK

TEXT_HERC:      MOV     DX,03BFH
                XOR     AL,AL
                OUT     DX,AL

                MOV     AL,20H
                MOV     SI,OFFSET TTABLE
                MOV     BX,720H
                MOV     CX,2000H
                CALL    HERC_MODE

TEXT_OK:        POP     BP
                RET
_TextMode       ENDP

;THIS ROUTINE SETS UP THE MODE FOR THE HERCULES CARD
HERC_MODE       PROC    NEAR
                PUSH    DS
                PUSH    ES

                PUSH    AX
                PUSH    BX
                PUSH    CX
```

```
                MOV     DX,3B8H
                OUT     DX,AL

                MOV     AX,DS
                MOV     ES,AX

                MOV     DX,3B4H
                MOV     CX,12
                XOR     AH,AH

HERC_MODE1:     MOV     AL,AH
                OUT     DX,AL
                INC     DX
                LODSB
                OUT     DX,AL

                INC     AH
                DEC     DX
                LOOP    HERC_MODE1

                POP     CX
                MOV     AX,0B000H
                CLD

                MOV     ES,AX
                XOR     DI,DI
                POP     AX
                REP     STOSW

                MOV     DX,03BAH         ;WAIT FOR VERTICAL RETRACE
HERC_MODE2:     IN      AL,DX
                SHL     AL,1
                JNC     HERC_MODE2

HERC_MODE3:     IN      AL,DX
                SHL     AL,1
                JC      HERC_MODE3

                MOV     DX,3B8H
                POP     AX
                ADD     AL,8
                OUT     DX,AL
                POP     ES
                POP     DS
                RET
HERC_MODE       ENDP

;GRAPHICS CARD INITIALIZATION DATA
;- NOTE THAT THESE THREE LINES GO IN THE _DATA SEGMENT OF MONOSCR.ASM
TTABLE          DB      61H,50H,52H,0FH,19H,06H,19H,19H,02H,0DH,0BH,0CH
GTABLE          DB      35H,2DH,2EH,07H,5BH,02H,57H,57H,02H,03H,00H,00H
GMODE           DW      ?
```

VIDEO HARDWARE DETECTION

Until now, the GraphicsMode and DoTable functions discussed in this chapter have assumed that someone would tell them what sort of video card and which graphics mode to work with. In some cases this is practical—in some cases this is largely unavoidable—but for many applications it's possible to let the program itself work out which graphics mode to use.

The problem of detecting graphics hardware is a bit tricky, inasmuch as it involves detecting what mode the card could be placed in, rather than the mode it happens to be in at the moment. In many cases this entails a certain amount of supposition, based on what is known about the available graphics cards and about what sort of graphics are to be displayed. For example, if your program detects a VGA card, quite a few graphics modes will be available to it. The mode it selects will be based on the sort of picture to be displayed—in the case of the examples in this chapter, a monochrome one.

The function to be discussed here, WhichCard, returns the mode constant that represents the highest resolution monochrome mode available on the video card that it detects. If it detects a VGA card it will return the constant MCGA, which has been used in this chapter to indicate the 640-by-480-pixel monochrome mode of a VGA card. However, the EGA and CGA graphics modes—640 by 350 pixels and 640 by 200 pixels, respectively—also would be available. The divinations of WhichCard should be regarded as suggestions rather than hard rules—you might find cause to override them from time to time.

Figure 8-11 illustrates the code for WhichCard.

Fig 8-11   A function to decide what type of display card is active at the moment

```
WhichCard()           /* return the card type or -1 if no graphics available */
{
        union REGS r;
        struct SREGS sr;
        char *p,sb[64];
        int rt=-1;

        /* let's look for an EGA BIOS */
        if(!memcmp(MK_FP(0xc000,0x0000),"\125\252",2)) {
                /* get the state information */
                r.x.ax=0x1b00;
                r.x.bx=0;
                r.x.di=FP_OFF(sb);
                sr.es=FP_SEG(sb);
                int86x(0x10,&r,&r,&sr);

                /* check to see it was supplied */
                if(r.h.al==0x1b) {
                        /* first four bytes are a pointer */
                        p=MK_FP((sb[3]<<8)+sb[2],(sb[1]<<8)+sb[0]);
```

```
                        r.x.ax=0x0f00;
                        int86(0x10,&r,&r);

                        if(r.h.al == 7 && p[0] & 0x80) {
                                if(isHerc()) rt=HERCMONO;
                                else rt=-1;
                        }
                        else if(p[2] & 0x02) {
                                /* perhaps it's a Paradise card */
                                if(!memcmp(MK_FP(0xc000,0x007d),"VGA=",4))
                                    rt=PARADISE;
                                else rt=MCGA;
                        } else if(p[1] & 0x80 || p[2] & 0x01) rt=EGA;
                        else rt=CGA;
                }
                else {
                        r.x.ax=0x0f00;
                        int86(0x10,&r,&r);

                        if(r.h.al==7) {
                                if(isHerc()) rt=HERCMONO;
                                else rt=-1;
                        } else rt=EGA;
                }
        }
        else {
                if(isRam(0xb000)) {
                        /* must be a Herc or MDA card */
                        if(isHerc()) rt=HERCMONO;
                        else rt=-1;
                }
                else if(isRam(0xb800)) rt=CGA;
                else rt=-1;
        }
        return(rt);
}

long tick()        /* fetch the BIOS tick count */
{
        union REGS r;

        r.x.ax = 0x0000;        /* get clock count */
        int86(0x1a,&r,&r);
        return(((long)r.x.cx<<16) | r.x.dx);
}

isHerc()  /* return true if there's Hercules card */
{
        long ts;
        int r=0;

        ts=tick();
        do {
                if(inp(0x03ba) & 0x80) {
```

Fig 8-11   continued

```
                        r=1;
                        break;
                }
        } while(ts==tick());
        return(r);
}

isRam(n)    /* test a segment for existance of memory */
        unsigned int n;
{
        static char t[8]="\125\252\125\252\125\252\125\252";
        char *p,b[8];

        p=MK_FP(n,0);
        memcpy(b,p,8);
        memcpy(p,t,8);
        if(memcmp(p,t,8)) return(0);
        else {
                memcpy(p,b,8);
                return(1);
        }
}
```

It might seem that something as simple as detecting which of a fairly small number of video cards is on hand would not require quite this much of a dog and pony show. In theory this should be the case. However, the rather wide diversity of display cards—especially the multi-mode cards that just about everyone uses—often complicates the task of a program that wants to find out what it's talking to.

The scope of the problem can be seen if you work through the code in WhichCard. This function begins with some observations about the EGA and VGA card BIOS.

When a PC compatible computer starts up, it looks for an extension BIOS, that is, something that bolts onto its regular ROM BIOS code to drive, for example, a type of display card it doesn't know how to handle. The EGA card BIOS is the most common example of such an extension. This is why most computers equipped with EGA or VGA cards will display two power-up messages. One is the copyright for the BIOS in the computer itself, and the other the copyright for the display card's extension BIOS.

Very early PC compatibles with very old BIOS revisions will not deal with BIOS extensions. These systems will need BIOS upgrades before an EGA or VGA card can be used in them.

To know whether an extension BIOS is available for its use, the BIOS looks at the two bytes at memory location C000:0000H, the base of the BIOS area. These will be 0x55 and 0xaa, respectively, if there's a BIOS extension on hand. This also will serve to tell any other program that's interested whether an EGA or VGA card BIOS has been installed. The existence of an EGA card BIOS presupposes the existence of an EGA card to plug it into.

The WhichCard code begins by performing this test. If an extension BIOS is not found, it assumes that the card is something fairly primitive, such as a Hercules or CGA card.

Unfortunately, the existence of an EGA BIOS does not necessarily preclude the possibility of the card in question being a Hercules card, or at least, of its behaving like one. Most of the recent generation of VGA cards— and many multimode EGA cards—are able to emulate Hercules monochrome graphics. To have such a card do this you usually have to run a utility to explicitly select the Hercules emulation mode. However, even in Hercules emulation mode, the BIOS extension will still be visible on most cards.

VGA cards provide an INT 10H BIOS function, function 0x1b, which returns all sorts of useful information about the capabilities of, among other things, the display card and its associated monitor—at least insofar as the BIOS knows these things itself. If you call this function, a 64-byte buffer pointed to by ES:DI will be loaded with a struct of information. The first four bytes of this struct consist of a pointer back into the BIOS where yet another collection of data can be found.

The first three bytes of the data pointed to consists of an array of bit fields that specify which screen modes the card in question will support. There is, predictably, no bit for the Hercules monochrome graphics mode.

These modes are defined in Fig. 8-12. This assumes that p is a pointer to the information in the BIOS.

Fig 8-12   The VGA display information data

p[0] & 0x01	-	40 by 25 monochrome text
p[0] & 0x02	-	40 by 25 colour text
p[0] & 0x04	-	80 by 25 monochrome text
p[0] & 0x08	-	80 by 25 colour text
p[0] & 0x10	-	320 by 200 CGA colour graphics
p[0] & 0x20	-	320 by 200 CGA monochrome graphics
p[0] & 0x40	-	640 by 200 CGA colour graphics
p[0] & 0x80	-	monochrome text
p[1] & 0x01	-	160 by 200 PCjr graphics
p[1] & 0x02	-	320 by 200 PCjr graphics
p[1] & 0x04	-	640 by 200 PCjr graphics
p[1] & 0x08	-	reserved
p[1] & 0x10	-	reserved
p[1] & 0x20	-	320 by 200 EGA colour graphics
p[1] & 0x40	-	640 by 200 EGA colour graphics
p[1] & 0x80	-	640 by 350 EGA monochrome graphics
p[2] & 0x01	-	640 by 350 EGA colour graphics
p[2] & 0x02	-	640 by 480 MCGA monochrome graphics
p[2] & 0x04	-	640 by 480 VGA colour graphics
p[2] & 0x08	-	320 by 200 VGA colour graphics

If function 0x1b returns 0x1b in the AL register, this information is available and determining which screen modes are available is pretty easy. In looking for a monochrome mode, the MCGA mode 0x11 has the highest resolution. In the case of WhichCard, the function includes code to look for a Paradise card as well by checking for the "VGA =" string in the BIOS. You will want to modify this to support whichever super VGA cards you want your software to work with.

As this function probably will still be available when a multimode card such as the Paradise Plus is in its Hercules mode, it's necessary to check for Herc mode too. The isHerc function will be discussed in a minute.

EGA cards do not support function 0x1b, and, as such, they're a bit trickier to deal with. It's reasonably safe to assume that if you find an EGA BIOS extension and if function 0x1b is not supported, your software will be dealing with a plain vanilla EGA card. The code must still check for Hercules mode, once again by checking the current video mode and then running isHerc.

If an EGA BIOS extension doesn't turn up, the detection process is a lot simpler. The choice is between a Herc card or a CGA card. Actually, there's a third possibility. Way back in the prehistory of PC design there was a text-only display card called the MDA, or monochrome display adapter. This uses screen mode seven and looks like a Hercules card except that it can't do graphics. These things still turn up on PCs that are designed for dedicated applications, such as electronic cash registers.

Differentiating between a Hercules card and a CGA card is fairly easy, and there are several ways to do it. The best one—usually—is to check for the existence of memory at segment 0xb000, the base of the Hercules video buffer. Simply write some data to this space and see if you can read it back. CGA cards, which have no memory at segment 0xb000, should return 0xff bytes. The function isRam checks for memory at a specified segment.

You also can differentiate between these two cards by checking the BIOS configuration switches—or, at least, you used to be able to. These can be read by executing an INT 11H instruction. The AX register returns with each bit representing one switch. Bits four and five deal with the display card.

The problem with this approach is that it represents the initial display card setting, that is, what the display card looked like when the computer was first turned on. Multimode cards such as the ATI Graphics Solution, which can emulate both a CGA card and a Hercules display, often make liars out of these bits by changing emulations behind their backs.

Trolling for screen memory is more reliable.

There are two ways to differentiate between a Hercules card and an MDA card—or three, if you're bold enough to assume that people with text-only displays won't attempt to run graphics software on their machines. Better make that two ways.

An MDA card only has four kilobytes of display memory. It runs from 0B000:0000H through 0B000:1000H. As such, checking for memory above this point will turn up any MDA cards that might be about, aspiring to greater things.

For reasons never fully discussed, the Hercules company suggests using a more complex approach. It seems that MDA cards lack the feature of a Hercules card that signals the start of the vertical retrace period. As such, if you sample the contents of port 0x3ba on a Herc card for at least the time it takes one full frame to be scanned—a fifteenth of a second is more than enough—the high order bit will be set some time during that interval if the card in question is a Hercules card.

The internal clock tick function of a PC serves as an accurate mechanism for measuring this interval.

INDEPENDENT MODE SWITCHING

Having worked out a way to detect which of the available monochrome graphics modes to use, the init and deinit functions in the GEM/IMG file viewer discussed earlier in this chapter can be rewritten and greatly simplified. They're shown in Fig. 8-13.

Fig 8-13   The init and deinit functions rewritten for use with the assembly language mode switching functions

```
init()                  /* turn on graphics mode */
{
        if(GraphicsMode(WhichCard())==-1) {
                puts("Graphics error");
                exit(1);
        }
        DoTable(n);
}

deinit()  /* turn off graphics card */
{
        TextMode();
}
```

Much of the work is being done by the assembly language code in MONOSCR.ASM. If you want to remove the #include statement for the "graphics.h" header file from this program you can safely do so now. You should, however, add the following #defines to your program to establish the mode constants:

```
#define CGA                 1
#define MCGA                2
```

```
#define EGA                 3
#define HERCMONO            7
#define PARADISE            0x59
```

Despite the convenience of allowing your software to work out which graphics mode to use, you probably should allow your users a mechanism for overriding its choices. Because of the variations in multimode cards available—especially among ones that aren't all that well designed—it's quite possible for WhichCard to come to the wrong conclusion about the display adapter to use. If the users of your programs can't talk it out of its errors—with a configuration file setting or a command line switch—they might be unable to use your software.

With the growing diversity of display cards, especially the super VGA cards, it's often a lot more practical to provide for user selectable display options. In many cases this means writing loadable machine language screen drivers. While a lot more work, these provide truly device independent screen handling. They also place the burden of deciding which sort of card to drive on the shoulders of your users, which is probably where it belongs.

The WhichCard function lacks the capability to reach out of your computer, rummage around in a drawer for some video card documentation, and consult the appropriate pages, all things that human beings are more or less capable of.

The next chapter of this book will discuss color displays. These are even more involved than monochrome ones, although you'll find that you probably understand most of the principles behind them by now.

9
CHAPTER

High-Speed Color
Screen Drivers

*When working toward the solution of a problem
it always helps if you know the answer.*
—Murphy's Laws of Computers

Color screen drivers are a lot like monochrome screen drivers except that
you'll need a more expensive monitor to debug one. Actually, the similar-
ity goes deeper than this. Almost all the principles are the same, and the
only real differences between them is in how they tickle their respective
display cards.

Because workable color display cards for the PC didn't appear until
fairly late in the evolution of microcomputer hardware—after the advent of
large scale integration and a general atmosphere of sympathy for systems
programmers—the interfacing peculiarities that marked a number of the
monochrome displays discussed in the last chapter don't have counterparts when dealing with color. All of the color displays to be looked at in
this chapter feature more or less linear memory mapping—and no interleaving to speak of—with pretty predictable relationships between what
you stuff in their buffers and what they put on their screens.

The EGA card is a little weird, but at least there seems to be a plan
behind it.

In one sense, there are really only two types of color displays for the
PC that are common enough to warrant discussion in this book, these
being the EGA and VGA cards. Unfortunately, there are probably upward
of a couple of dozen wholly incompatible variations on the latter card,
which clouds the issue at least a bit.

Interfacing bit-mapped graphics software to a color display is exceedingly easy most of the time because color image files usually turn out to
have been designed to make it this way. You will discover over the next few

pages that the hitherto apparently convoluted data structure of PC Paint-brush files matches perfectly the apparently convoluted data structure of an EGA card's graphics buffer. Likewise, the pixels of a 256-color GIF file are arranged in exactly the same way as are the pixels of a VGA card's buffer. Even the palette data is somewhat compatible.

In this chapter we will look at machine language display modules for four distinct displays, to wit, the EGA 640-by-350 pixel, 16-color display, the VGA 320-by-200 pixel, 256-color display, the VGA 640-by-480 pixel, 16-color display, and the Paradise 640-by-400 pixel, 256-color display. The latter case is an example of a color driver for a super VGA mode, and will serve as a boilerplate for writing your own if you happen to have a different sort of super VGA card.

If you've tried out the example GIF decoder programs in Chapter 5, you probably will already be at least passingly familiar with the code to be discussed here.

In this chapter, with one exception, all of the examples pertaining to VGA cards assume that they will be in one or another 256-color modes. The one exception is a driver for the 16-color VGA mode, which will be discussed toward the end of this chapter. In its 256-color mode, the VGA card is technically behaving like an MCGA card.

PALETTES REVISITED

The EGA card only has a single color graphics mode. It's the same one that has been used previously as its single monochrome mode—the 640-by-350-pixel mode. The unique structure of the EGA card's display buffer allows it to be used as both.

Color display cards need a mechanism for representing color as percentages of red, green, and blue light, the primary phosphor colors of a cathode ray tube. The obvious way to do this would be to simply comprise each pixel of 3 bytes, or registers, one each for the respective percentages of the primary additive colors. This would result in a display with enviable color facilities, but it would cost the earth and would require a very powerful computer to drive it at even modest speeds.

Allowing that many of the people who buy ATs and 386 systems would have gladly bought Cray supercomputers instead, if not for the substantial price break on a micro, the designers of display cards came up with the idea of palettes. A card that uses palettes can get by with much less memory and related hardware and still do a respectable number of colors.

People who work with Cray supercomputers will, naturally, scoff at this.

In a palette-driven display card, each pixel does not determine the color of the dot it represents directly, in that a pixel does not specify percentages of red, green, and blue light. Rather, it tells the card which entry in the current palette should be used to specify the requisite color components. A palette is just a lookup table, where each entry consists of three numbers.

If the number stored in a particular pixel is 12, this tells the card to go look at palette entry 12 and to display the pixel in the color that it finds there. In this way, a card can have any number of pixels but it will usually have a much smaller number of distinct colors that it can display at once.

Palette driven displays usually are described as being able to display some number of colors chosen from a much larger range. The EGA card can display 16 colors chosen from 64. A VGA card can display 256 colors chosen from something like a quarter of a million.

The number of different colors that a display card can display at one time is a function of the size of its palette, that is, the number of entries in it. This is 16 for an EGA card and 256 for a VGA card. The number of colors from which these colors are chosen is a factor of the degree of control the card has over the intensity of the three color guns of the picture tube it's attached to.

In the case of an EGA card, each gun can be set to one of four levels. There are three guns, so the total number of colors can be worked out as four raised to the power of three, or 64.

The VGA card design uses an analog monitor that has no specific gradations of intensity for its color guns. The intensity of each gun is controlled by an analog voltage. The analog voltages are generated by six-bit digital to analog converters in the VGA card attached to the monitor. A digital to analog converter is a circuit that takes a binary number and outputs a voltage level that corresponds to it.

A 6-bit number can have 64 discrete values, so a VGA card can define 64 steps of intensity for each of the three color guns of a picture tube. This works out to 64 raised to the power of three, or 262,144 possible colors. Obviously, with such fine control of the color components, a VGA card can create very subtle distinctions of color. It can reproduce a scanned photograph with enough color control to simulate realistic flesh tones, shadow detail and the color gradations created by natural lighting.

In practice, it's rarely necessary to have access to more than 256 different colors to digitize a color photograph accurately—or, at least convincingly.

THE *EGA* DISPLAY

The EGA card is palette driven, but in a very crude way. In order to fully understand it, you have to dig into its display memory structure first.

When it's first placed in its graphics mode, an EGA card behaves like a 640-by-350-pixel monochrome display, a facility that has been used extensively throughout this book. If you were to execute this bit of code, however, the appearance of the EGA display memory would change from the point of view of a program accessing it:

```
MOV     AL,02H
MOV     DX,03C4H
OUT     DX,AL
INC     DX
MOV     AL,02H
OUT     DX,AL
```

The second of the two OUT instructions causes the page of display memory that has been used in the monochrome EGA drivers thus far to vanish from the memory bus, to be replaced by a second page. The first page still exists, its contents intact—it simply can't be read from or written to anymore. If you were to write data to the memory at segment 0xa000, the base of the EGA's graphics buffer, the data would actually turn up in the second page.

This code would cause the second page to go away, to be replaced by the third page:

```
MOV     AL,02H
MOV     DX,03C4H
OUT     DX,AL
INC     DX
MOV     AL,04H
OUT     DX,AL
```

If you're looking for the difference between this code fragment and the last, note that the second OUT instruction has 04H in the AL register, rather than 02H. The page that is brought onto the bus by this code is determined by which of the first four bits of AL is set. If the first bit is set, that is, if AL contains 01H, the first page is made active. If the second bit is set—AL contains 02H—the second page is made active. To get the third page up you'd load AL with 04H, and the fourth page would require that AL contain 08H.

Only one page can be active at a time, and switching a page onto the bus switches off whatever page was active previously.

When an EGA card is first put into its graphics mode, all four pages of display memory are cleared and the first page is made active. For reasons that will be discussed in a moment, this causes white pixels to be displayed for any bits that are subsequently set in this page, making the card behave like a monochrome display by default.

Let's say that you wanted to turn on the first pixel of an EGA card so that it displayed palette color 12. It's not necessary to know what color this actually is—you're free to define which of the 64 possible colors the card can display will be represented by palette color 12. This will be dealt with shortly. At the moment, the problem is how to store the number 12 at pixel zero.

The binary representation of twelve is 1100B. This is the key to understanding how the EGA card's graphics memory works. To set the first pixel to hold this number, you would start by switching in page zero and setting the first bit of the first byte. Next, switch in page one and set the first bit of the first byte. Switch in page two and unset the first bit of the first byte. Finally, switch in page three and unset the first bit of the first byte.

The four bits of each pixel value are stored in the four separate image pages, or *planes*, of the EGA card's buffer. For this reason, setting individual pixels on an EGA card is fairly time-consuming, because the code that does so must flip through four pages. However, updating a large area of the display with a bitmap can be quite fast.

At worst, the card's pages would have to be flipped 1400 times to update the whole card line by line. This is the most attractive way to do it. A second approach is to write each of the planes in total before changing pages. This is the quickest approach, but it looks ugly as the display colors change while the four bitmaps are being written.

The code that will be discussed here to update an EGA card with a color bitmap will do so one line at a time, both for cosmetic reasons and because this is the form in which the lines come out of an image file. In practice, a well-written high-speed machine language driver can minimize the time spent in flipping EGA display pages.

It's important to bear in mind that each display page of an EGA card behaves just like a monochrome bitmap. You might have occasion to treat them this way. For example, you can capture an EGA screen into memory by bringing each of its four pages onto the bus in turn and simply copying 28,000 bytes from memory segment 0A000H for each one.

One of the positive features of the EGA card's somewhat peculiar graphics mode structure is that while it requires almost a quarter of a megabyte of memory to hold a complete 16-color image, no one bitmap occupies more than one memory segment. The individual pages can be dealt with using 16-bit numbers and simple pointer arithmetic, allowing the code driving an EGA display to be tight and fast.

One of the negative features of the EGA card's design is that graphics file formats that present their image data with one byte per pixel, as is the case with GIF files, require extensive bitwise manipulation to display them on an EGA card.

The EGA Driver

The EGA screen driver is shown in Fig. 9-1. It's called EGASCR.ASM. This is a complete assembly language module—once you've typed it in you can assemble it to produce a linkable object file, EGASCR.OBJ. It will add a number of useful functions to a C language program linked to it.

The first functions you'll probably have need of are EGAgraphics and Text. The first of these sets the card into the EGA graphics mode and creates a line start table for it, just as the Graphics function did in the last chapter. The second is used when you want to get out of the graphics mode—it just uses a BIOS call to restore the normal EGA text mode.

Fig 9-1 The assembly language EGA screen driver

```
;
;                   EGA Screen graphics routines
;

VERSION            EQU    1                        ;VERSION
SUBVERSION         EQU    0                        ;SUBVERSION

_AOFF              EQU    6                         ;FAR STACK OFFSET

;THIS MACRO FETCHES THE DATA SEGEMENT
DATASEG            MACRO
                   PUSH   AX
                   MOV    AX,_DATA
                   MOV    DS,AX
                   POP    AX
                   ENDM

;THIS MACRO SETS A BIT IN ES:DI FOR EGA GRAPHICS
SETBIT             MACRO  FIELD
                   PUSH   AX
                   PUSH   DS
                   MOV    AX,_DATA              ;POINT TO THE DATA SEGMENT
                   MOV    DS,AX
                   MOV    AL,80H                ;SET HIGH BIT
                   MOV    CL,DL
                   SHR    AL,CL                 ;SHIFTED DOWN TO MASK
                   MOV    BX,OFFSET EGATABLE    ;POINT TO LINE START TABLE
                   ADD    BX,FIELD
                   MOV    BX,[BX]
                   OR     ES:[DI+BX],AL
                   POP    DS
                   POP    AX
                   ENDM

;THIS MACRO SELECTS AN EGA PLANE
EGAPLANE           MACRO  ARG1
                   MOV    AL,2
                   MOV    DX,03C4H
                   OUT    DX,AL
                   INC    DX
                   MOV    AL,ARG1
                   OUT    DX,AL
                   ENDM

;THIS MACRO RETURNS SCREEN LINE OFFSET FOR LINE DX IN DI
TUBEOFF            MACRO
                   PUSH   DX
                   PUSH   SI
                   PUSH   DS
                   DATASEG
```

```
                MOV     SI,OFFSET SCREENTABLE
                SHL     DX,1
                ADD     SI,DX
                MOV     DI,[SI]
                POP     DS
                POP     SI
                POP     DX
                ENDM

;THIS MACRO DOES A FAR LOOP
LNGLOOP         MACRO   ADDR
                LOCAL   LAB1
                DEC     CX
                JZ      LAB1
                JMP     ADDR
LAB1:           NOP
                ENDM

;THIS MACRO TESTS AND SETS A PALETTE COMBINATION
PALETTEBITS     MACRO   OFFS,LOWMASK,HIGHMASK
                LOCAL   LABX
                CMP     BYTE PTR [SI + BX + OFFS],033H
                JBE     LABX
                OR      BYTE PTR ES:[DI],LOWMASK

                CMP     BYTE PTR [SI + BX + OFFS],077H
                JBE     LABX
                AND     BYTE PTR ES:[DI],NOT LOWMASK
                OR      BYTE PTR ES:[DI],HIGHMASK

                CMP     BYTE PTR [SI + BX + OFFS],0BBH
                JBE     LABX
                OR      BYTE PTR ES:[DI],LOWMASK + HIGHMASK
LABX:           NOP
                ENDM


EGA_TEXT        SEGMENT BYTE PUBLIC 'CODE'
                ASSUME  CS:EGA_TEXT,DS:_DATA


;THIS FUNCTION CONVERTS THE GIF PALETTE INTO AN EGA PALETTE
;               CALLED AS
;               Gif2EgaPALETTE(egapalette,gifpalette,number);
;               char *egapalette,gifpalette;
;               int number; /* number of valid colours */
;
                PUBLIC  _Gif2EgaPALETTE
_Gif2EgaPALETTE PROC    FAR
                PUSH    BP
                MOV     BP,SP

                MOV     DI,[BP + _AOFF + 0]    ;OFFSET OF DESTINATION
                MOV     ES,[BP + _AOFF + 2]    ;SEGMENT OF DESTINATION
```

Fig 9-1   continued

```
                MOV     SI,[BP + _AOFF + 4]     ;OFFSET OF SOURCE
                MOV     DS,[BP + _AOFF + 6]     ;SEGMENT OF SOURCE

                MOV     CX,[BP + _AOFF + 8]     ;NUMBER OF COLOURS
                SUB     BX,BX

GEP0:           MOV     BYTE PTR ES:[DI],0
                PALETTEBITS     0,20H,04H       ;RED
                PALETTEBITS     1,10H,02H       ;GREEN
                PALETTEBITS     2,08H,01H       ;BLUE

                ADD     BX,3
                INC     DI
                LOOP    GEP0
                DATASEG
                POP     BP
                RET
_Gif2EgaPALETTE ENDP


;THIS FUNCTION CHANGES THE CURRENT EGA PALETTE
;               CALLED AS
;               PaletteEGA(palette,number);
;               char *palette;
;               int number; /* number of valid colours */
;
                PUBLIC  _PaletteEGA
_PaletteEGA     PROC    FAR
                PUSH    BP
                MOV     BP,SP

                MOV     SI,[BP + _AOFF + 0]     ;OFFSET OF SOURCE
                MOV     DS,[BP + _AOFF + 2]     ;SEGMENT OF SOURCE

                MOV     CX,[BP + _AOFF + 4]     ;NUMBER OF COLOURS
                SUB     BX,BX
                CMP     CX,16
                JLE     PALETTE_EGA1
                MOV     CX,16

PALETTE_EGA1:   MOV     BH,[SI]
                MOV     AX,1000H
                INT     10H
                INC     BL
                INC     SI
                LOOP    PALETTE_EGA1

                DATASEG
                POP     BP
                RET
_PaletteEGA     ENDP
```

```
;THIS FUNCTION SETS THE DISPLAY CARD INTO EGA GRAPHICS MODE
;               CALLED AS
;               EGAgraphics();
;
                PUBLIC  _EGAgraphics
_EGAgraphics    PROC    FAR
                PUSH    BP
                DATASEG

                MOV     CX,350                  ;DEPTH OF SCREEN
                SUB     DX,DX
                MOV     SI,OFFSET SCREENTABLE

EGAG1:          PUSH    DX
                MOV     AX,80                   ;WIDTH OF SCREEEN
                MUL     DX
                MOV     [SI],AX
                ADD     SI,2
                POP     DX
                INC     DX
                LOOP    EGAG1
                MOV     AX,0010H
                INT     10H
                POP     BP
                RET
_EGAgraphics    ENDP


;THIS FUNCTION SETS THE DISPLAY CARD INTO TEXT MODE
;               CALLED AS
;               Text();
;
                PUBLIC  _Text
_Text           PROC    FAR
                PUSH    BP
                DATASEG
                MOV     AX,0003H
                INT     10H
                POP     BP
                RET
_Text           ENDP


;THIS FUNCTION DISPLAYS AN EGA LINE
;               CALLED AS
;               ShowEGA(line,length,linenumber);
;               char *line;
;               int length; /* bytes in one field */
;               int linennumber;
;
                PUBLIC  _ShowEGA
_ShowEGA        PROC    FAR
```

Fig 9-1 continued

```
                PUSH    BP
                MOV     BP,SP

                MOV     SI,[BP + _AOFF + 0]     ;OFFSET OF SOURCE
                MOV     DS,[BP + _AOFF + 2]     ;SEGMENT OF SOURCE

                MOV     DX,[BP + _AOFF + 6]     ;GET LINE NUMBER
                CMP     DX,350
                JGE     SHOWEGAX
                TUBEOFF

                MOV     AX,0A000H
                MOV     ES,AX
                MOV     BX,[BP + _AOFF + 4]     ;LENGTH OF MOVE IN BYTES

                MOV     CX,BX
                EGAPLANE        1
                CLD
                PUSH    DI
        REPNE   MOVSB
                POP     DI

                MOV     CX,BX
                EGAPLANE        2
                PUSH    DI
        REPNE   MOVSB
                POP     DI
                MOV     CX,BX
                EGAPLANE        4
                PUSH    DI
        REPNE   MOVSB
                POP     DI

                MOV     CX,BX
                EGAPLANE        8
                PUSH    DI
        REPNE   MOVSB
                POP     DI
                EGAPLANE        0FH

SHOWEGAX:       DATASEG
                POP     BP
                RET
_ShowEGA        ENDP

;THIS FUNCTION CONVERTS A GIF LINE TO AN EGA LINE
;               CALLED AS
;               Gif2Ega(*egaline,*gifline,length);
;               char *egaline,*gifline;
;               int length;
```

```
;
                PUBLIC   _Gif2Ega
_Gif2Ega        PROC     FAR
                PUSH     BP
                MOV      BP,SP

                MOV      DI,[BP + _AOFF + 0]     ;OFFSET OF DEST
                MOV      ES,[BP + _AOFF + 2]     ;SEGMENT OF DEST

                MOV      SI,[BP + _AOFF + 4]     ;OFFSET OF SOURCE
                MOV      DS,[BP + _AOFF + 6]     ;SEGMENT OF SOURCE
                MOV      CX,[BP + _AOFF + 8]     ;LENGTH IN BITS

                PUSH     DI
                PUSH     ES
                SHL      CX,1
                SHL      CX,1
                MOV      AL,0
        REPNE   STOSB                            ;ZERO ALL FOUR FIELDS OF DEST
                POP      ES
                POP      DI

                MOV      DX,[BP + _AOFF + 8]     ;LENGTH IN BITS
                SHR      DX,1
                SHR      DX,1
                SHR      DX,1                     ;WIDTH / 8 = BYTES IN DEST FIELD
                SUB      AX,AX
                PUSH     DS
                DATASEG
                MOV      EGATABLE+0,AX
                ADD      AX,DX
                MOV      EGATABLE+2,AX
                ADD      AX,DX
                MOV      EGATABLE+4,AX
                ADD      AX,DX
                MOV      EGATABLE+6,AX            ;INITIALIZE LINE START TABLE
                POP      DS

                MOV      CX,[BP + _AOFF + 8]     ;LENGTH IN BITS
                SUB      DX,DX                    ;ZERO THE BIT COUNTER
GIF2EGA2:       PUSH     CX
                LODSB                            ;GET A PIXEL

                TEST     AL,1
                JZ       GIF2EGA3
                SETBIT   0
GIF2EGA3:       TEST     AL,2
                JZ       GIF2EGA4
                SETBIT   2
GIF2EGA4:       TEST     AL,4
                JZ       GIF2EGA5
```

Fig 9-1   continued

```
                  SETBIT  4
GIF2EGA5:         TEST    AL,8
                  JZ      GIF2EGA6
                  SETBIT  6
GIF2EGA6:         INC     DL
                  CMP     DL,8
                  JL      GIF2EGA7
                  SUB     DL,DL
                  INC     DI
GIF2EGA7:         POP     CX
                  LNGLOOP GIF2EGA2
                  DATASEG

                  POP     BP
                  RET
_Gif2Ega          ENDP

EGA_TEXT          ENDS

DGROUP            GROUP   _DATA,_BSS
_DATA             SEGMENT WORD PUBLIC 'DATA'

EGATABLE          DW      4 DUP (0)          ;EGA BUFFER OFFSET TABLE
SCREENTABLE       DW      350 DUP (0)            ;EGA LINE START TABLE
EGAPALETTE        DB      256 DUP (0)            ;EGA PALETTE BUFFER

_DATA             ENDS

_BSS              SEGMENT WORD PUBLIC 'BSS'
_BSS              ENDS
                  END
```

The Gif2EgaPALETTE function is intended to convert a GIF palette into an EGA palette, although it will work with any palette data that is similarly structured. This includes the palettes in PCX files.

Most image file palette data is structured as a number of palette entries, each entry being three bytes. Each byte represents the percentage of red, green, or blue light needed for the particular color defined by the palette entry in question. The value in the byte is the numerator of a fraction in which 255 is the denominator.

On an EGA card, each palette entry is defined as a single byte. Because the EGA card only has 64 possible colors to choose from, eight bits is more than enough to represent them—there are actually only six used. On an EGA card, palette entries are often referred to as *color numbers*.

For any given EGA color, there are four possible settings for each of the three guns in the picture tube of the monitor the card drives. These are off, low level, high level, and high plus low level. The first three bits of a color

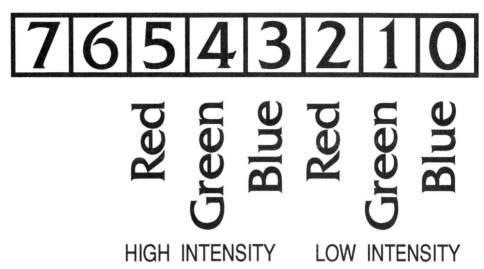

HIGH INTENSITY   LOW INTENSITY

Fig 9-2   The structure of an EGA color number

number represent the three guns at low level. The next three bits represent the guns at high level. The structure of a color number is illustrated in Fig. 9-2.

It's not too hard to see how this works. For example, if the two blue bits—bits zero and three—are both off, the blue gun of the picture tube will be off. If bit zero is set, the blue gun will be on at about one third of its maximum intensity. If bit three is set the blue gun will be on at about two thirds of its maximum intensity. If both bits zero and three are set, the blue gun will be full on.

The Gif2EgaPALETTE function can translate the 48 bytes of a conventional 16-color palette into 16 EGA color numbers. If the palette originally was designed for use with something having a bit finer color resolution—a VGA card, perhaps—this might require some extrapolation. As you'll see if you look at the code, the range of zero to 255, or 0FFH, is carved up into four chunks and the color values assigned accordingly.

The PALETTEBITS macro does most of the work.

One of the problems that you'll probably encounter in displaying images on an EGA card is in handling a picture that has more colors than an EGA card can represent at one time. You can reduce the 24 bits of color represented by a three byte palette entry down to the six bits allowed by an EGA card's color number and still wind up with acceptable colors in a surprising number of cases. However, dealing with having more colors than an EGA card has palette entries is a much larger problem.

You might want to think about how to get around this sort of difficulty. Obviously there is no perfect solution. One way is to group all the similar colors together, so that the total number of colors needed to represent the picture is correspondingly reduced.

The ShowEGA function is designed to take something that looks like one line of a PCX file and stuff it into the four pages of the EGA's display memory, swapping pages between each of the four actual lines. The operation of this code should be pretty easy to understand by now. The EGA-PLANE macro selects the EGA plane to be updated. In tight loops like this one, the use of macros is preferable to subroutines—they result in more code, but they execute a lot faster.

At this point, it's possible to see this screen driver in action. The program in Fig. 9-3 is a PCX file viewer that uses the functions just discussed.

Fig 9-3　A program to view 16-color PCX files using the EGA screen driver

```
/* A fast program to look at 16 colour
   PCX pictures - must link to EGASCR.OBJ */

#include "stdio.h"
#include "alloc.h"
#include "dos.h"

#define fastEGA          1          /* set false to see colour planes */

typedef struct   {
        char     manufacturer;
        char     version;
        char     encoding;
        char     bits_per_pixel;
        int      xmin,ymin;
        int      xmax,ymax;
        int      hres;
        int      vres;
        char     palette[48];
        char     reserved;
        char     colour_planes;
        int      bytes_per_line;
        int      palette_type;
        char     filler[58];
                 } PCXHEAD;

PCXHEAD header;                       /* where the header lives */
unsigned int width,depth;
unsigned int bytes;
char *farPtr();

main(argc,argv)
        int argc;
        char *argv[];
{
        FILE *fp;
        char *p;

        if(argc > 1) {
                /* attempt to open the file */
```

```
                if((fp=fopen(argv[1],"rb")) != NULL) {
                        /* read in the header */
                        if(fread((char *)&header,1,sizeof(PCXHEAD),fp)
                           == sizeof(PCXHEAD)) {
                                /* check to make sure it's a picture */
                                if(header.manufacturer==0x0a) {
                                        /* allocate a big buffer */
                                        width = (header.xmax-header.xmin)+1;
                                        depth = (header.ymax-header.ymin)+1;
                                        bytes=header.bytes_per_line;
                                        if((p=farmalloc((long)depth*(long)bytes*
                                          (long)header.colour_planes)) != NULL) {
                                                /* unpack the file */
                                                UnpackPcxFile(p,fp);
                                                /* look at the file */
                                                ShowPcxFile(p);
                                                free(p);
                                        }
                                } else printf("Not a PCX file.\n");
                        } else printf("Error reading %s.\n",argv[1]);
                        fclose(fp);
                } else printf("Error opening %s.\n",argv[1]);
        }
}


ShowPcxFile(p)                  /* show the picture in p */
        char *p;
{
        char pal[128],*s,*tp;
        int i,j;

        /* set the palette */
        init();

        Gif2EgaPALETTE(pal,header.palette,1<<header.colour_planes);
        PaletteEGA(pal,1<<header.colour_planes);

        #if fastEGA
        for(i=0;i<depth;++i) {
                ShowEGA(p,bytes,i);
                p=farPtr(p,(long)(bytes*header.colour_planes));
        }
        #else

        for(j=0;j<header.colour_planes;++j) {
                setpage(1<<j);
                s=MK_FP(0xa000,0);
                tp=p+(j*bytes);
                for(i=0;i<depth;++i) {
                        memcpy(s,tp,bytes);
                        s+=bytes;
                        tp=farPtr(tp,(long)(bytes * header.colour_planes));
                }
                delay(1000);
```

Fig 9-3   continued

```
            }
        setpage(0x0f);
        #endif
        getch();
        deinit();
}

setpage(n)                      /* set the EGA display page */
        int n;
{
        outportb(0x3c4,2);
        outportb(0x3c5,n);
}

UnpackPcxFile(p,fp)             /* open and unpack the image */
        char *p;
        FILE *fp;
{
        int i,j;

        for(i=0;i<depth;++i) {
                /* read lines in */
                for(j=0;j<header.colour_planes;++j) {
                        ReadPcxLine(p,fp);
                        p=farPtr(p,(long)bytes);
                }
        }
}

ReadPcxLine(p,fp)    /* read and decode a PCX line into p */
        char *p;
        FILE *fp;
{
        int n=0,c,i;

        /* null the buffer */
        memset(p,0,bytes);
        do {
                /* get a key byte */
                c=fgetc(fp) & 0xff;
                /* if it's a run of bytes field */
                if((c & 0xc0) == 0xc0) {
                        /* and off the high bits */
                        i=c & 0x3f;
                        /* get the run byte */
                        c=fgetc(fp);
                        /* run the byte */
                        while(i--) p[n++]=c;
                }
                /* else just store it */
                else p[n++]=c;
        } while(n < bytes);
        return(n);
```

```
}

init()                  /* turn on EGA graphics mode */
{
        EGAgraphics();
}

deinit()   /* turn off graphics card */
{
        Text();
}

char *farPtr(p,l) /* return a far pointer p + l */
        char *p;
        long l;
{
        unsigned int seg,off;

        seg = FP_SEG(p);
        off = FP_OFF(p);
        seg += (off / 16);
        off &= 0x000f;
        off += (unsigned int)(l & 0x000fL);
        seg += (l / 16L);
        p=MK_FP(seg,off);
        return(p);
}
```

This is a modification of one of the PCX viewers discussed in Chapter 4. It must be linked to the assembly language module EGASCR.OBJ.

This program can be compiled in one of two ways. If the fastEGA equate is true, the program will compile to use the ShowEGA function from EGASCR.OBJ. It will display one line at a time. This will look attractive, but it won't be quite as fast as it could be. If you set fastEGA to zero, the code will compile to write each of the four EGA planes in its totality before changing pages. There's a one second delay between the page changes. This will allow you to see what the picture looks like as it builds up.

Real world software probably should not handle EGA screen updates one page at a time like this.

Bitwise Line Conversion

There's one more function in the EGASCR.ASM module, Gif2Ega. It allows a line of image data stored in the VGA line format to be displayed on an EGA card. This code is exceedingly tricky to work out, especially if you don't know in advance quite what it's up to.

A line of data from a GIF file—that is, data stored in VGA format—is structured so that each byte holds the palette number for one pixel. If a picture stored this way is 640 pixels across, each line is 640 bytes long. It probably could be simpler, but one has a hard time imagining how.

If a 16-color picture is stored in this way, the first four bits of each byte hold the palette entry numbers. The upper four bits will be unused. To convert this format into something compatible with an EGA card, a lot of bitwise manipulation must be wrought on the source data. Each VGA line translates into four monochrome bit-map lines, one for each of the EGA planes.

To translate a 16-color VGA line into four monochrome lines, scan through the VGA bytes and extract the first bit from each. These bits would be used to set bits in the first monochrome bitmap line. A 640-pixel VGA line would result in four 80-byte-wide monochrome lines, so there's a lot of bit juggling to do. You might be able to see how the translation works in C a bit more readily.

The following fragment of code will create the first of the four bit-mapped lines at dest. The VGA line is at source. The value in width is the number of pixels across in the source line. The value in bytes is the number bytes in the destination line. Assuming that width is a reasonable number, bytes should be width divided by eight:

```
int i;

memset(dest,0,bytes);
for(i = 0;i < width; + +i)
    if(source[i] & 0x01)
        dest[i / 8] |= (0x80 > > (i & 0x07));
```

The first bit of each byte of the source line is tested to see if it's set. If it is, the corresponding bit in the destination bitmap is set. The byte that contains this bit can be found by dividing the location of the source byte by eight, and the bit position by rotating 0x80 right by the location mode eight.

To create the second bitmap line you would replace 0x01 in the test, above, with 0x02. The third line would use 0x04 and the fourth 0x08. A more complete function would work like this:

```
int i,j;

memset(dest,0,4*bytes);
for(j = 0;j < 4; +j) {
    for(i = 0;i < width; + +i)
        if(source[i] & (1 < < j))dest[(j * bytes) + (i / 8)]|= (0x80 > > (i & 0x07));
}
```

This would leave you with the four bit-mapped lines one after the other at dest. If you were to pass this to ShowEGA, it would display correctly.

This is actually what Gif2Ega in the EGASCR.ASM driver does. However, it uses assembly language and some careful coding to do it much faster than a C language function could manage the conversion. Its only drawback is that it's very nearly impossible to read.

You might want to look back at the EGA GIF file decoder in Chapter 5. The display section, which was left as a bit of a mystery at the time, should make reasonable sense now.

THE *VGA* DISPLAY

Displaying pictures on a VGA card in its 256-color mode is a lot easier than doing so on an EGA card in 16 colors. As has already been touched on, the data of a VGA card's screen buffer is simpler in structure. It's not interleaved, and the pixels and their corresponding bytes in memory have a one-to-one relationship. Of course, a stock VGA card can only display 320 by 200 pixels in this mode, which is not all that exciting.

This screen mode usually is referred to as mode 13H, or just mode 13 if you normally count in hex.

The VGASCR.ASM module shown in Fig. 9-4 is the equivalent of the EGA screen driver just discussed, this time written for a VGA card. There's a great deal less data conversion to be done. In fact, the only potential problem is that a VGA card's palette entries use six bits of resolution whereas most palettes—such as those in a GIF file—are defined with eight bits of resolution. Shifting each palette entry right by two bits—dividing it by four—solves this minor inconsistency.

Fig 9-4   The assembly language VGA screen driver

```
;
;                       VGA Screen graphics routines
;
;                       These routines will display graphics... most
;                       notably GIF files... in the 320 x 200 13H mode
;                       of a VGA card... in 256 glorious colours
;

VERSION         EQU     1                       ;VERSION
SUBVERSION      EQU     0                       ;SUBVERSION

_AOFF           EQU     6                       ;FAR STACK OFFSET

;DO 32 BIT MOVSB
MOVSB32         MACRO
                LOCAL   LAB1,LAB2
                MOV     BL,DS:[SI]
                INC     SI
                JNZ     LAB1
                MOV     AX,DS
                ADD     AX,4096
                MOV     DS,AX
LAB1:           MOV     ES:[DI],BL
                INC     DI
                JNZ     LAB2
                MOV     AX,ES
```

Fig 9-4   continued

```
                ADD     AX,4096
                MOV     ES,AX
LAB2:           NOP
                ENDM

;THIS MACRO FETCHES THE DATA SEGEMENT
DATASEG         MACRO
                PUSH    AX
                MOV     AX,_DATA
                MOV     DS,AX
                POP     AX
                ENDM

;THIS MACRO RETURNS SCREEN LINE OFFSET FOR LINE DX IN DI
TUBEOFF         MACRO
                PUSH    DX
                PUSH    SI
                PUSH    DS
                DATASEG
                MOV     SI,OFFSET SCREENTABLE
                SHL     DX,1
                ADD     SI,DX
                MOV     DI,[SI]
                POP     DS
                POP     SI
                POP     DX
                ENDM

;THIS MACRO ADJUSTS THE PALETTE PERCENTAGE
FIXPALETTE      MACRO
                SHR     AL,1
                SHR     AL,1
                ENDM
VGA_TEXT        SEGMENT BYTE PUBLIC 'CODE'
                ASSUME  CS:VGA_TEXT,DS:_DATA

;THIS FUNCTION SETS THE VGA PALETTE FROM A GIF COLOUR MAP
;               CALLED AS
;               SetVgaPalette(gifpalette,number);
;               char *gifpalette;
;               int number; /* number of valid colours */
;
                PUBLIC  _SetVgaPalette
_SetVgaPalette  PROC    FAR
                PUSH    BP
                MOV     BP,SP

                MOV     AX,1000H
                MOV     BX,0712H
                INT     10H

                MOV     SI,[BP + _AOFF + 0]     ;OFFSET OF SOURCE
                MOV     DS,[BP + _AOFF + 2]     ;SEGMENT OF SOURCE
```

```
                MOV     CX,[BP + _AOFF + 4]        ;NUMBER OF COLOURS
                MOV     AX,_DATA
                MOV     ES,AX
                MOV     DI,OFFSET VGAPALETTE

                CMP     CX,0                       ;CHECK FOR NASTIES
                JG      GVP0
                JMP     GVPX

GVP0:           PUSH    CX
                LODSB
                FIXPALETTE                         ;RED
                STOSB
                LODSB
                FIXPALETTE                         ;GREEN
                STOSB
                LODSB
                FIXPALETTE                         ;BLUE
                STOSB

                POP     CX
                LOOP    GVP0

                MOV     AX,1012H                   ;POINT TO THE PALETTE
                MOV     BX,0000H
                MOV     CX,256
                MOV     DX,OFFSET VGAPALETTE
                INT     10H

GVPX:           DATASEG
                POP     BP
                RET
_SetVgaPalette  ENDP

;THIS FUNCTION SETS THE DISPLAY CARD INTO VGA GRAPHICS MODE
;               CALLED AS
;               VGAgraphics();
;
                PUBLIC  _VGAgraphics
_VGAgraphics    PROC    FAR
                PUSH    BP
                DATASEG

                MOV     CX,200                     ;DEPTH OF SCREEN
                SUB     DX,DX
                MOV     SI,OFFSET SCREENTABLE

VGAG1:          PUSH    DX
                MOV     AX,320                     ;WIDTH OF SCREEEN
                MUL     DX
                MOV     [SI],AX
                ADD     SI,2
                POP     DX
                INC     DX
                LOOP    VGAG1
```

Fig 9-4   continued

```
                MOV       AX,0013H
                INT       10H
                POP       BP
                RET
_VGAgraphics    ENDP

;THIS FUNCTION SETS THE DISPLAY CARD INTO TEXT MODE
;               CALLED AS
;               VGAText();
;
                PUBLIC    _VGAText
_VGAText        PROC      FAR
                PUSH      BP
                DATASEG

                MOV       AX,1200H
                MOV       BX,0031H
                INT       10H

                MOV       AX,0003H
                INT       10H
                POP       BP
                RET
_VGAText        ENDP

;THIS FUNCTION DISPLAYS A VGA LINE
;               CALLED AS
;               ShowVGA(line,length,linenumber);
;               char *line;
;               int length; /* bytes in one field */
;               int linennumber;
;
                PUBLIC    _ShowVGA
_ShowVGA        PROC      FAR
                PUSH      BP
                MOV       BP,SP

                MOV       SI,[BP + _AOFF + 0]      ;OFFSET OF SOURCE
                MOV       DS,[BP + _AOFF + 2]      ;SEGMENT OF SOURCE
                MOV       DX,[BP + _AOFF + 6]      ;GET LINE NUMBER
                CMP       DX,200
                JGE       SHOWVGAX

                TUBEOFF

                CLD
                MOV       CX,[BP + _AOFF + 4]      ;LENGTH OF MOVE IN BYTES
                CMP       CX,0
                JE        SHOWVGAX                 ;CHECK FOR NASTIES
                CMP       CX,320
                JL        SHOWVGA1
                MOV       CX,320
SHOWVGA1:       MOV       AX,0A000H
```

```
                    MOV       ES,AX
          REPNE     MOVSB

SHOWVGAX:           DATASEG
                    POP       BP
                    RET
_ShowVGA            ENDP

;THUS FUNCTION MOVES MEMORY WITH LARGE POINTERS
;
;                   Move memory with large pointers
;                   FarMove(dest,src,l);
;
;                   char *dest,*src;
;                   unsigned int l;

                    PUBLIC    _FarMove
_FarMove            PROC      FAR
                    PUSH      BP
                    MOV       BP,SP

                    MOV       DI,[BP + _AOFF + 0]      ;OFFSET OF DESTINATION
                    MOV       ES,[BP + _AOFF + 2]      ;SEGMENT OF DESTINATIONS
                    MOV       SI,[BP + _AOFF + 4]      ;OFFSET OF SOURCE
                    MOV       DS,[BP + _AOFF + 6]      ;SEGMENT OF SOURCE
                    MOV       CX,[BP + _AOFF + 8]      ;NUMBER OF BYTES TO MOVE

FARMOVE1:           MOVSB32
                    LOOP      FARMOVE1

                    DATASEG

                    POP       BP
                    RET
_FarMove            ENDP

VGA_TEXT            ENDS

DGROUP              GROUP     _DATA,_BSS
_DATA               SEGMENT WORD PUBLIC 'DATA'

SCREENTABLE         DW        200 DUP (0)              ;VGA LINE START TABLE
VGAPALETTE          DB        300H DUP (0)             ;VGA PALETTE BUFFER

_DATA               ENDS
_BSS                SEGMENT WORD PUBLIC 'BSS'
_BSS                ENDS
                    END
```

A single VGA screen, despite having one byte per pixel, only occupies 60,000 bytes of memory, that is, it just fits into a single segment.

The VGA 256-color screen driver doesn't really do very much. Copying a line into the screen buffer merely involves moving it into graphics memory—there are no bit planes involved. It's still faster to use a line start table than it would be to calculate each line start value on the fly, but the structure of this table is exceedingly simple. One of the pleasing things about VGA graphics is that they look so stunning with so little work.

One of the less than pleasing things about VGA graphics is that the screen area encompasses relatively few pixels. Figure 9-5 illustrates the relationship between a typical 640-by-480-pixel GIF file and the 320-by-200-pixel VGA screen.

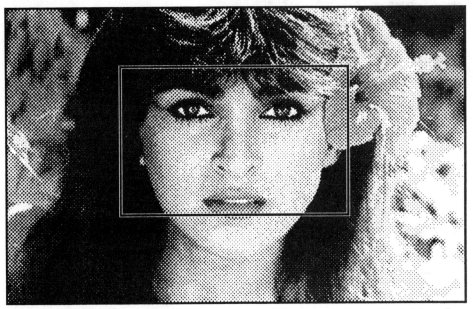

Fig 9-5   The VGA screen in relation to a large image. This picture was downloaded from Rose Media (416) 226-9260

To see a large image, you must either arrange to have the screen pan over the picture using a virtual screen page—or you'll have to figure out how to display more pixels on your screen. Both are possible.

Virtual screen paging was dealt with in detail in the discussion of monochrome image viewer programs. The principles remain the same in applying it to color. The entire image is unpacked into a large buffer and selected portions of it are updated to the screen to create the illusion of panning a small window over a big picture.

The only potentially complex aspect of this is in figuring out where in the big buffer to copy the screen data from. In the following discussion, let's allow that the picture to be panned over is IMAGEWIDE pixels wide and IMAGEDEEP pixels deep. Remember that a byte and a pixel are essentially the same in this mode. The screen is 320 by 200 pixels. The upper left corner of the screen in relation to the upper left corner of the picture will be represented by x and y. The big buffer with the image in it will be called p.

The first byte of data to be copied to the screen would be found at the following location:

```
p + (y*IMAGEWIDE) + x;
```

To copy this line to the screen, you would do the following:

```
memcpy(MK_FP(0xa000,y*320),
    farPtr(p,((long)y*(long)IMAGEWIDE)) + x,
    320);
```

The next line would be found by incrementing y and performing the calculation again.

In practice it's a lot faster to do all this in assembly language. The ShowVGA function in the VGASCR driver does the same thing as the foregoing C language code, but with a somewhat heavier foot.

Figure 9-6 illustrates the VGA GIF decoder from Chapter 5 modified to handle virtual screen paging. The cursor keys will move the window and the Esc key will return you to DOS. This program must link to VGASCR.OBJ and the GIF decoder module from Chapter 5.

Fig 9-6   A VGA GIF viewer that implements software panning

```
/*
        An example C language VGA GIF decoder.
        Loads the whole picture into a buffer and pages.
        Links to assembly language module.
*/

#include "stdio.h"
#include "dos.h"
#include "alloc.h"

#define HOME            71 * 256
#define CURSOR_UP       72 * 256
#define PG_UP           73 * 256
#define CURSOR_LEFT     75 * 256
#define CURSOR_RIGHT    77 * 256
#define END             79 * 256
#define CURSOR_DOWN     80 * 256
#define PG_DOWN         81 * 256

#define screenDeep      200
#define screenWide      320

extern char PALETTE[256][4],OUTROW[1024],COPYRIGHT[];
extern int INTERLACED,IMAGEWIDE,IMAGEDEEP;
extern int IMAGEX,IMAGEY,XLOC,YLOC;
extern int VERSION,SUBVERSION;
```

Fig 9-6   continued

```c
char *pbf=NULL;              /* pointer to line work space */
char *picture=NULL;
long size=0L;

main(argc,argv)
        int argc;
        char *argv[];
{
        char filename[65];
        int i,e,ShowIt(),Colourize();
        int ImageDone(),BadError(),BGround();

        SetShow(ShowIt);
        SetPalette(Colourize);
        SetImage(ImageDone);
        SetError(BadError);
        SetBackground(BGround);
        if(argc > 1) {
                if((pbf=malloc(4096)) != NULL) {
                        VGAgraphics();
                        for(i=1;i<argc;++i) {
                                strmfe(filename,argv[i],"GIF");
                                if((e=UnpackGIF(filename)) != 0) break;
                        }
                        VGAText();
                        if(e) printf("Error code %d",e);
                        free(pbf);
                } else puts("Error allocating memory");
        }
        ShowCopyright();
}
/* This function should do whatever is to be done when the
   image has been fully unpacked. The simplest thing is to
   do nothing, if the image was being displayed as it was
   unpacked. In this case, we'll beep. */
ImageDone()
{
        char f=0,*farPtr();
        int c,i,top=0,left=0;

        nosound();
        sound(660);
        delay(100);
        sound(880);
        delay(50);
        sound(440);
        delay(75);
        nosound();

        do {
                if(!f) for(i=0;i<screenDeep;++i)
                  ShowVGA(farPtr(picture,
                    left+(long)(i+top) *
```

```
                         (long)IMAGEWIDE),IMAGEWIDE,i);
                    f=1;
                    switch(c=GetKey()) {
                         case HOME:
                              top=left=0;
                              f=0;
                              break;
                         case END:
                              top=IMAGEDEEP-screenDeep;
                              left=IMAGEWIDE-screenWide;
                              f=0;
                              break;
                         case CURSOR_LEFT:
                              if(left > (screenWide/4))
                                   left-=(screenWide/4);
                              else left = 0;
                              f=0;
                                        break;
                         case CURSOR_RIGHT:
                              if(left+screenWide+(screenWide/4) < IMAGEWIDE)
                                   left+=(screenWide/4);
                              else left=IMAGEWIDE-screenWide;
                              f=0;
                              break;
                         case PG_DOWN:
                         case CURSOR_DOWN:
                              if(top+screenDeep+(screenDeep/4) < IMAGEDEEP)
                                   top+=(screenDeep/4);
                              else top=IMAGEDEEP-screenDeep;
                              f=0;
                              break;
                         case PG_UP:
                         case CURSOR_UP:
                              if(top > (screenDeep/4)) top-=(screenDeep/4);
                              else top = 0;
                              f=0;
                              break;
                    }
          } while(c != 27);

          farfree(picture);
}
/* This function should do whatever is needed to set the palette
   of the display card to the colour map in the palette buffer
   at palette. The n value is the number of valid colours. */
Colourize(n,palette)
          int n;
          char *palette;
{
          SetVgaPalette(palette,n);
}

/* This function is called after each line has been unpacked. It
   should show the line in the global buffer OUTROW on the screen
```

Fig 9-6 continued

```
        starting at line YLOC. To be really proper about it, it should
        add IMAGEX pixels to the left and IMAGEY pixels to the top. */
ShowIt()
{
        char *farPtr();

        FarMove(farPtr(picture,(long)YLOC*(long)IMAGEWIDE),OUTROW,IMAGEWIDE);
}

/* This function is called to set the background colour. The colour
   number will be found in n. This can be ignored if you like. */
BGround(n)
        int n;
{
        union REGS r;
        int i;

        size=(long)IMAGEWIDE * (long)IMAGEDEEP;
        if(size == 0L || (picture=farmalloc(size)) == NULL) {
                VGAText();
                printf("Error allocating memory - "
                        "requested %lu, %lu available",
                         size,coreleft());
                exit(1);
        }

        memset(pbf,n,320);
        for(i=0;i<200;++i) ShowVGA(pbf,IMAGEWIDE,i);

        r.x.ax=0x1001;
        r.x.bx=n << 8;
        int86(0x10,&r,&r);                              /* set overscan */
}

/* This function will be called if something bad happens in the process
   of unpacking a GIF file, such that the process really should not
   continue. It's passed the address of a string which describes the
   nature of the problem. It's not adviseable to return from this
   function. */
BadError(s)
        char *s;
{
        VGAText();
        printf("\007\007\007Fatal error - %s.\n",s);
        exit(1);
}

/* This function will access and print the copyright notice. Some version
   of this should exist in your program because CompuServe gripes if they
   aren't mentioned in GIF programs. You have been warned. */
ShowCopyright()
{
        char *p;
```

```
        p = COPYRIGHT;
        while(*p) {
                p += printf(p)+1;
                puts("");
        }
}

strmfe(new,old,ext)                     /* make file name with specific extension */
        char *new,*old,*ext;
{
        while(*old != 0 && *old != '.') *new++=*old++;
        *new++='.';
        while(*ext) *new++=*ext++;
        *new=0;
}

char *farPtr(p,l) /* return a far pointer p + l */
        char *p;
        long l;
{
        unsigned int seg,off;

        seg=FP_SEG(p);
        off=FP_OFF(p);
        seg+=(off / 16);
        off += (unsigned int)(l & 0x000fL);
        seg += (l / 16L);
        p=MK_FP(seg,off);
        return(p);
}

GetKey()
{
        int c;

        c = getch();
        if(!(c & 0x00ff)) c = getch() << 8;
        return(c);
}
```

This program works by allocating a very large buffer to hold the entire picture it decodes. A 640-by-480-pixel GIF file would require something on the order of 300k of memory. This is more memory than is free when you compile and run the program under Turbo C's integrated development environment.

To try the program with a large GIF file, you'll have to get out of Turbo C and run it from the command line.

Unlike the GIF viewers in Chapter 5, this program does not unpack its pictures directly to the screen. As such, it would normally appear to be doing nothing for a long time because it's busy filling its buffer. While you could put a message on the screen that explains this apparent inactivity, it's not very much more work to have the first 200 lines of the image being decoded stuffed into the screen buffer as well as being copied to the image buffer. This will give anyone using the program something to look at while the program is thinking.

The 16-Color VGA Display

There's a seldom used VGA mode that supports 640 by 480 pixels in 16 colors. This usually is referred to as mode twelve, meaning mode 12H. It's of questionable use for handling images, because one finds fairly few 16-color pictures with these dimensions. It works well for things such as Microsoft Windows or Ventura Publisher, though, as it has something closer to a one-to-one aspect ratio.

Mode 12 turns out to be easy to work with. It has four image planes and can be treated exactly like the EGA graphics mode save for its slightly larger vertical dimension. Figure 9-7 illustrates a screen driver for it.

Fig 9-7   The assembly language VGA 16-color screen driver

```
;
;        VGA 16 colour Screen graphics routines
;

VERSION         EQU     1                       ;VERSION
SUBVERSION      EQU     0                       ;SUBVERSION

_AOFF           EQU     6                       ;FAR STACK OFFSET

;THIS MACRO FETCHES THE DATA SEGEMENT
DATASEG         MACRO
                PUSH    AX
                MOV     AX,_DATA
                MOV     DS,AX
                POP     AX
                ENDM

;THIS MACRO SETS A BIT IN ES:DI FOR EGA GRAPHICS
SETBIT          MACRO   FIELD
                PUSH    AX
                PUSH    DS
                MOV     AX,_DATA                ;POINT TO THE DATA SEGMENT
                MOV     DS,AX
                MOV     AL,80H                  ;SET HIGH BIT
                MOV     CL,DL
                SHR     AL,CL                   ;SHIFTED DOWN TO MASK
                MOV     BX,OFFSET EGATABLE      ;POINT TO LINE START TABLE
                ADD     BX,FIELD
                MOV     BX,[BX]
                OR      ES:[DI+BX],AL
                POP     DS
                POP     AX
                ENDM
```

```
;THIS MACRO SELECTS AN EGA PLANE
EGAPLANE        MACRO   ARG1
                MOV     AL,2
                MOV     DX,03C4H
                OUT     DX,AL
                INC     DX
                MOV     AL,ARG1
                OUT     DX,AL
                ENDM


;THIS MACRO RETURNS SCREEN LINE OFFSET FOR LINE DX IN DI
TUBEOFF         MACRO
                PUSH    DX
                PUSH    SI
                PUSH    DS
                DATASEG
                MOV     SI,OFFSET SCREENTABLE
                SHL     DX,1
                ADD     SI,DX
                MOV     DI,[SI]
                POP     DS
                POP     SI
                POP     DX
                ENDM
;THIS MACRO DOES A FAR LOOP
LNGLOOP         MACRO   ADDR
                LOCAL   LAB1
                DEC     CX
                JZ      LAB1
                JMP     ADDR
LAB1:           NOP
                ENDM


;THIS MACRO TESTS AND SETS A PALETTE COMBINATION
PALETTEBITS     MACRO   OFFS,LOWMASK,HIGHMASK
                LOCAL   LABX
                CMP     BYTE PTR [SI + BX + OFFS],033H
                JBE     LABX
                OR      BYTE PTR ES:[DI],LOWMASK

                CMP     BYTE PTR [SI + BX + OFFS],077H
                JBE     LABX
                AND     BYTE PTR ES:[DI],NOT LOWMASK
                OR      BYTE PTR ES:[DI],HIGHMASK

                CMP     BYTE PTR [SI + BX + OFFS],0BBH
                JBE     LABX
                OR      BYTE PTR ES:[DI],LOWMASK + HIGHMASK
LABX:           NOP
                ENDM


VGA16_TEXT      SEGMENT BYTE PUBLIC 'CODE'
                ASSUME  CS:VGA16_TEXT,DS:_DATA
;THIS FUNCTION CONVERTS THE GIF PALETTE INTO AN EGA PALETTE
```

Fig 9-7 continued

```
;                   CALLED AS
;                   Gif2EgaPALETTE(egapalette,gifpalette,number);
;                   char *egapalette,gifpalette;
;                   int number; /* number of valid colours */
;
                    PUBLIC  _Gif2EgaPALETTE
_Gif2EgaPALETTE PROC FAR
                    PUSH    BP
                    MOV     BP,SP

                    MOV     DI,[BP + _AOFF + 0]     ;OFFSET OF DESTINATION
                    MOV     ES,[BP + _AOFF + 2]     ;SEGMENT OF DESTINATION

                    MOV     SI,[BP + _AOFF + 4]     ;OFFSET OF SOURCE
                    MOV     DS,[BP + _AOFF + 6]     ;SEGMENT OF SOURCE

                    MOV     CX,[BP + _AOFF + 8]     ;NUMBER OF COLOURS
                    SUB     BX,BX

GEP0:               MOV     BYTE PTR ES:[DI],0

                    PALETTEBITS     0,20H,04H       ;RED
                    PALETTEBITS     1,10H,02H       ;GREEN
                    PALETTEBITS     2,08H,01H       ;BLUE

                    ADD     BX,3
                    INC     DI
                    LOOP    GEP0
                    DATASEG
                    POP     BP
                    RET
_Gif2EgaPALETTE ENDP

;THIS FUNCTION CHANGES THE CURRENT EGA PALETTE
;                   CALLED AS
;                   PaletteVGA16(palette,number);
;                   char *palette;
;                   int number; /* number of valid colours */
;
                    PUBLIC  _PaletteVGA16
_PaletteVGA16   PROC FAR
                    PUSH    BP
                    MOV     BP,SP

                    MOV     SI,[BP + _AOFF + 0]     ;OFFSET OF SOURCE
                    MOV     DS,[BP + _AOFF + 2]     ;SEGMENT OF SOURCE

                    MOV     CX,[BP + _AOFF + 4]     ;NUMBER OF COLOURS
                    SUB     BX,BX
                    CMP     CX,16
                    JLE     PALETTE_VEGA1
                    MOV     CX,16
```

```
PALETTE_VEGA1:  MOV     BH,[SI]
                MOV     AX,1000H
                INT     10H
                INC     BL
                INC     SI
                LOOP    PALETTE_VEGA1

                DATASEG
                POP     BP
                RET
_PaletteVGA16   ENDP

;THIS FUNCTION SETS THE DISPLAY CARD INTO EGA GRAPHICS MODE
;               CALLED AS
;               VGA16graphics();
;
                PUBLIC  _VGA16graphics
_VGA16graphics  PROC    FAR
                PUSH    BP
                DATASEG

                MOV     CX,480                  ;DEPTH OF SCREEN
                SUB     DX,DX
                MOV     SI,OFFSET SCREENTABLE

VEGAG1:         PUSH    DX
                MOV     AX,80                   ;WIDTH OF SCREEEN
                MUL     DX
                MOV     [SI],AX
                ADD     SI,2
                POP     DX
                INC     DX
                LOOP    VEGAG1
                MOV     AX,0012H
                INT     10H
                POP     BP
                RET
_VGA16graphics  ENDP

;THIS FUNCTION SETS THE DISPLAY CARD INTO TEXT MODE
;               CALLED AS
;               Text();
;
                PUBLIC  _Text
_Text           PROC    FAR
                PUSH    BP
                DATASEG
                MOV     AX,0003H
                INT     10H
                POP     BP
                RET
_Text           ENDP

;THIS FUNCTION DISPLAYS AN EGA LINE
;               CALLED AS
```

Fig 9-7   continued

```
;                 ShowVGA16(line,length,linenumber);
;                 char *line;
;                 int length; /* bytes in one field */
;                 int linennumber;
;
                  PUBLIC   _ShowVGA16
_ShowVGA16        PROC     FAR
                  PUSH     BP
                  MOV      BP,SP

                  MOV      SI,[BP + _AOFF + 0]      ;OFFSET OF SOURCE
                  MOV      DS,[BP + _AOFF + 2]      ;SEGMENT OF SOURCE

                  MOV      DX,[BP + _AOFF + 6]      ;GET LINE NUMBER
                  CMP      DX,480
                  JGE      SHOWVEGAX

                  TUBEOFF

                  MOV      AX,0A000H
                  MOV      ES,AX
                  MOV      BX,[BP + _AOFF + 4]      ;LENGTH OF MOVE IN BYTES

                  MOV      CX,BX
                  EGAPLANE          1
                  CLD
                  PUSH     DI
      REPNE       MOVSB
                  POP      DI

                  MOV      CX,BX
                  EGAPLANE          2
                  PUSH     DI
      REPNE       MOVSB
                  POP      DI
                  MOV      CX,BX
                  EGAPLANE          4
                  PUSH     DI
      REPNE       MOVSB
                  POP      DI

                  MOV      CX,BX
                  EGAPLANE          8
                  PUSH     DI
      REPNE       MOVSB
                  POP      DI
                  EGAPLANE          0FH

SHOWVEGAX:        DATASEG
                  POP      BP
                  RET
_ShowVGA16        ENDP
```

```
;THIS FUNCTION CONVERTS A GIF LINE TO AN EGA LINE
;              CALLED AS
;              Gif2Ega(*egaline,*gifline,length);
;              char *egaline,*gifline;
;              int length;
;
               PUBLIC   _Gif2Ega
_Gif2Ega       PROC     FAR
               PUSH     BP
               MOV      BP,SP

               MOV      DI,[BP + _AOFF + 0]    ;OFFSET OF DEST
               MOV      ES,[BP + _AOFF + 2]    ;SEGMENT OF DEST

               MOV      SI,[BP + _AOFF + 4]    ;OFFSET OF SOURCE
               MOV      DS,[BP + _AOFF + 6]    ;SEGMENT OF SOURCE

               MOV      CX,[BP + _AOFF + 8]    ;LENGTH IN BITS

               PUSH     DI
               PUSH     ES
               SHL      CX,1
               SHL      CX,1
               MOV      AL,0
      REPNE    STOSB                           ;ZERO ALL FOUR FIELDS OF DEST
               POP      ES
               POP      DI

               MOV      DX,[BP + _AOFF + 8]    ;LENGTH IN BITS
               SHR      DX,1
               SHR      DX,1
               SHR      DX,1                   ;WIDTH / 8 = BYTES IN DEST FIELD
               SUB      AX,AX
               PUSH     DS
               DATASEG
               MOV      EGATABLE+0,AX
               ADD      AX,DX
               MOV      EGATABLE+2,AX
               ADD      AX,DX
               MOV      EGATABLE+4,AX
               ADD      AX,DX
               MOV      EGATABLE+6,AX          ;INITIALIZE LINE START TABLE
               POP      DS

               MOV      CX,[BP + _AOFF + 8]    ;LENGTH IN BITS
               SUB      DX,DX                  ;ZERO THE BIT COUNTER
GIF2EGA2:      PUSH     CX
               LODSB                           ;GET A PIXEL

               TEST     AL,1
               JZ       GIF2EGA3
               SETBIT   0
GIF2EGA3:      TEST     AL,2
```

Fig 9-7   continued

```
                    JZ        GIF2EGA4
                    SETBIT    2
GIF2EGA4:           TEST      AL,4
                    JZ        GIF2EGA5
                    SETBIT    4
GIF2EGA5:           TEST      AL,8
                    JZ        GIF2EGA6
                    SETBIT    6
GIF2EGA6:           INC       DL
                    CMP       DL,8
                    JL        GIF2EGA7
                    SUB       DL,DL
                    INC       DI
GIF2EGA7:           POP       CX
                    LNGLOOP   GIF2EGA2
                    DATASEG

                    POP       BP
                    RET
_Gif2Ega            ENDP

VGA16_TEXT          ENDS

DGROUP              GROUP     _DATA,_BSS
_DATA               SEGMENT   WORD PUBLIC 'DATA'

EGATABLE            DW        4 DUP (0)          ;EGA BUFFER OFFSET TABLE
SCREENTABLE         DW        480 DUP (0)             ;EGA LINE START TABLE
EGAPALETTE          DB        256 DUP (0)             ;EGA PALETTE BUFFER

_DATA               ENDS

_BSS                SEGMENT   WORD PUBLIC 'BSS'
_BSS                ENDS
                    END
```

The only meaningful difference between this module, VGA 16SCR.ASM, and the EGASCR.ASM module discussed at the beginning of this chapter is the substitution of 480 for 350 wherever it occurs, the use of graphics mode 12H rather than mode 10H and a few changes in the names of the functions.

Figure 9-8 is a GIF decoder that uses the mode twelve screen driver.

As with the other example GIF viewers in this chapter, this code must link to the GIF decoder module in Chapter 5.

WRITING A COLOR SUPER *VGA* DRIVER

Most VGA cards can display more pixels than the stock VGA mode 13H supports. A super VGA card with any self-respect at all will manage

Fig 9-8   A GIF viewer for use with screen mode 12H

```
/*
        An example C language GIF decoder for mode 12H
*/

#include "stdio.h"
#include "dos.h"
#include "alloc.h"

extern char PALETTE[256][4],OUTROW[1024],COPYRIGHT[];
extern int INTERLACED,IMAGEWIDE,IMAGEDEEP;
extern int IMAGEX,IMAGEY,XLOC,YLOC;
extern int VERSION,SUBVERSION;

char *pbf=NULL;          /* pointer to line work space */

main(argc,argv)
        int argc;
        char *argv[];
{
        char filename[65];
        int i,e,ShowIt(),Colourize();
        int ImageDone(),BadError(),BGround();

        SetShow(ShowIt);
        SetPalette(Colourize);
        SetImage(ImageDone);
        SetError(BadError);
        SetBackground(BGround);
        if(argc > 1) {
                if((pbf=malloc(4096)) != NULL) {
                        VGA16graphics();
                        for(i=1;i<argc;++i) {
                                strmfe(filename,argv[i],"GIF");
                                if((e=UnpackGIF(filename)) == 0) {
                                        if(getch()==27) break;
                                }
                                else break;
                        }
                        Text();
                        if(e) printf("Error code %d",e);
                        free(pbf);
                } else puts("Error allocating memory");
        }
        ShowCopyright();
}

ImageDone()
{
        nosound();
        sound(660);
        delay(100);
        sound(880);
```

Fig 9-8   continued

```
        delay(50);
        sound(440);
        delay(75);
        nosound();
}

Colourize(n,palette)
        int n;
        char *palette;
{
        char b[256];

        Gif2EgaPALETTE(b,palette,n);
        PaletteVGA16(b,n);
}

ShowIt()
{
        Gif2Ega(pbf,OUTROW,IMAGEWIDE);
        ShowVGA16(pbf,IMAGEWIDE>>3,YLOC);
}

BGround(n)
        int n;
{
        int i;

        memset(OUTROW,n,80);
        Gif2Ega(pbf,OUTROW,IMAGEWIDE);
        for(i=0;i<350;++i) ShowVGA16(pbf,IMAGEWIDE>>3,i);
}

BadError(s)
        char *s;
{
        Text();
        printf("\007\007\007Fatal error - %s.\n",s);
        exit(1);
}

ShowCopyright()
{
        char *p;

        p = COPYRIGHT;
        while(*p) {
                p += printf(p)+1;
                puts("");
        }
}

strmfe(new,old,ext)                     /* make file name with specific extension */
        char *new,*old,*ext;
```

```
{
        while(*old != 0 && *old != '.') *new++=*old++;
        *new++='.';
        while(*ext) *new++=*ext++;
        *new=0;
}
```

at least 640 by 400 pixels in 256 colors, and cards with 800-by-600-pixel resolution in 256 colors certainly exist. The latter mode presupposes having 512k of memory on the display card.

One immediate observation that springs to mind, in discussing these super modes, is that a 256-color 640-by-400 pixel screen will unquestionably require more that 64k of memory. Allowing that the graphics buffer of a hypothetical video card starts at location 0A000:0000H, that is, the first byte at memory segment 0A000H, such an image would require a graphics buffer that extended out to segment 0EB00H. This would overlay a number of useful things in high memory, including the EGA BIOS area and the LIM page frame area.

Clearly, this is not how super VGA cards actually handle their display buffers. In fact, what they really do is to page parts of their display buffers into the 64k at segment 0xa000. This is very much like what happens to the four display planes of an EGA card, except that a super VGA card's display is still pixel oriented, that is, each byte represents one pixel.

At 640 pixels across, a 64k screen buffer would hold about 100 lines. Thus, if you wanted to update one of the first 100 lines of the screen you would tell the card to put the first page of its display memory on line and write to it just as you would the normal VGA display buffer—save for the longer line length, of course. If you wanted to update a line in the range of 101 to 201, you would tell the card to take the first page off line and bring the second page on line. You would subtract 100 from the actual line number and write to the display memory as you did with the first line.

The super VGA modes of the various VGA cards are not standardized in the least bit. They all have their own unique characteristics, and in most cases you'll have to write a different driver for every super VGA card you want your programs to support.

There are several potentially troublesome aspects in writing a specific VGA driver, each of which can be resolved only with some inside information provided by the manufacturer of the card. You will need to know how to put the card into the super VGA mode you want to work with, how big each page of the screen buffer actually is in this mode and, finally, which registers in the card to tickle to make it change pages.

The first question usually involves knowing which screen mode to select with the by now familiar INT 10H function zero. The second question cannot be worked out logically in most cases. The pages usually will be something like 64k in size, but as 64k does not divide evenly by either

640 or 800—the two common line lengths for super VGA modes—it's usually the case that a slightly smaller page size will be used. It's a lot more convenient to allow a driver to change pages in between lines.

In the example to be discussed shortly, the paging is handled in such a way as to allow you to decide how big each page is to be.

Finally, the procedure for changing pages usually involves some low level meddling with the card's registers. The designer of a VGA card can implement this in any way he or she feels like.

Some VGA cards, such as the Tseng Labs QVA/8600, actually come with this information in their manuals. Most do not—you'll have to contact their manufacturers directly. The information, when it's available at all, is rarely designed to be easily comprehensible. Bear in mind that the same data sheet that deals with the graphics mode you're after probably will also talk about countless alphanumeric VGA modes, downloading characters and probably the use of a light pen.

The following program involves the creation of a super VGA driver for the 640-by-400-pixel mode of the Paradise VGA cards. This is a fairly typical example of the craft. The 400-line mode is common to all the Paradise VGA cards.

The Paradise Super VGA Driver

It's not too difficult to figure out how to put the Paradise card into its 640-by-400-pixel, 256-color mode once you've had a read of the data sheets. It's mode 5EH. The following code will handle the change:

```
MOV    AX,005EH
INT    10H
```

The Paradise documentation notes that you can see if this worked by calling the INT 10H function 0FH. The AL register should contain the current video mode after this call, 5EH.

The documentation surrounding VGA cards seems to have a tradition of using slightly obtuse terms to refer to the important concepts of programming this already obtuse hardware. The Paradise documentation calls the paged screen memory VRAM, presumably for virtual memory. In this case it's defined as being "virtual" because only some of it is accessible at one time.

The Paradise card allows you to define any place in its virtual screen buffer as being the start of the page that is switched into the bus. It will page 64k at a time, but this doesn't mean you have to update all 64k at once. It's a lot more convenient to work with chunks of 60k, which will hold 96 lines of 640 pixels. This means that you'll have to deal with four pages to update the entire screen.

Much of the information in the pertinent section of the Paradise technical documentation isn't actually relevant to writing a straight screen driver. There are examples that pertain to moving areas of the screen contents around in the card's virtual memory, something that isn't necessary in simply displaying bit-mapped images.

Selecting a page of virtual memory involves the use of a register that the documentation refers to as PROA. This isn't actually a hardware register per se. It's an internal memory register in the Paradise card that must be accessed through a hardware register, 03CEH. The following code will write the value in the AL register to PROA:

```
PUSH    AX              ;SAVE THE VALUE
MOV     DX,03CEH        ;GET THE REGISTER
MOV     AX,050FH        ;UNLOCK PROA
OUT     DX,AX           ;OUTPUT THE WORD
POP     AX              ;RESTORE THE VALUE
MOV     AH,AL           ;PUT THE VALUE IN AH
MOV     AL,9            ;INDEX FOR PROA
OUT     DX,AX           ;OUTPUT THE WORD
MOV     AX,000FH        ;LOCK PROA
OUT     DX,AX
```

The graphics memory on the Paradise card is not segmented like the main memory in a PC. You can think of it as being linear memory. It would require a five-digit hex number to address all of it. The lower three digits are provided by the register being used to deal with the memory. The upper two digits are set by the value written to PROA.

Let's say that you wanted to update the 200'th line of the screen buffer. This would start at the 128,000'th byte of the buffer, or byte 1F400H. To access this, you would set DS to 0A000H, the base of the graphics buffer, SI to 0400H and PROA to 1FH. Through the internal black magic of the card, writing to where SI points would update the 200'th line on your screen.

Figure 9-9 is a screen driver, PARSCR.ASM, for the 600-by-400-pixel, 256-color mode of a Paradise card.

Fig 9-9   The assembly language Paradise super VGA 640-by-400-pixel screen driver

```
;
;               Paradise Screen graphics routines
;
;               These routines will display graphics... most
;               notably GIF files... in the 640 x 400 5EH mode
;               of a Paradise VGA card... in 256 glorious colours
;

VERSION         EQU     1                       ;VERSION
SUBVERSION      EQU     0                       ;SUBVERSION

PROA_REG        EQU     9                       ;INDICES FOR SPECIAL

SCREEN_WIDE     EQU     640                     ;SCREEN WIDTH
```

Fig 9-9   continued

```
SCREEN_DEEP        EQU      400                    ;SCREEN DEPTH
COLOURS            EQU      256                    ;NUMBER OF COLOURS

_AOFF              EQU      6                      ;FAR STACK OFFSET

;SET THE PROA REGISTER TO THE VALUE IN AL
SET_PROA           MACRO
                   PUSH     AX
                   MOV      DX,03CEH
                   MOV      AX,050FH
                   OUT      DX,AX
                   POP      AX
                   MOV      AH,AL
                   MOV      AL,PROA_REG
                   OUT      DX,AX
                   MOV      AX,000FH
                   OUT      DX,AX
                   ENDM


;THIS MACRO FETCHES THE DATA SEGEMENT
DATASEG            MACRO
                   PUSH     AX
                   MOV      AX,_DATA
                   MOV      DS,AX
                   POP      AX
                   ENDM


;THIS MACRO RETURNS SCREEN LINE OFFSET FOR LINE DX IN DI
TUBEOFF            MACRO
                   PUSH     DX
                   PUSH     SI
                   PUSH     DS
                   DATASEG
                   MOV      SI,OFFSET SCREENTABLE
                   SHL      DX,1
                   ADD      SI,DX
                   MOV      DI,[SI]
                   POP      DS
                   POP      SI
                   POP      DX
                   ENDM


;THIS MACRO ADJUSTS THE PALETTE PERCENTAGE
FIXPALETTE         MACRO
                   SHR      AL,1
                   SHR      AL,1
                   ENDM

VGA_TEXT           SEGMENT BYTE PUBLIC 'CODE'
                   ASSUME  CS:VGA_TEXT,DS:_DATA

;THIS FUNCTION SETS THE VGA PALETTE FROM A GIF COLOUR MAP
;                  CALLED AS
```

```
;               SetVgaPalette(gifpalette,number);
;               char *gifpalette;
;               int number; /* number of valid colours */
;
                PUBLIC  _SetParPalette
_SetParPalette  PROC    FAR
                PUSH    BP
                MOV     BP,SP

                MOV     AX,1000H
                MOV     BX,0712H
                INT     10H

                MOV     SI,[BP + _AOFF + 0]     ;OFFSET OF SOURCE
                MOV     DS,[BP + _AOFF + 2]     ;SEGMENT OF SOURCE

                MOV     CX,[BP + _AOFF + 4]     ;NUMBER OF COLOURS
                MOV     AX,_DATA
                MOV     ES,AX
                MOV     DI,OFFSET VGAPALETTE

                CMP     CX,0                    ;CHECK FOR NASTIES
                JG      GVP0
                JMP     GVPX

GVP0:           PUSH    CX
                LODSB
                FIXPALETTE                      ;RED
                STOSB
                LODSB
                FIXPALETTE                      ;GREEN
                STOSB
                LODSB
                FIXPALETTE                      ;BLUE
                STOSB

                POP     CX
                LOOP    GVP0

                MOV     AX,1012H                ;POINT TO THE PALETTE
                MOV     BX,0000H
                MOV     CX,COLOURS
                MOV     DX,OFFSET VGAPALETTE
                INT     10H

GVPX:           DATASEG
                POP     BP
                RET
_SetParPalette  ENDP

;THIS FUNCTION SETS THE DISPLAY CARD INTO VGA GRAPHICS MODE
;               CALLED AS
;               PARgraphics();
;
```

Fig 9-9   continued

```
                PUBLIC   _PARgraphics
_PARgraphics    PROC     FAR
                PUSH     BP
                DATASEG

                MOV      CX,SCREEN_DEEP              ;DEPTH OF SCREEN
                SUB      BX,BX                      ;ZERO LINE COUNTER
                MOV      SI,OFFSET SCREENTABLE      ;POINT TO TABLE

VGAG1:          PUSH     CX
                MOV      AX,SCREEN_WIDE             ;WIDTH OF SCREEN
                MUL      BX                         ;TIMES LINE NUMBER

                MOV      CL,4                       ;SHIFT HIGH ORDER
                SHL      DX,CL                      ;WORD OVER BY A BYTE
                AND      DX,0070H

                CMP      AX,(0FFFEH-SCREEN_WIDE)     ;SEE IF WE WILL
                JB       VGAG2                      ;HIT A 64K BOUNDARY
                SUB      AX,1000H                   ;AND ADJUST THE
                INC      DX                         ;HIGH ORDER WORD

VGAG2:          MOV      [SI],AX                    ;SAVE THE VALUES
                MOV      [SI+2],DX                  ;IN OUR LOOKUP TABLE
                ADD      SI,4                       ;AND POINT TO THE
                INC      BX                         ;NEXT LINE AND
                POP      CX                         ;ENTRY
                LOOP     VGAG1

                MOV      AX,007EH                   ;USE SPECIAL PARADISE
                MOV      BX,SCREEN_WIDE             ;BIOS FUNCTION
                MOV      CX,SCREEN_DEEP             ;TO SET GRAPHICS
                MOV      DX,COLOURS                 ;MODE
                INT      10H

                MOV      AX,007FH                   ;READ PR1
                MOV      BH,1BH
                INT      10H

                MOV      AX,007FH
                AND      BL,0F7H                    ;DISABLE PROB
                MOV      BH,0BH
                INT      10H

                POP      BP
                RET
_PARgraphics    ENDP

;THIS FUNCTION SETS THE DISPLAY CARD INTO TEXT MODE
;               CALLED AS
;               PARtext();
;
                PUBLIC   _PARtext
```

```
_PARtext        PROC    FAR
                PUSH    BP
                DATASEG
                MOV     AX,1200H
                MOV     BX,0031H
                INT     10H

                MOV     AX,0003H
                INT     10H
                POP     BP
                RET
_PARtext        ENDP

;THIS FUNCTION DISPLAYS A VGA LINE
;               CALLED AS
;               ShowPAR(line,length,linenumber);
;               char *line;
;               int length; /* bytes in one field */
;               int linennumber;
;
                PUBLIC  _ShowPAR
_ShowPAR        PROC    FAR
                PUSH    BP
                MOV     BP,SP

                MOV     AX,_DATA
                MOV     ES,AX

                CMP     WORD PTR [BP + _AOFF + 6],SCREEN_DEEP
                JGE     SHOWVGAX                ;IS THIS A LEGAL LINE?
                MOV     SI,[BP + _AOFF + 0]     ;OFFSET OF SOURCE
                MOV     DS,[BP + _AOFF + 2]     ;SEGMENT OF SOURCE
                MOV     CX,[BP + _AOFF + 4]     ;LENGTH OF MOVE IN BYTES

                CMP     CX,SCREEN_WIDE          ;IS IT TOO LONG?
                JL      SHOWVGA0

                MOV     CX,SCREEN_WIDE

SHOWVGA0:       MOV     BX,[BP + _AOFF + 6]     ;GET INDEX INTO LINE TABLE
                SHL     BX,1
                SHL     BX,1

                MOV     DI,ES:[SCREENTABLE + BX]
                MOV     AX,ES:[SCREENTABLE + 2 + BX]
                SET_PROA                        ;SET HIGH ORDER WORD

SHOWVGA1:       MOV     AX,0A000H               ;POINT TO VIDEO BUFFER
                MOV     ES,AX                   ;WITH ES

                CLD
        REPNE   MOVSB                           ;MOVE IN THE LINE DATA

SHOWVGAX:       DATASEG
                POP     BP
```

Fig 9-9   continued

```
                        RET
_ShowPAR                ENDP

VGA_TEXT                ENDS

DGROUP                  GROUP     _DATA,_BSS

_DATA                   SEGMENT WORD PUBLIC 'DATA'

SCREENTABLE             DW        (SCREEN_DEEP * 2 )DUP (0)   ;VGA LINE START TABLE
VGAPALETTE              DB        300H DUP (0)                ;VGA PALETTE BUFFER

_DATA                   ENDS

_BSS                    SEGMENT WORD PUBLIC 'BSS'
_BSS                    ENDS
                        END
```

The only images that are commonly found with this sort of resolution are GIF pictures. As such, the program in Fig. 9-10 is a GIF viewer modified to use the Paradise screen driver.

This program must link to PARSCR.OBJ and the GIF decoder in Chapter 5.

Fig 9-10   A GIF viewer for use with the Paradise driver

```
/*
        An example C language Paradise SVGA GIF decoder
*/

#include "stdio.h"
#include "dos.h"
#include "alloc.h"

extern char PALETTE[256][4],OUTROW[1024],COPYRIGHT[];
extern int INTERLACED,IMAGEWIDE,IMAGEDEEP;
extern int IMAGEX,IMAGEY,XLOC,YLOC;
extern int VERSION,SUBVERSION;

char *pbf=NULL;          /* pointer to line work space */

main(argc,argv)
        int argc;
        char *argv[];
{
        char filename[65];
        int i,e,ShowIt(),Colourize();
        int ImageDone(),BadError(),BGround();

        SetShow(ShowIt);
        SetPalette(Colourize);
```

```
                SetImage(ImageDone);
                SetError(BadError);
                SetBackground(BGround);
                if(argc > 1) {
                        if((pbf=malloc(4096)) != NULL) {
                                PARgraphics();
                                for(i=1;i<argc;++i) {
                                        strmfe(filename,argv[i],"GIF");
                                        if((e=UnpackGIF(filename)) == 0) {
                                                if(getch()==27) break;
                                        }
                                        else break;
                                }
                                PARtext();
                                if(e) printf("Error code %d",e);
                                free(pbf);
                        } else puts("Error allocating memory");
                }
                ShowCopyright();
}

ImageDone()
{
        nosound();
        sound(660);
        delay(100);
        sound(880);
        delay(50);
        sound(440);
        delay(75);
        nosound();
}

Colourize(n,palette)
        int n;
        char *palette;
{
        SetParPalette(palette,n);
}

ShowIt()
{
        ShowPAR(OUTROW,IMAGEWIDE,YLOC);
}

BGround(n)
        int n;
{
        union REGS r;
        int i;

        memset(pbf,n,640);
        for(i=0;i<400;++i) ShowPAR(pbf,640,i);

        r.x.ax=0x1001;
```

Fig 9-10 continued

```
        r.x.bx=n << 8;
        int86(0x10,&r,&r);                      /* set overscan */
}


BadError(s)
        char *s;
{

        PARtext();
        printf("\007\007\007Fatal error - %s.\n",s);
        exit(1);
}


ShowCopyright()
{

        char *p;

        p = COPYRIGHT;
        while(*p) {
                p += printf(p)+1;
                puts("");
        }
}

strmfe(new,old,ext)                  /* make file name with specific extension */
        char *new,*old,*ext;
{

        while(*old != 0 && *old != '.') *new++=*old++;
        *new++='.';
        while(*ext) *new++=*ext++;
        *new=0;
}
```

PRACTICAL SCREEN DRIVERS

Even more so than with the monochrome screen drivers discussed in the last chapter, color drivers really seem to cry out for a loadable screen driver strategy. Having linked-in drivers for the standard EGA and VGA modes is pretty easy to manage, but if you want to write software that will deal with the growing number of super VGA cards you'll probably have to allow the users of your programs to choose their drivers. Linking in dozens of drivers is wasteful of space, and it requires that you release a new version of your program every time you want to add a new driver to your application.

10
CHAPTER

Printing and Encapsulated PostScript Files

Inside every small problem is a big problem struggling to get out.
—Murphy's Laws of Computers

One of the great drawbacks to glorious, 256-color monitors is that glorious, 256-color printers aren't nearly so plentiful. More to the point, at least at the programming level, displaying an image on your screen is a great deal easier than is having it roll out of your printer.

In printing bit-mapped graphics, you will have two principle things to consider. The first is that the printers that are likely to reproduce one's graphics vary enormously in their capabilities and in the way that they're communicated with. The second is that most of the more interesting images are multiple color ones, while most of the affordable printers are stuck with black and white. Of those printers that will reproduce color, only the really high end color PostScript printers and film recorders really can begin to duplicate the color capabilities of a VGA card. Color ink jet printers and other low-cost color devices are capable of more than one color, but they're hardly capable of reproduction quality.

In dealing with printing images, then, you must learn how to control various sorts of printers, and to deal with color in a workable way for black and white output devices. Surprisingly, the possibilities in this latter area are a lot more usable than you might initially think, especially if you're driving a laser printer.

THE THREE BASIC PRINTER TYPES

There are basically only three types of graphics compatible printers that PCs usually find themselves attached to. Everything else is a subset of them. This taxonomy is based more on how the printers work than on who makes them.

The first group consists of all graphics capable dot matrix printers. These behave largely like an Epson FX-80, and while your particular printer might or might not actually emulate an FX-80's control codes—most do to some extent—it probably prints in much the same manner as one when it's asked to handle graphics. Dot matrix printers handle graphics in a way that is perfectly sensible from the point of view of a printer and very nearly diabolical for everyone else.

The second group consists of laser printers that emulate the Hewlett Packard LaserJet Plus, or some superset thereof. These are basic, top down lasers with a fairly primitive page description language called PCL. In a sense, they're the laser equivalent of the Epson FX-80, although, of course, they have much more powerful font and graphics facilities built into them.

LaserJets print bit-mapped graphics in exactly the same format as you'll be used to seeing them stored in memory—at least, they do when they're trying to print straight monochrome bitmaps. While a tad arcane to program because of their propensity for wanting lots of obscure escape sequences, LaserJet compatible printers require the least amount of actual data manipulation and bit fiddling to get images from them.

The third group of printers comprises all PostScript devices. Now, PostScript usually makes one think of laser printers, but PostScript can be used to drive just about any hard copy device. There are PostScript typesetters, PostScript crystal printers and, through the use of off board PostScript interpreters like Freedom of Press and GoScript, even PostScript dot matrix printers. One of the beauties of PostScript is that you need not know what sort of a PostScript device you're outputting an image to code up the picture.

This is almost true, anyway. PostScript devices of varying resolutions tend to produce varying densities of grey for the same absolute numerical percentage of grey in a PostScript file—such that, for example, 30 percent grey looks lighter on a Linotronic PostScript typesetter than it does on a 300 dot per inch Apple LaserWriter.

PostScript offers you the most elegant way to deal with color images on a black and white output device.

Unlike the previous two sorts of output devices, a PostScript printer can be communicated with using nothing but straight ASCII. You don't print to a PostScript device, but, rather, you write a program in PostScript that describes what you want printed—PostScript is a very powerful programming language that is resident in any PostScript printer. If you're used to driving simple printers, the notion of having a language at the far end of your printer cable might require some head scratching for a while.

Writing PostScript programs is a fascinating area of programming, and one that will not be discussed very deeply at all in this book. You can get by with very little PostScript programming if you just want to print some pictures.

In dealing with monochrome bit-mapped images, it's quite reasonable to come up with three largely interchangeable functions that will print the same image to these three sorts printers. This makes supporting them relatively painless, because, at this level, they can all be said to have essentially the same capabilities. In reality, monochrome graphics on a dot matrix printer are pushing it to its limit, while printing the same image to a PostScript device is analogous to fetching groceries in an E type Jaguar. However, printers rarely complain about what they're given to print— unlike E type Jags, which commit car suicide when they're asked to perform menial chores.

Dot Matrix Printers

The ideal output device for bit-mapped graphics would be one that would accept data in the same form in which it's stored. The two sorts of laser printers we'll look at approach this facility. Dot matrix printers do not—they require that you manipulate your bit-mapped pictures rather savagely to print them.

This example deals with the Epson FX-80. Now, to begin with, note that Epson no longer actually makes the FX-80 per se—they long ago superseded it with newer, more powerful printers having supersets of its control codes and capabilities. However, the wonderful thing about programming for this printer is that most dot matrix printers emulate its basic control set. If your program will drive an FX-80, it will drive most dot matrix printers. Usually this means that it won't drive them as well as they could be driven, and in writing graphics applications it's usually essential that one have multiple printer drivers on hand for all the countless variations on the theme of printing bitmaps. However, by sticking to the FX-80 control codes you can see how things work and create software that will run with the lowest common denominator.

Most of the newer, more interesting dot matrix printers support 24 pins and near letter quality modes—and, of course, much nicer graphics modes too. While this chapter won't be discussing them in detail—mostly because there are no real standards for these higher resolution modes— the principles are the same as the ones for the FX-80.

One line of monochrome image data, as seen on a monitor, consists of some number of bytes laid end to end, so that each bit of each byte controls one pixel. The pixels are arranged horizontally along the screen of the monitor, as you will recall.

One line of a graphic image sent to a dot matrix printer is eight bits deep. One byte of a graphic image sent to the printer will result in eight pixels being reproduced on paper, but they'll be vertical. The first byte does the first dot of the first eight horizontal lines. The next byte does the next dot of the first eight lines—and so on, for the width of the image. The next byte after that starts with the first dot of each of eight lines starting with the ninth line, because the first eight lines will have been taken care of.

Figure 10-1 illustrates the relationship of screen data to printer data.

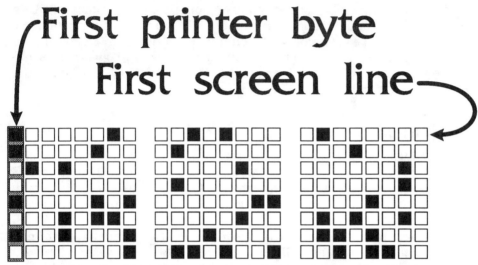

Fig 10-1   The relationship between a normal bitmap and dot matrix printer data

If it helps in understanding this process, consider that in printing text characters, the printer uses a matrix of pins, hence its name. In printing graphics, only the leftmost vertical row of pins is used, and which pins fire in that row is controlled by the data in the current byte of graphic information being printed. When that byte has been hammered into the paper, the print head moves over not by one character space but by the width of one dot.

This probably sounds difficult to program. It is. There's an enormous amount of bitwise data manipulation required to construct the appropriate bytes from a conventionally stored bitmap in memory and output them in the right order to the printer.

In addition to this, you also will have to control most of the things the printer does while it isn't actually printing graphics. This involves escape codes. Each line of graphic information is preceded by an escape sequence that tells the printer which resolution of graphics reproduction to drop into for that line and the number of subsequent bytes of information to process as graphics. When the line is complete, you must send the printer some escape codes to move its print head back to the left side of the page and down by exactly eight dots, so that the next pass of the print head will appear just below the first pass.

The most important set of escape codes to bear in mind for printing graphics to an FX-80 is the group that selects the graphics mode and tells the printer how long the next line is to be. There are several of these, because the printer is capable of printing graphics with several degrees of density. This first set of codes is for the simplest mode, normal density graphics. The maximum number of horizontal pixels you can put on an $8^1/_2$-by-11-inch sheet of paper in this mode is 640, or the width of an EGA graphics screen:

ESC K LO HI

The first byte, ESC, is character 27. The second is an uppercase K. The third, LO, is the low order byte of the integer that holds the length of the line in pixels. If you are going to print a 640-dot line, you can figure this out easily by looking at the hex value for this number, 280H. The low order byte is 80H, or 128.

The next byte, HI, is the high order part of this integer, 02H in this case.

There are several other useful graphics modes supported by a basic Epson FX-80 compatible printer. This next one gives you double the resolution of the normal mode, but at low speed, resulting in somewhat tighter looking dots than the high speed mode:

ESC L LO HI

And this, then, is the double resolution high speed mode:

ESC Y LO HI

Finally, this is quad mode. It will do more than 2,500 dots per line across $8^1/_2$-inch paper, but it's glacially slow:

ESC Z LO HI

Now, if this isn't enough, there's a sort of master graphics mode that allows you to access all of these modes plus a couple of others. Its form is:

ESC * MODE LO HI

In this case, the asterisk is, in fact, an asterisk. The LO and HI bytes are as they were described before, with one catch that we'll get into in just a moment. The MODE value can be one of seven numbers, to wit:

00H	Normal mode
01H	Low speed double
02H	High speed double
03H	Quad density
04H	Epson QX-10 emulation
05H	Plotter emulation
06H	Square pixels

In practice, only the last one is of any real use beyond what you could do with the aforementioned single mode escape sequences. It's what the Epson manuals call "CRT" mode, indicating that it's intended for use in screen dumps, one might suppose. Its density is somewhere between normal and double resolution, but pictures printed in it come up with a more or less one to one aspect ratio. All of the other modes result in printed images that look as if they'd been squeezed in one dimension or the other.

The catch regarding the lengths of lines has to do with a bit of common sense. Obviously, the same picture printed in normal mode and quad mode will occupy considerably different amounts of paper. In using the master graphics mode, you must take some care to see that the line length you've told the printer to reproduce isn't greater than what the paper can support in the density you've called for. This can get a little tricky if you're printing variable width pictures. You also might want to bear in mind that dot matrix printers come in narrow and wide carriage models.

Here's another catch of specific interest to C language programmers. This bit of code will create the escape sequence for any of the master graphics modes—or, it usually will. You might want to see if you can figure out what its problem is before you read on.

```
sprintf(b,"\x1b*%c%c%c",mode,width,width >> 8);
```

This mode works in everything but the normal mode, mode zero. In this mode, there would be a zero byte in the middle of the string, and C interprets zero bytes as being the ends of strings. As such, the two bytes for the length of the line would not be included in the string printed to buffer b.

Watch for this one when you're dealing with printer data from C.

Back when eight pin printers like the Epson FX-80 were a lot more popular than they are today, the phrase "Epson compatible" was bandied about quite a lot. In fact, very few so called Epson compatible printers really were, and they fell down most frequently in the area of printing graphics. Very often, you'll find that only the normal, single density mode is supported exactly, with subtle variations on the others. This is why programs that reproduce graphics on dot matrix printers usually have such extensive setup menus.

It's also worth pointing out that there's a healthy number of graphics printers that don't even try to emulate the Epson FX-80, although most use much the same structure for their escape codes. One example of this sort of device is a tiny little printer called the PN-101 which Yamaha had NEC build for their MSX music computers. It has escape codes for many of the Epson FX-80 facilities, but every one of them is just a bit different.

Having said all this, Fig. 10-2 is a function to print a bit-mapped image stored in a buffer to an Epson FX-80 printer. It uses the square pixel mode of the master graphics escape sequence, so its horizontal resolution is limited to about 720 or so dots. It's great for printing MacPaint images and things of about the same dimensions.

This will be the form of all the monochrome bit-map printing functions to be discussed here. The first argument, picture, is a pointer to where

Fig 10-2   A function to print small bitmaps to an Epson FX-80 compatible dot matrix printer

```
EPrint(picture,width,lines)
        char *picture;
        int width,lines;
{
        int i,j;

        p_string("\x1b@");
        for(i=0;i<lines;i+=8) {
                p_string("\x1b*\x06");
                p_char(width);
                p_char(width >> 8);
                for(j=0;j<width;++j)
                  p_char(~get_bit(picture+(i*(width/8)),j,width));
                p_string("\r\x1bJ\x18");
                if(kbhit()) if(getch()==0x1b) break;
        }
        p_string("\x1b@");
}

p_string(s)
        char *s;
{
        while(*s) p_char(*s++);
}

p_char(c)
        int c;
{
        struct REGS r;

        do {
                r.h.ah = 2;
                r.x.dx = 0;
                int86(0x17,&r,&r);
        } while(!(r.h.ah & 0x80));

        r.h.ah = 0;
        r.h.al = c;
        r.x.dx = 0;
        int86(0x17,&r,&r);
}

get_bit(p,n,w)
        char *p;
        int n,w;
{
        int b,i,r=0;

        p += (n / 8);
        for(i=7;i>>=0;--i) {
                b = *p;
```

Fig 10-2   continued

```
                if(b & (1<<(7-n%8)))  r |= (1 << i);
                p += (w/8);
        }
        return(r);
}
```

bitmap actually lives, presumably where you unpacked it into when you loaded it into memory from a graphics file. The width argument is the length of one line of the picture in pixels. The lines argument is the depth of the picture in pixels.

The EPrint function assumes that the picture will have been inverted, for reasons that have been discussed previously. If your application doesn't involve storing its bitmaps this way, you can change it quite easily. Just make this line:

p_char(~ get_bit(picture + (i*(width/8)),j,width));

into this line:

p_char(get_bit(picture + (i*(width/8)),j,width));

That is, remove the tilde in front of the call to get bit so that the result of the get bit function won't be NOTed.

This function uses several others to do some of the hard stuff. The get bit function performs all the fancy bitwise manipulation to rotate the bytes that will be printed. It's not too hard to see what it's up to if you care to work through it.

One of the unfortunate aspects of this code is how it's forced to communicate with the printer. It would be very handy indeed if you could send all this data to the printer port by simply using the fprintf function provided by C and printing to stdprn, the standard streamed print device. Having done so, you would have the facility of redirecting it to other devices with the DOS MODE command, as well as sending all the printer output to a disk file with almost no code changes. Regrettably, this doesn't work reliably in this application.

It turns out that DOS doesn't check to see if the printer is ready before it sends a character down the pipe. It only checks to see if there was an error after the fact. As such, because this function will be printing far more data than most printers will be able to buffer, the printer will be forever losing some of it as DOS sends it more than it can immediately handle. This makes a great cosmic hash of one's pictures very, very quickly.

The p char function provides a way around this—simply by going around DOS. It uses direct BIOS calls to talk to the printer 1 byte at a time. Now, if you look at it closely you'll notice that it's a little chilling, as the first of its two int86 calls to the BIOS will be an endless loop if the printer port never becomes ready. In practice this doesn't happen.

You could put a keyboard check or a time out in this loop if you wanted to.

The first call waits for the printer port to signal that the printer's buffer is sufficiently empty to allow it to accept one more byte, as indicated by the high order bit of the AH register when the BIOS call returns. The second call actually sends the byte.

Note that this—and all the other—printer functions in this chapter assume that the printer is connected to LPT1.

The whole EPrint function should be easily understandable now. It steps through the bit-mapped image at picture eight lines at a time, this being the number of vertical rows of bits that the printer will lay down in one pass of its print head. Prior to sending the data for each line, it prints the master graphics mode escape sequence of the printer for the square pixel mode followed by the low and high order bytes of the width value. It then steps through the line one pixel at a time, using get bit to assemble the bytes to be printed.

Finally, with the whole line printed, it must move the print head back to the left side of the page and down exactly eight lines. Getting back to the left side of the page is easy—a carriage return manages that. The rest of the sequence is:

ESC J AMOUNT

where the AMOUNT value is the number of 216ths of an inch that the print head must move down. The value here, 18H or 24 decimal—about .11 inches—was determined experimentally. Regrettably, this is another area in which compatible printers usually aren't, and you might find that this number wants changing if you use this routine to print to something other than an FX-80. It probably also will want changing if you use a different printer graphics mode.

This function is designed to print bitmaps that will fit into a single 64k memory segment. You can use far pointers to deal with larger bitmaps if you want to. The programs later in this chapter illustrate how to get this together.

If you have a laser printer, it's easy to think disparagingly of dot matrix printers. It's a task having to support their plethora of modes and models, and even when they work their output is funky and not very nice to look at. However, in writing commercial applications software that handles graphics, one must bear in mind that there are a lot more potential users with dot matrix printers on the planet than there are with lasers, and this is likely to remain so for quite a while.

Dot matrix support, as ugly as it might seem, is pretty well mandatory for most graphics applications that produce hard copy.

LaserJets

Writing programs that print monochrome bitmaps to Hewlett Packard LaserJet Plus compatible printers will seem breathtakingly simple after dealing with dot matrix printers. There's a pretty obvious reason for this, actually. A LaserJet stores its bitmaps in memory, just as you will have done in the computer that created them. Being a bear of very little brain, the LaserJet wants to be sent its graphics in a form that requires that it do the least amount of thinking when it gets them. As such, you can all but blast them over in their raw form.

Even with this simple device, however, there are a number of considerations to bear in mind. The first is that a straight LaserJet—without the Plus—doesn't have enough memory to reproduce full page graphics. The LaserJet needs at least a megabyte and a half of memory to handle big pictures. Not many of these early LaserJets still exist as such, though, so one probably need not worry about it.

More important is that the LaserJet supports four resolution modes for pictures. The coarsest, 75 dots to the inch, is analogous to basic dot matrix resolution. A MacPaint picture will fill a whole page in this mode. Things get progressively tighter at 100 and 150 dots per inch until you reach 300 dots per inch, which is the actual resolution of the laser printer engine. At this density, a MacPaint picture prints up at about two by two and a half inches. Most of the pictures in this book are printed at 150 dots per inch. For reasons that will be discussed in greater detail later on in this chapter, reproducing fine detail at 300 dots to the inch poses some problems if what you're printing is going to ultimately wind up being stuck to the drum of a printing press.

Figure 10-3 illustrates the four resolutions of a LaserJet.

Figure 10-4 is a simple printing routine for the LaserJet. It handles images that are small enough to fit in a single memory segment.

This routine uses the same arguments as the EPrint function discussed for the FX-80. However, because of the rather simpler data structure of the LaserJet's graphics modes, the horizontal dimensions that the various parts of the function use in dealing with the printer are in bytes, rather than in pixels. Also note that there's a new argument, an integer called mode. This must be set to one of 75, 100, 150, or 300. If it's something else, the printer usually defaults to its 75-dot-per-inch mode.

There's one caveat to programming the LaserJet for graphics. If you get anything wrong, so that the printer fails to recognize that it's supposed to go into its graphics mode, it usually will try to reproduce all the bytes of your picture as meaningless text. Because laser printers are very fast in text mode, it probably will get away with spewing out quite a bit of paper before you manage to shut it down.

If you're developing a LaserJet driver where other people can see you working, it's a good idea to debug this part of it when everyone else is at lunch.

The escape sequences for the LaserJet aren't a whole lot less complex than were those of the FX-80. However, there are substantially fewer of them to deal with when you're printing straight black and white graphics.

Fig 10-3   The four resolutions of a LaserJet Plus compatible laser printer: 300, 150, 100, and 75 dots to the inch

Fig 10-4   A function to print small bitmaps to a LaserJet

```
HPrint(picture,mode,width,lines)
        char *picture;
        int mode,width,lines;
{
        char s[64],*p,*farPtr();
        int i;

        width = width >> 3;
        sprintf(s,"\x1b*t%dR",mode);
        p_string(s);
        p_string("\x1b*r0A");
```

Fig 10-4   continued

```
        for(i=0;i<lines;++i) {
                sprintf(s,"\x1b*b%dW",width);
                p_string(s);
                p_buff(picture,width);
                picture += width;
        }

        p_string("\x1b*rB\n");
        p_string("\x0c");
}

p_buff(s,l)
        char *s;
        int l;
{
        while(l--) p_char(~(*s++));
}
```

The first one is the resolution command. It's of the form:

ESC * t MODE R

As with the dot matrix printers, ESC is character 27. The asterisk is actually an asterisk, and the lowercase ''t'' and the uppercase ''R'' are what they appear to be. The MODE value is one of the four legal resolution values just discussed. However, where the escape sequences for a dot matrix printer would have sent character 75 in this field, for example, the LaserJet wants the actual string ''75.'' Thus, to put the printer in its 75 dot-per-inch graphics mode, you would send it the following string from C:

" \x1b*t75R"

This example uses a hexadecimal constant for the ESC character—in classical C this would be written in octal as \033 instead of \x1b. Most contemporary C compilers let you have it either way.

Note that you shouldn't send a carriage return after this, or after any of the other LaserJet escape sequences.

The next sequence tells the printer that some graphic lines are coming. It goes like this:

ESC * r POSITION A

The POSITION value tells the printer where the left margin of the picture is to go. If it's zero, the image will start at the left margin of the paper. In fact, the printer can't print right out to any of the paper margins, so it actually starts 40 or 50 dots in from the left margin. If this value is one, the picture will start at the current cursor position—there are separate cursor positioning escape sequences for the LaserJet. In this example the picture starts at the left side of the page, but you might want to position it elsewhere, especially if it's smaller than the page.

The sequence:

ESC * p POSITION X

sets the horizontal value of the cursor to the specified number of dots over from the left. Likewise:

ESC * p POSITION Y

sets the vertical position of the cursor to the specified number of dots down from the top. For example, this string, in C notation, would position the cursor at (100,150) on the current page of the LaserJet:

" \x1b*p100X\x1b*p150Y"

Unlike as with a dot matrix printer, you can move the LaserJet's cursor back up the page as easily as moving it down. The position of graphics has little to do with any text on the page—you can create very complex pages by combining the two. However, this is beyond the scope of this discussion.

You're now ready to send some graphics to the printer. Each line of graphic data represents one horizontal line of the bitmap. If you want to print a picture that is 720 pixels across, the graphics line would consist of 90 bytes of bit-map information preceded by yet another escape sequence. At the end of the 90 bytes, the LaserJet automatically positions its internal graphics cursor at the left side of the page and down one line, all set for another line should one appear. In the meantime, it drops back into text mode to await either some text or another escape sequence.

The escape sequence that signals the start of a line of graphic information is:

ESC * b COUNT W

where the value of COUNT is the number of bytes in the line—90 in the case of this example. In C, this would be:

" \x1b*b90W"

and then 90 bytes of graphics. Having been presented with this sequence, the printer will interpret the next 90 bytes as graphics no matter what they are—it will ignore all its escape sequences for the next 90 bytes. As such, you must make sure that the length of your graphic lines agrees with what you've told the printer, lest it gobble up the next escape sequence as the end of its current graphic line.

When you're done printing the current picture you'd send the printer this sequence:

ESC * r B

This tells it that the bit-mapped graphics are over with. You also might want to send it character 12—or 0CH—which will cause it to spit its current sheet of paper out so you can have a look at it.

As will be discussed in greater detail in the chapter on dithering, it's very often necessary that you print pictures that are too big to fit in a single memory segment. You might think that a monochrome image of this size probably would not occur without some sort of spontaneous mutation, but large graphics files are quite common when one is dealing with image scanners—as well as with pictures that have been dithered down from color image files. For reasons to be discussed later in this book, dithering works best if you scale the color image to be dithered up by a few hundred percent. A monochrome image that is 640 by 400 pixels requires a mere 32k to store it. Scale it up by 300 percent and it suddenly swells to occupy a quarter of a megabyte.

Figure 10-5 illustrates how you would print a multiple segment image in a big buffer. This would require that the buffer has been allocated with farmalloc or directly through a call to DOS.

Fig 10-5   A function to print big bitmaps to a LaserJet

```
BigPrint(picture,width,lines)
        char *picture;
        int width,lines;
{
        char s[64],*farPtr();
        int i;

        p_string("\x1b*t300R");                /* set raster size mode */
        p_string("\x1b*r0A");            /* say graphics are coming */

        for(i=0;i<<lines;++i) {
                sprintf(s,"\x1b*b%dW",sourceBytes);
                p_string(s);
                p_buff(picture,width >> 3);
                picture = farPtr(picture,(long)width>>3);
        }
        p_string("\x1b*rB");
        p_string("\x0c");
}
```

This program copes with the rather awkward situation of large model pointers, which have cropped up at several other places in this book.

The various escape sequences used here are exactly as they were in the single segment example. However, this function assumes that the image will be printed at 300-dot-per-inch resolution, so there's no mode argument. A picture big enough to require a multiple segment buffer to contain it also would require pretty small pixels to fit it on a single page.

It's worth mentioning a bit of the terminology that goes along with LaserJets—if you consult a LaserJet manual you might find that some of the words used there differ from the ones in this book. First of all, bitmapped graphics probably will be called "raster" graphics. Secondly, because a LaserJet prints in multiple resolution modes when it does graphics, the manuals differentiate between pixels and dots. A dot is one point on the laser's scan, and always will be one 300'th of an inch across. A pixel will be equivalent only to a dot at 300 dots per inch. It's made up of four dots—two on a side—at a 150-dots-per-inch resolution. A 100-dot-per-inch pixel is three dots on a side, and so on.

Obviously, this discussion only deals with the graphics modes of the LaserJet. If you want to write programs that deal with the text mode of this complex little box, you'll need a complete escape code listing.

PostScript

The last of the three classifications of printers consists of all Post-Script devices. As you'll see in a little while, PostScript printers are not limited to simple bitmaps at all. In fact, if you're really well off, they're not even limited to black and white. However, color PostScript devices are seriously expensive, and they won't be discussed here.

As with the LaserJet, fully understanding the internal workings of a PostScript printer requires a lot more information than there's room for in this book. Rather than just a list of escape codes, you'll need several books to really understand everything there is to know about PostScript programming. Quite a few PostScript manuals exist.

Figure 10-6 illustrates a function that will print a single segment monochrome bitmap to a PostScript printer. As with the previous two examples, it assumes that the printer is connected to LPT1:. However, you'll notice that there are no escape sequences in this function. This bit of code actually writes a small PostScript program directly to the printer.

This program uses a PostScript operator called imagemask. To fully understand the syntax of this, you would have to get fairly deeply into PostScript coding. PostScript is a particularly obtuse little language if you aren't used to it. It is, as its name might imply, a postfix language. This means that it uses its stack to a great extent, pushing things onto it frequently. However, the actual structure of programs written in PostScript place one precariously close to the workings of the language itself, because everything must be written backward. For example, to print the string "Existential begonias," PostScript would have us do this:

(Existential begonias) show

This line means to push the address of the string onto the stack and then to call the show operator to print it. Although this is, in fact, exactly what C actually does behind your back, PostScript is a bit hard to deal with at first because of this rather convoluted structure.

There are two operators under PostScript that are specifically included in the language to deal with raw bitmaps. You've seen the simpler of the two here—the other one will turn up in just a while. This one, image-mask, is entirely devoted to monochrome bitmaps. In fact, it's intended for

Fig 10-6   A function to print small bitmaps to a PostScript printer

```
PPrint(picture,width,lines)
        char *picture;
        int width,lines;
{
        static char b[64];
        unsigned int i,j;

        p_string("%% Printing a picture\r\n");
        p_string("20 740 translate\r\n");
        sprintf(b,"%d %d scale\r\n",width,lines);
        p_string(b);
        p_string("0 setgray\r\n");

        sprintf(b,"%d %d true [%d 0 0 -%d 0 %d] \r\n {< ",
        width,lines,width,lines,0);
        p_string(b);
        for(i=0;i<((width/8) * lines);++i) {
                sprintf(b,"%02.2x",~(*picture++) & 0xff);
                p_string(b);
                if(!((i+1) % 64)) p_string("\r\n");
                if(kbhit()) if(getch()==0x1b) break;
        }
        p_string("> } \r\nimagemask\r\n");

        p_string("showpage\r\n");
}
```

use in creating masks rather than in actually printing images. However, because it wants to deal with data in precisely the format that monochrome bitmaps are stored in memory, it seems like a shame not to press it into service.

This is the basic structure of the call to imagemask:

ImageWidth ImageHeight true
[ImageWidth 0 0 ImageHeight 0 0]
%% lots of hex data
imagemask

The actual image is, of course, contained in the lots of hex data. The data is represented as a long string of two-digit hex numbers representing the bytes of the bitmap. There are no spaces or other punctuation between the hex digits, but the occasional carriage return is a good idea, because most PostScript printers have finite input buffers. PostScript ignores carriage returns and line feeds much as C does.

The line of numbers within the square brackets is a PostScript *transformation matrix*. It tells the imagemask operator how to process the data in the image. This is quite a complex subject—suffice it to say that this matrix causes imagemask to reproduce the image as you would expect it to be.

In the interest of fully understanding this bit of code, it should be noted that true is a predefined constant under PostScript. In this case, it's taken as a boolean value.

Finally, showpage causes the current page to be printed and spit from the printer.

If you have a relatively new Postscript printer and you want to play with this thing, you might have this bit of C code write the PostScript program it generates to a file rather than to the printer directly. Then you can see what happens when you change parts of it. Most newer PostScript printers have interactive modes that allow you to have a chat directly with the PostScript interpreter in the printer over a serial cable. A telecommunication program, such as Qmodem, works nicely for this purpose. Using the interactive mode you can send a program to the printer and read any error messages or complaints that the printer might send back as a result of trying to interpret it.

Consult your manual for the details of how to access the interactive mode of your particular printer.

COLOR IN BLACK AND WHITE

All of the forgoing code was, of course, limited to printing black and white bitmaps. Printing color is a very awkward thing at best. The possibilities seem to fall into two groups, to wit, the very ugly and the very expensive. Of the very ugly—ink jet and multiple color impact printers— the less said the better. These machines are ideal for doing business graphs and charts, but they don't make it for images with extensive color requirements.

The other group, color PostScript printers and film recorders, are not the sort of thing that most casual programmers can afford to play with.

In speaking of printing color images—at least until the technology gets a bit more affordable—most programmers will be looking at doing a decent job of creating black and white representations of color pictures that preserve as much of the original color images as possible. In fact, there are a number of areas where quite a lot can be done along these lines.

This section deals with printing color GIF images to a black and white laser printer. The techniques to be discussed are quite portable, however, and can be applied to any color image of up to 256 colors.

The simplest way to print a color image in black and white is to dither it into a black and white bitmap and print that using one of the printing routines already discussed. This works, and if you're using something other than a PostScript device it's probably as good as it gets. However, it's slow, and you unquestionably give up a fair bit of detail in the resulting images. See the chapter on dithering for some proper examples of dithering code.

If you have a PostScript printer you can do quite a bit better than this because PostScript printers have built-in halftone capabilities. It's fairly easy to convert the color palette of a GIF file into a lookup table of grey values and let the printer make these into variable sized dots.

Most computer users will have encountered halftones in some form or other. The most common example of them is found in newspapers and books, where continuous tone pictures—the kind that come back from a one hour photo place—are printed on paper by faking out grey shades with patterns of dots. Printing presses are just like laser printers in that they can only print black and white—they can't do actual grey.

The halftoning process is quite ancient, and is based on a clever system of cheating on various characteristics of photographic materials. If you have a piece of glass with a very fine cross hatch of lines on it, you'd think that light shining through it would leave black squares on a photographic emulsion beneath it. In fact, this doesn't actually happen—at least, not in all circumstances. If the light is somewhat faint, such as what that might be reflected from a grey surface, the "dots" produced by the spaces between the lines will be smaller than the actual space the light is shining through. As the light gets fainter, the dots will get smaller.

Shooting a photograph through a halftone screen such as this will create a facsimile of the picture with the greys represented by these variable sized dots.

You can do something like this in dithering a color image down to black and white, although the process is quite different and the results frequently are not as attractive as they might have been had the picture been mechanically screened. You might have some difficulty in imagining how one might get a monitor under a process camera to screen it, though.

In fact, you can synthesize a mechanical halftone in data quite simply. Given some arbitrary grey level, you can simply have your output device fill a suitable size box on the page it's printing with a corresponding grey tone, that is, a dot pattern just like the ones produced in a normal photographic halftone. If these boxes are small and numerous enough, they'll form pixels and the resulting image will look something like the original.

Figure 10-7 illustrates the same GIF image dithered and halftoned. Dithering will be discussed in detail in the next chapter.

The code to form reasonable dots and grey shades would be pretty frightening, but, fortunately, you don't have to worry about it. A PostScript printer is capable of generating up to 256 grey levels. It even provides you with a really elegant way to code up a bitmap to use them.

The PostScript image operator works a lot like the imagemask operator discussed a while ago, except that it's not confined to source images in which each bit of the data conforms to one pixel of the final image. In fact, it lets you have up to eight bits—one byte—per pixel. Given an image that is coded up with eight bits for each pixel, it prints a grey area for each eight

Fig 10-7   A dithered 256-color image (above) and the same image handled as a halftone (below). This picture was downloaded from Rose Media (416) 226-9260

bit "sample" in the image. Allowing that you've specified some dimensions that will make the grey areas small enough, the resulting halftoned picture can be strikingly good.

Figure 10-8 illustrates a simple PostScript program that will print a 256-color image. It omits most of the hundred or so kilobytes of hex data that was originally part of this file. You'll see how to create your own in a few minutes.

Fig 10-8   A PostScript program to produce a halftone. The hex data of the picture itself is missing

```
%!PS-Adobe-2.0 EPSF-1.2
%%Creator: PostGif/Alchemy Mindworks Inc.
%%Title: PICTURE.EPS
%%BoundingBox:0 0 320 200
/width 320 def
/height 200 def
/pixwidth 320 def
/pixheight 200 def
/picstr width string def
/dopic {
        gsave
        width height 8
        [width 0 0 height neg 0 height]
        { currentfile picstr readhexstring pop }
        image
        grestore
        } def
25 40 translate
pixwidth pixheight scale
dopic
5B43333333333333333333B ...
%% lots of hex data
... 3433B3B43434B5343
showpage
```

To begin with, the first few lines of the program are comments—in PostScript, any line beginning with a percent sign is disregarded by the PostScript interpreter. However, these are very important comments because they're not disregarded by quite a few other programs. With these comments at the start of the program, it qualifies as an *encapsulated* PostScript image. This means that it can be inhaled into just about anything that accepts PostScript files. For example, Ventura Publisher will accept a file such as this, allowing you to include fully screened halftones in a desktop publishing document.

Applications such as Ventura that will read encapsulated PostScript files look for the %!PS-Adobe and the %%BoundingBox comments. The first is a PostScript file's equivalent of an image header. The second tells the program reading the file what the maximum area the contents of the file might occupy. This is pretty obvious with an image, but a PostScript program can include all sorts of wild type effects and other sorts of graphics.

As an aside, one application that *won't* read these files is Adobe's own *Illustrator* package, which doesn't seem to be able to cope with this much hex data all at once.

The heart of this program is the image operator. It creates a halftone representation of the image stored in all the hex data that comes at the end of the file. This is the form of it:

ImageWidth ImageHeight Bits matrix procedure image

This line might take some explaining. The first two values are the width and height of the picture you want to print. The Bits value is the number of bits per pixel, which can be left at eight. In fact, to print pictures with fewer than 256 possible grey levels you can set this to something smaller, crunch the data, and make all that hex a bit less voluminous, but this gets complicated and would create a program too massive to be understood easily.

The matrix is the same as the one you looked at in imagemask.

The procedure is a PostScript routine to fetch the data that will make up the picture and present it to image. In this case, the data is to come from the current file, that is, from wherever the PostScript interpreter has acquired the program. The stuff in the curly brackets after the matrix arranges this. The image operator will call this repeatedly to fetch the hex data from the file.

Finally, showpage spits the whole works out.

A reasonable size image encoded this way can take a fair while to come sliding out of your printer. Be patient. It hasn't hung—it's just thinking.

Figure 10-9 is the actual C program that generated the program you've just looked at. Given a GIF image, it will decode the picture and generate a grey scaled PostScript version of it all set for porting to the PostScript printer of your choice. It writes the PostScript program to a file rather than directly to the printer because such files very often are useful for inclusion in other things, such as the aforementioned Ventura chapters.

Fig 10-9   A program to create halftoned EPS files from GIF images

```
/*
        An example C language GIF decoder.
        Creates a PostScript file to print GIF images
*/

#include "stdio.h"
#include "dos.h"
#include "alloc.h"
#include "graphics.h"

extern char PALETTE[256][4],OUTROW[1024],COPYRIGHT[];
extern int INTERLACED,IMAGEWIDE,IMAGEDEEP;
```

Fig 10-9   continued

```
extern int IMAGEX,IMAGEY,XLOC,YLOC;
extern int VERSION,SUBVERSION;

char greypalette[256];
char postfile[65];
FILE *POST;
char *buffer=NULL,*farPtr();

main(argc,argv)
        int argc;
        char *argv[];
{
        char filename[65];
        int i,e,ShowIt(),Colourize();
        int ImageDone(),BadError(),BGround();

        SetShow(ShowIt);
        SetPalette(Colourize);
        SetImage(ImageDone);
        SetError(BadError);
        SetBackground(BGround);
        if(argc > 1) {
                for(i=1;i<argc;++i) {
                        strmfe(filename,argv[i],"GIF");
                        strmfe(postfile,argv[i],"EPS");
                        strupr(postfile);
                        if((e=UnpackGIF(filename)) != 0) break;
                }
                if(e) printf("Error code %d",e);
        }
        ShowCopyright();
}

ImageDone()
{
        int i,j;

        for(i=0;i<IMAGEDEEP;++i) {
                memcpy(OUTROW,
                  farPtr(buffer,(long)i*(long)IMAGEWIDE),
                  IMAGEWIDE);
                for(j=0;j<IMAGEWIDE;++j)
                  fprintf(POST,"%02.2X",
                   greypalette[OUTROW[j]]& 0xff);
                fprintf(POST,"\r\n");
         }
        fprintf(POST,"\r\n%%%%Trailer\r\n");
        fprintf(POST,"\r\nshowpage\r\n");
        fclose(POST);
        farfree(buffer);
}

/* create a pallette lookup table with the palette
```

```
        colour values grey scale summed. */
Colourize(n,palette)
        int n;
        char *palette;
{
        double f;
        int i;

        for(i=0;i<n;++i) {
                f= (0.30 * (double)*palette++) +
                   (0.59 * (double)*palette++) +
                   (0.11 * (double)*palette++);
                if(f > 255.0) f=255.0;
                greypalette[i]=(char)f;
        }
}


ShowIt()
{
        int i;

        memcpy(farPtr(buffer,(long)YLOC*(long)IMAGEWIDE),
          OUTROW,IMAGEWIDE);
}

/* Write the PostScript EPS header. If the image is
   interlaced, allocate a big buffer for it. */
BGround()
{
        int i,sWide,sDeep;

        if((POST = fopen(postfile,"wb")) == NULL) {
                printf("Error creating %s\n",postfile);
                exit(1);
        }

        sWide = (int)((double)IMAGEWIDE * 1.25);
        sDeep = (int)((double)IMAGEDEEP * 1.25);

        fprintf(POST,"%%!PS-Adobe-2.0 EPSF-1.2\r\n");
        fprintf(POST,"%%%%Creator: PostGif\r\n");
        fprintf(POST,"%%%%Title: %s\r\n",postfile);
        fprintf(POST,"%%%%TemplateBox:0 0 %u %u\r\n",IMAGEWIDE,IMAGEDEEP);
        fprintf(POST,"%%%%BoundingBox:0 0 %u %u\r\n",sWide,sDeep);
        fprintf(POST,"%%%%PageOrigin:0 0\r\n");
        fprintf(POST,"%%%%PrinterName:\r\n");
        fprintf(POST,"%%%%PrinterRect:11 709 533 25\r\n");
        fprintf(POST,"/width %u def\r\n",IMAGEWIDE);
        fprintf(POST,"/height %u def\r\n",IMAGEDEEP);
        fprintf(POST,"/pixwidth %u def\r\n",sWide);
        fprintf(POST,"/pixheight %u def\r\n",sDeep);
        fprintf(POST,"/picstr width string def\r\n");
        fprintf(POST,"/dopic {\r\n");
        fprintf(POST,"gsave\r\n");
```

Fig 10-9   continued

```
        fprintf(POST,"width height 8\r\n");
        fprintf(POST,"[width 0 0 height neg 0 height]\r\n");
        fprintf(POST,"{currentfile picstr "
                    "readhexstring pop}\r\n");
        fprintf(POST,"image\r\n");
        fprintf(POST,"grestore\r\n");
        fprintf(POST,"} def\r\n");
        fprintf(POST,"25 40 translate\r\n");

        fprintf(POST,"pixwidth pixheight scale\r\n");
        fprintf(POST,"dopic\r\n");
        if((buffer=farmalloc((long)IMAGEWIDE*(long)IMAGEDEEP))== NULL) {
                puts("Error allocating memory");
                exit(1);
        }
}


BadError(s)
        char *s;
{
        printf("\007\007\007Fatal error - %s.\n",s);
        exit(1);
}


ShowCopyright()
{
        char *p;

        p = COPYRIGHT;
        puts("");
        while(*p) {
                p += printf(p)+1;
                puts("");
        }
}

strmfe(new,old,ext)   /* change file extension */
        char *new,*old,*ext;
{
        while(*old != 0 && *old != '.') *new++=*old++;
        *new++='.';
        while(*ext) *new++=*ext++;
        *new=0;
}

char *farPtr(p,l) /* return a far pointer p + l */
        char *p;
        long l;
{
        unsigned int seg,off;

        seg = FP_SEG(p);
        off = FP_OFF(p);
```

```
        seg += (off / 16);
        off &= 0x000f;
        off += (unsigned int)(l & 0x000fL);
        seg += (l / 16L);
        p=MK_FP(seg,off);
        return(p);
}
```

There are quite a few things happening in this little program. First of all, as you'll recognize unless you've been reading the chapters of this book out of order, this effort is yet another version of the basic GIF decoder that was discussed in Chapter 5. It must be linked to GIF1.OBJ, as described in that chapter, which handles all the actual image decoding and calls the various functions of this program to write the EPS file.

If you haven't read Chapter 5 yet, you probably should do so now. The GIF decoder is an example of convoluted programming at its most twisted, and you'll be well perplexed for a while if you don't know what it's up to.

This program is complicated somewhat by the observation that some of the GIF files that it will be asked to read will be interlaced, that is, that the image lines as they emerge from the GIF decoder will not be in the order that they will appear in the final picture. Given a noninterlaced image, you simply can write each line of the picture into the PostScript file as it comes out of the decoder. Interlaced files must be handled differently—you have to buffer them and write them only when all the lines have been decoded and stored in memory.

In other words, the image has to be deinterlaced by putting the whole thing in memory and then reading it out in the correct order.

There are a few really huge GIF images floating around that actually won't fit in memory if you have a few resident programs in there too and a reasonable contingent of files and buffers in the CONFIG.SYS file of your PC. Fortunately, these really big pictures tend not to be interlaced. As such, this program will handle noninterlaced pictures one line at a time and only buffer the ones that need buffering. Because there's no substantial amount of memory required by this program unless the image it's working on insists on being deinterlaced, it can cope with normal GIF pictures of any size.

The mechanism for buffering an image poses the same problems that have occurred earlier in this chapter when dealing with large pictures that wouldn't fit in a single segment—and this program uses the same solutions, too. The farPtr function will create true 32-bit pointers to allow you the illusion of a large block of contiguous, nonsegmented memory.

Converting a color GIF palette into a number of grey tones is quite a lot easier than it might seem to be. There's a fairly workable formula for doing this. It goes like this:

grey = .30 * red + .59 * green + .11 * blue

This is by no means foolproof. For example, it's quite possible to come up with two color values that are quite contrasting and distinct in a color picture and result in exactly the same grey levels when they're reduced to black and white. However, it's surprising how well this simple conversion works, and how seldom it creates inappropriate black and white pictures.

Later in this chapter you'll see how to improve on this conversion process by introducing it to grey scale remapping.

If you look at the code in ImageDone or ShowIt that actually writes the data to the PostScript file, you'll probably find that it seems to go through one more step than is called for—there's a lookup table, greypalette, involved in the works. In fact, if you think about it, this is actually how color pictures work. Normally, a color GIF file's pixel values are indices into three lookup tables for the three primary color values. In this case, as you will have converted the color palette to grey levels, you only need one table.

This program creates an eight bit per sample—or one byte per pixel—PostScript file. However, this does not mean that it can be used only with 256-color GIF images. Images with smaller palettes will simply waste the upper part of each hex number in the EPS file. PostScript allows you to improve on the packing of bits for the image operator when you have less than eight bits per pixel of valid image data—it would have been considerably more involved to have implemented this here, though. You might want to attempt it if you're adept at PostScript programming and feel like a protracted hack late one night.

There are, in fact, quite a few fairly clever things you can do at the PostScript level of this program if you want to enhance it a bit. PostScript allows data to be read from binary as well as hex strings—this will reduce the resultant EPS files by about half, although you won't be able to look at the works with a text editor. You also might want to include some intelligence in the program to scale down particularly wide pictures to keep them from spilling off the right side of the page. Finally, you can rotate images that are in "landscape" orientations so they use more of the paper.

This chapter could very easily degenerate into a PostScript tutorial.

EPS Preview

One of the drawbacks to using EPS files, such as the ones created by the previous program, as graphics in desktop publishing packages is that most of these packages won't be able to show you what the graphic looks like on your screen. This is changing gradually—Adobe has started to make noises to the effect that it has "screen" PostScript available, and that desktop publishing packages and other applications that allow for the importation of encapsulated PostScript files might want to use this facility to interpret the EPS images in real time.

At the time of this writing, no one had actually done this. Certain conceptual problems seem to arise in its implementation. For example, a PostScript interpreter in a laser printer is very large and very slow. In addition, it's very expensive to license. On screen, real time PostScript previewing might not be a reality for some time.

In the mean while, if you're creating encapsulated PostScript files of bit-mapped images for use with some other package, you'll find them awkward at best to deal with. The Ventura Publisher package, for example, certainly accepts EPS graphics, but confronted with the output of the previous program it will simply draw a large "X" on the screen where the picture is supposed to go. The picture will print properly—assuming that it's being printed to a PostScript device, of course—but accurately positioning it on the screen would be well nigh impossible because it can't be viewed directly.

There's a way around this. Most of the desktop publishing packages and word processors that accept encapsulated PostScript files support the use of preview images in EPS files. Regrettably, this facility isn't well documented, and few of the applications that generate EPS files know how to include a preview. It will be discussed here to modify the previous program to include previews with the halftone EPS files.

Figure 10-10 is a Ventura Publisher screen with the GIF file halftoned in Fig. 10-7 plainly visible as a preview. Versions of Ventura Publisher prior to 2.0 could not display EPS preview images.

A preview image is simply a TIFF file containing bit-mapped representation of whatever the actual PostScript graphic in the EPS file happens to

Fig 10-10   An EPS file with a TIFF preview imported into a Ventura Publisher chapter

be. It gets tacked onto the end of the EPS file, right after all the ASCII Post-Script code. The PostScript file also must acquire a binary header up front to tell any interested applications how to locate the TIFF image.

This might sound rather like a last minute hack. One suspects that it is. It has a lot of holes in it, not the least of which is that for just about any application except for the one we're going to look at here, generating a bit-mapped image of a PostScript graphic is very, very involved. However, that particular problem is someone else's.

Allowing that you want to encode a 256-color GIF image into an encapsulated PostScript file, the only serious problem in creating the TIFF image for the preview is that the TIFF image wants to be black and white. It also must conform to the dimensions of the original GIF image, so that it actually provides an accurate preview. Although you could dither the color image to create a monochrome preview, this probably is severe overkill. It's also not all that desirable, actually—dithered size-as pictures don't retain detail all that well, and it's to ascertain the location of the details of the picture in the EPS file that you will be going to the trouble of creating a preview in the first place.

A much simpler, and, as it happens, more useful solution is to simply turn the picture into a monochrome bitmap by setting a white threshold. The most obvious white threshold is 50 percent, and this happens to work out very well. Any pixel in the GIF image that represents less than the threshold level of grey becomes a black pixel in the preview. All the rest become white pixels in the preview.

You can see how this is done in the makebit function in Fig. 10-11.

Fig 10-11   A better halftoning program for GIF files. This version does grey scale remapping and includes a TIFF preview

```
/*
        An example C language GIF decoder.
        Creates a PostScript file to print GIF images
        Includes a TIFF file for previewing
*/

#include "stdio.h"
#include "dos.h"
#include "alloc.h"
#include "graphics.h"

#define TIFtags 7        /* how many tags in our TIF header */

typedef struct {          char head[4];
                          unsigned long psStart;
                          unsigned long psSize;
                          unsigned long mfStart;
                          unsigned long mfSize;
                          unsigned long tfStart;
                          unsigned long tfSize;
                          unsigned int checksum;
```

```c
        } EPSheader;

/* contrast expansion lookup table */
char greymap[256] = {
        /* 00-0f */
        0x01,0x01,0x01,0x01,0x01,0x01,0x01,0x01,
        0x01,0x01,0x01,0x01,0x01,0x01,0x01,0x01,
        /* 10-1f */
        0x01,0x01,0x01,0x01,0x01,0x01,0x01,0x01,
        0x01,0x01,0x01,0x01,0x01,0x01,0x01,0x01,
        /* 20-2f */
        0x01,0x01,0x01,0x01,0x01,0x01,0x01,0x02,
        0x03,0x04,0x05,0x06,0x07,0x08,0x09,0x0a,
        /* 30-3f */
        0x0b,0x0c,0x0d,0x0e,0x0f,0x10,0x11,0x12,
        0x13,0x14,0x15,0x16,0x17,0x18,0x19,0x1a,
        /* 40-4f */
        0x1b,0x1c,0x1d,0x1e,0x1f,0x20,0x20,0x21,
        0x22,0x23,0x23,0x24,0x25,0x27,0x27,0x28,
        /* 50-5f */
        0x29,0x2a,0x2b,0x2c,0x2d,0x2e,0x2f,0x2f,
        0x30,0x31,0x32,0x33,0x34,0x35,0x36,0x37,
        /* 60-6f */
        0x38,0x39,0x3a,0x3a,0x3b,0x3c,0x3d,0x3e,
        0x3f,0x40,0x41,0x42,0x43,0x44,0x45,0x46,
        /* 70-7f */
        0x47,0x48,0x49,0x4a,0x4b,0x4c,0x4d,0x4e,
        0x50,0x51,0x52,0x53,0x55,0x56,0x57,0x58,
        /* 80-8f */
        0x59,0x5a,0x5b,0x5d,0x5e,0x5f,0x60,0x61,
        0x63,0x64,0x65,0x66,0x67,0x69,0x6a,0x6b,
        /* 90-9f */
        0x6c,0x6e,0x70,0x72,0x73,0x74,0x76,0x78,
        0x7a,0x7c,0x7e,0x80,0x82,0x84,0x86,0x88,
        /* a0-af */
        0x8a,0x8c,0x8f,0x91,0x93,0x95,0x98,0x9a,
        0x9c,0x9f,0xa1,0xa4,0xa6,0xa9,0xab,0xae,
        /* b0-bf */
        0xb0,0xb2,0xb3,0xb5,0xb7,0xb9,0xba,0xbc,
        0xbd,0xbe,0xc0,0xc2,0xc4,0xc6,0xc8,0xca,
        /* c0-cf */
        0xcc,0xce,0xd0,0xd2,0xd4,0xd6,0xd9,0xdb,
        0xdd,0xe0,0xe3,0xe6,0xe8,0xeb,0xed,0xef,
        /* d0-df */
        0xf2,0xf5,0xf8,0xfb,0xfe,0xfe,0xfe,0xfe,
        0xfe,0xfe,0xfe,0xfe,0xfe,0xfe,0xfe,0xfe,
        /* e0-ef */
        0xfe,0xfe,0xfe,0xfe,0xfe,0xfe,0xfe,0xfe,
        0xfe,0xfe,0xfe,0xfe,0xfe,0xfe,0xfe,0xfe,
        /* f0-ff */
        0xfe,0xfe,0xfe,0xfe,0xfe,0xfe,0xfe,0xfe,
        0xfe,0xfe,0xfe,0xfe,0xfe,0xfe,0xfe,0xfe,
                };

extern char PALETTE[256][4],OUTROW[1024],COPYRIGHT[];
```

Fig 10-11   continued

```
extern int INTERLACED,IMAGEWIDE,IMAGEDEEP;
extern int IMAGEX,IMAGEY,XLOC,YLOC;
extern int VERSION,SUBVERSION;

EPSheader EPSH;
char greypalette[256];
char postfile[65];
FILE *POST;
char *buffer=NULL,*farPtr();
unsigned int destBytes;
char preview=0xff;

main(argc,argv)
        int argc;
        char *argv[];
{
        char filename[65];
        int i,e,ShowIt(),Colourize();
        int ImageDone(),BadError(),BGround();

        SetShow(ShowIt);
        SetPalette(Colourize);
        SetImage(ImageDone);
        SetError(BadError);
        SetBackground(BGround);
        if(argc > 1) {
                for(i=1;i<argc;++i) if(!stricmp(argv[i],"/P"))
                  preview=0;
                for(i=1;i<argc;++i) {
                        if(argv[i][0] != '/') {
                                strmfe(filename,argv[i],"GIF");
                                strmfe(postfile,argv[i],"EPS");
                                strupr(postfile);
                                if((e=UnpackGIF(filename)) != 0) break;
                        }
                }
                if(e) printf("Error code %d",e);
        }
        ShowCopyright();
}

ImageDone()
{
        int i,j;

        for(i=0;i<IMAGEDEEP;++i) {
                memcpy(OUTROW,
                  farPtr(buffer,(long)i*(long)IMAGEWIDE),
                  IMAGEWIDE);
                for(j=0;j<IMAGEWIDE;++j)
                  fprintf(POST,"%02.2X",
                   greypalette[OUTROW[j]]& 0xff);
                fprintf(POST,"\r\n");
```

```
                }

        fprintf(POST,"\r\n%%%%Trailer\r\n");
        fprintf(POST,"\r\nshowpage\r\n");
        if(preview) maketif(buffer);
        fclose(POST);
        farfree(buffer);
}

/* create a pallette lookup table with the palette
   colour values grey scale summed. */
Colourize(n,palette)
        int n;
        char *palette;
{
        double f;
        int i;

        for(i=0;i<n;++i) {
                f= (0.30 * (double)*palette++) +
                   (0.59 * (double)*palette++) +
                   (0.11 * (double)*palette++);
                if(f > 255.0) f=255.0;
                greypalette[i]=greymap[(char)f];
        }
}


ShowIt()
{
        int i;

        memcpy(farPtr(buffer,(long)YLOC*(long)IMAGEWIDE),
          OUTROW,IMAGEWIDE);
}

/* Write the PostScript EPS header. If the image is
   interlaced, allocate a big buffer for it. */
BGround()
{
        int i,sWide,sDeep;

        if((POST = fopen(postfile,"wb")) == NULL) {
                printf("Error creating %s\n",postfile);
                exit(1);
        }

        if(preview)
                printf("Writing %s with preview - "
                    "basic image size: %u x %u\n",
                  postfile,IMAGEWIDE,IMAGEDEEP);
    else
                printf("Writing %s without preview - "
                    "basic image size: %u x %u\n",
                  postfile,IMAGEWIDE,IMAGEDEEP);
```

Fig 10-11   continued

```
        sWide = (int)((double)IMAGEWIDE * 1.25);
        sDeep = (int)((double)IMAGEDEEP * 1.25);

        if(preview) for(i=0;i<sizeof(EPSheader);++i)
          fputc(0,POST);
        fprintf(POST,"%%!PS-Adobe-2.0 EPSF-1.2\r\n");
        fprintf(POST,"%%%%Creator: PostGif\r\n");
        fprintf(POST,"%%%%Title: %s\r\n",postfile);
        fprintf(POST,"%%%%TemplateBox:0 0 %u %u\r\n",
          IMAGEWIDE,IMAGEDEEP);
        fprintf(POST,"%%%%BoundingBox:0 0 %u %u\r\n",
          sWide,sDeep);
        fprintf(POST,"%%%%PageOrigin:0 0\r\n");
        fprintf(POST,"%%%%PrinterName:\r\n");
        fprintf(POST,"%%%%PrinterRect:11 709 533 25\r\n");
        fprintf(POST,"/width %u def\r\n",IMAGEWIDE);
        fprintf(POST,"/height %u def\r\n",IMAGEDEEP);
        fprintf(POST,"/pixwidth %u def\r\n",sWide);
        fprintf(POST,"/pixheight %u def\r\n",sDeep);
        fprintf(POST,"/picstr width string def\r\n");
        fprintf(POST,"/dopic {\r\n");
        fprintf(POST,"gsave\r\n");
        fprintf(POST,"width height 8\r\n");
        fprintf(POST,"[width 0 0 height neg 0 height]\r\n");
        fprintf(POST,"{currentfile picstr "
                     "readhexstring pop}\r\n");
        fprintf(POST,"image\r\n");
        fprintf(POST,"grestore\r\n");
        fprintf(POST,"} def\r\n");
        if(!preview) fprintf(POST,"25 40 translate\r\n");

        fprintf(POST,"pixwidth pixheight scale\r\n");
        fprintf(POST,"dopic\r\n");
        if((buffer=farmalloc((long)IMAGEWIDE*(long)IMAGEDEEP))
          == NULL) {
                puts("Error allocating memory");
                exit(1);
        }
}

BadError(s)
        char *s;
{
        printf("\007\007\007Fatal error - %s.\n",s);
        exit(1);
}

ShowCopyright()
{
        char *p;

        p = COPYRIGHT;
        puts("");
```

```
                while(*p) {
                        p += printf(p)+1;
                        puts("");
                }
        }

strmfe(new,old,ext)   /* change file extension */
        char *new,*old,*ext;
        {
                while(*old != 0 && *old != '.') *new++=*old++;
                *new++='.';
                while(*ext) *new++=*ext++;
                *new=0;
        }

char *farPtr(p,l) /* return a far pointer p + l */
        char *p;
        long l;
        {
                unsigned int seg,off;

                seg = FP_SEG(p);
                off = FP_OFF(p);
                seg += (off / 16);
                off &= 0x000f;
                off += (unsigned int)(l & 0x000fL);
                seg += (l / 16L);
                p=MK_FP(seg,off);
                return(p);
        }

/* create a TIF file for the preview */
maketif(buf)
        char *buf;
        {
                char *q,b[256];
                unsigned long offs,size;
                unsigned int i=0,k;
                static char p[1024];

                EPSH.tfStart = ftell(POST);

                putWord(0x4949,POST);
                putWord(0x002a,POST);
                putLong(8L,POST);
                i=8;

                putWord(TIFtags,POST);      /* number of tags */

                putWord(0x00ff,POST);       /* subfile type tag */
                putWord(0x0003,POST);       /* short type */
                putLong(0x0001L,POST);      /* one item */
                putLong(0x0001L,POST);      /* type one - single image */

                putWord(0x0100,POST);       /* image width tag */
```

Fig 10-11   continued

```
        putWord(0x0003,POST);        /* short type */
        putLong(0x0001L,POST);       /* one item */
        putLong((long)IMAGEWIDE,POST);        /* width in pixels */
        putWord(0x0101,POST);        /* image length tag */
        putWord(0x0003,POST);        /* short type */
        putLong(0x0001L,POST);       /* one item */
        putLong((long)IMAGEDEEP,POST);        /* depth in pixels */

        putWord(0x0103,POST);        /* image compression tag */
        putWord(0x0003,POST);        /* short type */
        putLong(0x0001L,POST);       /* one item */
        putLong(0x8005L,POST);       /* packbits compression */

        putWord(0x0106,POST);        /* photomtrc interpretation */
        putWord(0x0003,POST);        /* short type */
        putLong(0x0001L,POST);       /* one item */
        putLong(0x0001L,POST);       /* min sample is black*/

        putWord(0x0111,POST);        /* strip offsets */
        putWord(0x0004,POST);        /* long */
        putLong(1L,POST); /* number of strips */
        putLong((long)i+2L+(12L*(long)TIFtags),POST);

        putWord(0x0117,POST);        /* strips per image */
        putWord(0x0004,POST);        /* long */
        putLong(1L,POST);
        putLong(0x0c19L,POST);

        destBytes=IMAGEWIDE >> 3;
        if(IMAGEWIDE & 0x07) ++destBytes;

        for(k=0;k<IMAGEDEEP;++k) {
                makebit(p,farPtr(buf,(long)k*
                   (long)IMAGEWIDE),IMAGEWIDE);
                WriteLine(p,POST);
        }

        /* load the EPSheader with data */
        memcpy(EPSH.head,"\xc5\xd0\xd3\xc6",4);
        EPSH.psStart=(long)sizeof(EPSheader);
        EPSH.psSize=EPSH.tfStart-EPSH.psStart;
        EPSH.mfStart=0L;
        EPSH.mfSize=0L;
        EPSH.tfSize=ftell(POST)-EPSH.tfStart;
        EPSH.checksum = 0xffff;

        fseek(POST,0L,SEEK_SET);
        fwrite((char *)&EPSH,1,sizeof(EPSheader),POST);
}

WriteLine(p,fp)     /* encode / write the line in p to fp  */
        char *p;
        FILE *fp;
```

```
{
        char b[256];
        unsigned int bdex=0,i=0,j=0,t=0;

        do {
                i=0;
                while((p[t+i]==p[t+i+1]) &&
                  ((t+i) < (destBytes-1)))++i;
                if(i>0) {
                        if(bdex) {
                                fputc(((bdex-1) & 0x7f),fp);
                                j+=1;
                                fwrite(b,1,bdex,fp);
                                j+=bdex;
                                bdex=0;
                        }
                        fputc((~i+1),fp);
                        fputc(p[t+i],fp);
                        j+=2;
                        t+=(i+1);
                } else b[bdex++]=p[t++];
        } while(t<destBytes);
        if(bdex) {
                fputc(((bdex-1) & 0x7f),fp);
                j+=1;
                fwrite(b,1,bdex,fp);
                j+=bdex;
                bdex=0;
        }
}

putWord(w,fp)                   /* write word w to file fp */
        unsigned int w;
        FILE *fp;
{
        fputc(w,fp);
        fputc((w >> 8),fp);
}

putLong(l,fp)                   /* write long l to file fp */
        unsigned long l;
        FILE *fp;
{
        fputc((char)l,fp);
        fputc((char)(l >> 8),fp);
        fputc((char)(l >> 16),fp);
        fputc((char)(l >> 24),fp);
}

makebit(dest,source,l)
        char *dest,*source;
        int l;
{
        int i,m;
```

Fig 10-11   continued

```
        memset (dest, 0, destBytes);
        for(i=0;i<l;++i) {
               m= 0x80 >> (i % 8);
               if(greypalette[source[i]] > 0x80)
                 dest[i / 8 ] |= m;
        }
  }
```

It probably is not necessary to get into the mechanics of actually generating the TIFF file itself, because this was gone over at great length in Chapter 7. In fact, the preview image is a completely stripped down TIFF format, with just enough tag information to define the picture. Because the image will never be manipulated, or even read directly, you need not include much additional data about it in the tag directory. As in Chapter 7, the TIFF images for EPS previews are stored using MacPaint-style byte compression.

The binary header at the front of the PostScript file is fairly simple, and was touched on in Chapter 7. It consists of these fields:

```
DB      0C5H,0D0H,0D3H,0C6H
DD      START_OF_POSTSCRIPT
DD      LENGTH_OF_POSTSCRIPT
DD      START_OF_METAFILE
DD      LENGTH_OF_METAFILE
DD      START_OF_TIFF
DD      LENGTH_OF_TIFF
DW      CHECKSUM
```

The first 4 bytes are constant, and tell an application reading this file that there is, in fact, a binary header available. These bytes are, in fact, the letters "EPSF" with their high order bits set.

The next field is a long integer—four bytes—that specifies how far into the file the PostScript code starts. Because the header is 14 bytes long and the PostScript starts immediately after this, the contents of this field will be 14L.

The next field is a long integer representing the length of the Post-Script part of the file which, of course, must be filled in by the application. This is done most easily by figuring out how much data has been written to the file when the last of the PostScript code has been dealt with—the ftell function under C is a convenient way to do this—and then subtracting 14L from this number.

The next two fields are long integers that will both contain zeros. The preview image can be stored either as a TIFF file or as a Windows Metafile. This program will be using a TIFF file, so the Metafile fields don't concern it.

The next field is a long integer indicating the offset of the start of the TIFF image, and the field after that is a long integer containing its length. If a program reading the file were to seek into the file by the number of bytes stored in the start field, it should find 2 bytes of either "I" or "M," as discussed in the chapter on TIFF files.

Finally, there's an integer that holds a checksum of the header, or 0xffff if the checksum is to be ignored. This can be set to 0xffff here, because the start of the TIFF image is a sufficient check on the integrity of the file.

There is one potential area of confusion in the creation of a preview image. The TIFF standard defines several things as existing at offsets relative to the start of the file. In the case of a stand-alone TIFF file, the start of the file is pretty easy to find. However, in this case there are two of them— the start of the EPS file and the start of the TIFF image file at the end of it. In the case of the binary header for the EPS file, when you talk about the offset of the TIFF image, the start of the file is the start of the EPS file itself. When you're busy writing the TIFF image, though, the start of the file actually is the start of the TIFF data.

The rest of this program works in exactly the same way as the previous one did, writing data for the PostScript image operator to read and make pictures out of.

One of the additional enhancements to this version of the program is a grey scale remapping table. This will be discussed at greater length in Chapter 11. For the moment, suffice it to say that a linear conversion of color to grey values produces a faithful but rather lifeless halftone. Remapping the grey scale expands the center of the contrast range to make the resulting picture look more interesting.

This code must be linked to the GIF decoder assembly language module from Chapter 5. Given any number of GIF files as command line arguments, it will create corresponding EPS files.

Because there are all sorts of cases in which it isn't appropriate to include a preview image in an EPS file, this version of the program includes a way to disable the generation of previews. If you invoke it as:

POSTGIF PARROT

where PARROT.GIF is the source image, the resulting PARROT.EPS file will contain a preview and will be suitable for including in a desktop publishing file. If you invoke it as:

POSTGIF PARROT /P

the preview will be disabled. This both saves some space in the file and eliminates the binary header, which can confuse a PostScript printer if the encapsulated PostScript file this program generates is copied directly to the printer.

LaserJet Halftones

Users of LaserJet compatible printers probably will observe that a LaserJet should be capable of doing much the same thing with a color GIF picture as has been discussed here for PostScript. In a sense this is true, but the implementation is quite a lot more involved. The LaserJet will print rectangular areas of varying grey tones, and this could certainly serve as the basis for a halftoning process analogous to what happens in the PostScript halftoning programs. Unfortunately, it can only print eight distinct levels of grey, which is hardly sufficient to represent even a rudimentary color picture. The results look posterized and not very attractive.

You could, of course, create your own halftones one pixel at a time, but this would require an extremely involved program.

Screens and Halftones

One important note in printing bitmaps concerns the *screens* used to produce halftone images. This can affect any bit-mapped picture that is destined to be reproduced on a mechanical printing press.

In printing terminology, a screen refers to the actual mechanical glass or plastic sheet with lines on it that is used to generate a halftone and also the resultant halftone image. The halftone will have the same number of dots to the inch as does the screen it's made from.

Printers choose the screens they make mechanical halftones with based on the sort of paper and press that the pictures being halftoned will be printed on. The cheapest sort of printing is newsprint run through a web press. A screen of 80 lines to the inch—or just an ''80 line screen''—is appropriate for this type of printing. Coated paper on a web press usually calls for a 110 line screen. Coated paper on a sheet-fed press can support as much as 144 line screens. Some of the really exacting print houses can do better still.

In creating pictures that will be reproduced on a printing press, you will want to use the tightest screens possible so that the pictures look as much like photographs as they can—this is true whether the screen is a sheet of plastic or a halftoning algorithm in a PostScript printer. However, choosing too tight a screen will cause the white spaces in between the dots of the halftone to fill up with ink in denser areas because the paper will not be able to actually print the dot structure, and the resulting picture will look muddy.

To further complicate the screening process, printing presses cannot reliably print grey shades of less than about five percent or more than about ninety-five percent. In the first case the black dots will have grown too small to print, and in the latter the white areas will have become so small as to fill up with ink from the surrounding black areas.

Just as a 300-line halftone would print up as an awful mess on most printing presses, so too will many complex bit-mapped images if they're printed at the maximum resolution of a 300-dot-per-inch laser printer.

Dithered pictures that look just fine when you output them can look dreadful when they come back from the printers because they contain, in effect, 300-dot-per-inch screened areas. The dithered images in this book have been printed at 150 dots per inch in most cases for this reason.

You might want to have another look at the four pictures in Fig. 10-3, which represent the various resolutions of a LaserJet printer. The first one, at three hundred dots per inch, illustrates what can happen when a printing press is asked to print a tighter screen than it's really up to. The press that printed this book was unable to reproduce 300-dot-per-inch screens, with the result that some of the details of this picture have been lost.

GRAPHICS CATALOG

Having determined that LaserJets aren't much use for printing half-tones—at least, they can't print them without an excessive amount of code—you might want to look for something else to do with a LaserJet that's at least as interesting.

A particularly interesting LaserJet graphics program is the graphics catalog, which is a good bit of code both because it produces very useful output and because it illustrates how to handle very complex graphics of several types on a LaserJet printer. In reality, this really means a LaserJet Plus printer—as you'll recall, a stock old style LaserJet—will not have enough memory to do useful graphics.

The graphics catalog grew out of the observation that there were about 10 megabytes of undeniably interesting image files on one of the hard drives here, but that no one could recall what most of them actually were.

Further observation of these files revealed that most of them had started life as MacPaint files, and had retained the dimensions of a Mac-Paint image even though they were all now IMG files converted for use with Ventura. Of those that were not, a block the size of a MacPaint file centered in the middle of the image area invariably revealed enough about the picture to deduce what it was.

If you print MacPaint files at three hundred dots to the inch they come out very small. In fact, they come out so small that you can just barely fit 16 of them on a single 8^1/$_2$-by-11-inch page. With careful positioning, there will be room for the file names in there too.

The graphics catalog program, then, accepts a file specification and prints all the image files it finds as catalog pages, sixteen to a page. The image files themselves can be a mixture of IMG files, PCX files, and Mac-Paint files. It creates a list of the files in memory, sorts them into alphabetical order, and loads and prints each one in turn.

Figure 10-12 illustrates a whole page of the graphics catalog program's output. It has been shot down for reproduction in this book, so that the pictures are a little hard to see. Figure 10-13 is the upper left corner of the same page reproduced size as.

ANIMALS.IMG CARLOGO.IMG CAROL3.IMG CHEETAH.IMG

CORNCOCK.IMG DRAGON5.IMG EURO5.IMG HYDRA.IMG

JAGUAR.IMG KNIGHT.IMG PANEL.IMG SKULLROS.IMG

SPACE3.IMG STUFF.IMG WABBIT.IMG WATERFAL.IMG P1

Fig 10-12   One page of output from the graphics catalog program, shot down to fit in its entirety

ANIMALS.IMG CARLOGO.IMG CAROL3.IMG

CORNCOCK.IMG DRAGON5.IMG EURO5.IMG

JAGUAR.IMG KNIGHT.IMG PANEL.IMG

Fig 10-13   Part of a page from the graphics catalog program shown

The results of the graphics cataloging program are exceedingly pleasing—the pages look very slick and professional, even through the code that generated them isn't actually all that complicated.

There are a number of important elements in the graphics cataloging program that you can see in the accompanying source code. The program is a little long, but it breaks down nicely into easily understandable functional sections.

A typical invocation of the graphics cataloging program—for example GRAFCAT.EXE when it has been compiled—might go something like this:

```
GRAFCAT \GEMART\P*.IMG
```

This would print all the IMG files that start with the letter P and reside in a subdirectory called \GEMART. As you'll see, if you pass GRAFCAT, a totally ambiguous file specification such as "*.*" it will look through all the files it finds but it will print only the PCX, PCC, IMG, and MAC files, handling each one appropriately.

To handle multiple files in alphabetical order the program must find all the file names that match the file specification passed to GRAFCAT, sort them, and then step through the list one name at a time, printing each file.

You'll see how the files actually are printed in a moment.

The file name handling mechanism of GRAFCAT has absolutely nothing to do with graphics, of course, although it—or something like it—probably will become part of any program you write that deals with multiple files.

To handle multiple file names, a program must read the name of each file into a big buffer that can be sorted later. In fact, in this application the program really only needs the file names themselves, but DOS happens to return a whole struct of information about the files in an ambiguous search, and it's easiest to store the whole thing. The program itself is not particularly demanding of memory in its operation, so it doesn't matter if it wastes some.

A file information struct in Turbo C is called an ffblk.

There's a basic problem in allocating the buffer that will hold the file information structs. At the outset, the program doesn't know how many files will match the ambiguous specification passed to it. As such, it can't know how big the buffer needs to be. There are two ways to cope with this—it can either allocate a big buffer and not allow any more names into it than will fit or it can count the files, allocate a suitable size buffer and then read through the list a second time, loading the information into the by now allocated buffer.

There actually is a third way. It could read in each file name and realloc the buffer to make it bigger each time, but this is dreadfully slow.

The first approach is a bit crude for a program that might be asked to print hundreds of images—especially if you have an image subdirectory like the one that gave birth to GRAFCAT. The second one is much faster than you might imagine, because while the program has to read the directory twice, DOS actually buffers the directory data during the first read. As such, it only has to be read from the disk once, and things are pretty quick after that.

If the size of one directory name struct is sizeof(struct ffblk) and the program has found i names, it can allocate a suitable buffer like this:

```
p = malloc(i * sizeof(struct ffblk));
```

If p isn't NULL, the program is ready to load the actual names into the buffer.

You can see the way this works in the source code by looking at count for and look for, which respectively count and load the names of files based on whatever file specifications are passed to them. This assumes that the same specification will be passed to both.

These functions use the Turbo C findfirst and findnext functions to scan the directory of whatever area the files have been specified in. These functions return zero and load the ffblk struct passed to them with data about each file found if, in fact, a file is found and return a nonzero value when no more files can be found. The way they're used in these functions might seem a bit convoluted at first, but it works very elegantly.

The complete structure of the ffblk data structure is defined by DOS—the 4EH and 4FH subfunctions of interrupt 21H return it. It can be defined in C like this:

```
struct        ffblk    {
              char              ff_reserved[21];
              char              ff_attrib;
              unsigned          ff_ftime;
              unsigned          ff_fdate;
              long              ff_fsize;
              char              ff_name[13];
};
```

You will be using only the ff name element of the struct in this program. If the program was tight for space, it could just buffer the actual file names. However, the count_for and look_for functions are handy general purpose tools as they stand—you might need some of the other information in the struct in other programs.

The sortlist function sorts the list into alphabetical order. This is a straight implementation of the Turbo C qsort function and, for that matter, everyone else's qsort function as well. It uses the dircheck function to compare entries in the file name list. If you haven't run across it before, you might want to check out your compiler's manual to familiarize yourself with how qsort uses a compare function—dircheck in this case—to facilitate sorting different types of data.

The dircheck function is the first place where you can see some pointer manipulation for use with the structs that have been copied into the file name buffer. As dircheck must compare the name elements of the structs passed to it, not the whole structs, it must use struct pointer notation to get at the appropriate bits of each struct. If p is a pointer to an ffblk struct, then p–>ff_name can be treated like any C string. Because qsort passes generic char pointers to dircheck, you must cast them to ffblk pointers.

Anyone who questions why computer programs are written in C rather than in English will note that it has taken a lot more English to describe this than it did C code to write it.

If you pass an argument such as \GEMART*.IMG to count for, it will return a buffer full of file names, but the file names will have no path components. As such, you must isolate the path component of the initial file specification so it can be tacked onto each name when you go to open the actual image files later on. The parse function does this using the Turbo C fnsplit function.

There's a bit of other preliminary housekeeping to attend to. Up at the top of the program there's the definition for a data type called POINT that holds the horizontal and vertical coordinates of a point on the LaserJet's page, as well as an array of POINTs called point array. The upper-left-hand corner of each of the sixteen images on the final page created by GRAF-CAT is loaded into a corresponding element in point array by the function make frames. This will make it a lot easier to figure out where to place each image when the program finally gets around to some printing.

There are three functions in the program that will print IMG, Mac-Paint, and PC Paintbrush files, respectively. In the case of PC Paintbrush files, which might be in color, the program actually only prints the first bit plane of the file if there happens to be more than one of them.

There's a very simple loop in the main function of the program that steps through each file name in the file name buffer, calling print_image for each. The print image function gets the file extension of the file it's given to work with and dispatches the print request to whichever of the three actual printing functions is appropriate.

If it's confronted with a file that has an unrecognized extension, print_image just ignores it and goes on to the next entry in the list. Thus, passing a "*.*" argument to the program in a directory with file types other than PCC, PCX, IMG, and MAC will not confuse the works.

Each of the actual file printing functions works identically. This discussion will deal with print IMG. This function starts by adding the access path to the file name passed to it and opening the file. It then reads in the header of the file and makes sure that the file in question is actually what it purports to be. This process varies a bit between the three printing functions. In the case of IMG files, it need only look at the first 16 bytes. The IMG header has been discussed in detail earlier in this book.

There are three or four global parameters to be set based on the file header read in—it's three for MacPaint and PC Paintbrush files and four for IMG files. The other routines that work with the data in each image file will need to know the width and height of the image in pixels and the number of bytes that each of the lines actually occupies. The IMG format also requires that the pattern size be determined, a value that is read from the header.

The number of bytes that a line of monochrome bit-mapped information occupies is a bit tricky, as you'll recall from several other examples we've seen. If the number of pixels in a line happens to be an even multiple of eight, this value will be the number of pixels divided by eight. However, if it's not even, it will be this value plus one. The pixels2bytes function sorts this out.

Once it knows how big a line of the image being decoded will be, the function allocates a buffer to hold one line of data. In the case of images that are wider than the size of the frame in which it will be printing, it will need only part of each line of information. However, it's a great deal more convenient to unpack each line completely and throw away the parts it doesn't need.

The inner loop of the function reads each line from the file and prints it. There also is some housekeeping, such as calling showbar to maintain a bar graph display on the screen as the printing process continues.

The three readline functions that correspond to the image printing functions will be quite familiar—you will have seen them all at work in the early chapters of this book. The only part that might take a bit of explaining is the PC Paintbrush version—depending upon how many color planes exist in the PCX file being decoded, the printing function might call the readline PCX function multiple times for each line of printed data. In this case, it's reading and printing the first plane of data and then reading and throwing away up to three more lines.

This does not allow for the new PCX files, by the way—the ones with 256 colors. You might want to add this facility to the program.

There's a lot of tickling of the LaserJet going on here. It's handled by three principle functions, startprint, printline, and endline. There's also showname, which prints the name of the file being unpacked using the LaserJet's default text font.

The workings of these functions should be pretty easy to understand by now, based on what was discussed earlier in this chapter. The startprint function sets the print resolution to 300 dots per inch and places the upper-left-hand corner of the printable page—as the LaserJet sees it—at the point designated by the appropriate entry in point array. It then tells the printer to expect some graphics.

The endprint function just sends an end of graphics escape sequence.

The printline function is equally simple—it sends the printer an escape sequence telling it how many bytes of graphic information to expect and then sends the line itself. The LaserJet takes care of positioning its internal cursor for the next line.

Once 16 images have been printed, the printing function calls eject_page, which handles numerous aspects of polishing up the page, spitting it out and the setting up for the next page.

In ejecting the page, the program must print the page number. Because space is very tight on the page, this number will get printed quite close to the name of the sixteenth image. To make it easy to spot, it will be underlined and printed in bold.

Unfortunately, the LaserJet does not provide a facility to print its default Courier font in bold. However, you can come up with a pretty respectable synthetic bold font by simply overprinting the page number twice, with the second pass moved to the right by two dots. Underlining it simply involves overprinting it with underscore characters.

After printing the page number, this function must print the ruling boxes around each of the images. Now, this turns out to be exceedingly tricky on a LaserJet. The printer will print rectangles, but it won't do hollow ones. If you print a black box, you get a black area. The LaserJet has a ''black only'' engine—once a dot has been set, overprinting it with white does not unset it. As such, you could not simply print a slightly smaller white box within a black one to arrive at a frame.

The framerect function illustrates how to get around this. It prints a frame by printing four very thin rectangles—so thin that they look like individual ruling lines.

Finally, eject_page spits out the page by printing a form feed character.

There are two optional command line parameters for the graphics catalog program. These allow you to set the start and stop pages for printing, so that you can print part of a catalog if you want to. This is handy if you discover that your LaserJet has run out of toner or otherwise lunched out on a page part way through a large collection of images.

Figure 10-14 is the complete catalog program. It's all written in C, so you won't need a project file to link in other object modules for this one.

Fig 10-14   The LaserJet graphics catalog program

```
/*
        GRAFCAT - Graphics catalog program
*/

#include "stdio.h"
#include "alloc.h"
#include "dir.h"
#include "dos.h"
#include "string.h"

#define resolution      300     /* dots per inch */
#define pagewide         2400    /* width of actual page */
#define pagedeep         3450    /* depth of actual page */
#define margin           5       /* padding in from edge */
#define framewide        576     /* maximum image width */
#define framedeep        720     /* maximum image depth */
```

```
#define h_gutter        16      /* horizontal space between images */
#define v_gutter        48      /* vertical space between images */

#define number_left     2250    /* horizontal page number position */

#define line_width      2       /* thickness of ruling box lines*/
#define line_gap         2       /* thickness of gap between image and rule */
#define line_shade      100     /* percent density of ruling lines */

#define xframes         (pagewide / (framewide+h_gutter))
#define yframes         (pagedeep / (framedeep+v_gutter))

#define max_frame       (xframes * yframes)
#define font_fudge      38      /* fudge actor for type */

#define barsize         20      /* size of bar graph */

typedef struct { unsigned int x,y; } POINT;

char path[81];                  /* path where files are */
char *buffer=NULL;              /* buffer for names */
char linebuffer[4096];          /* line buffer - make it big */
char *filename();

POINT point_array[max_frame];

unsigned int width,depth,bytes,planes;
unsigned int patternsize=1;
unsigned int current=0;

unsigned int countfor();
unsigned int pixels2bytes();

unsigned int page_number=1;
unsigned int start_page;
unsigned int stop_page;
unsigned int count=0;

main(argc,argv)
        int argc;
        char *argv[];
{
        unsigned int i;
puts("Graphics Catalog version 1.0");

if(argc > 1) {
        strlwr(argv[1]);
        make_frames();
        i=countfor(argv[1]);
        if((buffer=malloc(i*sizeof(struct ffblk))) != NULL) {

                /* extract the path if the argument for later */
                parse(argv[1]);

                /* find all the files specified */
                lookfor(argv[1]);
```

Fig 10-14   continued

```
            printf("%u files in %s\n",i,path);

            /* sort the list */
            sortlist();

            /* clear out the printer */
            reset_printer();
            start_page=0;
            stop_page=count;

            /* go through possible command line options */
            for(i=1;i<argc;++i) {
              if(argv[i][0]=='/') {
                switch(toupper(argv[i][1])) {
                  case 'S':
                    start_page=((unsigned int)atoi(argv[i]+2) *
                      max_frame)-max_frame;
                      break;
                  case 'E':
                    stop_page=(((unsigned int)atoi(argv[i]+2) *
                      max_frame));
                      break;
                }
              }
            }

            /* chack page ranges */
            if(start_page > count) {
                    printf("\nBad news - printing "
                        "starts after end of list");
                    exit(1);
            }
            if(stop_page < start_page) {
                    printf("\nBad news - printing "
                        "stops before it starts");
                    exit(1);
            }
            if(stop_page > count) stop_page=count;

            /* set current page number */
            page_number=(start_page / max_frame)+1;

            for(i=start_page;i<stop_page;++i) print_image(i);
            if(current) eject_page();
                    free(buffer);
            } else puts("Bad news... can't allocate memory");
      } else puts("An argument would be handy. "
            "How about the path to some picture files...\n"
            " Examples:    GRAFCAT *.IMG\n"
            "                 catalogs GEM/IMG files\n"
            "              GRAFCAT \\PAINT\\B*.MAC\n"
            "                 catalogs MacPaint files starting with B\n"
            "              GRAFCAT D:*.PCX\n,"
```

```
                       "                  catalogs all the PC Paintbrush files on D:\n"
                       " Options:    /S<n> start with page n\n"
                       "             /E<n> end after page n\n");
}


print_image(n)                /* dispatch request to print image */
{
        struct ffblk *f;
        char s[MAXEXT];

        f=(struct ffblk*)(buffer+(n*sizeof(struct ffblk)));
        fnsplit(f->ff_name,NULL,NULL,NULL,s);

        if(!strcmp(s,".IMG")) print_IMG(n);
        else if(!strcmp(s,".MAC")) print_MAC(n);
        else if(!strcmp(s,".PCX")) print_PCX(n);
        else if(!strcmp(s,".PCC")) print_PCX(n);

}


print_IMG(n)            /* open and print GEM/IMG image n */
        unsigned int n;
{
        FILE *fp;
        struct ffblk *f;
        char s[81],b[16];
        unsigned int i;

        f=(struct ffblk*)(buffer+(n*sizeof(struct ffblk)));

        if((fp=fopen(filename(f->ff_name),"rb")) != NULL) {
                clear_line();
                printf("Printing %-14.14s - %u of %u - page %u ",
                    f->ff_name,(n+1)-start_page,stop_page-start_page,
                    page_number);
                showgraph();
                if(fread(b,1,16,fp) == 16 &&
                    !memcmp("\x00\x01\x00\x08\x00\x01",b,6)) {
                        patternsize = (b[7] & 0xff)+((b[6] & 0xff)<<8);
                        width = (b[13] & 0xff)+((b[12] & 0xff)<<8);
                        depth = (b[15] & 0xff)+((b[14] & 0xff)<<8);
                        bytes=pixels2bytes(width);
                        pushloc();
                        showname(f->ff_name,current);
                        startprint(current++);
                        for(i=0;i<depth;++i) {
                                if(i >= framedeep) break;
                                readline_IMG(linebuffer,fp);
                                if(width <= framewide)
                                    printline(linebuffer,bytes);
                                    else printline(linebuffer+((bytes/2)-
                                        (pixels2bytes(framewide)/2)),
                                        pixels2bytes(framewide));
                                showbar(i,framedeep);
```

Fig 10-14   continued

```
                            }
                            endprint();
                            poploc();
                            if(current >= max_frame) eject_page();
                    } else printf("\nError reading header in %s\n",s);
                    fclose(fp);
                    return(1);
        }
        else {
                    printf("\nError opening %s\n",s);
                    return(0);
        }
}

print_MAC(n)              /* open and print MacPaint image n */
        unsigned int n;
{
        FILE *fp;
        struct ffblk *f;
        char s[81],b[128];
        unsigned int i;

        f=(struct ffblk*)(buffer+(n*sizeof(struct ffblk)));

        if((fp=fopen(filename(f->ff_name),"rb")) != NULL) {
                    clear_line();
                    printf("Printing %-14.14s - %u of %u - page %u ",
                        f->ff_name, (n+1)-start_page,stop_page-start_page,
                        page_number);
                    showgraph();
                    if(fread(b,1,128,fp) == 128) {
                            if(!memcmp("PNTG",b+65,4))
                                fseek(fp,640L,SEEK_SET);
                            else if(!memcmp("\000\000\000\002",b,4))
                                fseek(fp,512L,SEEK_SET);
                            if(!memcmp("PNTG",b+65,4) ||
                                !memcmp("\000\000\000\002",b,4)) {
                                    width = 576;
                                    depth = 720;
                                    bytes=pixels2bytes(width);
                                    pushloc();
                                    showname(f->ff_name,current);
                                    startprint(current++);
                                    for(i=0;i<depth;++i) {
                                            if(i >= framedeep) break;
                                            readline_MAC(linebuffer,fp);
                                            printline(linebuffer,bytes);
                                            showbar(i,framedeep);
                                    }
                                    endprint();
                                    poploc();
                                    if(current >= max_frame) eject_page();
                        } else printf("\nCorrupted header in %s\n",s);
```

```
                } else printf("\nError reading header in %s\n",s);
                fclose(fp);
                return(1);
        }
        else {
                printf("\nError opening %s\n",s);
                return(0);
        }
}

print_PCX(n)            /* open and print PC Paintbrush image n */
        unsigned int n;
{
        FILE *fp;
        struct ffblk *f;
        char s[81],b[128];
        unsigned int i,j;

        f=(struct ffblk*)(buffer+(n*sizeof(struct ffblk)));

        if((fp=fopen(filename(f->ff_name),"rb")) != NULL) {
                clear_line();
                printf("Printing %-14.14s - %u of %u - page %u ",
                    f->ff_name,(n+1)-start_page,stop_page-start_page,
                    page_number);
                showgraph();
                if(fread(b,1,128,fp) == 128 && b[0] == 0x0a) {
                        width = (b[8] & 0xff)+((b[9] & 0xff)<<8);
                        depth = (b[10] & 0xff)+((b[11] & 0xff)<<8);
                        bytes = (b[66] & 0xff)+((b[67] & 0xff)<<8);
                        planes = b[65];
                        pushloc();
                        showname(f->ff_name,current);
                        startprint(current++);
                        for(i=0;i<depth;++i) {
                                if(i >= framedeep) break;
                                readline_PCX(linebuffer,fp);
                                if(width <= framewide)
                                  printline(linebuffer,bytes);
                                else printline(linebuffer+((bytes/2)-
                                  (pixels2bytes(framewide)/2)),
                                    pixels2bytes(framewide));
                                showbar(i,framedeep);
                                for(j=1;j<planes;++j)
                                  readline_PCX(linebuffer,fp);
                        }
                        endprint();
                        poploc();
                        if(current >= max_frame) eject_page();
                } else printf("\nError reading header in %s\n",s);
                fclose(fp);
                return(1);
        }
        else {
```

Fig 10-14   continued

```
                     printf("\nError opening %s\n",s);
                     return(0);
          }
}

sortlist()                    /* sort the file list by file size */
{
        int dircheck();

        qsort(buffer,count,sizeof(struct ffblk),dircheck);
}

dircheck(e1,e2)               /* compare two files */
        char *e1,*e2;
{
        struct ffblk *p1,*p2;

        p1=(struct ffblk *)e1;
        p2=(struct ffblk *)e2;
        return(strcmp(p1->ff_name,p2->ff_name));
}

lookfor(b)         /* find all the file names which match spec b */
        char *b;
{
        struct ffblk f;

        if(!findfirst(b,&f,0)) {
                do {
                        memcpy(buffer+(count*sizeof(struct ffblk)),
                               (char *)&f,sizeof(struct ffblk));
                        ++count;
                } while(!findnext(&f));
        }
}

unsigned int countfor(b)
        char *b;
{
        struct ffblk f;
        unsigned int i=0;

        if(!findfirst(b,&f,0)) {
                do {
                        ++i;
                } while(!findnext(&f));
        }
        return(i);
}

parse(s)
        char *s;
{
        char drive[MAXDRIVE],dir[MAXDIR];
```

```
        fnsplit(s,drive,dir,NULL,NULL);
        sprintf(path,"%s%s",drive,dir);
}

readline_IMG(p,fp)                      /* read and decode a GEM/IMG line into p */
        char *p;
        FILE *fp;
{
        char *pr;
        int r,j,k,n=0,c,i;
memset(p,0,bytes);
r=1;
do {
        c=fgetc(fp) & 0xff;
        if(c==0) {                              /* it's a pattern or a rep */
                c=fgetc(fp) & 0xff;
                if(c==0) {                      /*it's a rep count change*/
                        fgetc(fp);              /* throw away the ff */
                        r=fgetc(fp) & 0xff;
                }
                else {
                        i=c & 0xff;
                        pr=p+n;

                        j=patternsize;
                        while(j--) p[n++]=fgetc(fp);

                        k=i-1;
                        while(k--) {
                                memcpy(p+n,pr,patternsize);
                                n+=patternsize;
                        }
                        j=r-1;
                        while(j--) {
                                k=i;
                                while(k--) {
                                        memcpy(p+n,pr,patternsize);
                                        n+=patternsize;
                                }
                        }
                        r=1;
                }
        }
        else if(c==0x80) {
                i=fgetc(fp) & 0xff;
                pr=p+n;
                j=i;
                while(j--) p[n++]=fgetc(fp);
                j=r-1;
                while(j--) {
                        memcpy(p+n,pr,i);
                        n+=i;
                }
                r=1;
```

Fig 10-14 continued

```
                }
        else if(c & 0x80) {
                i = c & 0x7f;
                pr=p+n;
                j=i;
                while(j--) p[n++]=0xff;
                j=r-1;
                while(j--) {
                        memcpy(p+n,pr,i);
                        n+=i;
                }
                r=1;
        }
        else {
                i = c & 0x7f;
                        pr=p+n;
                        j=i;
                        while(j--) p[n++]=0x00;
                        j=r-1;
                        while(j--) {
                                memcpy(p+n,pr,i);
                                n+=i;
                        }
                        r=1;
                }
        } while(n < bytes);
        return(n);
}

readline_MAC(p,fp)                      /* read and decode a MacPaint line into p */
        char *p;
        FILE *fp;
{
        int n=0,c,i;

        memset(p,0,bytes);
        do {
                c=fgetc(fp) & 0xff;
                if(c & 0x80) {
                        i = ((~c) & 0xff)+2;
                        c=fgetc(fp);
                        while(i--) p[n++] = c;
                }
                else {
                        i=(c & 0xff)+1;
                        while(i--) p[n++] = fgetc(fp);
                }
        } while(n < bytes);
        return(n);
}

readline_PCX(p,fp)                      /* read and decode a PCX line into p */
        char *p;
```

```
        FILE *fp;
{
        int n=0,c,i;

        memset(p,0,bytes);
        do {
                c=fgetc(fp) & 0xff;
                if((c & 0xc0) == 0xc0) {
                        i=c & 0x3f;
                        c=fgetc(fp);
                        while(i--) p[n++]=~c;
                }
                else p[n++]=~c;
        } while(n < bytes);
        return(n);
}


startprint(n)              /* prepare the printer for action for frame n*/
        int n;
{
        char s[65];

        sprintf(s,"\x1b*t%uR",resolution);
        p_string(s);                              /* set resolution */
        sprintf(s,"\x1b*p%uX",point_array[n].x);
        p_string(s);                              /* set left page frame */
        sprintf(s,"\x1b*p%uY",point_array[n].y);
        p_string(s);

        p_string("\x1b*r1A");        /* say graphics are coming */
}

endprint()
{
        p_string("\x1b*rB");              /* end raster graphics */
}

printline(p,l)             /* print one line of the image */
        char *p;
        unsigned int l;
{
        char s[80];

        sprintf(s,"\x1b*b%dW",l);
        p_string(s);
        p_buff(p,l);
}

p_string(s)
        char *s;
{
        while(*s) p_char(*s++);
}
```

Fig 10-14   continued

```
p_buff(s,l)
        char *s;
        int l;
{
        while(l--) p_char(*s++);
}


p_char(c)
        int c;
{
        union REGS r;

        do {
                r.h.ah = 2;
                r.x.dx = 0;
                int86(0x17,&r,&r);
        } while(!(r.h.ah & 0x80));

        r.h.ah = 0;
        r.h.al = c;
        r.x.dx = 0;
        int86(0x17,&r,&r);
}


eject_page()        /* finish the page and eject it */
{
        char b[65];
        int i;

        /* select the courier font */
        p_string("\x1b(sp10h12vsb3T");

        /* position the text */
        sprintf(b,"\x1b*p%ux%uY",number_left,
            point_array[max_frame-1].y+framedeep+font_fudge);
        p_string(b);

        /* print the text */
        sprintf(b,"P%u",page_number);
        p_string(b);

        /* go back to the beginning of the text and bold it */
        sprintf(b,"\x1b*p%ux%uY",2+number_left,
            point_array[max_frame-1].y+framedeep+font_fudge);
        p_string(b);
        i=sprintf(b,"P%u",page_number);
        p_string(b);

        /* finally, underline it */
        sprintf(b,"\x1b*p%ux%uY",number_left,
            point_array[max_frame-1].y+framedeep+font_fudge);
        p_string(b);
        while(i--) p_char('_');
```

```
        clear_line();
        printf("Ejecting page %u",page_number++);

        for(i=0;i<max_frame;++i)
                framerect(point_array[i].x,point_array[i].y,
                            point_array[i].x+framewide,
                            point_array[i].y+framedeep);

        current=0;
        p_string("\x0c");
}
make_frames()      /* calculate the frame origins */
{
        int x,y;

        for(y=0;y<yframes;++y) {
                for(x=0;x<xframes;++x) {
                        point_array[(y*yframes)+x].x=
                            margin+(x*(framewide+h_gutter));
                        point_array[(y*yframes)+x].y=
                            margin+(y*(framedeep+v_gutter));
                }
        }
}

unsigned int pixels2bytes(n)   /* return number of bytes in number of pixels */
        unsigned int n;
{
        if(n & 0x0007) return((n >> 3) + 1);
        else return(n >> 3);
}

framerect(l,t,r,b)
        unsigned int l,t,r,b;
{
        char s[65];

        /* draw top line */
        sprintf(s,"\x1b*p%uX",l-(line_width+line_gap));
        p_string(s);
        sprintf(s,"\x1b*p%uY",t-(line_width+line_gap));
        p_string(s);
        sprintf(s,"\x1b*c%uA",(r-l)+(2*(line_width+line_gap)));
        p_string(s);
        sprintf(s,"\x1b*c%uB",line_width);
        p_string(s);
        sprintf(s,"\x1b*c%uG",line_shade);
        p_string(s);
        p_string("\x1b*c2P");

        /* draw bottom line */
        sprintf(s,"\x1b*p%uX",l-(line_width+line_gap));
        p_string(s);
        sprintf(s,"\x1b*p%uY",b+line_gap);
```

Fig 10-14   continued

```
          p_string(s);
          sprintf(s,"\x1b*c%uA",(r-l)+(2*(line_width+line_gap)));
          p_string(s);
          sprintf(s,"\x1b*c%uB",line_width);
          p_string(s);
          sprintf(s,"\x1b*c%uG",line_shade);
          p_string(s);
          p_string("\x1b*c2P");

          /* draw left line */
          sprintf(s,"\x1b*p%uX",l-(line_width+line_gap));
          p_string(s);
          sprintf(s,"\x1b*p%uY",t-(line_width+line_gap));
          p_string(s);
          sprintf(s,"\x1b*c%uA",line_width);
          p_string(s);
          sprintf(s,"\x1b*c%uB",(b-t)+(2*(line_width+line_gap)));
          p_string(s);
          sprintf(s,"\x1b*c%uG",line_shade);
          p_string(s);
          p_string("\x1b*c2P");

          /* draw right line */
          sprintf(s,"\x1b*p%uX",r+line_gap);
          p_string(s);
          sprintf(s,"\x1b*p%uY",t-(line_width+line_gap));
          p_string(s);
          sprintf(s,"\x1b*c%uA",line_width);
          p_string(s);
          sprintf(s,"\x1b*c%uB",(b-t)+(2*(line_width+line_gap)));
          p_string(s);
          sprintf(s,"\x1b*c%uG",line_shade);
          p_string(s);
          p_string("\x1b*c2P");
}

showname(s,i)                /* print the file name */
          char *s;
          unsigned int i;
{
          char b[65];

          p_string("\x1b(sp10h12vsb3T");

          sprintf(b,"\x1b*p%ux%uY",point_array[i].x,
                  point_array[i].y+framedeep+font_fudge);
          p_string(b);
          p_string(s);
}

reset_printer()
{
          p_string("\033E");
```

```
}

pushloc() /* save the current printer cursor position */
{
        p_string("\x1b&f0S");
}

poploc()  /* restore the current printer cursor position */
{
        p_string("\x1b&f1S");
}

clear_line()
{
        int i=79;

        putchar('\r');
        while(i--) putchar(' ');
        putchar('\r');
}

showbar(n,max)     /* show the bar graph */
        int n,max;
{
        static int l;
        int i;

        i=(n*barsize)/max;
        if(i != l) putchar(219);
        l=i;
}

showgraph()
{
        int i;

        for(i=0;i<barsize;++i) putchar(178);
        for(i=0;i<barsize;++i) putchar(8);
}
char *filename(s) /* create a file name with the path installed */
        char *s;
{
        static char b[129];
        char *p;

        while(*s == 32) ++s;
        if((p=strchr(s,10)) != NULL) *p=0;
        if((p=strchr(s,13)) != NULL) *p=0;
        if((p=strchr(s,32)) != NULL) *p=0;

        strcpy(b,path);
        strcat(b,s);
        return(b);
}
```

Enhancements to the Catalog Program

There are a number of things you might want to consider adding to this program once you understand how it functions. If you have a printer that handles both a LaserJet emulation and PostScript—or if you lack a LaserJet altogether—you could try making the catalog program drive a PostScript printer. However, PostScript printers are pretty slow in dealing with bit-mapped images, and this program sends down an awful lot of bit-mapped data. A PostScript version of this thing takes ages to print.

It would be useful to have the catalog program accept color image formats. Obviously, it can't print in color, but there are several ways in which it could manage a representative image of a full color GIF or PCX file—at least you'd be able to tell what the picture was.

If you're looking for an interesting way to expand on the basic code for the catalog program, consider adding the facility for decoding and dithering GIF and full color PCX files. You will need several of the modules discussed in this book, but the task is essentially a simple one. The program will get quite a bit bigger, of course.

OUT OF PAPER

This chapter is by no means the last word in printing bit-mapped images. It has, of necessity, been restricted to a common group of output devices. There are all sorts of others, and when you get into some of the specialized ones, such as film recorders, you can encounter some very interesting programming challenges indeed. It's useful to note, however, that even very esoteric hard copy devices most often behave in much the same ways that the printers we've discussed in this chapter do. There are, after all, just so many ways to print a pixel.

11
CHAPTER

Dithering

If at first you don't succeed, transform your data.
—Murphy's Laws of Computers

In discussing the applications of bit-mapped graphics to printers, one of the things that came up in Chapter 10 was the difficulties inherent in printing color images on monochrome output devices. This also will be a problem if you wish to view color images on a monochrome monitor.

Representing color in black and white would seem to be an insurmountable problem on the surface, but this is hardly so if you look up from your monitor for a moment and consider some other approaches to graphics. Photography, one of the oldest visual technologies in use, has been managing it for more than a century. A black and white photograph manages to reduce color to grey scales.

Newspapers have been further reducing grey scales to halftones for almost as long. Before the advent of halftones, the artists who created commercial etchings learned to represent grey with patterns of lines.

Hand-drawn mechanical halftones date back to the seventeenth century in the form of mezzotints.

Halftones, although manageable in the PostScript imaging example in Chapter 10, are not really practical when one is dealing with pure image files. It would be possible, for example, to render a full color GIF file as a graphic halftone in an IMG file, but the result would be one of the most enormous IMG files imaginable. Consider that to be able to represent 256 shades of grey, such a file would have to be able to manage halftone dots of 256 different sizes. This would require that each pixel in the original picture be represented by at least a 16-pixel square area in the halftoned file.

A 320-by-200-pixel GIF file would require a 5120-by-3200-pixel IMG file to hold even a rudimentary halftone of its former glory.

In addition, of course, the software to generate the dots of a halftone would be ponderous indeed—not to mention being fairly slow.

There is another way to transform color pictures into black and white, one that has been mentioned earlier in this book. It involves one of the more arcane areas of bit-mapped images, that of dithering.

Dithering is an algorithmic process of reducing a color image to a series of black and white dots, such that the original grey scale of the source image is preserved to some extent. Dithering is fascinating in that it seems to do the impossible. By applying a suitable dither to a color image, you can create a monochrome image of the same dimensions with what seems to be much of its original grey scale information preserved.

Figure 11-1 illustrates a halftone and a dither of the same 256-color source file.

The example dithering programs in this chapter will use GIF files as their source images and output monochrome IMG files. However, you can apply the code to be discussed to any bit-mapped file format.

BASIC DITHERING CONCEPTS

Any color image can be reduced to a grey scaled image by simply summing the primary additive colors. The formula for doing so is as follows:

grey = .30 * red + .59 * green + .11 * blue

If you apply this formula to the palette of a GIF file, you can replace the palette numbers in the actual GIF images with grey values.

In fact, although theoretically this is all you have to do to convert a color image to a grey scale, the results don't look all that exciting. As was touched on in the last chapter, it's necessary to cheat on this process somewhat by remapping the shades of grey a bit. This expands the contrast of the source image and makes it look more interesting.

Remapping the grey scale involves expanding the center portion of the range. Although it's certainly possible to handle this by devising a function to do it, the best results can be had by using a lookup table of values. The original grey value from the previous expression is used as an index into the table. Inasmuch as there are only 256 possible shades of grey returned by this expression—at least, there are when it's applied to the palette of a GIF files—the mapping table need only have 256 entries.

Figure 11-2 illustrates the way the grey scale is remapped.

The table is a bit enormous to write down. You'll be able to see it in total, shortly. This is by no means the definitive table—the values in it were determined largely by trial and error. Feel free to adjust the values if you want to.

Approaches to Dithering

The simplest way to create a monochrome image from a color picture that has been reduced to a grey scale is to use a *threshold*. This simply

Fig 11-1   A halftoned 256-color image (above) and a dither of the same picture. This picture was downloaded from Canada Remote Systems (416) 629-0136

means to assign an arbitrary level below which a pixel will be regarded as being black and above which it will be considered white. This is how the preview images for the PostScript EPS file generator in the last chapter were created.

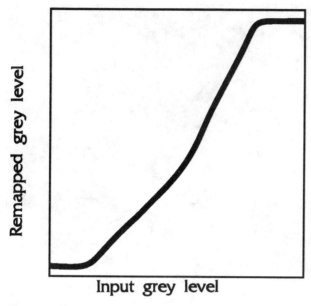

Fig 11-2   The grey scale remapping used in this chapter

Here's how this would work. Let's allow that the threshold is midway between black and white. Because white would be 255, the threshold will be 127. Any pixel with a grey level of greater than 127 will be plotted as white.

Figure 11-3 illustrates a picture that has been converted to black and white in this way.

Fig 11-3   Thresholding the parrot. It's not dead—merely resting

The drawback to this approach is fairly obvious. An enormous amount of detail from the color source image has vanished in this monochrome image, and the resulting picture is exceedingly contrasty. Different results can be had by changing the threshold value, but the resulting picture will never look particularly good.

Early scanner designers were frequently faced with this problem. Their scanners could handle 32 or 64 levels of grey, but the image file formats of the time—MacPaint, for example—were inherently monochrome. To avoid turning everything into line art, they adopted some rudimentary dithering.

One of the earliest forms of dithering used in microcomputers was pattern dithering. The Bayer dither is one of the commonly found pattern dithers. It might be easier to understand what it's doing if you look at the code that makes it go—it's illustrated in Fig. 11-4.

The principle of a Bayer dither is to compare the grey levels of the source image to the fixed dither pattern. This pattern is an eight by eight matrix, so the grey levels are reduced to 64 possible levels of grey. Having done this, each eight by eight block of the image is essentially compared to

Fig 11-4   How a Bayer dither works

```
/* dither an image using a Bayer pattern dither. See the
   later examples for the workings of the getPixel and
   bitPixel functions. */

dither(dest,source)
      char *dest,*source;
{
      static char pattern[8][8] =
            {  0,32, 8,40, 2,34,10,42,
              48,16,56,24,50,18,58,26,
              12,44, 4,36,14,46, 6,38,
              60,28,52,20,62,30,54,22,
               3,35,11,43, 1,33, 9,41,
              51,19,59,27,49,17,57,25,
              15,47, 7,39,13,45, 5,37,
              63,31,55,23,61,29,53,21 };
      int x,y,n;

      for(y=0;y<IMAGEDEEP;++y) {
            for(x=0;x<IMAGEWIDE;++x) {
                  n=getPixel(source,x,y);
                  /* note that pixel value is shifted
                     right by two for 0-63 range */
                  if((n >> 2) > pattern[x & 7][y & 7])
                        bitPixel(dest,x,y,1);
                  else bitPixel(dest,x,y,0);
            }
      }
}
```

the pattern. Those pixels in the source image that are greater than the corresponding elements in the matrix will be white pixels in the destination image. Those that are not will be black pixels.

Figure 11-5 is an example of an image passed through a Bayer dither.

One of the most notable things about the Bayer dither is that it doesn't work all that well. The pictures it creates have a lot of things that are characteristic of this approach to dithering. Contemporary dithering techniques usually can outperform the Bayer dither as far as their results go. They can't outperform it for speed, however. Dithering, as you'll see, gets slower as it gets better.

Fig 11-5   The parrot having been Bayer dithered. Now it's dead

Artifacts and Errors

The problem with Bayer dithering is that it imposes a rigid pattern on the images it processes, regardless of the content of the image. Applied to a large image, Bayer dithering frequently results in a recognizable pattern if the image is printed and viewed as a whole. The easiest way to see the pattern is to apply Bayer dithering to a large, uniform 50 percent grey area.

Many of the early Macintosh scanners, such as the ubiquitous ThunderScan, which turns the Macintosh's ImageWriter dot matrix printer into a pretty respectable scanner, used this sort of dithering. MacPaint files with the familiar cross hatching of Bayer dithering abound.

The pattern that Bayer dithering impresses on an image is called an *artifact*. Artifacts are unwanted visual byproducts of image processing. In dithering, one attempts to create a dithering process that results in a faithful illusion of continuous tone grey scales with no visible artifacts. In a real sense this is impossible, but you will find that by applying a bit of cunning to the problem you can reduce the occurrence of artifacts to the point where they aren't obvious unless you're looking for them.

The most productive way to arrive at a usable dithering procedure that does not impose any obvious artifacts on an image is to employ *error diffusion*. This is both elegantly simple in principle and a little mysterious in practice.

You have to consider the situation from the point of view of a pixel to really understand error diffusion. Let's allow that there's a grey scale pixel about to be turned to a monochrome pixel by comparing it against a threshold. The threshold is halfway between black and white, which will be 127. The pixel in question has a grey level of 150, so it will be white. However, there's an error of 23 here—the difference between the real grey level of the pixel and the level of the threshold.

If this error is *diffused* out to the surrounding pixels, its effects will be less noticeable in the final dither. Bear in mind that each of these pixels will have errors too. The result—if it's done properly—will be to set up a series of alternating black and white pixels that look a lot like the grey scale of the original.

This approach has lots of potential problems, not the least of which is finding a realistic approach to diffusing the pixel errors. One of the more troublesome byproducts of the process—and one that none of the dithering approaches in this chapter really addresses perfectly—is the tendency of formerly hard boundaries between areas of widely varying grey levels to soften and diffuse along with the threshold errors. Images that involve some text, for example, don't usually dither very well.

Dithering Algorithms

The most popular error diffusion approach is the Floyd-Steinberg filter, perhaps not surprisingly the result of some work by R.W. Floyd and L. Steinberg. This is quite an old filter actually, having been presented in 1975.

This is how the Floyd-Steinberg filter works:

```
    X    7
3   5    1
```

It might take you a moment to figure out how to read error diffusion diagrams. In this case, note that all the numbers add up to 16. Given that there is an error between the pixel at X and the threshold between white and black, you would add 7/16ths of the error to the pixel directly to the right of X. You would add 3/16ths of the error to the pixel to the left of X and one pixel down. You would add 5/16ths of the error to the pixel directly below X, and the remaining 1/16th of the error to the pixel to the right and one pixel down from X.

Having done this, you'd move to the next pixel in the source image and repeat the process.

The results of the Floyd-Steinberg filter are really quite good. You can improve on them, however, by using a filter that "communicates" with a larger number of pixels, spreading the error out over more dots. This usually results in a final image that has better detail at the boundaries between areas of different grey levels in the source image, such as with text.

The Stucki filter improves on the performance of Floyd-Steinberg to some extent. Actually, it might not be quite right to say that it improves on anything. It produces different results that might work out better with some images. The results of dithering are always a bit subjective.

This is how a Stucki dither works:

```
            X     8     4
2     4     8     4     2
1     2     4     2     1
```

These numbers add up to 42, so the pixel to the right of X would get $8/42$ths of the error, and so on.

The drawback to the Stucki dither is that it's slow. It entails dealing with lots of pixels in three lines. However, more than this it requires a lot of integer multiplication and division. By comparison, the Floyd-Steinberg dither can be implemented with bit shifts and subtraction.

C compilers tend to handle this sort of thing for you. For example, if you divide an integer by 16 in C, Turbo C will actually shift it right by four bits in the final program. The 8088 series processors can do a bit shift in eight or so machine cycles, as compared to more than 100 cycles for an IDIV instruction. Spread over a 640-by-480-pixel GIF file—307,200 individual pixels with 12 calculations for each—this can make a substantial difference in the time it takes to dither a picture.

Images that have been dithered with a Stucki filter generally look more acceptable than those handled with a Floyd-Steinberg filter, but the time increase in using the Stucki filter is often prohibitive, especially on large images.

The third commonly found dithering filter is the Burkes filter. This was designed as a compromise between the Floyd-Steinberg filter and the Stucki filter. It communicates with more pixels than the former, but it does so using simple math that can be handled with bit shifts and subtraction. Its results lie, predictably, somewhere between the two previous filters.

The Burkes filter can be represented like this:

```
            X     8     4
2     4     8     4     2
```

Figure 11-6 illustrates the same image dithered with these three filters. Note the differences in the time it took to perform these dithers. The

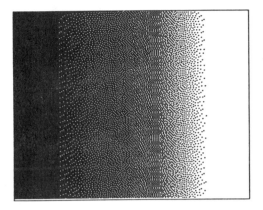

Floyd-Steinberg dither — 16 seconds

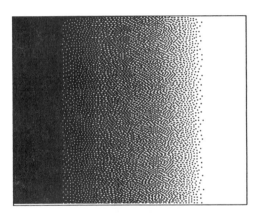

Burkes dither — 22 seconds

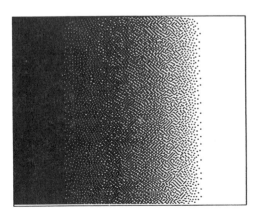

Stucki dither — 33 seconds

Fig 11-6   The three error diffusion filters discussed in this chapter and their results

source image was a 640-by-480-pixel GIF file and the dithering program was run on a 16 megahertz 386 system.

There are numerous other filters that have turned up over the years. The example programs in this chapter will only implement the previous three error diffusion filters, but you can add some additional ones if you like. You can also try to concoct your own filter.

This is the Sierra filter:

```
            X    5    3
2     4     5    4    2
      2     3    2
```

It parcels out errors in 30 seconds. This is the Jarvis, Judice, and Ninke filter:

```
            X    7    5
3     5     7    5    3
1     3     5    3    1
```

It uses forty-eighths of the original error.

Finally, this is the Stevenson and Arce filter. It uses two hundredths of the error. The results it produces are notably more attractive than those of any of the other filters discussed this far, but it's so processor intensive as to make it impractical for use on a microcomputer:

```
              X         32
12      26         30         16
     12         26         12
5       12         12         5
```

One of the common causes of artifacts in using error diffusion techniques is the tendency of the errors on one line to simply transfer themselves to next line and gather along vertical objects in the image. You'll frequently encounter them there, playing poker, annoying passers-by, and ultimately having to be diffused by the police.

The filters discussed here lend themselves to a fairly effective solution to this problem in that none of them is completely symmetrical. Rather than scanning through the lines of the source image from left to right for each line, it's desirable to use a *serpentine* scan. This means that the first line would be scanned from left to right with one of the filters discussed. The next line would be scanned from right to left with a mirror image of the filter.

Again, this does not necessarily produce better results. It does produce different ones, though, which might be more suitable for some images.

It's probably worth noting that despite all of the foregoing, this chapter barely scratches the surface of the subject of dithering. If you're interested in improving on the techniques discussed herein, you're urged to read Robert Ulichney's *Digital Halftoning*, listed at the end of this chapter. It's an exhaustive and definitive guide to this area of image processing.

Test File Generator

Before discussing the first of the dithering programs, you might want to look at the program in Fig. 11-7. This is a simple GIF file generator. It will write out a GIF file called GRAYSCAL.GIF, which contains a smooth grey scale fountain running horizontally across the image. This is a useful test file to work with if you're investigating different dithering filters.

In practice, one usually devises dithering filters to deal with hard edges rather than smooth tones, and you'll want real digitized images to test them. However, the mechanics of working the bugs out of a dithering program usually involve tracking down things like spurious pixels at pathological grey levels, for which the GRAYSCAL.GIF file is exceedingly useful.

This program must link to the GIF encoder module from Chapter 6.

Fig 11-7   A program to create a test GIF file

```
/*
        An example GIF encoder
        Create a grey scale fountain
*/

#include "stdio.h"
#include "alloc.h"
#include "dos.h"

#define width    256
#define depth    200

typedef struct {          unsigned int screenwide;
                          unsigned int screendeep;
                          unsigned int imageleft;
                          unsigned int imagetop;
                          unsigned int imagewide;
                          unsigned int imagedeep;
                          unsigned int background;
                          unsigned int bits;
                          unsigned long imagesize;
                          char *palette;
                          char *image;
                          char *path;
                } GIFDATA;

char gifFile[]="GRAYSCAL.GIF";
char palette[768];

main()
{
        GIFDATA gd;
        char *p;
        int i,j,n;
```

Fig 11-7   continued

```
        gd.screenwide=width;
        gd.screendeep=depth;
        gd.imageleft=0;
        gd.imagetop=0;
        gd.imagewide=width;
        gd.imagedeep=depth;
        gd.background=0;
        gd.bits=8;
        gd.palette=palette;
        gd.path=gifFile;
        gd.imagesize=(long)depth*(long)width;

        if((p=malloc(width*depth)) != NULL) {
                gd.image=p;
                memset(palette,0,768);
                for(i=0;i<256;++i) memset(palette+(i*3),i,3);

                for(j=0;j<depth;++j) {
                        for(i=0;i<width;++i) p[(j*width)+i]=i;
                }
                if((n=PackGIF(&gd)) != 0)
                    printf("Error %d writing GIF file",n);
                free(p);
        }
}
```

DITHERING SIZE AS

The easiest way to investigate dithering is to write a program that will generate a dithered monochrome image from a color source file. The program in Fig. 11-8 does this. It embodies three of the filters discussed earlier in this chapter—the Floyd-Steinberg, Stucki, and Burkes. It has a number of command line options that let you select the filter to be used, whether the raster will be scanned unidirectionally or in a serpentine pattern and, finally, a quick and nasty graphics display that will allow you to see the file as it's being dithered—assuming that you have an EGA display in your computer.

Fig 11-8   A program to dither GIF files into monochrome IMG files using conventional memory

```
/*
        An example C language GIF decoder.
        Dithers GIF file to black and white
        Copyright (c) 1989 Alchemy Mindworks
*/

#include "stdio.h"
#include "dos.h"
#include "dir.h"
#include "alloc.h"
```

```
#include "time.h"

#define     maxline         2048     /* longest GIF line */

/* dithering procedures */
#define     FLOYD           1
#define     BURKES          2
#define     STUCKI          3

extern char PALETTE[256][3],OUTROW[1024],COPYRIGHT[];
extern int INTERLACED,IMAGEWIDE,IMAGEDEEP;
extern int IMAGEX,IMAGEY,XLOC,YLOC;

extern int VERSION,SUBVERSION;

/* this is the IMG file header - familiar sight */

char IMGheader[16] = {
0x00,0x01,0x00,0x08,0x00,0x01,0x00,0x01,
0x00,0x55,0x00,0x55,0x02,0x40,0x02,0xd0
        };

/* contrast expansion lookup table */

char greymap[256] = {
    /* 00-0f */
    0x01,0x01,0x01,0x01,0x01,0x01,0x01,0x01,
    0x01,0x01,0x01,0x01,0x01,0x01,0x01,0x01,
    /* 10-1f */
    0x01,0x01,0x01,0x01,0x01,0x01,0x01,0x01,
    0x01,0x01,0x01,0x01,0x01,0x01,0x01,0x01,
    /* 20-2f */
    0x01,0x01,0x01,0x01,0x01,0x01,0x01,0x02,
    0x03,0x04,0x05,0x06,0x07,0x08,0x09,0x0a,
    /* 30-3f */
    0x0b,0x0c,0x0d,0x0e,0x0f,0x10,0x11,0x12,
    0x13,0x14,0x15,0x16,0x17,0x18,0x19,0x1a,
    /* 40-4f */
    0x1b,0x1c,0x1d,0x1e,0x1f,0x20,0x20,0x21,
    0x22,0x23,0x23,0x24,0x25,0x27,0x27,0x28,
    /* 50-5f */
    0x29,0x2a,0x2b,0x2c,0x2d,0x2e,0x2f,0x2f,
    0x30,0x31,0x32,0x33,0x34,0x35,0x36,0x37,
    /* 60-6f */
    0x38,0x39,0x3a,0x3a,0x3b,0x3c,0x3d,0x3e,
    0x3f,0x40,0x41,0x42,0x43,0x44,0x45,0x46,
    /* 70-7f */
    0x47,0x48,0x49,0x4a,0x4b,0x4c,0x4d,0x4e,
    0x50,0x51,0x52,0x53,0x55,0x56,0x57,0x58,
    /* 80-8f */
    0x59,0x5a,0x5b,0x5d,0x5e,0x5f,0x60,0x61,
    0x63,0x64,0x65,0x66,0x67,0x69,0x6a,0x6b,
    /* 90-9f */
    0x6c,0x6e,0x70,0x72,0x73,0x74,0x76,0x78,
```

Fig 11-8 continued

```
      0x7a,0x7c,0x7e,0x80,0x82,0x84,0x86,0x88,
      /* a0-af */
      0x8a,0x8c,0x8f,0x91,0x93,0x95,0x98,0x9a,
      0x9c,0x9f,0xa1,0xa4,0xa6,0xa9,0xab,0xae,
      /* b0-bf */
      0xb0,0xb2,0xb3,0xb5,0xb7,0xb9,0xba,0xbc,
      0xbd,0xbe,0xc0,0xc2,0xc4,0xc6,0xc8,0xca,
      /* c0-cf */
      0xcc,0xce,0xd0,0xd2,0xd4,0xd6,0xd9,0xdb,
      0xdd,0xe0,0xe3,0xe6,0xe8,0xeb,0xed,0xef,
      /* d0-df */
      0xf2,0xf5,0xf8,0xfb,0xfe,0xfe,0xfe,0xfe,
      0xfe,0xfe,0xfe,0xfe,0xfe,0xfe,0xfe,0xfe,
      /* e0-ef */
      0xfe,0xfe,0xfe,0xfe,0xfe,0xfe,0xfe,0xfe,
      0xfe,0xfe,0xfe,0xfe,0xfe,0xfe,0xfe,0xfe,
      /* f0-ff */
      0xfe,0xfe,0xfe,0xfe,0xfe,0xfe,0xfe,0xfe,
      0xfe,0xfe,0xfe,0xfe,0xfe,0xfe,0xfe,0xfe,
         };

char *sourceBuf,*destBuf;      /* buffers */
char *farPtr();
char GIFname[81],IMGname[81];      /* file names */
char greypalette[256];         /* grey palette */
char outbuf[maxline];          /* work space for dither */

char ditherType=FLOYD;            /* flag for dither type */
char raster=0;                 /* serpentine raster? */
char display=0;                /* on screen graphics? */

int black,white;          /* global black and white */
int bytes;                /* monochrome line size */

main(argc,argv)
    int argc;
    char *argv[];
{
    int i,e,ShowIt(),Colourize();
    int ImageDone(),BadError(),BGround();
    int breakout();

    /* usual GIF stuff */
    SetShow(ShowIt);
    SetPalette(Colourize);
    SetImage(ImageDone);
    SetError(BadError);
    SetBackground(BGround);

    /* handler for breaks */
    ctrlbrk(breakout);

    printf("DITHER version 1.0\n"
```

```
                "_____\n");
if(argc > 1) {

    for(i=0;i<argc;++i) {

        /* check for options */
        if(argv[i][0]=='/') {
            switch(toupper(argv[i][1])) {
                case 'F':
                    ditherType=FLOYD;
                    break;
                case 'S':
                    ditherType=STUCKI;
                    break;
                case 'B':
                    ditherType=BURKES;
                    break;
                case 'R':
                    raster=1;
                    break;
                case 'D':
                    display=1;
                    break;
            }
        }
    }

    for(i=1;i<argc;++i) {
        if(argv[i][0]!='/') {
            strmfe(GIFname,argv[i],"GIF");
            strmfe(IMGname,argv[i],"IMG");
            strupr(GIFname);
            strupr(IMGname);
            if((e=UnpackGIF(GIFname)) != 0) break;
        }
    }

    if(e) printf("Error code %d",e);
}

else {

    puts("Needs a path to a GIF file to dither\n"
        "Options:    /F - Floyd/Steinberg dither\n"
        "            /S - Stucki dither\n"
        "            /B - Burkes dither\n"
        "            /R - Unidirectional raster\n"
        "            /D - Show image on an EGA card\n"
        );

}

/* might want to kill this */
```

Fig 11-8 continued

```
    ShowCopyright();
}

/* this function dithers the image at source
   and makes a monochrome version of it at dest
   by dithering it into submission. */
dither(dest,source)
    char *dest,*source;
{
    long Tstart,Tstop,Telapsed;
    char *p,tbufr[80];
    int err,x,y,n;

    /* say what we're up to... */
    if(raster) printf("Unidirectional raster scan, ");
    else printf("Serpentine raster scan, ");

    switch(ditherType) {
        case FLOYD:
            puts("Floyd-Steinberg dither");
            break;
        case STUCKI:
            puts("Stucki dither");
            break;
        case BURKES:
            puts("Burkes dither");
            break;
    }

    /* go for graphics */
    if(display) {
        puts("Hit any key...");
        getch();
        init();
    }

    time(&Tstart);

    for(y=0;y<IMAGEDEEP;++y) {

        if(!display) printf("\rLine %d of %d",y,IMAGEDEEP);

        if(kbhit()) if(getch()==27) breakout();

        if((y & 1) || raster) {
            for(x=0;x<IMAGEWIDE;++x) {
                if((n=getPixel(source,x,y)) > ((black+white) / 2)) {
                    bitPixel(dest,x,y,0);
                    err=n-white;
                }
                else {
                    bitPixel(dest,x,y,n);
                    err=n-black;
```

```
                        }
                        ditherPixel(source,x,y,err);
                    }
                }

            else {
                for(x=IMAGEWIDE-1;x>=0;--x) {
                    if((n=getPixel(source,x,y)) > ((black+white) / 2)) {
                        bitPixel(dest,x,y,0);
                        err=n-white;
                    }
                    else {
                        bitPixel(dest,x,y,n);
                        err=n-black;
                    }
                    ditherPixel(source,x,y,err);
                }
            }

            if(display) {
                if(y < 350) {
                    p=farPtr(dest,((long)y*(long)bytes));
                    if(bytes > 80) {
                        for(x=0;x<80;++x) tbufr[x]=~p[x];
                        memcpy(MK_FP(0xa000,(long)y*80L),tbufr,80);
                    }
                    else {
                        for(x=0;x<bytes;++x) tbufr[x]=~p[x];
                        memcpy(MK_FP(0xa000,(long)y*80L),tbufr,bytes);
                    }
                }
            }
        }
    time(&Tstop);
    if(display) {
        putchar(7);
        getch();
        deinit();
    }
    Telapsed = (long)difftime(Tstop,Tstart);
    printf("\nElapsed time for dither: %ld seconds (%ld:%02.2ld)\n",
        Telapsed,Telapsed/60L,Telapsed%60L);
    printf("Black = %d     White = %d\n",black,white);
}

/* diffuse the error for one pixel */
ditherPixel(source,x,y,err)
  char *source;
  int x,y,err;
{
  switch(ditherType) {
    case FLOYD:
      if((y & 1) || raster) {
          setPixel(source,x+1,y,getPixel(source,x+1,y) + ((7 * err) / 16));
```

Fig 11-8 continued

```
        setPixel(source,x-1,y+1,getPixel(source,x-1,y+1) + ((3 * err) / 16));
        setPixel(source,x,y+1,getPixel(source,x,y+1) + ((5 * err) / 16));
        setPixel(source,x+1,y+1,getPixel(source,x+1,y+1) + (err / 16));

    }
    else {
        setPixel(source,x-1,y,getPixel(source,x-1,y) + ((7 * err) / 16));
        setPixel(source,x+1,y+1,getPixel(source,x+1,y+1) + ((3 * err) / 16));
        setPixel(source,x,y+1,getPixel(source,x,y+1) + ((5 * err) / 16));
        setPixel(source,x-1,y+1,getPixel(source,x-1,y+1) + (err / 16));

    }
    break;
case STUCKI:
    if((y & 1) || raster) {
        setPixel(source,x+2,y,getPixel(source,x+2,y) + ((8 * err) / 42));
        setPixel(source,x+1,y,getPixel(source,x+1,y) + ((4 * err) / 42));
        setPixel(source,x-2,y+1,getPixel(source,x-2,y+1) + ((2 * err) / 42));
        setPixel(source,x-1,y+1,getPixel(source,x-1,y+1) + ((4 * err) / 42));
        setPixel(source,x,y+1,getPixel(source,x,y+1) + ((8 * err) / 42));
        setPixel(source,x+1,y+1,getPixel(source,x+1,y+1) + ((4 * err) / 42));
        setPixel(source,x+2,y+1,getPixel(source,x+2,y+1) + ((2 * err) / 42));

        setPixel(source,x-2,y+2,getPixel(source,x-2,y+2) + ((1 * err) / 42));
        setPixel(source,x-1,y+2,getPixel(source,x-1,y+2) + ((2 * err) / 42));
        setPixel(source,x,y+2,getPixel(source,x,y+2) + ((4 * err) / 42));
        setPixel(source,x+1,y+2,getPixel(source,x+1,y+2) + ((2 * err) / 42));
        setPixel(source,x+2,y+2,getPixel(source,x+2,y+2) + ((1 * err) / 42));

    }
    else {
        setPixel(source,x-2,y,getPixel(source,x-2,y) + ((8 * err) / 42));
        setPixel(source,x-1,y,getPixel(source,x-1,y) + ((4 * err) / 42));

        setPixel(source,x+2,y+1,getPixel(source,x+2,y+1) + ((2 * err) / 42));
        setPixel(source,x+1,y+1,getPixel(source,x+1,y+1) + ((4 * err) / 42));
        setPixel(source,x,y+1,getPixel(source,x,y+1) + ((8 * err) / 42));
        setPixel(source,x-1,y+1,getPixel(source,x-1,y+1) + ((4 * err) / 42));
        setPixel(source,x-2,y+1,getPixel(source,x-2,y+1) + ((2 * err) / 42));

        setPixel(source,x+2,y+2,getPixel(source,x+2,y+2) + ((1 * err) / 42));
        setPixel(source,x+1,y+2,getPixel(source,x+1,y+2) + ((2 * err) / 42));
        setPixel(source,x,y+2,getPixel(source,x,y+2) + ((4 * err) / 42));
        setPixel(source,x-1,y+2,getPixel(source,x-1,y+2) + ((2 * err) / 42));
        setPixel(source,x-2,y+2,getPixel(source,x-2,y+2) + ((1 * err) / 42));

    }
    break;
case BURKES:
    if((y & 1) || raster) {
        setPixel(source,x+2,y,getPixel(source,x+2,y) + ((8 * err) / 32));
        setPixel(source,x+1,y,getPixel(source,x+1,y) + ((4 * err) / 32));

        setPixel(source,x-2,y+1,getPixel(source,x-2,y+1) + ((2 * err) / 32));
        setPixel(source,x-1,y+1,getPixel(source,x-1,y+1) + ((4 * err) / 32));
        setPixel(source,x,y+1,getPixel(source,x,y+1) + ((8 * err) / 32));
        setPixel(source,x+1,y+1,getPixel(source,x+1,y+1) + ((4 * err) / 32));
```

```
            setPixel(source,x+2,y+1,getPixel(source,x+2,y+1) + ((2 * err) / 32));
        }
        else {
            setPixel(source,x-2,y,getPixel(source,x-2,y) + ((8 * err) / 32));
            setPixel(source,x-1,y,getPixel(source,x-1,y) + ((4 * err) / 32));

            setPixel(source,x+2,y+1,getPixel(source,x+2,y+1) + ((2 * err) / 32));
            setPixel(source,x+1,y+1,getPixel(source,x+1,y+1) + ((4 * err) / 32));
            setPixel(source,x,y+1,getPixel(source,x,y+1) + ((8 * err) / 32));
            setPixel(source,x-1,y+1,getPixel(source,x-1,y+1) + ((4 * err) / 32));
            setPixel(source,x-2,y+1,getPixel(source,x-2,y+1) + ((2 * err) / 32));
        }
        break;
    }
}

/* write the monochrome image to a file */
ImageDone()
{
    FILE *fp;
    char *pr;
    int i,r=0;
    dither(destBuf,sourceBuf);

    if((fp=fopen(IMGname,"wb")) != NULL) {
        IMGheader[12]=IMAGEWIDE >> 8;
        IMGheader[13]=IMAGEWIDE;
        IMGheader[14]=IMAGEDEEP >> 8;
        IMGheader[15]=IMAGEDEEP;

        if(fwrite(IMGheader,1,16,fp)==16) {
            for(i=0;i<IMAGEDEEP;++i) {

                pr=farPtr(destBuf,(long)i*(long)bytes);

                if(!WriteImgLine(pr,fp,bytes)) {
                    r=0;
                    break;
                } else r=1;
            }
        }
        fclose(fp);
        if(!r) {
            printf("\nError writing %s",IMGname);
            remove(IMGname);
        }
    } else printf("\nError creating %s",IMGname);
    freeBuffer();
}

/* create a pallette lookup table with the palette
   colour values grey scale summed. */
Colourize(n,palette)
    int n;
```

Fig 11-8   continued

```
    char *palette;
{
    double f;
    int i;

    black=255;
    white=0;

    for(i=0;i<n;++i) {
        f= (0.30 * (double)*palette++) +
            (0.59 * (double)*palette++) +
            (0.11 * (double)*palette++);
        if(f > 255.0) f=255.0;
        /* do grey scale expansion */
        greypalette[i]=greymap[(char)f];

        /* establish black and white levels */
        if(greypalette[i] < black) black = greypalette[i];
        if(greypalette[i] > white) white = greypalette[i];
    }
}

/* copy the line into memory */
ShowIt()
{
    int i;
    for(i=0;i<IMAGEWIDE;++i) OUTROW[i]=greypalette[OUTROW[i]];
    memcpy(farPtr(sourceBuf,(long)YLOC*(long)IMAGEWIDE),
        OUTROW,IMAGEWIDE);
}

/* do some initial housekeeping */
BGround()
{
    bytes=pixels2bytes(IMAGEWIDE);
    allocateBuffer();
    printf("\r Unpacking...\r");
}

BadError(s)
    char *s;
{
    printf("\007\007\007Fatal error - %s.\n",s);
    exit(1);
}

ShowCopyright()
{
    char *p;

    p = COPYRIGHT;
    puts("");
    while(*p) {
```

```
                   p += printf(p)+1;
           puts("");
       }
}

strmfe(new,old,ext)     /* make file name with specific extension */
    char *new,*old,*ext;
{
    while(*old != 0 && *old != '.') *new++=*old++;
    *new++='.';
    while(*ext) *new++=*ext++;
    *new=0;
}

char *farPtr(p,l)     /* return a far pointer p + l */
    char *p;
    long l;
{
    unsigned int seg,off;

    seg = FP_SEG(p);
    off = FP_OFF(p);
    seg += (off / 16);
    off &= 0x000f;
    off += (unsigned int)(l & 0x000fL);
    seg += (l / 16L);
    p=MK_FP(seg,off);
    return(p);
}

writeImgLine(p,fp,n)     /* IMG encode and write the line in p to fp */
    char *p;
        FILE *fp;
    int n;
{
    char b[0x0080];
    unsigned int bdex=0,i=0,j=0,t=0;

    do {
        i=0;
        while((p[t+i]==p[t+i+1]) &&
            ((t+i) < (n-1)) && i < 0x7e) ++i;

        if(i>0 || bdex >= 0x7e) {

            if(bdex) {
                fputc(0x80,fp);
                fputc(bdex,fp);
                j+=2;
                fwrite(b,1,bdex,fp);
                j+=bdex;
                bdex=0;
            }
```

Fig 11-8 continued

```
                if(i) {
                    if(p[t+i]==0xff) {
                        fputc(0x80+i+1,fp);
                        j+=1;
                    }
                    else if(p[t+i]==0x00) {
                        fputc(i+1,fp);
                        j+=1;
                    }
                    else {
                        fputc(0x00,fp);
                        fputc(i+1,fp);
                        fputc(p[t+i],fp);
                        j+=3;
                    }
                    t+=(i+1);
                }
            } else b[bdex++]=p[t++];
        } while(t<n);

        if(bdex) {
            fputc(0x80,fp);
            fputc(bdex,fp);
            j+=2;
            fwrite(b,1,bdex,fp);
            j+=bdex;
        }
}

init()          /* turn on graphics mode */
{
    union REGS r;

    r.x.ax=0x0010;
    int86(0x10,&r,&r);
}
deinit()     /* turn off graphics card */
{
    union REGS r;

    r.x.ax=0x0003;
    int86(0x10,&r,&r);
}

pixels2bytes(n)     /* return number of bytes in number of pixels */
    unsigned int n;
{
    if(n & 0x0007) return((n >> 3) + 1);
    else return(n >> 3);
}

getPixel(buf,x,y)    /* get a pixel from the source image */
    char *buf;
```

```
        int x,y;
{
    char *p;

    p=farPtr(buf,((long)y*(long)IMAGEWIDE));
    return(p[x]);
}

setPixel(buf,x,y,n)      /* place a pixel in the source image */
    char *buf;
    int x,y,n;
{
    char *p;

    if(x >= 0 && x < IMAGEWIDE &&
       y >= 0 && y < IMAGEDEEP) {

        if(n < black) n=black;
        if(n > white) n=white;
        p=farPtr(buf,((long)y*(long)IMAGEWIDE));
        p[x]=n;

    }

}

bitPixel(buf,x,y,n)      /* place a pixel in the destination image */
    char *buf;
    int x,y,n;
{
    char *p;

    if(x >= 0 && x < IMAGEWIDE &&
       y >= 0 && y < IMAGEDEEP) {

        p=farPtr(buf,((long)bytes*(long)y));

        if(n) p[x >> 3] |= (0x80 >> (x & 0x0007));
        else p[x >> 3] &= ~(0x80 >> (x & 0x0007));

    }
}
/* find a way to create scratch buffers */
allocateBuffer()
{
    if((sourceBuf=farmalloc((long)IMAGEWIDE*(long)IMAGEDEEP)) == NULL ||
       (destBuf=farmalloc((long)bytes*(long)IMAGEDEEP)) == NULL) {
        puts("Can't allocate memory");
        exit(1);
    }
}

/* free all the allocated memory */
freeBuffer()
```

Fig 11-8   continued

```
{
    farfree(sourceBuf);
    farfree(destBuf);
}

/* do housekeeping for abnormal end */
breakout()
{
    freeBuffer();
    if(display) deinit();
    exit(0);
}
```

You can add graphics drivers for the other display cards discussed in this book if you want to. Because this feature is more of a debugging tool rather than a functional part of the program, you might want to leave it off entirely if you ultimately use this code for something practical.

The process of dithering involves fetching pixels from the source image, setting the adjoining pixels based on the error so derived and setting the pixels in the destination monochrome image. There's nothing at all complicated about any of this. However, the way in which you implement it will have a lot to do with the ultimate speed of your dithering program.

The dithering functions in this chapter have been written in C. The alternative—writing them in assembly language—would have unquestionably resulted in faster code. However, the resulting programs would have been all but unreadable without considerable effort. Unlike, for example, the GIF decoder in Chapter 5, you probably will want to meddle with the dithering programs. Having programs understandable is arguably more important than having them fast.

You will find that you can do quite a lot to optimize this code without reverting to assembly language.

There's nothing terribly complicated about the dithering program. You will notice the skeleton of the C language GIF decoder in it—it links to the GIF decoder module from Chapter 5, as have several earlier programs. You will probably recognize a number of familiar code fragments in this program—for example, the IMG packing function at ImageDone is identical to the code discussed in Chapter 3.

The EGA graphics display—down toward the bottom of the dither function—also should be familiar. It simply stuffs the image lines into the EGA card's video buffer by copying them to a far pointer. This, too, is by no means as fast as it could be.

Assuming that you call this program DITHER.C, leaving you with DITHER.EXE when the whole works is compiled and linked, you would dither a file called JENNIFER.GIF into JENNIFER.IMG like this:

DITHER JENNIFER

Dithering this way is a very slow process, especially if you're running with an XT or an early AT. If you get interested in dithering, you probably will want to work on optimizing this thing before you go much further. There are a few fairly simple things you can do to improve it, some of which are discussed in conjunction with the next program.

DITHERING EXPANDED IMAGES

If you scale a picture up and then dither it, something magical often happens. The process of error diffusion tends to enhance the details of expanded images, finding details that weren't really there but look as if they should have been. You can frequently enhance an image considerably this way.

Figure 11-9 illustrates three dithers of the same picture. The left one is a size as dither. The right two are the same source file scaled up and then dithered.

Scaling up a picture by an integral amount is easy, especially when you're working with a one byte per pixel format like a GIF file. Where things start to get a bit awkward, however, is in providing memory to expand an image into. A 640-by-480-pixel GIF file requires 307,200 bytes of memory, which should fit in DOS memory if there's nothing else of any size in there too. Expand this by a factor of two and it will need 1,228,800 bytes.

The dithering filters discussed in this chapter only work with two or three lines at a time, but they must be contiguous lines. GIF files are not constrained to unpack in the order they want to be displayed—as you will recall from Chapter 5, they can be interlaced. This being the case, it's necessary to actually have a megabyte and a quarter of some type of storage to handle an expanded file.

This is all scratch space, to be sure. You only need it for a while.

Obviously, there's no way to get this much of a picture into DOS memory. Even if you lose all your resident programs and keep your dithering program itself stripped to the bone, you won't be able to count on having much more than half a megabyte of DOS memory available. This huge scratch space will have to come from somewhere else.

There are three ways of dealing with a huge block of data like this, to wit, extended memory, expanded memory, and virtual memory. One of these will be essential if you want to dither expanded image files.

Extended Memory

The two types of extra memory available for PC compatible systems are unfortunate in that their names are quite similar. Extended memory, also called XMS memory, is only applicable to AT compatible machines and 386 systems. It exists on the extended memory bus that starts above

Size as dither — 16 seconds

200% expansion — 60 seconds

Fig 11-9 The results of scaling and dithering. Note how the detail around the parrot's eye has improved

300% expansion — 142 seconds

Fig 11-9   continued

the normal PC BIOS, that is, beyond memory segment 0FFFFH.

Extended memory is not contiguous with DOS memory. If you plug two megabytes of extended memory into a 640k AT, you will still have 640k of DOS memory. The extended memory will be useful only for data storage, and then only for programs specifically written to use it.

Extended memory is arguably the least complicated way to work with huge buffers of the sort you'll need for dithering expanded images.

To work with extended memory, you will have to be able to perform four functions relating to it. You must be able to allocate a buffer, write data to the buffer, read data from the buffer, and finally deallocate the buffer when you no longer need it.

Accessing extended memory at the assembly language level is a bit complicated, involving some of the 80286-specific instructions and registers. Fortunately, you don't have to do this yourself—and, in fact, you shouldn't even if you are up for figuring out how to. To coexist with other programs that might want to use extended memory too, all communication with it is handled through an extended memory driver.

The extended memory driver is a small program that DOS loads in through your CONFIG.SYS file when your system boots up. The most common one is HIMEM.SYS, which was written by Microsoft. It comes with Windows, and is available by itself from Microsoft at a nominal cost. It also appears on bulletin boards from time to time along with its source code.

Several other extended memory drivers exist that behave in the same way that HIMEM.SYS does. The 386^{MAX} package from Qualitas, for example, provides a compatible extended memory driver for 80386 based systems.

With an extended memory driver installed in your system, the aforementioned functions are handled by the driver. If your program needed a 2-megabyte buffer, for example, it would negotiate with the driver for one. The driver passes memory "handles" around to give applications access to extended memory buffers.

The driver also provides a way for a program to detect whether there is, in fact, a driver present and what version of the extended memory specification it supports. The extended memory functions to be discussed in this chapter presuppose that they'll be talking to a driver that supports the version 2.0 extended memory standard or better.

There is a moderately serious catch to using extended memory. The VDISK.SYS driver supplied with DOS, a RAM disk, can be instructed to place its RAM disk contents in extended memory. However, it's a bit brain damaged, having been written under the assumption that it would have exclusive use of all the extended memory it could find. As such, any attempt to allocate an extended memory buffer through the driver on a machine with VDISK.SYS installed will fail, even if VDISK isn't actually using all the extended memory.

The RAMDRIVE.SYS program that comes with DOS 3.3 and better overcomes this problem. However, if you want to use extended memory for something other than a RAM disk and you don't have RAMDRIVE.SYS, you'll have to remove VDISK.SYS from your CONFIG.SYS file.

Changes to your CONFIG.SYS file do not take effect until after you've rebooted your computer.

The process of accessing extended memory is a bit cumbersome from within C. As such, the expanded dithering program (to be discussed later in this chapter) will use a small assembly language interface for extended memory access.

Expanded Memory

Early on in the history of PC's, users of spreadsheet packages—most notably Lotus 1-2-3—began to become aware of the rather nasty trick that had been played upon them by some unnamed engineer at IBM. The 640k memory limit of a stock PC severely cut into what could be done with Lotus. The Lotus package is capable of handling financial planning right down to the cost of paper clips and coffee, but detailed spreadsheets require lots of storage.

The solution to this problem was one of the most intriguing of hacks, something called *expanded* memory. It's also called LIM memory, LIM standing for Lotus, Intel, and Microsoft, the three companies that perpetrated it. Because the then contemporary 8088 based PC's could not address extended memory, any sort of memory solution had to involve space within the one megabyte basic memory bus of the PC.

LIM memory works a bit like the video buffer of a super VGA card. A LIM memory card might have two megabytes of memory on it, but only a small part of it, one *page*, can appear on the bus at a time. It appears in the LIM *page frame*, which could be anywhere, but usually is situated somewhere around segments 0C000H to 0E000H, up above the video card buffers.

To access LIM memory, then, you would figure out which page you wanted to get at and tell your LIM memory card to make it appear in the page frame. You can read and write to the memory in the page frame just like you would normal memory, which is what it appears to be.

When it comes time to access a different page, you would tell the memory card to take the current page away and put a different page in the page frame so you can have a shot at it.

As with extended memory, expanded memory is handled through a driver loaded through your CONFIG.SYS file. This forces all the programs that want to use it to communicate with the LIM memory hardware through a common interface. In turn, this keeps you from having to know how to tickle the LIM memory to make it page. It also allows multiple programs to use the LIM memory simultaneously without having to worry about stomping on each others' data.

The program in this chapter presumes that it will be talking to a LIM driver of version 3.2 or better.

If your application calls for dealing with many large data objects—large, in this case, being bigger than the LIM page frame—extended memory is considerably faster to use than expanded memory. In the case of a dithering program, however, the biggest object you'll have to move around at a time will be one scan line. Running the same dither in extended and expended memory actually times out almost identically.

If you have an 80386-based machine and one of the smart 80386 memory managers, such as 386^{MAX}, you can set up your system to have both extended and expanded memory in any proportion you like.

Talking to a LIM driver is a bit more civilized than talking to an extended memory driver. It can all be managed in C.

Virtual Memory

The least desirable option in handling a large buffer is to use virtual memory. This is a term that gets bandied about a lot, and it sounds like some magical way to use memory that isn't there. It's not.

Virtual memory simply involves using a disk file as an overflow for whatever real memory you can scare up. In the case of working with an expanded color image to be dithered, you would unpack the source GIF file into a big disk file and then read and write individual lines from the file into memory to work on them.

Virtual memory has many drawbacks. It's exceedingly slow, of course, because your program must access the disk every time it wants to get some data from the virtual memory file. It also presupposes that you'll have lots of disk space free. In practice, these two requirements really assume that you'll be working with a hard drive.

Using virtual memory also imposes considerably more demands on the program you write to use it—there is, after all, no convenient virtual memory driver to simply pass a few parameters to.

Dithering Large Files

The next dithering program to be discussed allows you to specify an expansion factor for the files to be dithered. This simply means that the GIF file being unpacked will be scaled up by some value and then dithered. The resulting IMG file also will have dimensions that are a multiple of those of the original GIF file.

Scaling an image up by an integral amount is easy. Each line of the source image is transformed into a destination line by replicating each source pixel by the expansion factor. The resulting line is then duplicated in the destination buffer by the expansion factor as well. If the expansion factor is three, then, the destination image will require nine times as much memory as the source image originally did.

It's worth noting that as you expand a picture, dithering it will produce more complex and much less regular image data. This means that the compression techniques used to pack simple monochrome formats like IMG files will become decidedly less effective. Expanding a GIF file and dithering it will not only take up more scratch memory, it will also produce much bigger final monochrome files than you might have anticipated.

In the first dithering program, the getPixel and setPixel functions worked by creating a far pointer into the image buffer each time they wanted to get or place a pixel. This was not terribly elegant—or terribly fast—although it served to illustrate the principle. There's a better way to handle this process, and because the expanded dither program works with larger images and at least nominally slower storage, it's worth doing to keep the code from slowing to a crawl.

Using the Floyd-Steinberg filter as an example, you will notice that in dithering a line the dithering function only actually communicates with two lines of data. The Stucki filter uses three. Even for very large images it's practical to keep three lines of the image in memory at a time. As such, the main loop of the dither function can simply fetch three lines from the image buffer at the top of the loop and put them back at the bottom.

In fact, this can be optimized still further. Each successive pass through the loop simply moves down a line, so only one line at a time really has to be exchanged with the image buffer. However, this is somewhat more complex to write and doesn't actually turn out to save a meaningful amount of time.

The getPixel and setPixel functions in the next dithering program simply work with the data in the local line store, trusting that it will be returned to the image buffer at the end of each pass through the dithering loop. This reduces the number of accesses to the image buffer to twice the number of lines in the file, a 10-fold improvement for the Floyd-Steinberg filter and a correspondingly better one for more complex filters, such as Stucki.

This approach to writing the dithering program also means that the parts of the code that actually deal with the image buffer can be kept pretty modular. It becomes simple to write the program to use whichever of the three types of extra memory you happen to have on hand. Only a few selected parts of it actually have to change.

Interfacing to Extended Memory

Extended memory uses the most obtuse interface, and it's the most difficult one to debug if something goes wrong. You can't simply boot up DEBUG and check to see if the data you've moved into extended memory actually turned up there. Extended memory can't be accessed directly by DEBUG.

The extended memory driver is communicated with initially through its private interrupt—INT 2FH. After some handshaking, however, it will allow you to deal with itself using a vector into its internal code, which is a lot faster than calling an interrupt would be.

The first thing to do in establishing communication with the extended memory driver is to see if it's there. This bit of code handles the task:

```
MOV     AX,4300H
INT     2FH
CMP     AL,80H
JE      DRIVER_OK
JMP     NO_DRIVER
```

Assuming that a driver turns out to be present, you can pry the secret of its control vector from it like this:

```
MOV     AX,4310H
INT     2FH
MOV     WORD PTR CS:[_CONTOFF],BX
MOV     WORD PTR CS:[_CONTSEG],ES
```

The two words where ES and BX are stored can be defined like this: In the real extended memory interface, to be discussed in a moment, these will initially be set to point into a dummy return function much like the ones found in the process handlers of the GIF decoder. This will keep your computer from jumping into the twilight zone if you happen to call the extended memory controller before it's initialized:

```
CONTROL     LABEL   DWORD
_CONTOFF    DW      ?
_CONTSEG    DW      ?
```

The ES:BX registers point to the control code in the driver. You will have to call this location with various parameters in the 8088 registers to get things done.

The first thing you might want to do is to find out the driver version number. This must be better than 2.0. The version is returned in AX, with AH being the version and AL the revision level:

```
XOR      AX,AX
CALL     CS:[CONTROL]
```

Extended memory is allocated in one kilobyte blocks. There's no limit to the number of blocks you can allocate, save for that of the amount of extended memory you have on hand. The memory allocation system behaves much like the familiar C language malloc function, in that if you attempt to allocate a buffer bigger than the largest block of free contiguous extended memory, the driver will simply refuse to do it and return an illegal result.

Blocks of allocated extended memory are accessed through *handles*. This is another of those terms that gets bandied about a lot, and it tends to mean different things in different contexts. In this case, a handle is an integer.

The extended memory driver is quite clever, in that it can do "garbage collection" to ensure that the maximum amount of extended memory is available for your use. Here's how this works:

Consider that you allocate three 1-megabyte extended memory buffers from a total pool of four megabytes. Later on, you deallocate the second block. There now will be two 1-megabyte blocks available, the first of which is trapped between the two blocks that are still allocated.

In fact, this won't actually happen—or, at least, things won't stay like this very long. The driver will move down the third block until it rests where the second block used to live before it was deallocated. It will collect all the free memory into a contiguous block.

The extended memory driver can do this because it never lets you get at your buffers directly. If you wanted some of the contents of the first block sent down into DOS memory, you would pass the handle of that block to the driver. The driver keeps track of where the memory that the handle refers to actually is.

There is one very important distinction between the allocation scheme of extended memory and that of conventional DOS memory. When your program terminates, any DOS memory that has been allocated and has not been freed explicitly by your program will be freed by DOS. This also happens if you crash out of a program by hitting Ctrl Break, for example. This is not the case for extended memory. If you have an allocated block of extended memory that you fail to deallocate before your program finishes, both the block and the handle that accessed it will become orphans—and essentially inaccessible—until you reboot your computer.

Extended memory handles are quite scarce. The exact number available varies from driver to driver. However, you should be frugal in using them, because once you have tied up all of them you will be unable to allocate any more extended memory until you free one up.

To allocate a block of extended memory, you would load the number of kilobytes you'd like to have into the DX register and do this:

```
MOV       AH,9
CALL      CS:[CONTROL]

OR        AX,AX
JZ        NO_MEMORY
JMP       OK_MEMORY
```

If this is successful, the number in DX would represent the handle for the allocated block of extended memory.

This will deallocate a block of extended memory. The handle should be in DX:

```
MOV       AH,10
CALL      CS:[CONTROL]
```

You can move data around between blocks of extended memory, within blocks of extended memory, and between extended and conventional memory. The dither program only calls for the latter case, although the same approach is used for all three.

The memory to be moved is specified with an XMOVE struct. This is what it looks like in C:

```
typedef struct {
        unsigned long length;
        unsigned int sourceH;
        unsigned long sourceOff;
        unsigned int destH;
        unsigned long destOff;
        } XMOVE;
```

The sourceH and destH members of the struct are the handles of the memory blocks to be moved between. If you want to deal with conventional memory, use the handle zero. The sourceOff and destOff members are the offsets into the blocks in question. This would be a C language far pointer for conventional DOS memory. The length member is the number of bytes to move.

If you want to move data from a conventional memory buffer in C called buff to an extended memory buffer with a handle in Xhandle, you would do this:

```
XMOVE x;

x.sourceH = 0;
```

```
x.sourceOff = ptr2long(p);
x.destH = Xhandle;
x.destOff = 0L;
x.length = bytes_to_move;
```

The ptr2long function is part of the extended memory assembly language interface, to be discussed in a moment. It just takes the two integer components of a C pointer and stores them in a long integer for the struct to use.

Having set this up, you would do the actual move like this: The DS:SI pointer should be set to point to the base of the XMOVE struct:

```
MOV     AH,11
CALL    CS:[CONTROL]
```

The AX register will contain zero if the move was unsuccessful. This can happen, for example, if you attempt to move data beyond the end of an allocated block. The extended memory driver is very meticulous.

The complete extended memory interface module is shown in Fig. 11-10. The source file is called XMEM.ASM, assembling down to XMEM.OBJ. It can be linked to any program that will need access to extended memory. The use of the functions it provides can be seen in the expanded dithering program, to be discussed shortly.

Fig 11-10   The assembly language extended memory interface

```
;
;          Extended memory control functions
;

VERSION          EQU     1                          ;VERSION
SUBVERSION       EQU     0                          ;SUBVERSION

_AOFF            EQU     6                          ;FAR STACK OFFSET

;THIS MACRO FETCHES THE DATA SEGEMENT
DATASEG          MACRO
                 PUSH    AX
                 MOV     AX,_DATA
                 MOV     DS,AX
                 POP     AX
                 ENDM

XMEM_TEXT        SEGMENT BYTE PUBLIC 'CODE'
                 ASSUME  CS:XMEM_TEXT,DS:_DATA

;THIS FUNCTION INITIALIZES THE DRIVER
;                CALLED AS
;                get_xmem();
;
;                Returns the version number or -1 if no driver
;
```

```
                PUBLIC    _get_xmem
_get_xmem       PROC      FAR
                PUSH      BP
                MOV       BP,SP

                MOV       AX,4300H        ;CALL FOR THE DRIVER
                INT       2FH
                CMP       AL,80H          ;WAS IT THERE?
                JE        GETX1

                MOV       AX,0FFFFH
                JMP       GETX2

GETX1:          MOV       AX,4310H        ;THE VECTOR, PLEASE...
                INT       2FH
                MOV       WORD PTR CS:[_CONTOFF],BX
                MOV       WORD PTR CS:[_CONTSEG],ES

                XOR       AX,AX           ;GET THE VERSION NUMBER
                CALL      CS:[CONTROL]

GETX2:          DATASEG
                POP       BP
                RET
_get_xmem       ENDP

;THIS FUNCTION MOVES EXTENDED MEMORY
;               CALLED AS
;               move_xmem(p);
;               p = pointer to move structure
;                       /* returns true if successfull */
;
                PUBLIC    _move_xmem
_move_xmem      PROC      FAR
                PUSH      BP
                MOV       BP,SP

                MOV       SI,[BP + _AOFF + 0]     ;OFFSET OF STRUCTURE
                MOV       DS,[BP + _AOFF + 2]     ;SEGMENT OF STRUCTURE

                MOV       AH,11           ;DO THE MOVE
                CALL      CS:[CONTROL]

                DATASEG
                POP       BP
                RET
_move_xmem      ENDP

;THIS FUNCTION DEALLOCATES EXTENDED MEMORY
;               CALLED AS
;               dealloc_xmem(h);
;               int h;  /* handle to deallocate */
;                       /* returns true if successfull */
;
```

Fig 11-10   continued

```
                  PUBLIC   _dealloc_xmem
_dealloc_xmem     PROC     FAR
                  PUSH     BP
                  MOV      BP,SP

                  MOV      DX,[BP + _AOFF + 0]      ;HANDLE
                  MOV      AH,10
                  CALL     CS:[CONTROL]             ;BYE, MEMORY...

                  DATASEG
                  POP      BP
                  RET
_dealloc_xmem     ENDP

;THIS FUNCTION ALLOCATES EXTENDED MEMORY
;                 CALLED AS
;                 alloc_xmem(n);
;                 int n;  /* number of kilobytes to allocate */
;                         /* returns handle or -1 if error */
;
                  PUBLIC   _alloc_xmem
_alloc_xmem       PROC     FAR
                  PUSH     BP
                  MOV      BP,SP

                  MOV      DX,[BP + _AOFF + 0]      ;NUMBER OF KILOBYTES
                  MOV      AH,9
                  CALL     CS:[CONTROL]             ;SOME MEMORY, PLEASE...

                  OR       AX,AX
                  JZ       ALLOC1

                  MOV      AX,DX
                  JMP      ALLOC2

ALLOC1:           MOV      AX,0FFFFH

ALLOC2:           DATASEG
                  POP      BP
                  RET
_alloc_xmem       ENDP

;THIS FUNCTION CONVERTS A POINTER TO AN INTEL LONG
;                 CALLED AS
;                 long ptr2long(p);
;                 char *p
;
                  PUBLIC   _ptr2long
_ptr2long         PROC     FAR
                  PUSH     BP
                  MOV      BP,SP

                  MOV      AX,[BP + _AOFF + 0]      ;OFFSET OF POINTER
```

```
                MOV     DX,[BP + _AOFF + 2]      ;SEGMENT OF POINTER

                DATASEG
                POP     BP
                RET
_ptr2long       ENDP

;THIS FUNCTION IS A DUMMY RETURN FOR UNSET PROCEDURES
_DUMMY          PROC    FAR
                MOV     AX,0FFFFH
                RET
_DUMMY          ENDP

CONTROL         LABEL   DWORD
_CONTOFF        DW      _DUMMY
_CONTSEG        DW      XMEM_TEXT

XMEM_TEXT       ENDS

DGROUP          GROUP   _DATA,_BSS
_DATA           SEGMENT WORD PUBLIC 'DATA'

_DATA           ENDS

_BSS            SEGMENT WORD PUBLIC 'BSS'
_BSS            ENDS
                END
```

There are a number of other things the extended memory driver can do, functions that are not required for the dithering program—or for most other applications of extended memory. If you're interested in the complete XMS 2.0 specification, you might want to contact Microsoft.

Interfacing to Expanded Memory

The expanded memory interface uses a device driver just like extended memory does. The device drivers for EMS boards tend to be specific to the particular boards they're written for, but the interface that your program will see is standardized.

Communication with the expanded memory driver is handled through the rather more conventional avenue of an interrupt. The EMS interrupt is 67H. You can deal with expanded memory equally well from either C or assembly language, and as there is no advantage to undertaking the added complexity of an assembly language interface, the EMS functions for the expanded dithering program will be dealt with in C.

The C language functions for handling expanded memory do roughly the same things as the extended memory functions just discussed, with the addition of functions to handle the memory paging and the page frame.

In checking for the existence of expanded memory, you must look for both the memory itself and for the driver. Checking for the driver is a bit mysterious. If it's in place, attempting to open a file called "EMMXXXX0" for reading will be successful, even though no such file actually exists on your disk. This is the code that handles this check:

```
int fh;
union REGS rg;

if((fh = open("EMMXXXX0",O_RDONLY,&fh)) = = - 1)
    /* no EMS driver */

rg.h.ah = 0x44;
rg.h.al = 0x00;
rg.x.bx = fh;
int86(0x21,&rg,&rg);

close(fh);
if(rg.x.cflag) /*... it isn't there */
if(rg.x.dx & 0x80) /*... it is there */
else /*... it isn't there */
```

Because it's possible for this rather peculiar file to actually exist as a real directory entry, the subsequent INT 21H call is used to check the nature of the opened file.

Having determined that an EMS driver exists, it's safe to use the expanded memory interrupt, INT 67H. This can be used to check for the existence of some actual expanded memory:

```
union REGS rg;

rg.h.ah = 0x40;
int86(0x67,&rg,&rg);
if(rg.h.ah = = 0) /* it's there */
else /* it's missing */
```

The next thing you probably will want to do is to locate the expanded memory page frame. This is a standard C language far pointer that will point to the bottom of the page frame up in high memory:

```
union REGS rg;

rg.h.ah = 0x41;
int86(0x67,&rg,&rg);
if(rg.h.ah != 0) /*... it couldn't be found */
else /* this is the pointer */ MK_FP(rg.x.bx,0)
```

In some applications, it's useful to map up to four logical pages onto the physical page in the expanded memory page frame. This is not one of them. For the purpose of the dithering program, one EMS page is 16,384 bytes long, a value that is defined in the constant pagesizeEMS.

Here's how expanded memory is allocated. The smallest unit of allocation for expanded memory is one 16k page. The variable *n* holds the number of pages to allocate:

```
union REGS rg;

rg.h.ah = 0x43;
rg.x.bx = n;
int86(0x67,&rg,&rg);
if(rg.h.ah) /* oops ... allocation failed */
else /* rg.x.dx is the handle */
```

The handle returned by this code is used to address the allocated block of memory.

When you're done with expanded memory you must deallocate it explicitly. As with extended memory, the memory you allocate will stay allocated even after your program has given up and returned you to DOS unless you deallocate it. If you fail to do so, the memory and its handle will become orphaned until you reboot your machine.

In theory it's possible to walk through all the orphaned handles in a driver and deallocate them, but this should not be necessary if the programs that use expanded memory are well behaved. One important area to keep in mind in this respect is the possibility of a program failing to clear up its memory allocation if it's interrupted by a user hitting Ctrl Break. Turbo C allows you to specify a control break handler with the ctrlbreak function, and you should do so in programs that use extended or expanded memory, the handler being a function that will deallocate any memory the program has called for.

The expanded dither program will illustrate how this is done.

Here's the code to deallocate some expanded memory:

```
rg.h.ah = 0x45;
rg.x.dx = handle;
int86(0x67,&rg,&rg);
if (rg.h.ah = = 0) /*... it's done */
else /*... deallocation failed */
```

Finally, the following code is the code to map pages. This actually handles the mapping of physical and logical pages, something that you won't have to do in the dithering program. The use of this code will be in its simplest sense, swapping pages in and out of the page frame:

```
rg.h.ah = 0x44;
rg.h.al = 0;
rg.x.bx = page_number;
rg.x.dx = handle;
```

```
int86(0x67,&rg,&rg);
if(rg.h.ah == 0) /*... good move */
else /*... something went wrong */
```

In using expanded memory, one usually is confronted with the awkwardness of having to use paged memory for things that do not necessarily lend themselves to being chopped up into pages. Unlike true segmented memory, where one can fudge the segment value to make the offset range big enough to overcome any local boundaries, an EMS page is a fixed quantity.

In moving image lines in and out of expanded memory, the page boundary gets in the way quite often. If the line in question is 640 bytes long and you're 600 bytes from the end of the page, the last 40 bytes will get lost if you use the available memory. The proper way to deal with this situation is to switch to the next available page and write the line to the base of the page frame. Alternately, of course, you could use the last 600 bytes and change pages part way through the line. This would, however, slow down the data movement code a lot, forcing it to deal with the memory one byte at a time, rather than as memory strings.

In practice, it's a lot faster to waste the top few bytes of each page. However, it's tricky to know what the page number and offset value for each line in an image file is to be before hand, and time-consuming to calculate them on the fly. If this problem sounds somewhat familiar, it probably is because something like it cropped up in addressing the lines of video display memory earlier in this book. The solution to it is the same, too—the dithering program will construct a table that specifies the page and offset for each line to be written to or read from expanded memory.

Figure 11-11 illustrates the complete expanded memory functions. You could compile these and link them to your program as an object module, but in the cause of keeping the project file for the expanded dithering program down to a manageable immensity, this version will be handled as a header file. These functions are based on a similar header written by Richard Bowler and placed in the public domain. It's called EMS.H here.

Fig 11-11   The expanded memory interface functions

```
/*
        Expanded memory functions
        derived from EMSFUNC by Richard Bowler
*/

#include "fcntl.h"
#include "io.h"
#include "dos.h"

#define pagesizeEMS      0x4000

int pagesAllocated = 0;
int totalPages;
```

```
/* return true if an EMS driver is available */
isEMS()
{
        int fh;
        union REGS rg;

        if((fh=open("EMMXXXX0",O_RDONLY,&fh)) ==-1)
            return(0);

        rg.h.ah = 0x44;
        rg.h.al = 0x00;
        rg.x.bx = fh;
        int86(0x21,&rg,&rg); /* issue interrupt  */
        close(fh);
        if(rg.x.cflag) return(0);
        if(rg.x.dx & 0x80) return(1);
        else return(0);
}

/* return true if the EMS hardware is available */
checkEMS()
{
    union REGS rg;

    rg.h.ah = 0x40;
    int86(0x67,&rg,&rg);
    if(rg.h.ah == 0) return(1);
    else return(0);
}

/* return the toatl number of pages */
coretotalEMS()
{
    union REGS rg;

    rg.h.ah = 0x42;
    int86(0x67,&rg,&rg);
    if(rg.x.cflag) return(-1);
    if(!pagesAllocated) {
        pagesAllocated = 1;
        totalPages = rg.x.dx;
    }
    return(rg.x.bx);
}
/* return the number of free pages */
coreleftEMS()
{
    union REGS rg;

    if(pagesAllocated) return(totalPages);
    rg.h.ah = 0x42;
    int86(0x67,&rg,&rg);
    if(rg.x.cflag) return(-1);
    pagesAllocated = 1;
```

Fig 11-11   continued

```
     totalPages = rg.x.dx;
     return(totalPages);
}

/* return the EMS page frame */
char *pageframeEMS()
{
     union REGS rg;

     rg.h.ah = 0x41;
     int86(0x67,&rg,&rg);
     if(rg.h.ah != 0) return (NULL);
     else return(MK_FP(rg.x.bx,0));
}

/* allocate n pages - returns a
   handle or zero if request failed */
unsigned int mallocEMS(n)
        int n;
{
        union REGS rg;

        if(n > coreleftEMS()) return(0);
        rg.h.ah = 0x43;
        rg.x.bx = n;
        int86(0x67,&rg,&rg);
        if(rg.h.ah) return(0);
        else return(rg.x.dx);
}

/* deallocate memory block pointed to by
   the handle in h */
freeEMS(h)
        unsigned int h;
{
        union REGS rg;
        int i;

        for(i=0;i<5;i++) {
                rg.h.ah = 0x45;
                rg.x.dx = h;
                int86(0x67,&rg,&rg);
                if (rg.h.ah == 0) break;
        }
        if(rg.h.ah == 0) return(1);
        else return(0);
}

/* map a logical page to a physical page */
mapEMS(h,Ppage,Lpage)
        unsigned int h;
        int Ppage,Lpage;
{
```

```
        union REGS rg;

        if(Ppage < 0 || Ppage > 3) return (0);
        rg.h.ah = 0x44;
        rg.h.al = Ppage;
        rg.x.bx = Lpage;
        rg.x.dx = h;
        int86(0x67,&rg,&rg);
        if(rg.h.ah != 0) return(0);
        else return(1);
}
```

Using Virtual Memory

Virtual memory requires no exotic code or hitherto unknown inter-
rupts. It's dealt with entirely through the use of the C file functions. It's
handled in the expanded dithering program as a streamed file to make it
easy to understand, but you'll find that it works a lot faster if you use the
unbuffered functions, that is, open rather than fopen.

Because the initial data that will be written to the virtual memory
temporary file might not appear in the order it's to be written, a file of sufficient size to accept it must be created before any virtual memory operations can be performed. If the GIF image to be unpacked by the dithering
program will occupy 256,000 bytes—the unpacked size of a 320-by-200-
pixel image expanded by a factor of two—you'll have to write this many
bytes to the temporary file.

The temporary file can be deleted as soon as your program has finished with it, the virtual memory equivalent of deallocating a buffer.

There are functions provided in Turbo C that will supply you with a
guaranteed unique scratch file for things like this, but in this application
it's probably sufficient to simply work with an unlikely file name. It's
called "TEMP_$$.$$$" in the expanded dithering program. If you have a
RAM disk you can make it a path to a file there, although if it's a RAM disk
in either extended or expanded memory you could use the appropriate
version of the dither program for your extra memory and not bother with
virtual memory.

Virtual memory running into an extended memory RAM disk is notably slower than direct access to the same expanded memory, as DOS has
to deal with the data moving in and out of the file even though it's actually
in memory. On the other hand, if you have VDISK.SYS installed in your
computer and don't want to disable it, forcing your virtual memory operations to take place in your RAM disk will allow you to achieve most of the
performance of an XMS buffer.

THE EXPANDED DITHERING PROGRAM

The dithering program in Fig. 11-12 embodies all of the enhancements discussed so far. Depending on which of the three memory option

Fig 11-12   A program to scale and dither GIF files

```
/*
    An example C language GIF decoder.
    Dithers GIF file to black and white
    Copyright (c) 1989 Alchemy Mindworks

    Uses extended, exanded and virtual memory
*/

#include "stdio.h"
#include "dos.h"
#include "dir.h"
#include "alloc.h"
#include "time.h"

#define     maxline        2048    /* longest GIF line */
#define     neighbours     3    /* maximum neighbouring lines */

#define     XMS        0    /* set true for extended memory */
#define     EMS        1    /* set true for expanded memory */
#define     VMS        0     /* set true for virtual memory */

/* dithering procedures */
#define     FLOYD          1
#define     BURKES         2
#define     STUCKI         3

#define     max_exp        4    /* biggest expansion factor */

extern char PALETTE[256][3],OUTROW[1024],COPYRIGHT[];
extern int INTERLACED,IMAGEWIDE,IMAGEDEEP;
extern int IMAGEX,IMAGEY,XLOC,YLOC;
extern int VERSION,SUBVERSION;

#if XMS
/* struct used for XMS memory moves */
typedef struct {
    unsigned long length;
    unsigned int sourceH;
    unsigned long sourceOff;
    unsigned int destH;
    unsigned long destOff;
    } XMOVE;
long ptr2long();
int XMShandle;          /* handle for extended memory */
#endif

#if EMS
#include "ems.h"    /* the EMS functions live here */

unsigned int EMShandle;    /* handle for expanded memory */
char *EMSpageframe;    /* pointer to EMS page frame */
char *EMSlinestart;    /* line start table for EMS */
```

```
#endif

#if VMS

#define    tempFile    "TEMP__$$.$$$"
FILE *VMShandle;      /* not really a handle, is it... */
#endif

/* this is the IMG file header - familiar sight */

char IMGheader[16] = {
0x00,0x01,0x00,0x08,0x00,0x01,0x00,0x01,
0x00,0x55,0x00,0x55,0x02,0x40,0x02,0xd0
        };

/* contrast expansion lookup table */

char greymap[256] = {
    /* 00-0f */
    0x01,0x01,0x01,0x01,0x01,0x01,0x01,0x01,
    0x01,0x01,0x01,0x01,0x01,0x01,0x01,0x01,
    /* 10-1f */
    0x01,0x01,0x01,0x01,0x01,0x01,0x01,0x01,
    0x01,0x01,0x01,0x01,0x01,0x01,0x01,0x01,
    /* 20-2f */
    0x01,0x01,0x01,0x01,0x01,0x01,0x01,0x02,
    0x03,0x04,0x05,0x06,0x07,0x08,0x09,0x0a,
    /* 30-3f */
    0x0b,0x0c,0x0d,0x0e,0x0f,0x10,0x11,0x12,
    0x13,0x14,0x15,0x16,0x17,0x18,0x19,0x1a,
    /* 40-4f */
    0x1b,0x1c,0x1d,0x1e,0x1f,0x20,0x20,0x21,
    0x22,0x23,0x23,0x24,0x25,0x27,0x27,0x28,
    /* 50-5f */
    0x29,0x2a,0x2b,0x2c,0x2d,0x2e,0x2f,0x2f,
    0x30,0x31,0x32,0x33,0x34,0x35,0x36,0x37,
    /* 60-6f */
    0x38,0x39,0x3a,0x3a,0x3b,0x3c,0x3d,0x3e,
    0x3f,0x40,0x41,0x42,0x43,0x44,0x45,0x46,
    /* 70-7f */
    0x47,0x48,0x49,0x4a,0x4b,0x4c,0x4d,0x4e,
    0x50,0x51,0x52,0x53,0x55,0x56,0x57,0x58,
    /* 80-8f */
    0x59,0x5a,0x5b,0x5d,0x5e,0x5f,0x60,0x61,
    0x63,0x64,0x65,0x66,0x67,0x69,0x6a,0x6b,
    /* 90-9f */
    0x6c,0x6e,0x70,0x72,0x73,0x74,0x76,0x78,
    0x7a,0x7c,0x7e,0x80,0x82,0x84,0x86,0x88,
    /* a0-af */
    0x8a,0x8c,0x8f,0x91,0x93,0x95,0x98,0x9a,
    0x9c,0x9f,0xa1,0xa4,0xa6,0xa9,0xab,0xae,
    /* b0-bf */
    0xb0,0xb2,0xb3,0xb5,0xb7,0xb9,0xba,0xbc,
    0xbd,0xbe,0xc0,0xc2,0xc4,0xc6,0xc8,0xca,
```

Fig 11-12   continued

```
      /* c0-cf */
      0xcc,0xce,0xd0,0xd2,0xd4,0xd6,0xd9,0xdb,
      0xdd,0xe0,0xe3,0xe6,0xe8,0xeb,0xed,0xef,
      /* d0-df */
      0xf2,0xf5,0xf8,0xfb,0xfe,0xfe,0xfe,0xfe,
      0xfe,0xfe,0xfe,0xfe,0xfe,0xfe,0xfe,0xfe,
      /* e0-ef */
      0xfe,0xfe,0xfe,0xfe,0xfe,0xfe,0xfe,0xfe,
      0xfe,0xfe,0xfe,0xfe,0xfe,0xfe,0xfe,0xfe,
      /* f0-ff */
      0xfe,0xfe,0xfe,0xfe,0xfe,0xfe,0xfe,0xfe,
      0xfe,0xfe,0xfe,0xfe,0xfe,0xfe,0xfe,0xfe,
          };

/* work space for dither */
char outbuf[neighbours][maxline*max_exp];

char *destBuf;              /* IMG buffer */
char *farPtr();
char GIFname[81],IMGname[81];    /* file names */

char greypalette[256];         /* grey palette */
char ditherType=FLOYD;          /* flag for dither type */
char raster=0;              /* serpentine raster? */
char display=0;              /* on screen graphics? */

int black,white;           /* global black and white */
int bytes;               /* monochrome line size */
int expansion=1;            /* amount to expand image */
int gotline;             /* last line got */

main(argc,argv)
    int argc;
    char *argv[];
{
    int i,e,ShowIt(),Colourize();
    int ImageDone(),BadError(),BGround();
    int breakout();

    /* usual GIF stuff */
    SetShow(ShowIt);
    SetPalette(Colourize);
    SetImage(ImageDone);
    SetError(BadError);
    SetBackground(BGround);

    /* handler for breaks */
    ctrlbrk(breakout);

    #if XMS

    printf("EXTENDED DITHER version 1.0\n"
        "_____\n");
```

```
#endif

#if EMS

printf("EXPANDED DITHER version 1.0\n"
       "_____\n");

#endif

#if VMS

printf("VIRTUAL DITHER version 1.0\n"
       "_____\n");

#endif
if(argc > 1) {
    for(i=0;i<argc;++i) {

        /* check for options */
        if(argv[i][0]=='/') {
            switch(toupper(argv[i][1])) {
                case 'F':
                    ditherType=FLOYD;
                    break;
                case 'S':
                    ditherType=STUCKI;
                    break;
                case 'B':
                    ditherType=BURKES;
                    break;
                case 'R':
                    raster=1;
                    break;
                case 'D':
                    display=1;
                    break;
                case 'X':
                    expansion = atoi(argv[i]+2);
                    if(expansion < 1)
                        expansion=1;
                    if(expansion > max_exp)
                        expansion=max_exp;
                    break;
            }
        }
    }

    for(i=1;i<argc;++i) {
        if(argv[i][0]!='/') {
            strmfe(GIFname,argv[i],"GIF");
            strmfe(IMGname,argv[i],"IMG");
            strupr(GIFname);
            strupr(IMGname);
            if((e=UnpackGIF(GIFname)) != 0) break;
```

Fig 11-12   continued

```
              }
        }

        if(e) printf("Error code %d",e);

    }

    else {
        puts("Needs a path to a GIF file to dither\n"
              "Options:    /F - Floyd/Steinberg dither\n"
              "            /S - Stucki dither\n"
              "            /B - Burkes dither\n"
              "            /R - Unidirectional raster\n"
              "            /D - Show image on an EGA card\n"
              "            /X - Expansion factor\n"
              );
    }

    ShowCopyright();
}
/* this function dithers the image at source
   and makes a monochrome version of it at dest
   by dithering it into submission. */
dither(dest)
    char *dest;
{
    long Tstart,Tstop,Telapsed;
    char *p,tbufr[80];
    int err,x,y,z,n,ln;

    /* say what we're up to... */
    if(raster) printf("\nUnidirectional raster scan, ");
    else printf("\nSerpentine raster scan, ");

    switch(ditherType) {
        case FLOYD:
            ln=2;
            puts("Floyd-Steinberg dither");
            break;
        case STUCKI:
            ln=3;
            puts("Stucki dither");
            break;
        case BURKES:
            ln=3;
            puts("Burkes dither");
            break;
    }

    printf("Expansion factor %u\n",expansion);

    /* go for graphics */
    if(display) {
```

```
        puts("Hit any key...");
        getch();
        init();
    }

    time(&Tstart);        /* record the start time */

    for(y=0;y<(IMAGEDEEP*expansion);++y) {

        /* record the base line */
        gotline=y;

        /* copy the next few lines from the temporary */
        for(z=0;z<ln;++z) {
            if((y+z) < (IMAGEDEEP*expansion))
                getLine(outbuf[z],y+z,IMAGEWIDE*expansion);
        }

        if(!display) printf("\rLine %d of %d",y,IMAGEDEEP*expansion);

        if(kbhit()) if(getch()==27) breakout(":Aborted");

        /* do the actual dither */
        if((y & 1) || raster) {
            for(x=0;x<(IMAGEWIDE*expansion);++x) {
                if((n=getPixel(x,y)) > ((black+white) / 2)) {
                    bitPixel(dest,x,y,0);
                    err=n-white;
                }
                else {
                    bitPixel(dest,x,y,1);
                    err=n-black;
                }
                ditherPixel(x,y,err);
            }
        }
        else {
            for(x=(IMAGEWIDE*expansion)-1;x>=0;--x) {
                if((n=getPixel(x,y)) > ((black+white) / 2)) {
                    bitPixel(dest,x,y,0);
                    err=n-white;
                }
                else {
                    bitPixel(dest,x,y,1);
                    err=n-black;
                }
                ditherPixel(x,y,err);
            }
        }

        if(display) {
            if(y < 350) {
                p=farPtr(dest,((long)y*(long)bytes));
                if(bytes > 80) {
```

Fig 11-12 continued

```
                        for(x=0;x<80;++x) tbufr[x]=~p[x];
                        memcpy(MK_FP(0xa000,(long)y*80L),tbufr,80);
                    }
                    else {
                        for(x=0;x<bytes;++x) tbufr[x]=~p[x];
                        memcpy(MK_FP(0xa000,(long)y*80L),tbufr,bytes);
                    }
                }
            }

            /* put the the lines back in the temporary */
            for(z=0;z<ln;++z) {
                if((y+z) < (IMAGEDEEP*expansion))
                    putLine(outbuf[z],y+z,IMAGEWIDE*expansion);
            }
        }
        time(&Tstop);
        if(display) {
            putchar(7);
            getch();
            deinit();
        }
        Telapsed = (long)difftime(Tstop,Tstart);
        printf("\nElapsed time for dither: %ld seconds (%ld:%02.2ld)\n",
            Telapsed,Telapsed/60L,Telapsed%60L);
        printf("Black = %d    White = %d\n",black,white);
}

/* diffuse the error for one pixel */
ditherPixel(x,y,err)
    int x,y,err;
{
  switch(ditherType) {
    case FLOYD:
      if((y & 1) || raster) {
        setPixel(x+1,y,getPixel(x+1,y) + ((7 * err) / 16));
        setPixel(x-1,y+1,getPixel(x-1,y+1) + ((3 * err) / 16));
        setPixel(x,y+1,getPixel(x,y+1) + ((5 * err) / 16));
        setPixel(x+1,y+1,getPixel(x+1,y+1) + (err / 16));
      }
      else {
        setPixel(x-1,y,getPixel(x-1,y) + ((7 * err) / 16));
        setPixel(x+1,y+1,getPixel(x+1,y+1) + ((3 * err) / 16));
        setPixel(x,y+1,getPixel(x,y+1) + ((5 * err) / 16));
        setPixel(x-1,y+1,getPixel(x-1,y+1) + (err / 16));
      }
      break;
    case STUCKI:
      if((y & 1) || raster) {
        setPixel(x+2,y,getPixel(x+2,y) + ((8 * err) / 42));
        setPixel(x+1,y,getPixel(x+1,y) + ((4 * err) / 42));
        setPixel(x-2,y+1,getPixel(x-2,y+1) + ((2 * err) / 42));
        setPixel(x-1,y+1,getPixel(x-1,y+1) + ((4 * err) / 42));
```

```
              setPixel(x,y+1,getPixel(x,y+1) + ((8 * err) / 42));
              setPixel(x+1,y+1,getPixel(x+1,y+1) + ((4 * err) / 42));
              setPixel(x+2,y+1,getPixel(x+2,y+1) + ((2 * err) / 42));

              setPixel(x-2,y+2,getPixel(x-2,y+2) + ((1 * err) / 42));
              setPixel(x-1,y+2,getPixel(x-1,y+2) + ((2 * err) / 42));
              setPixel(x,y+2,getPixel(x,y+2) + ((4 * err) / 42));
              setPixel(x+1,y+2,getPixel(x+1,y+2) + ((2 * err) / 42));
              setPixel(x+2,y+2,getPixel(x+2,y+2) + ((1 * err) / 42));
            }
          else {
            setPixel(x-2,y,getPixel(x-2,y) + ((8 * err) / 42));
            setPixel(x-1,y,getPixel(x-1,y) + ((4 * err) / 42));

            setPixel(x+2,y+1,getPixel(x+2,y+1) + ((2 * err) / 42));
            setPixel(x+1,y+1,getPixel(x+1,y+1) + ((4 * err) / 42));
            setPixel(x,y+1,getPixel(x,y+1) + ((8 * err) / 42));
            setPixel(x-1,y+1,getPixel(x-1,y+1) + ((4 * err) / 42));
            setPixel(x-2,y+1,getPixel(x-2,y+1) + ((2 * err) / 42));

            setPixel(x+2,y+2,getPixel(x+2,y+2) + ((1 * err) / 42));
            setPixel(x+1,y+2,getPixel(x+1,y+2) + ((2 * err) / 42));
            setPixel(x,y+2,getPixel(x,y+2) + ((4 * err) / 42));
            setPixel(x-1,y+2,getPixel(x-1,y+2) + ((2 * err) / 42));
            setPixel(x-2,y+2,getPixel(x-2,y+2) + ((1 * err) / 42));
            }
          break;
        case BURKES:
          if((y & 1) || raster) {
            setPixel(x+2,y,getPixel(x+2,y) + ((8 * err) / 32));
            setPixel(x+1,y,getPixel(x+1,y) + ((4 * err) / 32));

            setPixel(x-2,y+1,getPixel(x-2,y+1) + ((2 * err) / 32));
            setPixel(x-1,y+1,getPixel(x-1,y+1) + ((4 * err) / 32));
            setPixel(x,y+1,getPixel(x,y+1) + ((8 * err) / 32));
            setPixel(x+1,y+1,getPixel(x+1,y+1) + ((4 * err) / 32));
            setPixel(x+2,y+1,getPixel(x+2,y+1) + ((2 * err) / 32));
            }
          else {
            setPixel(x-2,y,getPixel(x-2,y) + ((8 * err) / 32));
            setPixel(x-1,y,getPixel(x-1,y) + ((4 * err) / 32));

            setPixel(x+2,y+1,getPixel(x+2,y+1) + ((2 * err) / 32));
            setPixel(x+1,y+1,getPixel(x+1,y+1) + ((4 * err) / 32));
            setPixel(x,y+1,getPixel(x,y+1) + ((8 * err) / 32));
            setPixel(x-1,y+1,getPixel(x-1,y+1) + ((4 * err) / 32));
            setPixel(x-2,y+1,getPixel(x-2,y+1) + ((2 * err) / 32));
            }
          break;
        }
    }

/* write the monochrome image to a file */
ImageDone()
```

Fig 11-12   continued

```
{
    FILE *fp;
    char *pr;
    int i,r=0;

    dither(destBuf);

    if((fp=fopen(IMGname,"wb")) != NULL) {

        IMGheader[12]=(IMAGEWIDE*expansion) >> 8;
        IMGheader[13]=(IMAGEWIDE*expansion);
        IMGheader[14]=(IMAGEDEEP*expansion) >> 8;
        IMGheader[15]=(IMAGEDEEP*expansion);

        if(fwrite(IMGheader,1,16,fp)==16) {

            for(i=0;i<(IMAGEDEEP*expansion);++i) {
                pr=farPtr(destBuf,(long)i*(long)bytes);
                if(!WriteImgLine(pr,fp,bytes)) {
                    r=0;
                    break;
                } else r=1;
            }

        }

        fclose(fp);

        if(!r) {
            printf("\nError writing %s",IMGname);
            remove(IMGname);
        }

    } else printf("\nError creating %s",IMGname);

    freeBuffer();
}

/* create a pallette lookup table with the palette
   colour values grey scale summed. */
Colourize(n,palette)
    int n;
    char *palette;
{
    double f;
    int i;

    black=255;
    white=0;

    for(i=0;i<n;++i) {
        f= (0.30 * (double)*palette++) +
```

```
                (0.59 * (double)*palette++) +
                (0.11 * (double)*palette++);
        if(f > 255.0) f=255.0;
        /* do grey scale expansion */
        greypalette[i]=greymap[(char)f];

        /* establish black and white levels */
        if(greypalette[i] < black) black = greypalette[i];
        if(greypalette[i] > white) white = greypalette[i];
    }
}

/* copy the line into memory */
ShowIt()
{
    int i;

    for(i=0;i<IMAGEWIDE;++i) OUTROW[i]=greypalette[OUTROW[i]];
    if(expansion==1)
        putLine(OUTROW,YLOC,IMAGEWIDE);
    else {
        for(i=0;i<IMAGEWIDE;++i)
            memset(outbuf[0]+(expansion*i),OUTROW[i],expansion);
        for(i=0;i<expansion;++i)
            putLine(outbuf[0],(YLOC*expansion)+i,IMAGEWIDE*expansion);
    }
}

/* do some initial housekeeping */
BGround()
{
    bytes=pixels2bytes(IMAGEWIDE)*expansion;
    allocateBuffer();
    printf("Unpacking...\r");
}

BadError(s)
    char *s;
{
    char b[65];

    sprintf(b,":GIF error %s",s);
    breakout(b);
}

ShowCopyright()
{
    char *p;
    p = COPYRIGHT;
    puts("");
    while(*p) {
        p += printf(p)+1;
        puts("");
    }
```

Fig 11-12   continued

```
}

strmfe(new,old,ext)      /* make file name with specific extension */
    char *new,*old,*ext;
{
    while(*old != 0 && *old != '.') *new++=*old++;
    *new++='.';
    while(*ext) *new++=*ext++;
    *new=0;
}

char *farPtr(p,l)      /* return a far pointer p + l */
    char *p;
    long l;
{
        unsigned int seg,off;

    seg = FP_SEG(p);
    off = FP_OFF(p);
    seg += (off / 16);
    off &= 0x000f;
    off += (unsigned int)(l & 0x000fL);
    seg += (l / 16L);
    p=MK_FP(seg,off);
    return(p);
}

writeImgLine(p,fp,n)      /* IMG encode and write the line in p to fp */
    char *p;
        FILE *fp;
    int n;
{
    char b[0x0080];
    unsigned int bdex=0,i=0,j=0,t=0;

    do {
        i=0;
        while((p[t+i]==p[t+i+1]) &&
            ((t+i) < (n-1)) && i < 0x7e) ++i;

        if(i>0 || bdex >= 0x7e) {

            if(bdex) {
                fputc(0x80,fp);
                fputc(bdex,fp);
                j+=2;
                fwrite(b,1,bdex,fp);
                j+=bdex;
                bdex=0;
            }

            if(i) {
```

```
                      if(p[t+i]==0xff) {
                          fputc(0x80+i+1,fp);
                          j+=1;
                      }
                      else if(p[t+i]==0x00) {
                          fputc(i+1,fp);
                          j+=1;
                      }
                      else {
                          fputc(0x00,fp);
                          fputc(i+1,fp);
                          fputc(p[t+i],fp);
                          j+=3;
                      }
                      t+=(i+1);
                  }
            } else b[bdex++]=p[t++];
    } while(t<n);

    if(bdex) {
        fputc(0x80,fp);
        fputc(bdex,fp);
        j+=2;
        fwrite(b,1,bdex,fp);
        j+=bdex;
    }
}

init()          /* turn on graphics mode */
{
    union REGS r;

    r.x.ax=0x0010;
    int86(0x10,&r,&r);
}

deinit()     /* turn off graphics card */
{
    union REGS r;

    r.x.ax=0x0003;
    int86(0x10,&r,&r);
}

pixels2bytes(n)     /* return number of bytes in number of pixels */
    unsigned int n;
{
    if(n & 0x0007) return((n >> 3) + 1);
    else return(n >> 3);
}

getPixel(x,y)     /* get a pixel from the source image */
    int x,y;
{
```

Fig 11-12   continued

```
    return(outbuf[y-gotline][x]);
}

setPixel(x,y,n)    /* place a pixel in the source image */
    int x,y,n;
{

    if(x >= 0 && x < (IMAGEWIDE*expansion) &&
        y >= 0 && y < (IMAGEDEEP*expansion)) {
        if(n < black) n=black;
        if(n > white) n=white;
        outbuf[y-gotline][x]=n;
    }
}

bitPixel(buf,x,y,n)    /* place a pixel in the destination image */
    char *buf;
    int x,y,n;
{
    char *p;

    if(x >= 0 && x < (IMAGEWIDE*expansion) &&
        y >= 0 && y < (IMAGEDEEP*expansion)) {
        p=farPtr(buf,((long)bytes*(long)y));
        if(n) p[x >> 3] |= (0x80 >> (x & 0x0007));
        else p[x >> 3] &= ~(0x80 >> (x & 0x0007));
    }
}

/* set up the temporary buffer or file */
allocateBuffer()
{
    int i;

    #if XMS
    long size;

    /* figure out how much memory will be needed */
    size = (long)IMAGEWIDE*(long)IMAGEDEEP*(long)(expansion*expansion);
    XMShandle=-1;

    /* is there an XMS driver on tap? */
    i=get_xmem();

    /* check the version number - must be 2.0 or better */
    if(i >= 0x0200 && i != -1)

        /* try to allocate some memory */
        XMShandle=alloc_xmem((size / 1024L)+1);

    /* -1 is a bad handle */
    if(XMShandle == -1)
```

```
            breakout(":Error allocating extended memory");
    #endif

    #if EMS
    unsigned int page=0,offset=0;

    EMShandle = 0;
    EMSlinestart = NULL;

    /* check for EMS memory and for a driver */
    if(isEMS()) {
        if(checkEMS()) {
            /* get the page frame pointer */
            EMSpageframe=pageframeEMS();

            /* make a table of line starts and pages */
            if((EMSlinestart=malloc(4*IMAGEDEEP*expansion))
                != NULL) {
                for(i=0;i<(IMAGEDEEP*expansion);++i) {
                    offset+=(IMAGEWIDE*expansion);
                    if(offset+(IMAGEWIDE*expansion) >=
                        pagesizeEMS) {
                        ++page;
                        offset=0;
                    }
                    setLinestart(i,page,offset);
                }
            } else breakout(":Error allocating EMS linestart");

            /* allocate some EMS memory */
            if((EMShandle=mallocEMS(page+1)) == 0)
                breakout(":Error allocating expanded memory");

        } else breakout(":No EMS hardware");
    } else breakout(":No EMS driver");
    #endif

    #if VMS
    long size;

    /* create a temporary file and fill it with zeros */
    if((VMShandle=fopen(tempFile,"wb+")) != NULL) {
        size = (long)IMAGEWIDE*(long)IMAGEDEEP*
            (long)(expansion*expansion);
        while(size--) if(fputc(0,VMShandle))
            breakout(":Error writing temporary file");
    } else breakout(":Error creating temporary file");
    #endif

    /* allocate an image buffer for the IMG file */
    if((destBuf=farmalloc((long)bytes*(long)(IMAGEDEEP*expansion))) == NULL)
        breakout(":Can't allocate destination memory");

}
```

Fig 11-12 continued

```
/* free all the allocated memory */
freeBuffer()
{
    #if XMS
    if(XMShandle != -1) dealloc_xmem(XMShandle);
    #endif
    #if EMS
    if(EMShandle) freeEMS(EMShandle);
    if(EMSlinestart != NULL) free(EMSlinestart);
    #endif
    #if VMS
    if(VMShandle != NULL) {
        fclose(VMShandle);
        remove(tempFile);
    }
    #endif
    if(destBuf != NULL) farfree(destBuf);
}

/* do housekeeping for abnormal end */
breakout(s)
    char *s;
{
    freeBuffer();
    if(display) deinit();
    if(*s==':') puts(s+1);
    exit(0);
}

/* write a line to extended memory */
putLine(p,n,l)
    char *p;
    int n,l;
{
    #if XMS
    XMOVE xmove;

    xmove.length = (long)l;
    xmove.sourceH=0;
    xmove.sourceOff=ptr2long(p);
    xmove.destH=XMShandle;
    xmove.destOff=(long)n*(long)IMAGEWIDE*(long)expansion;
    if(!move_xmem(&xmove))
        breakout(":Error moving line into buffer");
    #endif

    #if EMS
    unsigned int page,offset;

    getLinestart(n,&page,&offset);
    if(!mapEMS(EMShandle,0,page))
        breakout(":Error moving line into buffer");
    memcpy(EMSpageframe+offset,p,l);
```

```
    #endif

    #if VMS
    if(!fseek(VMShandle,(long)n*(long)IMAGEWIDE*
        (long)expansion,SEEK_SET)) {
        if(fwrite(p,1,1,VMShandle) != 1)
            breakout(":Error writing to temporary file");
    } else breakout(":Error seeking in temporary file");
    #endif
}

/* get a line from extended memory */
getLine(p,n,l)
    char *p;
    int n,l;
{
    #if XMS
    XMOVE xmove;

    xmove.length = (long)l;
    xmove.sourceH=XMShandle;
    xmove.sourceOff=(long)n*(long)IMAGEWIDE*(long)expansion;
    xmove.destH=0;
    xmove.destOff=ptr2long(p);
    if(!move_xmem(&xmove))
        breakout(":Error getting line from buffer");
    #endif

    #if EMS
    unsigned int page,offset;

    getLinestart(n,&page,&offset);
    if(!mapEMS(EMShandle,0,page))
        breakout(":Error getting line from buffer");
    memcpy(p,EMSpageframe+offset,l);
    #endif

    #if VMS
    if(!fseek(VMShandle,(long)n*(long)IMAGEWIDE*
        (long)expansion,SEEK_SET)) {
        if(fread(p,1,1,VMShandle) != 1)
            breakout(":Error reading from temporary file");
    } else breakout(":Error seeking in temporary file");
    #endif
}

#if EMS
setLinestart(n,page,offset)     /* store one EMS line start */
    int n,page,offset;
{
    EMSlinestart[n*4]=page;
    EMSlinestart[n*4+1]=page>>8;
    EMSlinestart[n*4+2]=offset;
    EMSlinestart[n*4+3]=offset>>8;
```

Fig 11-12   continued
```
}

getLinestart(n,page,offset)     /* fetch one EMS line start */
    int n,*page,*offset;
{
    *page=EMSlinestart[n*4]+(EMSlinestart[n*4+1] << 8);
    *offset=EMSlinestart[n*4+2]+(EMSlinestart[n*4+3] << 8);
}
#endif
```

---

defines you set true, it can be compiled to work with extended, expanded or virtual memory. In the first case you'll have to add XMEM.OBJ to your project file. In the second you'll need EMS.H handy. In the third case, plan on having a lot of free disk space.

You also will have to link in the GIF decoder module, as with the previous dithering program.

The considerably more efficient way of handling pixels in this version of the dithering program means that it will run faster than the conventional memory version, even for images that would have fit comfortably into a conventional memory buffer. If you want to do anything practical with the original dithering program you might want to go back and add this strategy to it.

The dithering options in this program are unchanged from the previous version. However, there's now a new command line switch, /X, which allows you to specify the expansion factor. It's limited to a maximum of four here, but you can certainly increase this if you have lots of extra memory to work with. A 640-by-480-pixel GIF file expanded by a factor of four will require about five megabytes of memory, not to mention a considerable period of time to dither.

FURTHER DITHERING

This chapter has touched on the techniques for dithering, as well as some of the related hardware issues. Dithering is a large and potentially fascinating subject. The programs discussed here will serve you well as a starting point—you will find that they lend themselves to all sorts of hacking and experimentation.

There are many filters extant in addition to the ones discussed here. There also are a number of enhancements to the basic error diffusion techniques, such as blue noise perturbation, which can considerably improve the appearance of a dithered image.

REFERENCES

Ulichney, R. "Digital Halftoning," MIT Press. This is a seminal reference on all aspects of dithering and related subjects.

Burkes, D.F. "Presentation of the Burkes error filter." This is an article written by the author of the Burkes filter discussed in this chapter. It was contributed to the public domain, and is hence a little hard to find. As of this writing, Daniel Burkes could be reached at TerraVision Inc., 2351 College Station Road Suite 563, Athens, GA 30305.

Floyd, R.W. and Steinberg, L. "An Adaptive Algorithm for Spatial Gray Scale." SID International Symposium Digest of Technical Papers, volume 1975m. This is the description of the Floyd-Steinberg error diffusion filter discussed in this chapter.

Stucki, P. "MECCA—a multiple-error correcting computation algorithm for bilevel image hard copy reproduction." Research Report RZ1060, IBM Research Laboratory, Zurich, Switzerland.

12
CHAPTER

Format Translation

Old programming wizards never die. They just recurse.
—Murphy's Laws of Computers

There are other epigrams from the font of Murphy's laws that would have suited this chapter equally as well. Consider "if nobody uses it there's probably a reason," "interchangeable parts aren't" and, perhaps most piquant, "if the shoe fits, it's ugly." All of these seem to suit the multiplicity of image file formats that plague PC-based software.

The multiplicity of image file formats seems to bespeak a multiplicity of applications to use them, and one of the unwritten clauses of Murphy's laws of computers is that the file you have will never be readable by the application you want to use it with. Image file format conversion is an important facet of reality for anyone who uses picture files on a PC.

Although all of the image file formats discussed in this book are at heart incompatible, image data itself essentially is universal. There are relatively few ways to represent a pixel, and each of them can be converted into any of the others with simple, low level techniques.

The problems involved in writing file format conversion programs, or *bridges*, are quite trivial compared to many of the things that have been dealt with in this book. Assuming that you know how to unpack the format you want to convert from and pack the format you want to convert to, there usually is very little more to worry about.

Some potential problems do crop up. For example, you might have to deal with the problem of converting a format having variable dimensions, such as IMG, into one having fixed dimensions, such as MacPaint. Color formats can present you with related sorts of problems, such as converting a 32-color GIF file into a PCX file, the PCX format being unable to support a 32-color palette.

All of these things require a bit of forethought to deal with.

The real art of writing image file format converters is usually not so much in getting them to work, which isn't particularly difficult if you know how to deal with the formats involved, but rather in getting them to work quickly and in all possible cases.

This chapter will discuss several sorts of image file converters, ranging from simple monochrome data *swabbers* right up to 256-color file converters that use many of the functions discussed in the previous chapters of this book.

After working your way through the five programs in this chapter you should be able to apply the encoding and decoding functions discussed in this book to any permutation of image file format conversion you encounter.

MONOCHROME FILE FORMAT CONVERTERS

There's only one way to represent monochrome bit-mapped data, which makes writing a program to convert between monochrome formats pretty painless. By comparison, color can be represented as either a series of bit planes or as a packed array of pixels, a problem that will crop up later.

In looking at the problem of converting between two monochrome image file formats, you'll be able to see virtually all of the techniques that you'll ultimately need if you want to deal with color formats. However, as was the case with the other purely monochrome phenomena that have appeared in this book, 2-color code is a lot easier to understand.

The most obvious way to convert between two dissimilar monochrome images file is to unpack the source file into a buffer and then pack the contents of the buffer into the destination format. This is pretty easy to understand—very easy to accomplish—and is the ultimate last resort when there's no other way to deal with a particularly awkward conversion problem.

There are several drawbacks to this approach at file conversion. To begin with, it involves using a large memory buffer. It might be exceedingly large if the two formats involved tend to support big pictures—consider converting TIFF files into IMG files, for example. In addition, it probably will involve the use of far pointers, which will slow things down a bit.

You usually can get away without having the entire source image unpacked at one time. Recall that images usually are packed one line at a time and, hence, can be expected to unpack into the same convenient packets. As such, you can unpack one line of the source image and immediately pack it into the destination file, repeating the process for as many times as there are source lines.

This certainly saves on memory and it can be a lot faster than working with a whole image in memory. However, the largest part of the time taken to convert an image in this way is tied up in uncompressing the source image lines and recompressing them to write them to the destination image file.

In some cases, it's possible to avoid doing this. If the source image compression format has fields that all can be represented by equivalent fields of the destination format, you can convert between the files in question by simply extracting the compressed data from the source file and applying it to the appropriate fields in the destination format.

This sort of conversion is called data *swabbing*. The data itself is left unchanged—only the way it's stored is modified.

MacPaint File Conversion

The MacPaint format seems to cry out for image conversion. It represents a huge body of interesting—if fairly small—images, but there are few commercial applications that will import it reliably. Of those that do, most impose some sort of penalty on it. For example, Ventura Publisher will import a MacPaint file, but it converts it to an IMG file before using it, leaving you with two files containing the same information kicking around your hard drive.

There's a lot to be said for converting MacPaint images into the formats they're to be used in before you go to use them.

Converting from MacPaint into the IMG format is a good example of a data swabber. It allows you to apply a bit of cunning to the problem, with the result being a very fast way to manage the conversion between these two formats.

As was discussed in Chapter 2, MacPaint image data is stored in two types of fields, to wit, string fields and run-of-byte fields. The first byte of each field tells the decoding software how to interpret the rest of the field.

The IMG format has equivalent fields, as well as several other types that can be ignored for the sake of this discussion. If you were to compress the same image into a MacPaint file and an IMG file, in the various fields of the two files could be the same, even though the index bytes and the other field related regalia would be different.

To convert a MacPaint file into an IMG file, then, all you have to do is to step through the source file's fields and copy the actual data into IMG style fields. The data itself actually never has to be unpacked. Figure 12-1 shows the two ends of the conversion process—a picture in MacPaint on a Macintosh being teleported to a page in Ventura Publisher.

The program to manage this translation is exceedingly simple. It's illustrated in Fig. 12-2. It's also exceedingly fast, as it really doesn't do any meaningful amount of work. Because MacPaint files conveniently fit into a single memory segment, the program works by loading the whole affair into a small buffer and then converting it on the fly as it's written out to the destination IMG file.

The IMG file header, stored at the top of the program, doesn't have any fields to fill in. Because the dimensions of a MacPaint file—and hence of any IMG file created from one—are constant, the bytes in the header never change. This header is set up to tell Ventura that the image files created by

Flower Girl in MacPaint

Flower Girl in Ventura Publisher

Fig 12-1   A MacPaint picture in FullPaint on a Macintosh and in Ventura Publisher on a PC

Fig 12-2   A program to translate MacPaint files to IMG files

```
/*
        MacPaint to Gem/IMG file translator
*/

#include "stdio.h"
#include "dos.h"
#include "stdlib.h"
```

```
char *buf;               /* pointer to load buffer    */
char *pnt;               /* pointer for unpack        */

long bsize;              /* index into load buffer    */
unsigned int PICT;       /* where the picture starts  */

char macfile[81];        /* file names */
char imgfile[81];
char *pas2c();

/* IMG file header */
char imghead[16] = "\x00\x01\x00\x08\x00\x01\x00\x01"
                   "\x00\x55\x00\x55\x02\x40\x02\xd0";

main(argc,argv)
        int argc;
        char *argv[];
{
        puts("MacPaint to IMG converter");
        if(argc > 1) {
                strupr(argv[1]);
                load(argv[1]);
                strmfe(imgfile,argv[1],"IMG");
                pnt = buf + PICT;
                if(PICT==0x280)
                    printf("The MacPaint picture in %s was called %s.\n",
                    macfile,pas2c(buf+1));
                printf("Writing to %s.\n",imgfile);
                save(imgfile);
                free(buf);
        }
        else {
                puts("This program translates MacPaint files "
                    "into IMG files for use"
                    "with such things as Ventura. Very handy, this."
                    "Invoke this program as"
                    "    MAC2IMG PICTURE.MAC"
                    "and it will create PICTURE.IMG");
        }
}

/* return a C string from a Pascal string */
char *pas2c(p)
        char *p;
{
        static char b[65];
        int i,j;

        i=*p++;
        for(j=0;j<i;j++) b[j]=*p++;
        b[i]=0;
        return(b);
}

/* load the MacPaint file into the buffer */
```

Fig 12-2   continued

```
load(f)
        char *f;
{

        FILE *fp;
        long s;

        strcpy(macfile,f);
        fp=fopen(macfile,"rb");
        if(fp==NULL) {
                strmfe(macfile,f,"MAC");
                fp=fopen(macfile,"rb");
        }

        if(fp != NULL) {
                fseek(fp,0L,SEEK_END);
                s = ftell(fp);
                rewind(fp);
                if(s < 0x0000ffffL) {
                        if((buf=malloc((int)s)) != NULL) {
                                if(fread(buf,1,(unsigned int)s,fp) !=
                                  (unsigned int)s) {
                                        printf("McError reading %s.\n",f);
                                        exit(1);
                                }
                                else {
                                        if(!memcmp(buf+0x0041,"PNTG",4))
                                            PICT=0x280;
                                        else
                                          if(!memcmp(buf,"\000\000\000\002",4))
                                            PICT=0x200;
                                        else {
                                                printf("%s is not a "
                                                        "MacPaint file.\n",f);
                                                exit(1);
                                        }
                                        bsize=s-(long)PICT;
                                }
                        }
                        else {
                                printf("McMemory allocation error.\n");
                                exit(1);
                        }
                }
                else {
                        printf("File %s is too McBig.\n",f);
                        exit(1);
                }
        }
        else {
                printf("Can't find McFile %s.",f);
                exit(1);
        }
}
```

```
/* save the MacPaint file loaded into the buffer
   in IMG format */
save(f)
        char *f;
{
        FILE *fp;
        long s;
        int i;

        if((fp=fopen(f,"wb")) != NULL) {
                fwrite(imghead,1,16,fp);
                s=bsize;
                do {
                        if(*pnt & 0x80) {
                                i=(~(*pnt++) & 0xff)+2;
                                fputc(0,fp);
                                fputc(i,fp);
                                fputc(*pnt++,fp);
                                s-=2;
                        }
                        else {
                                i=((*pnt++) & 0xff)+1;
                                fputc(0x80,fp);
                                fputc(i,fp);
                                while(i--) {
                                        fputc(*pnt++,fp);
                                        --s;
                                }
                                --s;
                        }
                } while(s > 0L);
                fclose(fp);
        }
        else {
                printf("Can't create McFile %s.",f);
                exit(1);
        }
}

/* make file name with a new extension */
strmfe(new,old,ext)
        char *new,*old,*ext;
{
        while(*old != 0 && *old != '.') *new++=*old++;
        *new++='.';
        while(*ext) *new++=*ext++;
        *new=0;
}
```

the conversion program are to have 55 micron pixels, that is, that they're to be displayed at 300 dots to the inch initially. They will have a horizontal dimension of 1.93 inches in this case. If you have cause to change this, you'll find a complete description of the header fields in Chapter 3.

An even more painless example of data swabbing—or perhaps just plain data stealing—can be found in a similar program to translate MacPaint files into TIFF files. Recall from the TIFF file discussion in Chapter 7 that the image data in a TIFF file can be compressed using the same run length encoding scheme as MacPaint files use. As such, you can create a TIFF file very simply by lifting the entire block of compressed image data from a MacPaint file and simply placing it in a TIFF file with the appropriate tags.

If you look at the program in Fig. 12-3, the MacPaint to TIFF file converter, you'll notice that it does even less than the MacPaint to IMG converter did. It uses the TIFF packing code from Chapter 7, but because the data is already compressed it doesn't actually have to read or write any strips. The original version of this program had a fairly extensive shareware notice on it—it took longer to print the notice than it did to convert a file.

Fig 12-3   A program to translate MacPaint files to TIFF files

```
/*
          MacPaint to TIFF file translator
*/

#include "stdio.h"
#include "alloc.h"
#include "tiff.h"

#define bytes           72
#define wide            576
#define deep            720

char *buf;                  /* pointer to load buffer     */

long bsize;                 /* index into load buffer     */
unsigned int PICT;          /* where the picture starts   */

char macfile[81];           /* file names */
char tiffile[81];

main(argc,argv)
        int argc;
        char *argv[];
{
        puts("MacPaint to TIFF converter");
        if(argc > 1) {
                strupr(argv[1]);
                load(argv[1]);
                save(argv[1]);
                free(buf);
        }
        else {
                puts("This program translates MacPaint files into TIFF files"
                        "Invoke this program as"
```

```
                                "      MAC2TIF PICTURE.MAC"
                                "and it will create PICTURE.TIF");
                }
        }

/* load the MacPaint file into the buffer */
load(f)
        char *f;
{
        FILE *fp;
        long s;

        strcpy(macfile,f);
        fp=fopen(macfile,"rb");
        if(fp==NULL) {
                strmfe(macfile,f,"MAC");
                fp=fopen(macfile,"rb");
        }

        if(fp != NULL) {
                fseek(fp,0L,SEEK_END);
                s = ftell(fp);
                rewind(fp);
                if(s < 0x0000ffffL) {
                        if((buf=malloc((int)s)) != NULL) {
                            if(fread(buf,1,(unsigned int)s,fp) !=
                                (unsigned int)s) {
                                    printf("McError reading %s.\n",f);
                                    exit(1);
                            }
                            else {
                                    if(!memcmp(buf+0x0041,"PNTG",4))
                                        PICT=0x280;
                                    else
                                      if(!memcmp(buf,"\000\000\000\002",4))
                                        PICT=0x200;
                                    else {
                                            printf("%s is not a MacPaint file,\n",f);
                                            exit(1);
                                    }
                                    bsize=s-(long)PICT;
                            }
                        }
                        else {
                                printf("McMemory allocation error.\n");
                                exit(1);
                        }
                }
            else {
                    printf("File %s is too McBig.\n",f);
                    exit(1);
            }
        }
    else {
```

Fig 12-3   continued

```
                   printf("Can't find McFile %s.",f);
                   exit(1);
          }
}

/* save the MacPaint file loaded into the buffer
   in TIF format */
save(f)
          char *f;
{
          FILE *fp;
          char b[81];

          strmfe(b,f,"TIF");

          if((fp=fopen(b,"wb")) != NULL) {
                   PackTifFile(fp,buf+PICT);
                   fclose(fp);
          }
          else {
                   printf("Error creating %s.\n",b);
                   exit(1);
          }
}

/* make file name with a new extension */
strmfe(new,old,ext)
          char *new,*old,*ext;
{
          while(*old != 0 && *old != '.') *new++=*old++;
          *new++='.';
          while(*ext) *new++=*ext++;
          *new=0;
}

/* pack in image into a TIFF file */
PackTifFile(fp,p)
          FILE *fp;
          char *p;
{
          int i;

          /* write the header */
          WriteTifHeader(fp);
          fwrite(p,1,(int)bsize,fp);
          /* write the dictionary */
          WriteTifDict(fp);
}

/* write a TIFF header */
WriteTifHeader(fp)
          FILE *fp;
{
```

```
        fputWord(fp,'II');                      /* intel packing */
        fputWord(fp,42);            /* version 42 */
        fputLong(fp,0L);            /* filler for offset */
}

/* write a TIFF IFD */
WriteTifDict(fp)
        FILE *fp;
{
        long l;

        /* remember where we parked */
        l=ftell(fp);
        /* there will be six tags */
        fputWord(fp,6);
        /* write the tags */
        WriteTifTag(fp,ImageWidth,TIFFshort,0L,(long)wide);
        WriteTifTag(fp,ImageLength,TIFFshort,0L,(long)deep);
        WriteTifTag(fp,BitsPerSample,TIFFshort,0L,1L);
        WriteTifTag(fp,Compression,TIFFshort,0L,(long)COMPmpnt);
        WriteTifTag(fp,PhotometricInterp,TIFFshort,0L,0L);
        WriteTifTag(fp,StripOffsets,TIFFlong,1L,8L);
        /* point to offset field of header */
        fseek(fp,4L,SEEK_SET);
        /* point to the start of the IFD */
        fputWord(fp,l);
}

/* write one TIFF tag to the IFD */
WriteTifTag(fp,tag,type,length,offset)
        FILE *fp;
        int tag,type;
        long length,offset;
{
        fputWord(fp,tag);
        fputWord(fp,type);
        fputLong(fp,length);
        fputLong(fp,offset);
}

/* return number of bytes in number of pixels */
pixels2bytes(n)
        int n;
{
        if(n & 0x0007) return((n >> 3) + 1);
        else return(n >> 3);
}

fputWord(fp,n)                  /* write one word to the file */
        FILE *fp;
        int n;
{
        fputc(n,fp);
        fputc((n >> 8),fp);
}
```

Fig 12-3 continued

```
fputLong(fp,n)                  /* write one long to the file */
        FILE *fp;
        long n;
{
        fputc(n,fp);
        fputc((n >> 8),fp);
        fputc((n >> 16),fp);
        fputc((n >> 24),fp);
}
```

Converting from MacPaint files to PCX files is the first example of real data conversion. The field structure of a PCX file does not lend itself to simply swabbing the fields, as was done with IMG files. A single field of a MacPaint file can unpack into a complete 72-byte line if need be. The PCX format limits the unpacked size of a single field to 63 bytes.

Figure 12-4 illustrates the ongoing peregrinations of our MacPaint picture, having now come to rest in the Windows version of PC Paintbrush.

Fig 12-4   The original MacPaint file now in PC Paintbrush

To convert a MacPaint picture to a PCX file, the conversion routine must actually uncompress the MacPaint line data into real binary lines and then recompress it into PCX lines. All of the code to do this has been discussed earlier in this book, and none of it will be particularly exciting by now. However, you'll note that the process does not require any substantial amount of memory, because only one line of the image ever exists in an unpacked state at a time. This program will run in much less memory than the simple data swabbers.

Figure 12-5 is the MacPaint to PCX file converter.

Fig 12-5   A program to translate MacPaint files to PCX files

```
/*
        MacPaint to PC Paintbrush file translator
        For Turbo C
        Copyright (c) 1987, 1988 Alchemy Mindworks
*/

#include "stdio.h"

#define bytes           72
#define wide            576
#define deep            720

FILE *OpenMacFile();

typedef struct  {
        char    manufacturer;
        char    version;
        char    encoding;
        char    bits_per_pixel;
        int     xmin,ymin;
        int     xmax,ymax;
        int     hres;
        int     vres;
        char    palette[48];
        char    reserved;
        char    colour_planes;
        int     bytes_per_line;
        int     palette_type;
        char    filler[58];
        } PCXHEAD;

typedef struct {
        char zerobyte;          /* always zero */
        char name[64];          /* name and some filler */
        char type[4];           /* Mac file type */
        char creator[4];        /* Mac file creator */
        char filler[10];
        long datafork_size;     /* length of Mac data fork */
        long rsrcfork_size;     /* length of Mac resource fork */
        long creation_date;     /* time of file's creation */
        long modif_date;        /* time of file's modification */
        char filler2[29];
        } MACBINARY;

PCXHEAD header;                 /* where the header lives */

main(argc,argv)
        int argc;
        char *argv[];
{
        puts("MacPaint to PCX converter");
        if(argc > 1) {
```

Fig 12-5   continued

```
                strupr(argv[1]);
                ConvertMacPcx(argv[1]);
        }
        else {
                puts("This program translates MacPaint files into PCX files"
                     "Invoke this program as"
                     "      MAC2PCX PICTURE.MAC"
                     "and it will create PICTURE.PCX");
        }
}

/* load the MacPaint file into the buffer */
FILE *OpenMacFIle(f)
        char *f;
{
        FILE *fp;
        MACBINARY m;
        char b[81];

        strcpy(b,f);
        fp=fopen(b,"rb");
        if(fp==NULL) {
                strmfe(b,f,"MAC");
                fp=fopen(b,"rb");
        }

        if(fp != NULL) {
                if(fread((char *)&m,1,sizeof(MACBINARY),fp) ==
                   sizeof(MACBINARY)) {
                        if(!memcmp(m.type,"PNTG",4))
                                fseek(fp,0x0280L,SEEK_SET);
                        else if(!memcmp((char *)&m,"\000\000\000\002",4))
                                fseek(fp,0x0200L,SEEK_SET);
                        else {
                                printf("%s is not a MacPaint file.\n",f);
                                exit(1);
                        }
                }
                else {
                        printf("Error reading McHeader.\n");
                        exit(1);
                }
        }
        else {
                printf("Can't find McFile %s.",f);
                exit(1);
        }
        return(fp);
}

ConvertMacPcx(f)
        char *f;
{
```

```
        FILE *dest,*source;
        char s[81],b[bytes];
        int i;

        strmfe(s,f,"PCX");
        if((source=OpenMacFile(f)) != NULL) {
                if((dest=fopen(s,"wb")) != NULL) {
                        /* write the header */
                        WritePcxHeader(dest);
                        /* read and write each line */
                        for(i=0;i<deep;++i) {
                                if(ReadMacLine(b,source)==72)
                                        WritePcxLine(b,dest);
                        }
                        fclose(dest);
                }
                else {
                        printf("Error creating %s.\n",s);
                        exit(1);
                }
                fclose(source);
        }
        else {
                printf("Error opening %s.\n",s);
                exit(1);
        }
}

ReadMacLine(p,fp)
        char *p;
        FILE *fp;
{
        int c,i,n=0;

        do {
                c=fgetc(fp) & 0xff;
                if(c & 0x80) {
                        i = ((~c) & 0xff)+2;
                        c=fgetc(fp);
                        while(i--) p[n++] = c;
                }
                else {
                        i=(c & 0xff)+1;
                        while(i--) p[n++] = fgetc(fp);
                }
        } while(n < 72);
        if(c==EOF) n=0;
        return(n);
}

WritePcxLine(p,fp)
        char *p;
        FILE *fp;
{
```

Fig 12-5   continued

```
        char b[64];
        unsigned int i=0,j=0,t=0;

        do {
                i=0;
                while((p[t+i]==p[t+i+1]) && ((t+i) < bytes) && (i<63)) ++i;
                if(i>0) {
                        fputc(i | 0xc0,fp);
                        fputc(~p[t],fp);
                        t+=i;
                        j+=2;
                }
                else {
                        if(((~p[t]) & 0xc0)==0xc0) {
                                fputc(0xc1,fp);
                                ++j;
                        }
                        fputc(~p[t++],fp);
                        ++j;
                }
        } while(t<bytes);
        return(j);
}

/* write a PCX header */
WritePcxHeader(fp)
        FILE *fp;
{
        memset((char *)&header,0,sizeof(PCXHEAD));
        header.manufacturer=0x0a;
        header.version=2;
        header.encoding=1;
        header.bits_per_pixel=1;
        header.xmin=header.ymin=0;
        header.xmax=wide-1;
        header.ymax=deep-1;
        header.colour_planes=1;
        header.bytes_per_line=bytes;
        header.palette_type=2;
        return(fwrite((char *)&header,1,sizeof(PCXHEAD),fp));
}

/* make file name with a new extension */
strmfe(new,old,ext)
        char *new,*old,*ext;
{
        while(*old != 0 && *old != '.') *new++=*old++;
        *new++='.';
        while(*ext) *new++=*ext++;
        *new=0;
}
```

All of these translators work in essentially the same way. Given that you have a MacPaint image file called PICTURE.MAC and have named the MacPaint to IMG converter MAC2IMG.EXE, typing the following will perform the conversion:

```
MAC2IMG PICTURE
```

This will create PICTURE.IMG in the same directory as PICTURE.MAC exists.

It's worth noting that these programs will read either traditional Mac-Paint files, as were discussed extensively in Chapter 2, or First Publisher style MAC files. This second version of the format is identical with the first except that it lacks the MacBinary header. The first four bytes of the file are:

```
00 00 00 02
```

The image data starts 512 bytes into the file.

MacPaint files are a convenient subject for file conversion, but the approaches discussed here for translating monochrome formats will work for any file type.

COLOR FILE CONVERTERS

The two color image file formats that have been discussed in this book are GIF and PCX. It actually is quite handy to be able to translate image files between them. GIF files are generally more easily passed around, and they're compressed a lot more efficiently than are PCX files. On the other hand, PCX files can be edited and generally meddled with using PC Paintbrush or Deluxe Paint. Deluxe Paint can do some especially interesting things to PCX files.

The two programs to translate between these formats, GIFTOPCX-.EXE and PCXTOGIF.EXE, are simply applications of the code discussed earlier in this book. They use the PCX functions from Chapter 4 and the GIF decoder and encoder modules from Chapters 5 and 6. You might find the application of the GIF encoder module here to be a more interesting example of its use than the one in Chapter 6 was. This actually does something practical.

GIF to PCX Translation

PCX files can appear as two specific data structures. Those with 16 colors or less will be stored as interleaved image planes, that is, in a structure similar to the graphics buffer of an EGA card. Those with 256 colors will be stored as packed arrays of pixels, as is the image buffer of a VGA card. In either case, the actual data compression scheme is the same, as was discussed in Chapter 4.

The new 256-color PCX files have their palettes tacked onto the end of their image data. This leaves the normal palette area of the header at something of a loss for what to do with itself. In this program we'll fill it with a default palette just in case some application comes along and tries to use the palette data it expects to find there.

The variations on the file format from version to version were discussed extensively in Chapter 4.

One potential complexity in converting GIF files into PCX files is that GIF files can have several permutations of color palette sizes that PCX files can't support. Specifically, GIF files can exist with palette sizes of 2, 4, 8, 16, 32, 64, 128, and 256 colors. PCX files can only deal with palettes of 2, 4, 8, 16, and 256 colors. In the case of a 32-color GIF file, for example, the conversion program must "promote" the palette to a 256-color table. Because PC Paintbrush will use part of the palette to display its menus and dialogs, as well as displaying the image, it's important that the smaller palette be replicated to fill the entire 256-entry palette table. Leaving it blank can result in PC Paintbrush showing you black menus on a black background—a tricky thing to read, this.

It's desirable to maintain compatibility with older versions of the PC Paintbrush format whenever possible. Applications that were written to work exclusively with the image plane structure of older PCX files—Ventura Publisher, Corel Draw and, of course, older versions of PC Paintbrush itself—will make no sense at all of the packed pixel format of the 256-color files. On the other hand, a 16-color GIF file will come out of the GIF decoder in a packed pixel format.

If the converter encounters a 16-color GIF file it should do the bitwise data manipulation to convert it into the older image plane format, rather than simply promoting it to a 256-color file and leaving the data as it is. Not only will this make the file readable by software that does not support the newer format, but it also will make for a much smaller PCX file. Keep in mind that PCX files don't compress their data all that well at the best of times.

Figure 12-6 illustrates the GIFTOPCX program.

Fig 12-6   A program to translate GIF files into PCX files

```
/*
        GIFTOPCX version 1.2
        Translates GIF to 256 colour PCX
*/

#include "stdio.h"
#include "dos.h"
#include "alloc.h"

#define maxline        1024          /* biggest GIF line allowed */

typedef struct  {
```

```
          char     manufacturer;
          char     version;
          char     encoding;
          char     bits_per_pixel;
          int      xmin,ymin;
          int      xmax,ymax;
          int      hres;
          int      vres;
          char     palette[48];
          char     reserved;
          char     colour_planes;
          int      bytes_per_line;
          int      palette_type;
          char     filler[58];
                   } PCXHEAD;

extern char PALETTE[256][4],OUTROW[1024],COPYRIGHT[];
extern int INTERLACED,IMAGEWIDE,IMAGEDEEP;
extern int IMAGEX,IMAGEY,XLOC,YLOC;
extern int VERSION,SUBVERSION;

char *linebuffer;
char *thepalette,*buffer=NULL,*farPtr();
char GIFname[80],PCXname[80];
char errors[4][16] = {  "Ok",
                        "File not found",
                        "Not a GIF file",
                        "File corrupted"
                        };
char PCXdefpal[48]= {
              0x00,0x00,0x0E,0x00,0x52,0x07,0x2C,0x00,
              0x0E,0x00,0x00,0x00,0xF8,0x01,0x2C,0x00,
              0x85,0x0F,0x42,0x00,0x21,0x00,0x00,0x00,
              0x00,0x00,0x6A,0x24,0x9B,0x49,0xA1,0x5E,
              0x90,0x5E,0x18,0x5E,0x84,0x14,0xD9,0x95,
              0xA0,0x14,0x12,0x00,0x06,0x00,0x68,0x1F
              };

int palette_size=0;

main(argc,argv)
       int argc;
       char *argv[];
{
       int i,e,ShowIt(),Colourize();
       int ImageDone(),BadError(),BGround();
       puts("GIF to PCX translator version 1.2");

       SetShow(ShowIt);
       SetPalette(Colourize);
       SetImage(ImageDone);
       SetError(BadError);
       SetBackground(BGround);
       if(argc > 1) {
```

Fig 12-6   continued

```
                for(i=1;i<argc;++i) {
                        strmfe(GIFname,argv[i],"GIF");
                        strmfe(PCXname,argv[i],"PCX");
                        strupr(GIFname);
                        strupr(PCXname);
                        if((e=UnpackGIF(GIFname)) != 0) break;
                }
                if(e) BadError(errors[e]);
        }
        else printf("I need the path to at least one GIF file.\n");

        printf("\nGIF is a trademark of CompuServe. "
                "PCX is a trademark of ZSoft Corporation.\n"
                "We're going to copyright the letter C... "
                "just thought you'd like to know.\n");
        exit(e);
}


ImageDone()
{
        FILE *fp;
        PCXHEAD h;
        char mask,*p,b[maxline];
        int x,y,pl,width;

        memset((char *)&h,0,sizeof(PCXHEAD));

        h.manufacturer=0x0a;
        h.version=5;
        h.encoding=1;
        h.xmin=0;
        h.ymin=0;
        h.xmax=IMAGEWIDE-1;
        h.ymax=IMAGEDEEP-1;
        h.hres=0;
        h.vres=0;
        h.palette_type=1;

        width=IMAGEWIDE >> 3;
        if(IMAGEWIDE & 0x0007) ++width;

        if(palette_size < 5) {
                h.bits_per_pixel=1;
                h.colour_planes=palette_size;
                h.bytes_per_line=width;
                memcpy(h.palette,thepalette,(1 << palette_size)*3);
        }

        else if (palette_size == 8) {
                h.bits_per_pixel=palette_size;
                h.colour_planes=1;
        h.bytes_per_line=IMAGEWIDE;
        memcpy(h.palette,PCXdefpal,48);
```

```
        }
        else {
                h.bits_per_pixel=8;
                h.colour_planes=1;
                h.bytes_per_line=IMAGEWIDE;
                memcpy(h.palette,PCXdefpal,48);
        }

        printf("Writing %s\n",PCXname);
        printf("Image size: %u x %u, %u colours\nWait...\n",
            IMAGEWIDE,IMAGEDEEP,1<<palette_size);
        if((fp=fopen(PCXname,"wb")) != NULL) {
                fwrite((char *)&h,1,sizeof(PCXHEAD),fp);
                for(y=0;y<IMAGEDEEP;++y) {
                        /* point to the GIF line to encode */
                        p=farPtr(buffer,(long)y*(long)IMAGEWIDE);

                        if(palette_size > 4) {
                                if(!write_line(p,fp,IMAGEWIDE))
                                        BadError("Can't write file");
                        }
                        else {
                                for(pl=0;pl<palette_size;++pl) {
                                        mask= 1 << pl;
                                        memset(b,0,maxline);
                                        for(x=0;x<IMAGEWIDE;++x) {
                                            if(p[x] & mask)
                                                b[(x >> 3)] |=
                                                  (0x80 >> (x & 0x0007));
                                        }
                                        if(!write_line(b,fp,width))
                                            BadError("Can't write file");
                                }
                        }
                }
                switch(palette_size) {
                        case 8:
                                fputc(12,fp);
                                fwrite(thepalette,1,
                                    3 * (1 << palette_size),fp);
                                break;
                        case 7:
                                fputc(12,fp);
                                for(x=0;x<2;++x)
                                    fwrite(thepalette,1,
                                        3 * (1 << palette_size),fp);
                                break;
                        case 6:
                                fputc(12,fp);
                                for(x=0;x<4;++x)
                                    fwrite(thepalette,1,
                                        3 * (1 << palette_size),fp);
                                break;
                        case 5:
                                fputc(12,fp);
```

Fig 12-6   continued

```
                        for(x=0;x<8;++x)
                            fwrite(thepalette,1,
                                    3 * (1 << palette_size),fp);
                            break;
                }
                fclose(fp);
        } else BadError("Can't create destination file.");
        farfree(buffer);
        free(linebuffer);
}
Colourize(n,palette)
        int n;
        char *palette;
{
        switch(n) {
                case 256:
                        palette_size=8;
                        break;
                case 128:
                        palette_size=7;
                        break;
                case 64:
                        palette_size=6;
                        break;
                case 32:
                        palette_size=5;
                        break;
                case 16:
                        palette_size=4;
                        break;
                case 8:
                        palette_size=3;
                        break;
                case 4:
                        palette_size=2;
                        break;
                case 2:
                        palette_size=1;
                        break;
        }

        thepalette=palette;
}

ShowIt()
{
        memcpy(farPtr(buffer,(long)YLOC*(long)IMAGEWIDE),OUTROW,IMAGEWIDE);
}

BGround()
{
        if((buffer=farmalloc((long)IMAGEWIDE*(long)IMAGEDEEP)) == NULL)
```

```
                    BadError("Can't allocate memory");
              if((linebuffer=malloc((IMAGEWIDE >> 3) * palette_size)) == NULL)
                    BadError("Can't allocate line buffer");

              printf("Reading %s\r",GIFname);
}

BadError(s)
       char *s;
{
       printf("\007\007\007Fatal error - %s.\n",s);
       exit(4);
}

strmfe(new,old,ext)                   /* make file name with specific extension */
       char *new,*old,*ext;
{
       while(*old != 0 && *old != '.') *new++=*old++;
       *new++='.';
       while(*ext) *new++=*ext++;
       *new=0;
}

char *farPtr(p,l) /* return a far pointer p + l */
       char *p;
       long l;
{
       unsigned int seg,off;

       seg = FP_SEG(p);
       off = FP_OFF(p);
       seg += (off / 16);
       off &= 0x000f;
       off += (unsigned int)(l & 0x000fL);
       seg += (l / 16L);
       p = MK_FP(seg,off);
       return(p);
}

write_line(p,fp,n)            /* write one line of a PCX file */
       char *p;
       FILE *fp;
       unsigned int n;
{
       unsigned int i=0,j=0,t=0;

       do {
              i=0;
              while((p[t+i]==p[t+i+1]) && ((t+i) < n) && (i<63))++i;
              if(i>0) {
                     fputc(i | 0xc0,fp);
                     fputc(p[t],fp);
                     t+=i;
                     j+=2;
```

Fig 12-6   continued

```
                }
                else {
                        if(((p[t]) & 0xc0)==0xc0) {
                                fputc(0xc1,fp);
                                ++j;
                        }
                        fputc(p[t++],fp);
                        ++j;
                }
        } while(t<n);
        if(ferror(fp)) j=0;
        return(j);
}
```

This program must link to the GIF decoder module from Chapter 5. If you give it a path to a GIF file, it will create a corresponding PCX file with the same name but with the extension PCX. This program can create PCX files of any size—including some that are a lot bigger than the current version of PC Paintbrush can deal with.

The GIFTOPCX program is an example of the worst possible situation for file conversion. Because a GIF file can be interlaced—and the lines might not come out of the decoder in the order they're to go into the PCX file being created from them—the entire image must be buffered before it can be recompressed. This requires that the program have a lot of memory available for it to run.

If you run this program from the Turbo C integrated development environment, bear in mind that Turbo C ties up a lot of the otherwise free memory in your machine. You'll probably have to use a fairly small GIF file to test it under Turbo C to avoid having the program complain about insufficient memory for its image buffer. You can use much larger GIF files once you've left Turbo C.

PCX to GIF Conversion

Having edited your pictures with PC Paintbrush, you'll probably want to convert them back into GIF files. The process is quite a lot simpler when you're converting from PCX to GIF files. The question of unsupported palette sizes doesn't crop up, because GIF files can support all the palette permutations that PCX files can. Once again, however, the program must allow for PCX files that are packed in both of the possible PCX image formats.

In the case of, say, a 16-color PCX file, it's once again necessary to do some bitwise manipulation of the PCX data to turn it into the packed pixel format of a GIF file. As with any image that uses a color palette of less than 256 colors, the upper half of each of the bytes in the resulting GIF image will be wasted. However, the LZW compression procedure used in packing a GIF file lets you get this space back, and the resulting GIF file will still be a lot smaller than the PCX file it was converted from.

Figure 12-7 is the PCXTOGIF program.

This program must link to the GIF encoder discussed in Chapter 6.

The PCXTOGIF program works in much the same way as GIFTOPCX did, in that it unpacks the entire PCX file into a buffer and then compresses the image into a GIF file from there. In this case it's not really necessary to do it this way. The lines that emerge from a PCX file can be packed into a GIF file in the same order. However, the GIF encoder module is designed to work with a complete image. If you encounter an application where you have to do this conversion in fairly restricted memory, you might want to try modifying the LZW encoding function in Chapter 6 to allow you to work with one line at a time.

Fig 12-7   A program to translate PCX files into GIF files

```
/*
        PCX to GIF translator version 1.2
*/

#include "stdio.h"
#include "alloc.h"
#include "dos.h"

#define maxline         1024

typedef struct  {
        char    manufacturer;
        char    version;
        char    encoding;
        char    bits_per_pixel;
        int     xmin,ymin;
        int     xmax,ymax;
        int     hres;
        int     vres;
        char    palette[48];
        char    reserved;
        char    colour_planes;
        int     bytes_per_line;
        int     palette_type;
        char    filler[58];
                } PCXHEAD;

typedef struct {
        unsigned int screenwide;
        unsigned int screendeep;
        unsigned int imageleft;
        unsigned int imagetop;
        unsigned int imagewide;
        unsigned int imagedeep;
        unsigned int background;
```

Fig 12-7   continued

```
            unsigned int bits;
            unsigned long imagesize;
            char *palette;
            char *image;
            char *path;
                    } GIFDATA;

 char PCXname[80],GIFname[80];
 char *farPtr();
 char *buffer;
 char thepalette[768];

 main(argc,argv)
            int argc;
            char *argv[];
 {

         PCXHEAD ph;
         GIFDATA gd;

         unsigned int i,n;

         puts("PCX to GIF translator version 1.2");

         if(argc > 1) {
                 for(i=1;i<argc;++i) {
                         strmfe(PCXname,argv[i],"PCX");
                         strmfe(GIFname,argv[i],"GIF");
                         strupr(GIFname);
                         strupr(PCXname);

                         unpackPCX(PCXname,&gd,&ph);

                         printf("Writing %s\n",GIFname);

                         printf("Image size: %u x %u, %u colours\nWait...\n",
                             gd.imagewide,gd.imagedeep,1 << gd.bits);

                         if((n=PackGIF(&gd)) != 0)
                             printf("Error %d writing GIF file",n);
                         farfree(gd.image);
                 }
         }
         else printf("I need the path to at least one PCX file.\n");

         printf("\nGIF is a trademark of CompuServe. "
                 "PCX is a trademark of ZSoft Corporation.\n"
 }

 unpackPCX(n,g,h)
         char *n;
         GIFDATA *g;
         PCXHEAD *h;
 {
```

```
FILE *fp;
char *p,b[maxline];
int i,mask,pl,x;

memset((char *)g,0,sizeof(GIFDATA));
memset((char *)h,0,sizeof(PCXHEAD));

printf("Reading %s\r",n);
if((fp=fopen(n,"rb")) != NULL) {
        if(fread((char *)h,1,sizeof(PCXHEAD),fp) == sizeof(PCXHEAD)) {
                g->screenwide=g->imagewide=(h->xmax+1)-h->xmin;
                g->screendeep=g->imagedeep=(h->ymax+1)-h->ymin;
                g->imageleft=g->imagetop=0;
                g->background=0;
                if(h->bits_per_pixel==1) g->bits=h->colour_planes;
                else g->bits=h->bits_per_pixel;
                g->path=GIFname;
                g->imagesize=(long)g->screenwide*(long)g->screendeep;
                if((g->image=farmalloc(g->imagesize)) == NULL)
                    BadError("Can't allocate memory");
                g->palette=thepalette;

                for(i=0;i<g->screendeep;++i) {
                        if(g->bits > 4) {
                                if(!read_line(farPtr(g->image,
                                  (long)i*(long)g->imagewide),
                                 fp,h->bytes_per_line))
                                    BadError("Can't read image");
                        }
                        else {
                                p=farPtr(g->image,
                                  (long)i*(long)g->imagewide);

                                memset(p,0,g->screenwide);
                                for(pl=0;pl<g->bits;++pl) {
                                        if(!read_line(b,fp,
                                          h->bytes_per_line))
                                            BadError("Can't read image");
                                        mask= 1 << pl;
                                        for(x=0;x<g->screenwide;++x) {
                                          if(b[(x >> 3)] &
                                             (0x80 >> (x & 0x0007)))
                                                p[x] |= mask;
                                        }
                                }

                        }

                }

                if(h->version >= 5) {
                        fseek(fp,-769L,SEEK_END);
                        i=fgetc(fp);
                        if(i==12) {
                                if(fread(thepalette,1,
```

Fig 12-7   continued

```
                                    3 * (1 << g->bits),fp)
                                    != (3 * (1 << g->bits)))
                                        BadError("Can't read palette");
                        } else memcpy(thepalette,h->palette,48);
                    } else memcpy(thepalette,h->palette,48);
                } else BadError("File corrupted");
                fclose(fp);
        } else BadError("File not found");
}

strmfe(new,old,ext)               /* make file name with specific extension */
        char *new,*old,*ext;
{
        while(*old != 0 && *old != '.') *new++=*old++;
        *new++='.';
        while(*ext) *new++=*ext++;
        *new=0;
}

char *farPtr(p,l) /* return a far pointer p + l */
        char *p;
        long l;
{
        unsigned int seg,off;

        seg = FP_SEG(p);
        off = FP_OFF(p);
        seg += (off / 16);
        off &= 0x000f;
        off += (unsigned int)(l & 0x000fL);
        seg += (l / 16L);
        p = MK_FP(seg,off);
        return(p);
}
BadError(s)
        char *s;
{
        printf("\007\007\007Fatal error - %s.\n",s);
        exit(4);
}

read_line(p,fp,max)               /* read and decode a line into p */
        char *p;
        FILE *fp;
        int max;
{
        int n=0,c,i;

        memset(p,0,max);
        do {
                c=fgetc(fp) & 0xff;
                if((c & 0xc0) == 0xc0) {
                        i=c & 0x3f;
```

```
                        c=fgetc(fp);
                        while(i--) p[n++]=c;
                }
                else p[n++]=c;
        } while(n < max);
        if(c==EOF) n=0;
        return(n);
}
```

INSTANT IMAGE CONVERSION

Using the code discussed earlier in this book and the techniques for applying it in this chapter, you should be able to write a program that will convert between any two image file formats. If you successfully puzzle out the workings of some of the formats that have not been discussed in this book, you can probably write conversion programs for them as well.

Image file converters tend to be quick 'n nasty little programs created to solve particular problems. The MacPaint to IMG converter, for example, was written back when the MacPaint bridge in Ventura 1.1 didn't work reliably, and it was a lot more practical to use IMG files with it.

If you use the programs in this chapter as boilerplates, you'll be able to create format converters pretty quickly.

APPENDIX

Using Microsoft Quick C and Other C Compilers

The example programs in this book have been developed using the Borland C integrated development environment version 2.0. One of the frequently expounded upon benefits of C is the ability to port source code from one environment to another with little effort. In practice, this is somewhat illusory. No two C compilers, even two compilers running under the same operating system, can share anything beyond trivial source code without some retouching.

With this in mind, the example programs in this book have been written to use as few of the Turbo C-specific library functions as possible, such that most of what gets ported will be "pure" C, that is, without leaning on any specific implementation of the language. As such, if you want to use the programs with a different compiler you should encounter a minimum of problems.

It also is worth noting that even among competing C compilers, a lot of the language specific functions and conventions have been standardized.

This appendix deals specifically with porting the example programs in this book to Microsoft's Quick C. However, the information here will help you overcome any minor snags you encounter in porting these programs to whatever implementation of C you're using.

GRAPHICS FUNCTIONS

The major area where you might encounter porting problems for the examples in this book is in using the graphics functions. Fortunately, none of the programs use a lot of graphics functions—in a sense, much of the purpose of this book is to find ways around using the graphics libraries that come with C compilers.

putimage

The graphics function that turns up frequently in this book is put-image, which is used to copy bit map fragments from memory to the screen. This has both the same name and the same syntax under Microsoft C, except that it has acquired a leading underbar ... _putimage rather than putimage. The only difference in its use are the operational constants passed as the last argument. These are the equivalents:

Turbo C	Quick C
COPY_PUT	_GPSET
XOR_PUT	_GXOR
OR_PUT	_GOR
AND_PUT	_GAND
NOT_PUT	_GPRESET

Changing Modes

Under Turbo C, the procedure for changing screen modes is quite complex. This is the generalized function for selecting a graphics mode:

```
init( )
{
    int d,m,e = 0;

    detectgraph(&d,&m);
    if(d<0) {
            puts("No graphics card");
            exit(1);
    }
    initgraph(&d,&m,"");
    e = graphresult( );
    if(e<0) {
            printf("Graphics error %d: %s",e,grapherrormsg(e));
            exit(1);
    }
}
```

This is how you would return to the standard text mode:

```
deinit( )
{
    closegraph( );
}
```

Under Quick C, the procedure is a lot simpler. To select a specific graphics mode, you simply call the function _setvideomode. To select the 256-color VGA graphics mode, for example, you would write the above function line this:

```
init( )
{
    _setvideomode(_MRES256COLOR);
}
```

Likewise, to return to text mode, you would do this:

```
deinit( )
{
    _setvideomode(_DEFAULTMODE);
}
```

This might leave you with some difficulties in Chapter 8, when the code gets into the tricky details of the Turbo C mode functions. Because the object of this chapter is to create functions that eliminate the need for any compiler dependent mode switching functions, you might want to just skip the intermediate steps and use the final form of the code.

OTHER FUNCTIONS

The directory search functions findfirst and findnext undergo a few lexical changed under Quick C. They are handled like this under Turbo C:

```
findfirst(char *path,struct ffblk *ffblk,int attribute);
findnext(struct ffblk *ffblk);
```

They look like this under Quick C:

```
_dos_findfirst(char *path,int attribute,struct find_t *buffer);
_dos_findnext(struct find_t *buffer);
```

A find_t struct is the same as the ffblk struct under Turbo C, but it has its members named differently.

```
struct find_t {
    char reversed[21];
    char attrib;
    unsigned int wr_time;
    unsigned int wr_date;
    long size;
    char name[13];
}
```

ASSEMBLY LANGUAGE

Assembly language itself is the same everywhere—at least, it is on a PC. The assembler directives for large model Quick C programming are the same as those for Turbo C.

The only thing you should note is that Quick C expects your assembly language functions to preserve the SI, DI, DS, and SS registers. The first three will be of interest in relation to the functions in this book. After you have saved BP and copied SS into it, you should execute these three instructions:

```
PUSH      SI
PUSH      DI
PUSH      DS
```

Before you go to restore BP and return from the assembly language function in question, you must do this:

```
POP       DS
POP       DI
POP       SI
```

Make sure you add these lines to any assembly language function you use from this book that mangles these registers.

A USEFUL MACRO

Microsoft C users will find that the MK_FP function, or macro, which is used throughout this book, has no convenient counterpart under Microsoft C. You might wish to include this macro definition in those programs which use it.

```
#define MK_FP(seg,ofs) ((void far *) \
    (((unsigned long) (seg) << 16 ) | (unsigned) (ofs)))
```

B

The TIFF 4.0 Tag Set

This appendix is abstracted from the TIFF 4.0 standard description. It provides a detailed list of those TIFF tags that might pertain to the sort of TIFF files discussed in this book, quite a few which were too exotic to pertain to a general overview of the subject have been omitted.

There are several interesting aspects of TIFF files that have not been discussed here because of lack of space. If you're interested in learning more about the TIFF standard, you are urged to contact one of the following. (Of necessity, this book has only dealt with a small part of this complex file format.)

Aldus Corporation
411 First Ave. South
Suite 200
Seattle, WA 98104

Windows Marketing Group
Microsoft Corporation
16011 NE 36th Way
Box 97017
Redmond, WA 98073-9717

A SELECTION OF TAGS

SubfileType
Tag = 255
Type = SHORT
N = 1

This tag defines what sort of image is in this file.

1. A full resolution image, ImageWidth, ImageLength, and StripOffsets are required fields.
2. A reduced resolution image.
3. Single page of a multiple page image.

ImageWidth
Tag = 256
Type = SHORT
N = 1

This tag defines the image width in pixels. No default.

ImageLength
Tag = 257
Type = SHORT
N = 1

This tag defines the image length in pixels. No default.

RowsPerStrip
Tag = 278
Type = SHORT or LONG
N = 1

This tag defines the number of rows per strip. The default is $2^{**}32 - 1$, which is effectively infinity. In this case, the entire image is one strip.

StripOffsets
Tag = 273
Type = SHORT or LONG
N = StripsPerImage for PlanarConfiguration equal to one or
SamplesPerPixel * StripsPerImage for PlanarConfiguration equal to two.

This tag defines the offset into the file for each strip. No default.

StripByteCounts
Tag = 279
Type = LONG
N = StripsPerImage for PlanarConfiguration equal to one or
SamplesPerPixel * StripsPerImage for PlanarConfiguration equal to two.

This tag defines the number of bytes in each strip. No default.

SamplesPerPixel
Tag = 277
Type = SHORT
N = 1

This tag defines the number of samples per pixel. This usually will be one for monochrome data and three for color data. The default is one.

BitsPerSample
Tag = 258
Type = SHORT
N = SamplesPerPixel

This tag defines the number of bits per sample. The default is one.

PlanarConfiguration
Tag = 284
Type = SHORT
N = 1

1. The sample values for each pixel are stored contiguously, so that there is a single image plane.
2. The samples are stored in separate sample planes. The values in StripOffsets and StripByteCounts are then arranged as a two-dimensional array, with SamplesPerPixel rows and StripsPerImage columns. PhotometricInterpretation describes the type of data that is stored in each sample plane. No default.

Compression
Tag = 259
Type = SHORT
N = SamplesPerPixel for PlanarConfiguration equal to 1 or 2.

This tag defines the compression type used.
1. No compression. Rows are required to begin on byte boundaries.
2. CCITT Group 3 one-dimensional modified Huffman run length encoding.
3. Facsimile-compatible CCITT Group 3, as specified in Standardization of Group 3 facsimile apparatus for document transmission, Recommendation T.4, Volume VII, Fascicle VII.3, Terminal Equipment and Protocols for Telematic Services, The International Telegraph and Telephone Consultative Committee (CCITT), Geneva, 1985, pages 16 through 31.
4. Facsimile-compatible CCITT Group 4, as specified in Facsimile Coding Schemes and Coding Control Functions for Group 4 Facsimile Apparatus, Recommendation T.6, Volume VII, Fascicle VII.3, Terminal Equipment and Protocols for Telematic Services, The International Telegraph and Telephone Consultative Committee (CCITT), Geneva, 1985, pages 40 through 48.
32771. No compression, but rows begin on even word boundaries.
32773. MacPaint compression.

FillOrder
Tag = 266
Type = SHORT
N = 1

This tag defines the order of data values within a byte.
1. Most significant bits of the byte are filled first.
2. Least significant bits of the byte are filled first. The default is one.

Threshholding
Tag = 263
Type = SHORT
N = 1

1. The image is a bilevel line art scan. BitsPerSample must be one.
2. The image is a halftone or dithered scan. BitsPerSample must be one.
3. The image is an error diffused dither. The default is one.

CellWidth
Tag = 264
Type = SHORT
N = 1

This tag defines the width of the dithering matrix used. No default.

CellLength
Tag = 265
Type = SHORT
N = 1

This tag defines the length of the dithering matrix used. No default.

MinSampleValue
Tag = 280
Type = SHORT
N = SamplesPerPixel

This tag defines the minimum valid sample value. The default is zero.

MaxSampleValue
Tag = 281
Type = SHORT
N = SamplesPerPixel

This tag defines the maximum valid sample value. The default is $2^{**}(\text{BitsPerSample}) - 1$.

PhotometricInterpretation
Tag = 262
Type = SHORT
N = 1

0. MinSampleValue should be imaged as white. MaxSampleValue should be imaged as black.
1. MinSampleValue should be imaged as black. MaxSampleValue should be imaged as white.
2. RGB.
   No default.

DocumentName

Tag = 269
Type = ASCII

This tag defines the name of the document from which this image was scanned. No default.

PageName
Tag = 285
Type = ASCII

This tag defines the name of the page from which this image was scanned. No default.

ImageDescription
Tag = 270
Type = ASCII

This tag defines useful or interesting information about the image. No default.

Make
Tag = 271
Type = ASCII

This tag defines the name of the scanner manufacturer. No default.

Model
Tag = 272
Type = ASCII

This tag defines the model name and number of the scanner. No default.

Index

Bit-Mapped Graphics

If you are intrigued with the possibilities of the programs included in *Bit-Mapped Graphics* (TAB Book No. 3558), you should definitely consider having the ready-to-run disk containing the software applications. This software is guaranteed free of manufacturer's defects. (If you have any problems, return the disk within 30 days, and we'll send you a new one.) Not only will you save the time and effort of typing the programs, but also the disk eliminates the possibility of errors in the data. Interested?

Available on a 5¼″ or 3½″ disk requiring 512K at $24.95, plus $2.50 shipping and handling. (A free disk of sample images is included.)

YES, I'm interested. Please send me:

_____ copies 5¼″ disks requiring 512K (#6750S), $24.95 each . . . . $ _____

_____ copies 3½″ disks requiring 512K (#6751S), $24.95 each . . . . $ _____

_____ TAB BOOKS catalog (free with purchase; otherwise send $1.00
in check or money order and receive coupon worth $1.00 off your next
purchase). . . . . $ _____

Shipping & Handling: $2.50 per disk in U.S.
($5.00 per disk outside U.S.) $ _____

Please add applicable state and local sales tax. $ _____

TOTAL $ _____

☐ Check or money order enclosed made payable to TAB BOOKS

Charge my ☐ VISA ☐ MasterCard ☐ American Express

Acct No. _____ Exp. Date _____

Signature _____

Name _____

Address _____

City _____ State _____ Zip _____

TOLL-FREE ORDERING: 1-800-822-8158
(in PA, AK, and Canada call 1-717-794-2191)
or write to TAB BOOKS, Blue Ridge Summit, PA 17294-0840

Prices subject to change. Orders outside the U.S. must be paid in international money order in U.S. dollars.

TAB-3558